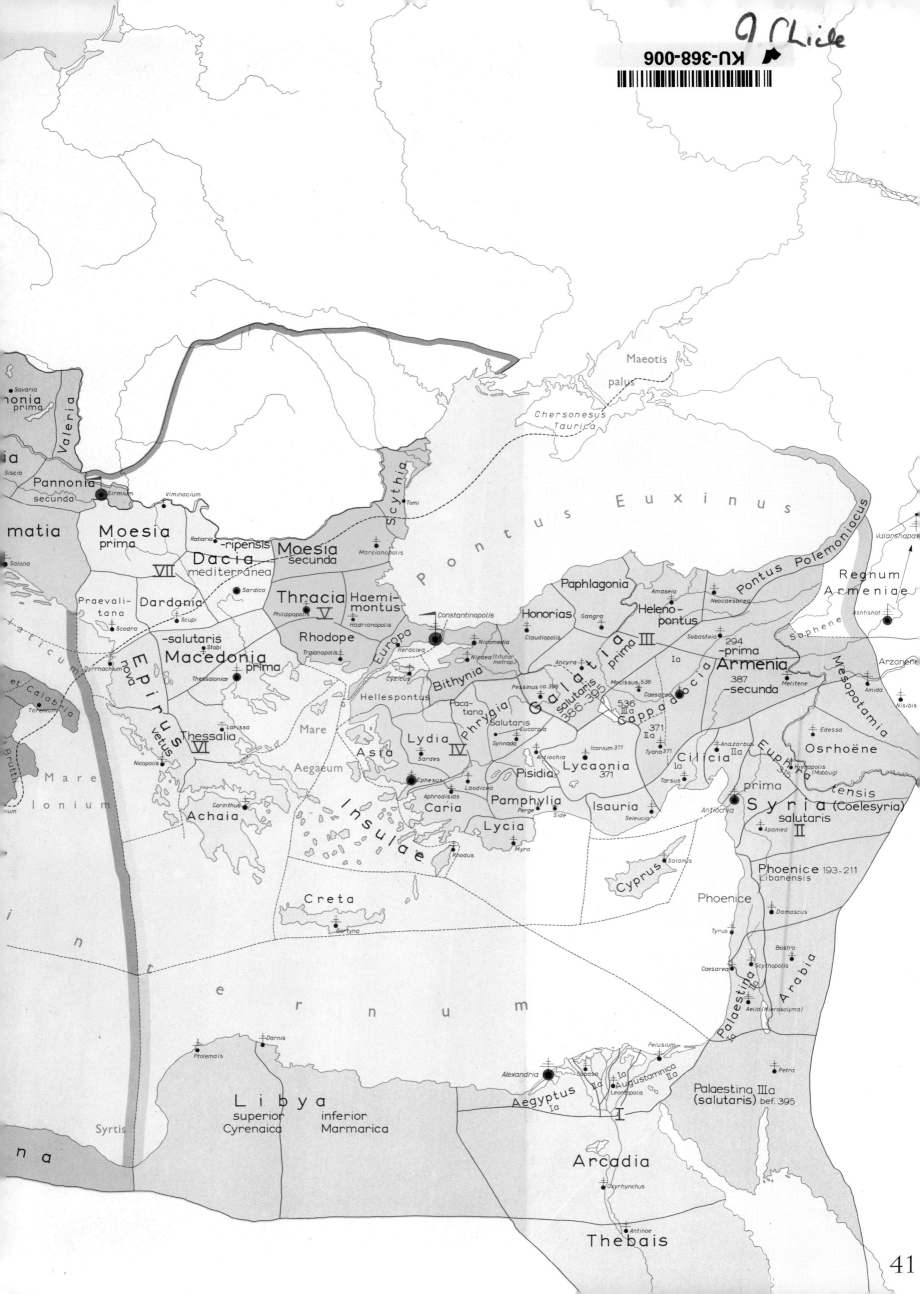

Savaria
nonia
prima
Valeria
ia
Siscia
Pannonia
secunda
Sirmium
matia
Moesia
prima
Salona
Viminacium
Ratiaria -ripensis
Dacia
mediterranea
VII
Praevali-
tana
Dardania
Scodra
Scupi
-salutaris
Stobi
Dyrrhachium
Epirus
nova
Macedonia
prima
Thessalonice

Moesia
secunda
Marcianopolis
Sardica
Thracia
V
Philippopolis
Hadrianopolis
Rhodope
Traianopolis

Scythia
Tomi

Pontus Euxinus

Maeotis
palus

Chersonesus
Taurica

Haemi-
montus
Europa
Constantinopolis
Heraclea
Nicomedia
Nicaea (titular
metrop.)
Cyzicus
Hellespontus
Bithynia

Paphlagonia
Amaseia
Honorias
Gangra
Claudiopolis
Ancyra
Pessinus ca.399
Galatia
prima
III
Neocaesarea

Heleno-
pontus
Sebasteia
294
-prima

Pontus Polemoniacus

Regnum
Armeniae
Valarshapat

Ishtishat
Armenia
387
-secunda
Sophene
Arzanene

et Calabria
Tarentum
Brutt
Mare
Ionium

Ionium

Epirus
vetus
VI
Nicopolis
Thessalia
Larissa

Corinthus
Achaia

Mare
Aegaeum

Insulae

Creta
Gortyna

Asia
Sardes
Lydia
IV
Ephesus
Aphrodisias
Laodicea
Caria

Pacatiana
Phrygia
Salutaris
Synnada
Eucaria
Antiochia
Pisidia
Perge
Pamphylia
Side
Lycia
Myra

Salutaris
386-395
536
IIIa
Iconium 371
Lycaonia
371
Isauria
Seleucia

536
Ia
Caesarea
371
IIa
Tyana 371
Ia

Cappadocia
Mocissus 536

Melitene
Mesopotamia
Amida
Nisibis
Edessa
Osrhoëne
Anazarbus
IIa
Cilicia
Ia
Tarsus

Euphra-
tensis
315
Hierapolis
(Mabbug)
prima
Syria (Coelesyria)
salutaris
II
Antiochia
Apamea

Rhodus

Cyprus
Salamis

Phoenice 193-211
Libanensis
Phoenice
Damascus
Tyrus
Bostra
Caesarea
Scythopolis
Arabia
Palaestina

Aelia (Hierasolyma)

Darnis
Ptolemais

Pelusium
Palaestina IIIa
(salutaris) bef. 395
Petra

Libya
superior
Cyrenaica
inferior
Marmarica

Syrtis

na

Alexandria
Copaso
Ia
Augustamnica
IIa
Leontopolis
Ia
Aegyptus
Ia
I

Arcadia

Oxyrhynchus

Antinoe
Thebais

ATLAS OF THE
EARLY CHRISTIAN WORLD

Καρποφορήσωμεν ἡμᾶς αὐτούς,
τὸ τιμιώτατον Θεῷ κτῆμα καὶ οἰκειότατον
Ἀποδῶμεν τῇ εἰκόνι τὸ κατ'εἰκόνα,
γνωρίσωμεν ἡμῶν τὸ ἀξίωμα
τιμήσωμεν τὸ ἀρχέτυπον,
γνῶμεν τοῦ μυστηρίου τὴν δύναμιν,
καὶ ὑπὲρ τίνος Χριστός ἀπέθανε.
Γενώμεθα ὡς Χριστός
ἐπεὶ καὶ Χριστός ὡς ἡμεῖς
γενώμεθα θεοὶ δι'αὐτόν,
ἐπειδὴ κἀκεῖνος δι'ἡμᾶς ἄνθρωπος.

LET US OFFER OURSELVES TO GOD AS A GIFT,
HIS MOST PRECIOUS POSSESSION AND MOST PROPER TO HIMSELF.
LET US GIVE BACK TO THE IMAGE WHAT IS MADE UNTO THAT IMAGE.
LET US RECOGNISE THE PRINCIPLE OF OUR BEING.
LET US HONOUR OUR FIRST PROTOTYPE.
LET US RECOGNISE THE FORCE OF THE MYSTERY
AND FOR WHOM CHRIST DIED.
LET US BECOME LIKE UNTO CHRIST,
SINCE CHRIST BECAME LIKE UNTO US.
LET US BECOME GODS FOR HIS SAKE,
SINCE HE BECAME MAN FOR OURS.

GREGORY OF NAZIANZUS, 'FIRST HOMILY ON EASTER NIGHT', 4

Θαυμαστὴν καὶ ὁμολογουμένως παράδοξον ἐνδείκνυνται τὴν κατάστασιν τῆς ἑαυτῶν πολιτείας

THEY [THE CHRISTIANS] DISPLAY A SURPRISING AND BY GENERAL AGREEMENT
ADMIRABLE WAY OF LIFE.

'AD DIOGNETUM' (ANONYMOUS TREATISE, PERHAPS OF SECOND CENTURY), 5, 5.

F. van der Meer

Christine Mohrmann

ATLAS OF THE
EARLY CHRISTIAN
WORLD

TRANSLATED AND EDITED BY

MARY F. HEDLUND
M.A. (OXON.)

AND

H. H. ROWLEY FORMER
M.A., B.LITT., D.D., LL.D., F.B.A.
PROFESSOR OF HEBREW LANGUAGE AND LITERATURE
UNIVERSITY OF MANCHESTER

NELSON
1966

THOMAS NELSON AND SONS LTD
36 Park Street London W1
· Parkside Works Edinburgh 9
10 Warehouse Road Apapa Lagos
P.O. Box 25012 Nairobi
THOMAS NELSON (AUSTRALIA) LTD
597 Little Collins Street Melbourne C1
THOMAS NELSON AND SONS (SOUTH AFRICA) (PROPRIETARY) LTD
P.O. Box 9881 Johannesburg
THOMAS NELSON AND SONS (CANADA) LTD
81 Curlew Drive Don Mills Ontario
THOMAS NELSON AND SONS
Copewood and Davis Street Camden 3, N. J.

first printed in this edition 1958
second impression 1959

Foreword

IN RECENT YEARS WE HAVE BECOME ACCUSTOMED TO WORKS BEARING THE title of 'Atlas', which offer much more than a collection of maps. The outstanding such work available to English readers is Grollenberg's *Atlas of the Bible*, whose wealth of illustrations has delighted, and whose text has instructed, many on both sides of the Atlantic. Here, by the enterprise of the same publishers, we have another ATLAS of the same kind, containing text, illustrations, and maps, skilfully associated with one another, designed to shed light on the story of the Early Church.

Probably everyone who handles this volume will turn first to the plates, to be fascinated by their number and variety. Emperors, monuments, mosaics, churches, baptisteries, and manuscripts figure among the subjects of these illustrations, which will be studied by historians of Christian art no less than by those who are interested in the life of the Church during the first six centuries of its existence. The authors can safely claim that in its scope and quality this magnificent collection of illustrations is unique.

The illustrations have been chosen and the text written by two distinguished professors of the University of Nijmegen, whose acknowledged scholarship is a guarantee of the reliability of the information given, and who provide the reader with the background of the story of the Church in the history of the Roman empire, and then introduce him to the martyrs, leaders, and writers by whose labours and sufferings the Church was established and spread throughout the ancient world. The association of the text with the illustrations will give it a vividness for the reader which will make this volume valuable to the serious student no less than to the general reader, and there will be few who will not learn much from every page. The many quotations of passages from Early Christian writers will be especially appreciated, and the most instructed readers will admire most the labour, knowledge, and insight that lie behind their selection.

The maps, again, are more than outlines of countries, filled in with names of rivers and towns. By the skilful use of symbols a vast amount of information is conveyed to the diligent reader - information which could be collected elsewhere only by arduous research over a wide field. For this alone, students of the subject will eagerly welcome the work.

It is fitting that an ATLAS OF THE EARLY CHRISTIAN WORLD should accompany an *Atlas of the Bible*, since it was by the Church that the Bible was treasured and preserved. It is good to have an Atlas so ably planned and executed as this, and I am happy to commend it to English readers. Approached from various points of view it will both nourish and satisfy interest, and I am confident that many will find pleasure and profit in its use.

H. H. ROWLEY
MANCHESTER, 1966

THIS BOOK IS AN ATLAS: A COLLECTION OF MAPS BALANCED BY A COLLECTION of plates with copious notes. It is a cultural and historical document and as such does not attempt to provide an exhaustive history of Christianity during the first six centuries of its existence nor a systematic survey of Early Christian literature - subjects more appropriately reserved for specialist manuals.

This work is one of general interest, and in it the point of departure is visual: maps of places, persons and things, and photographs of monuments and remains. The maps are all original and are the work of Professor van der Meer. The photographs have been chosen not essentially for the beauty of the reproduction or the fame of the monument, but because of their significance and illustrative power. These two criteria - significance and illumination - also explain the classification and grouping of motifs and themes - a valuable device of presentation rarely found elsewhere. The text and notes also follow this system: the text quotations accompanying the illustrations explain and clarify them as much as possible. Both authors have collaborated in this. A great deal of material which is only to be found scattered elsewhere is here gathered together. Purely archaeological documentation, however - such as ground-plans, reconstructions, and other data provided by excavation - has been deliberately omitted as being of less interest to the non-specialist. A selection of aerial photographs may perhaps be considered as bridging the gap to a certain extent.

The world of Early Christendom is one which must be understood from within. It is not the prevailing form - which is usually still that of late Classical times - but the Christian content which plays the determining rôle. The classical forms of life and thought, through which we perceive the life of the Early Church, are nothing more than an outer garment: nothing more than the Graeco-Roman robes, the *tunica* and *pallium*, in which Christ Himself appears upon the monuments of the pictorial arts. This 'earliest attire' is important, for the things of the spirit are most plain at their origin: nowhere is the water so clear as close by the source. But if anything can ever be said to be in some sense immortal, then this is true of the Early Christian ideas and motifs and even of their form. This fact serves to explain the great interest which they arouse even in our times, and that not only among Christians.

The period dealt with by this atlas is a traditional one: it begins with the post-Apostolic times and ends around the year 600, when the Greek East loses its hinterlands and the Latin West sees the disappearance of classical society and enters upon the Middle Ages. The result is the permanent separation of East and West, even though Christians in each are unanimous in looking back upon the centuries of the martyrs, the Councils, and the Apostolic Fathers as upon a classical age.

Seven years have elapsed since the appearance of the second edition. For their critical assistance in the preparation of this third edition I should like to express my thanks to Professor W. M. Calder, Edinburgh; Mr. D. R. Wilson, Oxford; and Professor J. Palanque, Aix-en-Provence.

F. VAN DER MEER
CHRISTINE MOHRMANN
NIJMEGEN, 1966

ATLAS OF THE EARLY CHRISTIAN WORLD

LIST OF MAPS

CONTENTS

LEGEND

THE MAPS

The maps adopt the divisions of the Roman Empire introduced by Diocletian, with the slight modifications made up to *ca* 600. The front endpaper gives a general survey of the political divisions of the Empire. All Early Christian bishoprics, in so far as they are known, are included. Those of which the position is unknown – this happens frequently in Africa – are included in the Index but not in the Maps. Only those bishoprics lying far outside the imperial boundaries, notably in the Parthian kingdom and farther east, are not included as falling outside the compass of the book. The maps upon which the Imperial dioceses are given are drawn up as far as is practicable in the Latin of the age depicted; the modern names can be found in the Index, after the classical names. In those maps which are chiefly devoted to the monuments, it has been thought preferable to give the modern names of towns, excavations, and other sites: these are also included in the Index. Much additional information may be found in the NOTES ON THE MAPS, page 213

As far as the Early Christian authors are concerned, they are given in red upon special maps, one for each century. They are collected on the back endpaper. In the text they are dealt with upon pages 173-82.

SYMBOLS

✝	episcopal see	∴	ruin; after placename or monument, destroyed or disappeared
✝	archdiocese	♆	Jewish monument
✝	patriarchate	†	died (with date)
🜊	castle or royal residence	✳	stresses importance
🜊	monastery		

ABBREVIATIONS

aft.	=	after	m., mon.	=	monastery
B.	=	bishop	m(m).	=	martyr(s)
b.	=	born	M.	=	Mons, mount(ain)
bapt.	=	baptistery	MS, MSS	=	manuscript(s)
bas.	=	basilica	necr.	=	necropolis, burial place
bef.	=	before	N.T.	=	New Testament
catac.	=	catacomb	O.T.	=	Old Testament
Chr.	=	Christian, Christianity	p.	=	poet
conc.	=	concilium, council	P.	=	Porta
cons.	=	consecrated	pal.	=	palace, *palatium*
diac.	=	diaconus, deacon	patr.	=	patriarchus, Patriarch
ep.	=	episcopus, bishop	phil.	=	philosopher
episc.	=	episcopium	presb.	=	presbyter
epist.	=	epistula(e), letter(s)	recons.	=	reconsecrated
f.	=	founded	syn.	=	synodus, synod
fre.	=	fresco	S.	=	San, Sanctus, Sancta, Sankt
Gr.	=	Greek	St	=	Saint
H.E.	=	Historia Ecclesiastica, Church History, (after name of author)	Ste	=	Sainte
			T	=	Templum
			t.	=	titulus
hist.	=	historian	theol.	=	theologian
i., ins	=	insula, island	trans.	=	translation, translated
l., lac	=	lacus, lake	IV, V	=	from the 4th, 5th century
mos.	=	mosaic	Ia, IIa, etc.	=	prima, secunda

TEXT

The text is planned to accompany the plates closely; the extracts from Early Christian texts that complement the descriptions of the plates, are all new translations, and the sources are given. For a few extracts, mainly poems, the Latin original is given. The original is also given for inscriptions and epitaphs.

THE EARLIEST CHURCHES

RECORDED CONGREGATIONS
OF THE FIRST CENTURY

⊕ Church
⊞ Jewish diaspora
Clem. Christian books underl.
(all in Greek - see back endpaper)

1 : 12 000 000

0   50   300 miles

Macedonia

*NT: 61-3 Eph.Col.Phil.
64 Gospel of Mark
I Pet.?
66-7 2 Tim.
67 Heb.
67 I Pet.(Silvanus?)
96 I Clem.(to the Cor.)*

51 Jews expelled
aft. 63 captives from Iudaea

al in Spain

Puteoli
Herculaneum
Pompei

Epirus

Thessalonica

Apollonia

Beroea
(Act 17,12-14)

NT: Philippi 57 II Cor.

Mysia
Troas

Pergamum
Thyatira
Sardes
Smyrna
Philadelphia
Ephesus
Tralles
Magnesia
Miletus
Hierapolis
Colossae
Laodicea

Asia

Phrygia

Nicopolis
NT: I Tim, Tit.

*NT: 56-57 Phil., I Cor., Gal.
100 Jo. I II III Jo.*

Patrae
Corinthus
Cenchreae

Athenae
Aegina

*NT: 50-51, I II Thess.
57-58, Rom.*

Achaia
*NT (Mt. Greek)
Lc. Gospel, Acts*

Patmus
NT: 95 Rev.

Creta

Bithynia

Galatia

Lycaonia

Antiochia Pisidiae
Iconium
Lystra
Derbe

Cappadocia

Pisidia
Pamphylia
Attalia?
Perge

Seleucia?

Cilicia
Tarsus

Sinope?

Amastris?
Amisus?

Pontus

Sophene

Beit Zabde
(Zabdizene)

Edessa

Osrhoëne

Syria
Antiochia

Cyprus
Salamis
Paphus

Tripolis?

Sidon
Tyrus
Ptolemais

Damascus

Capharnaum

Caesarea Pal.
Samaria (Sebaste)
Ioppe
Azotus
Diospolis (Lydda)

Pella

Palaestina
Liber Iubilaeorum
Apoc. Baruch

Khirbet Qumran: writings
of the Essenes
found 1947 sqq.

Hierosolyma
*NT: 49 Jds., 75 Jude
62 † James
66 revolt; Christians flee to Pella
70 destruction of the city
70-135 10th legion ("Fretensis")
107 † Simeon ep.
37-97 Flavius Iosephus*

Cyrene

Pentapolis

Alexandria

Aegyptus

1

THE DISTRIBUTION OF CHRISTIANITY

BY A.D. 300

For the individual congregations see Map 3/4

� Majority or large number of the people Christian
A smaller proportion Christian
Minority Christian
Very few people Christian
No record of Christians

1 : 20 000 000

0   100   400 miles

Hibernia

Britannia

Germania
magna

Germania

Belgica

Gallia

Aquitania

Raetia
Noricum
Pannonia

Dacia

Chersonesus
Taurica

Iberia

Hispania

Baetica

Mauretania

Numidia

Africa

Italia

Sicilia

Dalmatia

Moesia

Thracia

Macedonia

Achaia

Creta

Asia
Phrygia
Pisidia

Bithynia

Galatia

Pontus

Cappadocia

Cilicia

Cyprus

Armenia

Sophene

Zabdizene
Adiabene

Osrhoëne

Mesopotamia

Syria

Arabia

Libya

Aegyptus

2

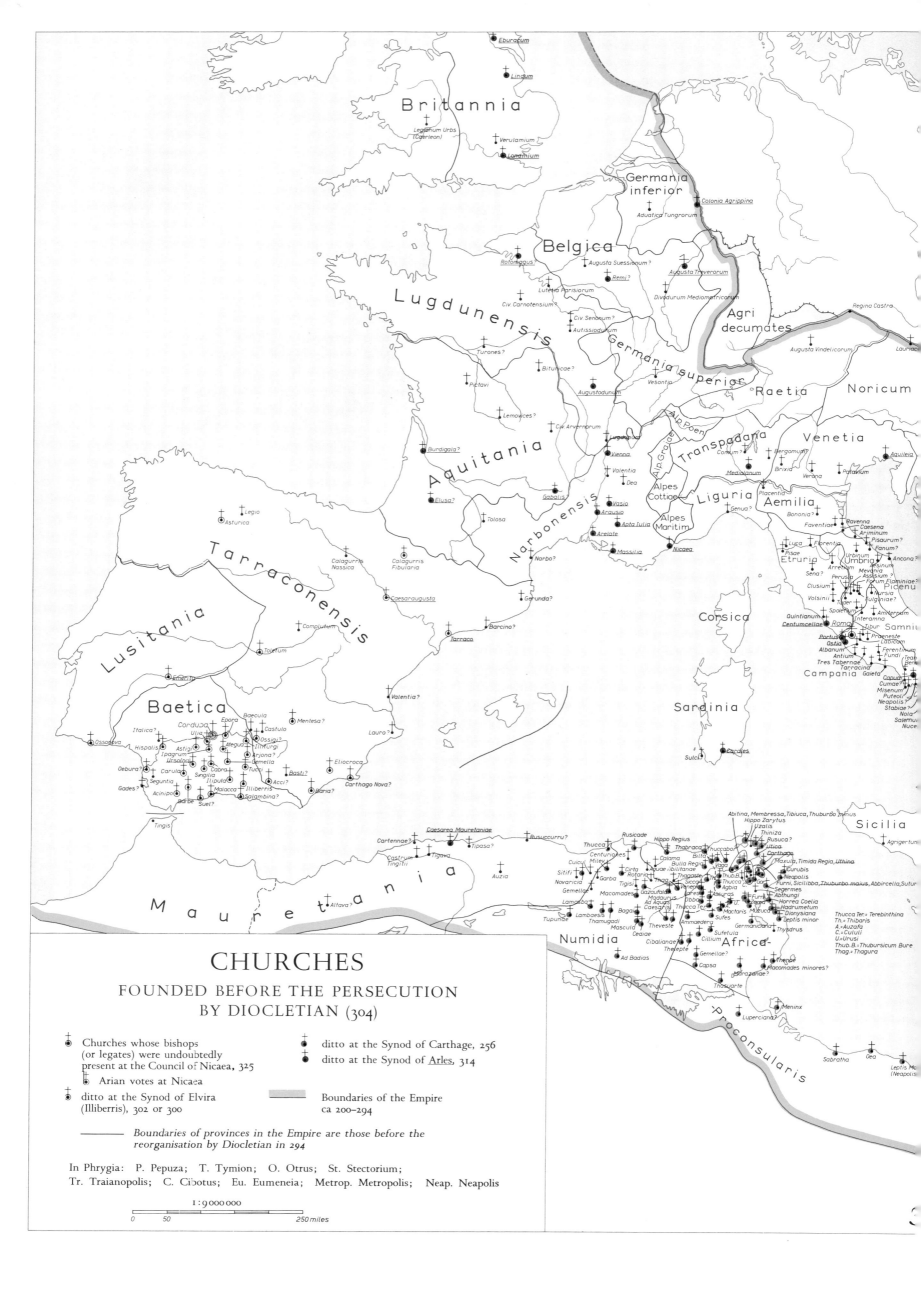

Britannia

Eburacum

Lindum

Legionium Urbs
(Caerleon)

Verulamium

Londinium

Germania inferior

Colonia Agrippina

Aduatica Tungrorum

Belgica

Rotomagus

Augusta Suessionum?

Augusta Treverorum

Remi?

Lutetia Parisiorum

Divodurum Mediomatricorum

Agri decumates

Regina Castra

Civ. Carnotensium?

Civ. Senonum?

Autissiodurum

Lugdunensis

Germania superior

Turones?

Bituricae

Vesontio

Augusta Vindelicorum

Laur...

Raetia

Noricum

Pictavi

Alp. Poen.

Lemovices?

Augustodunum

Venetia

Civ. Arvernorum

Lugdunum

Alp. Graiae

Comum

Bergomum

Aquileia

Transpadana

Burdigaia?

Vienna

Mediolanum

Brixia

Verona

Patavium

Aquitania

Valentia

Dea

Legio

Asturica

Elusa?

Gabalis

Vasio

Arausio

Alpes Cottiae

Genua

Placentia

Liguria

Aemilia

Ravenna

Narbonensis

Tolosa

Alpes Maritim.

Bononia

Faventiae

Caesena

Ariminum

Pisaurum?

Fanum?

Calagurris Nassica

Calagurris Fibularia

Arelate

Apta Iulia

Nicaea

Luca

Florentia

Pisae

Urbinum

Ancona?

Tarraconensis

Massilia

Narbo?

Etruria

Arretium

Sena?

Perusia

Assisium?

Forum Flaminiae

Umbria

Mevania

Picenu..

Caesaraugusta

Gerunda?

Clusium

Volsinii

Nursia

Fulginiae?

Lusitania

Complutum

Barcino?

Quintianum

Spoletium

Amiternum

Interamna

Centumcellae

Roma

Tibur

Samniu...

Toletum

Tarraco

Portus

Ostia

Praeneste

Lanicum

Ferentium

Albanum

Antium

Tres Tabernae

Tarracina

Emerita

Fundi

Gaieta

Campania

Tea...

Ben...

Capu...

Corsica

Baetica

Valentia?

Cumae

Misenum

Puteoli

Neapolis

Italica?

Mentesa?

Corduba

Epora

Baecula

Stabiae?

Nola

Castulo

Lauro?

Salernum

Nuce...

Ulia

Ossigi?

Ategua

Illurgi

Arjona?

Hispalis

Astigi?

Ipagrum

Gemella

Ursaonia

Cabra

Tucci

Basti?

Eliocroca

Oebura?

Carula

Singilia

Ilipula

Acci?

Segentia

Illiberris

Carthago Nova?

Gades?

Acinipo

Malacca

Baria?

Barbe

Salambina?

Sardinia

Suel?

Sulci

Caralis

Tingis

Caesarea Mauretaniae

Busuccurru?

Sicilia

Cartennae?

Tipasa

Abitina, Membressa, Tibiuca, Thuburbo minus

Agrigentu..

Castrum Tingitii

Tigava

Altava?

Hippo Zarytus

Uzalis

Thiniza

Thucca

Rusicade

Hippo Regius

Rusuca?

Thabraca

Utica

M a u r e t a n i a

Auzia

Centuriones

Bulla Regia

Thuccabori

Carthago

Cuicul

Milev

Bitta

Maxula, Timida Regia, Uthina

Sitifi

Cirta

Rotarii

Aquae Tibilitanae

Curubis

Novaricia

Garba

Tigisi

Vaga

Neapolis

Furni, Sicilibba, Thuburbo maius, Abbircella, Sutur...

Gemellae

Macomades

Gazaufala

Segermes

Abthungi

Lamasba

Madaurus

Thagaste

Agbia

Horrea Coelia

Ad Aquas

Furni

Hadrumetum

Tupunde

Lambaesis

Bagai

Caesar(is)

Thucca Ter.

Mactaris

Muzuca

Dionysiana

Leptis minor

Thamugadi

Mascula

Sufes

Germaniciana

Thysdrus

Theveste

Ammaedera

Numidia

Gemellae

Cibalianae

Thelepte

Sufetula

Cillium

Africa-

Ad Badias

Capsa

Gemellae

Macomades minores?

Proconsularis

Marazanae?

Thasuarte

Thucca Ter.=Terebinthina
Th.=Thibaris
A.=Auzafa
C.=Cululi
U.=Urusi
Thub.B.=Thubursicum Bure
Thag.=Thagura

Theno..

Lupercianu...

Meninx

Sabratha

Oea

Leptis Ma...
(Neapolis)

CHURCHES

FOUNDED BEFORE THE PERSECUTION
BY DIOCLETIAN (304)

✝ Churches whose bishops
(or legates) were undoubtedly
present at the Council of Nicaea, 325

✝ Arian votes at Nicaea

⊙ ditto at the Synod of Elvira
(Illiberris), 302 or 300

● ditto at the Synod of Carthage, 256

● ditto at the Synod of <u>Arles</u>, 314

▬▬ Boundaries of the Empire
ca 200–294

——— *Boundaries of provinces in the Empire are those before the
reorganisation by Diocletian in 294*

In Phrygia: P. Pepuza; T. Tymion; O. Otrus; St. Stectorium;
Tr. Traianopolis; C. Cibotus; Eu. Eumeneia; Metrop. Metropolis; Neap. Neapolis

1 : 9 000 000

0   50   250 miles

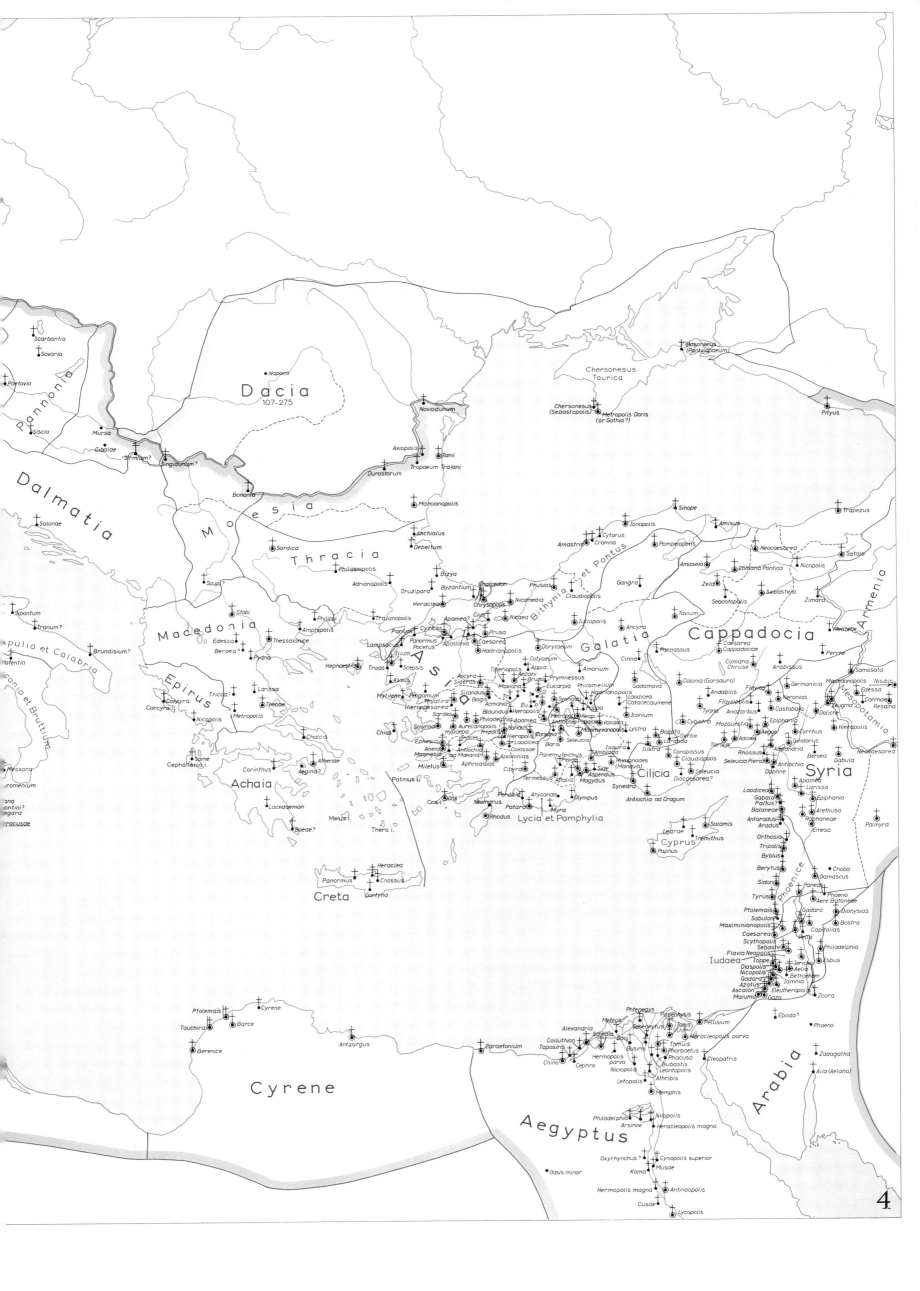

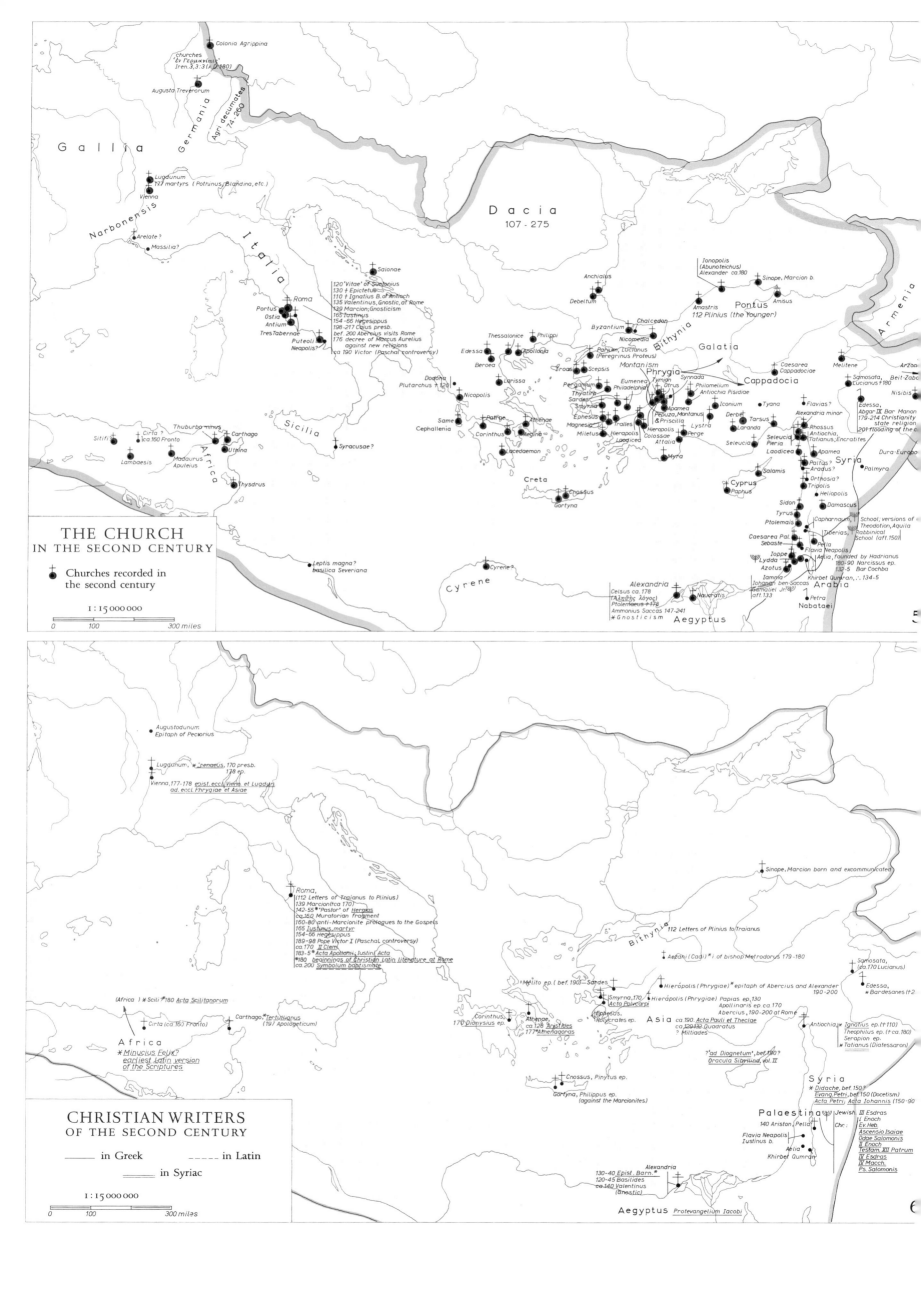

THE CHURCH IN THE SECOND CENTURY

✝ Churches recorded in the second century

1 : 15 000 000

0   100   300 miles

Upper map labels:

Colonia Agrippina

churches 'ἐν Γερμανίαις' Iren.3,3,3 (A.D.180)

Augusta Treverorum

Gallia

Germania

Agri decumates 74-200

Lugdunum 177 martyrs (Potinus, Blandina, etc.)
Vienna

Narbonensis

Arelate ?
Massilia?

Italia

Dacia 107-275

Salonae

Roma
120 'Vitae' of Suetonius
130 † Epictetus
110 † Ignatius B. of Antioch
135 Valentinus, Gnostic, at Rome
139 Marcion; Gnosticism
165 Iustinus
154-66 Hegesippus
198-217 Caius presb.
bef. 200 Abercius visits Rome
176 decree of Marcus Aurelius against new religions
ca 190 Victor (Paschal controversy)

Portus
Ostia
Antium
TresTabernae
Puteoli
Neapolis

Sicilia

Syracusae ?

Cirta ?
Thuburbo minus
Sitifis   Ica 160 Fronto   Carthago
Utnina
Lambaesis
Madaurus Apuleius
Africa
Thysdrus

Leptis magna?
basilica Severiana

Cyrene

Cyrene ?

Anchialus
Debeltum

Ionopolis (Abunoteichus) Alexander ca.180
Sinope, Marcion b.
Amastris
Amisus
Pontus
112 Plinius (the Younger)

Byzantium
Chalcedon
Nicomedia
Bithynia
Galatia

Thessalonice   Philippi
Edessa   Apollonia
Beroea
Troas   Scepsis
Parium, Lucianus (Peregrinus Proteus)
Pergamum
Thyatira
Sardes
Smyrna
Ephesus
Magnesia
Miletus
Tralles
Hierapolis
Colossae
Laodicea
Montanism
Eumenea
Philadelphia
Tymion
Otrus
Apamea
Pepuza, Montanus & Priscilla
Phrygia
Synnada
Philomelium
Antiochia Pisidia
Iconium
Derbe
Lystra
Perge
Attalia
Laranda

Caesarea Cappadociae
Cappadocia
Tyana

Armenia
Melitene
Arz...
Samosata, Lucianus †180
Beit-Zabo
Nisibis
Edessa, Abgar IX Bar Manon 179-214 Christianity 201 flooding state religion

Rhossus
Seleucia Pieria
Antiochia, Tatianus; Encratites
Seleucia
Laodicea
Paltus ?
Aradus ?
Orthosias?
Tripolis
Heliopolis
Syria
Dura-Europos
Palmyra
Damascus

Dodona
Plutarchus † 120
Nicopolis
Larissa

Same
Cephallenia
Patrae
Athenae
Corinthus
Aegina
Lacedaemon
Myra

Creta
Cnossus
Gortyna

Cyprus
Paphus
Salamis
Sidon
Tyrus
Ptolemais
Capharnaum; School; versions of Theodotion, Aquila
Tiberias, Rabbinical School (aft.150)
Caesarea Pal.
Sebaste
Pella
Flavia Neapolis
Aelia, founded by Hadrianus 180-90 Narcissus ep. 132-5 Bar Cochba
Ioppe
Lydda
Azotus
Iamnia
Khirbet Qumran, ∴ 134-5
Johanan ben-Saccas
Gamaliel Jr. aft.133
Arabia
Petra
Nabataei

Alexandria
Celsus ca. 178
('Ἀληθὴς λόγος)
Ptolemaeus † 178
Ammonius Saccas 147-241
* Gnosticism
Aegyptus
Naucratis

CHRISTIAN WRITERS OF THE SECOND CENTURY

— in Greek   - - - in Latin

═══ in Syriac

1 : 15 000 000

0   100   300 miles

Lower map labels:

Augustodunum: Epitaph of Pectorius

Lugdunum, * Irenaeus, 170 presb. 178 ep.
Vienna, 177-178 epist. eccl. Vienna et Lugdun ad. eccl. Phrygiae et Asiae

Roma,
(112 Letters of Trajanus to Plinius)
139 Marcion(ca 170)
142-55 * 'Pastor' of Hermas
ca.160 Muratorian fragment
160-80 anti-Marcionite prologues to the Gospels
165 Iustinus, martyr
154-66 Hegesippus
189-98 Pope Victor I (Paschal controversy)
ca.170   II Clem.
183-5 * Acta Apollonii, Iustini Acta
* 180 beginnings of Christian Latin Literature at Rome
ca 200 Symbolum baptismale

(Africa) * Scili *180 Acta Scilitanorum

Cirta (ca 160 Fronto)

Carthago,*Tertullianus (197 Apologeticum)

Africa
* Minucius Felix? earliest Latin version of the Scriptures

Sinope, Marcion born and excommunicated

Bithynia   112 Letters of Plinius to Trajanus

Aezani (Cadi) * i of bishop Metrodorus 179-180

Samosata, (ca.170 Lucianus)

* Melito ep.(bef.190) Sardes

Hierapolis (Phrygia) * epitaph of Abercius and Alexander 190-200

Edessa, * Bardesanes (†...

Smyrna,170, Acta Polycarpi

Hierapolis (Phrygia) Papias ep.130
Apollinaris ep. ca.170
Abercius, 190-200 at Rome

Corinthus, 170 Dionysius ep.

Ephesus, Polycrates ep.

Athenae, ca 128 Aristides 177 Athenagoras

Asia   ca.190 Acta Pauli et Theclae
ca.129-132 Quadratus
? Miltiades

Antiochia * Ignatius ep.(†110)
Theophilus ep.(† ca.180)
Serapion ep.
* Tatianus (Diatessaron)

?'ad Diognetum', bef.190?
Oracula Sibyllina, vol.II

Cnossus, Pinytus ep.

Gortyna, Philippus ep. (against the Marcionites)

Syria
* Didache, bef 150?
* Evang. Petri, bef 150 (Docetism)
Acta Petri, Acta Iohannis (150-90

Palaestina   Jewish: III Esdras
II. Enoch
Chr.: Ev. Heb.
Ascensio Isaiae
Odae Salomonis
II Enoch
Testam. XII Patrum
IV Esdras
IV Macch.
Ps. Salomonis

140 Ariston Pella

Flavia Neapolis
Iustinus b.

Aelia
Khirbet Qumran

Alexandria
130-40 Epist. Barn. *
120-45 Basilides
ca 140 Valentinus (Gnostic)

Aegyptus   Protevangelium Iacobi

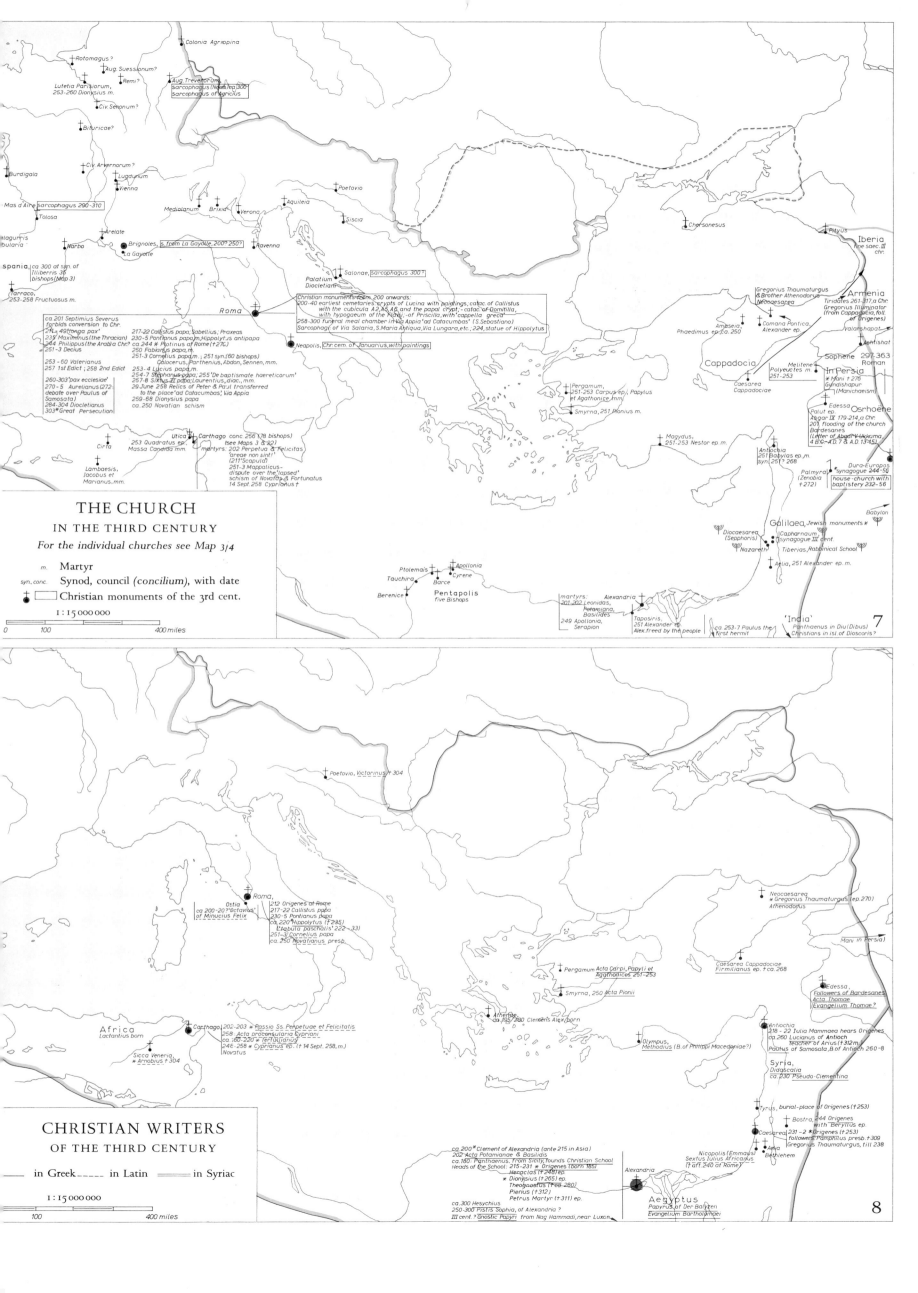

THE CHURCH IN THE THIRD CENTURY
For the individual churches see Map 3/4

m. Martyr
syn., conc. Synod, council (concilium), with date
Christian monuments of the 3rd cent.
1 : 15 000 000

7

CHRISTIAN WRITERS OF THE THIRD CENTURY
—— in Greek - - - - in Latin ===== in Syriac
1 : 15 000 000

8

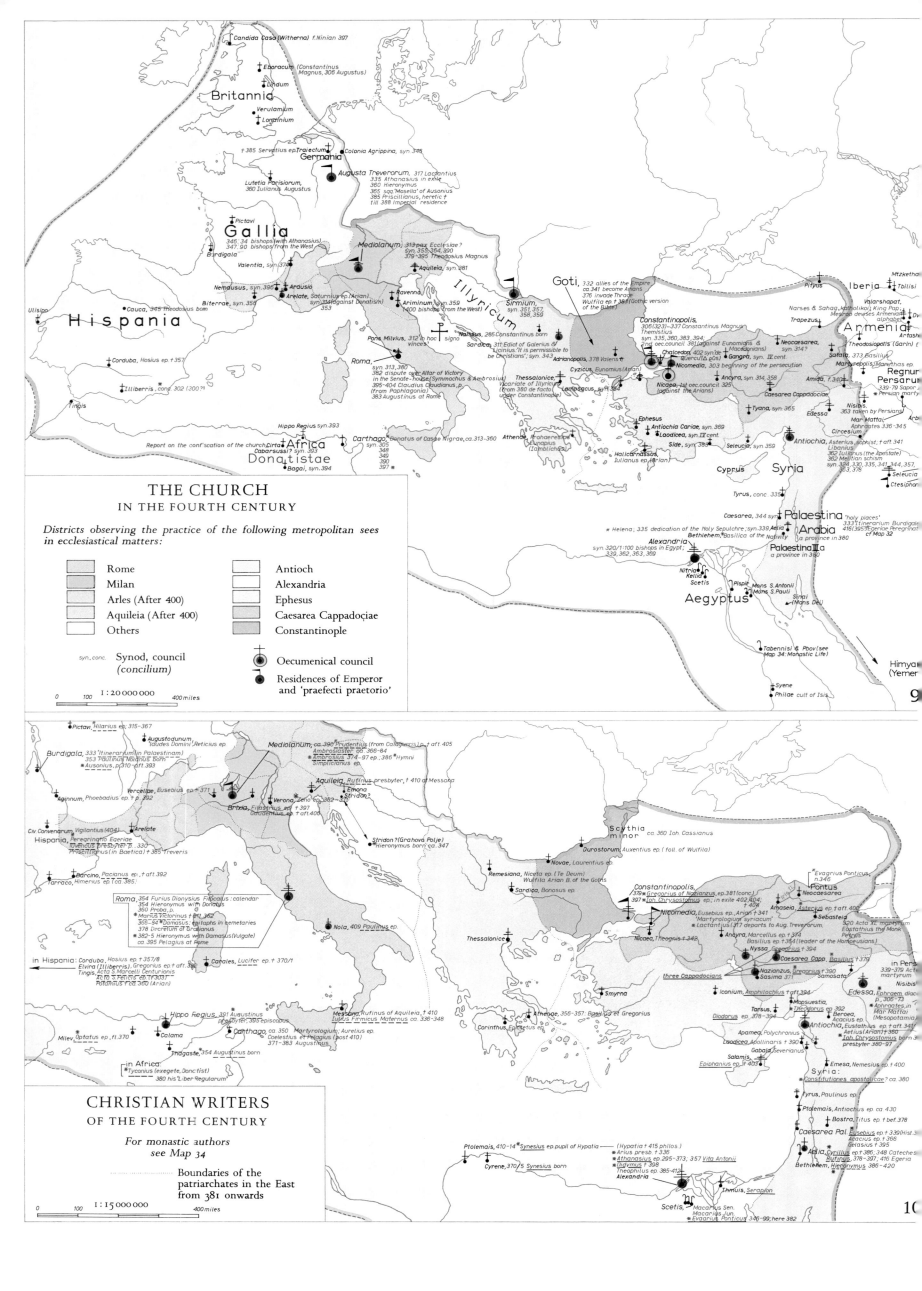

THE CHURCH
IN THE FOURTH CENTURY

Districts observing the practice of the following metropolitan sees in ecclesiastical matters:

- Rome
- Milan
- Arles (After 400)
- Aquileia (After 400)
- Others

- Antioch
- Alexandria
- Ephesus
- Caesarea Cappadociae
- Constantinople

syn., conc. — Synod, council (concilium)

⊙ Oecumenical council

◉ Residences of Emperor and 'praefecti praetorio'

0   100   1 : 20 000 000   400 miles

Map 1 labels (selection):

Candida Casa (Witherna) f.Ninian 397 · Eboracum (Constantinus Magnus, 306 Augustus) · Lindum · Britannia · Verulamium · Londinium · †385 Servatius ep.Traiectum · Germania · Colonia Agrippina, syn.345 · Lutetia Parisiorum, 360 Iulianus Augustus · Augusta Treverorum, 317 Lactantius / 335 Athanasius in exile / 360 Hieronymus / 365 sqq.'Mosella' of Ausonius / 385 Priscillianus, heretic † / till 388 Imperial residence · Pictavi · Gallia · 346: 34 bishops (with Athanasius) / 347: 90 bishops (from the West) · Burdigala · Mediolanum, 313 pax Ecclesiae? / syn.355,364,390 / 379-395 Theodosius Magnus · Aquileia, syn.381 · Illyricum · Goti, 332 allies of the Empire / ca.341 become Arians / 376 invade Thrace / Wulfila ep.†381(Gothic version of the Bible) · Valentia, syn.374 · Nemausus, syn.396 · Arausio · Biterrae, syn.356 · Arelate, Saturninus ep.(Arian) 314(against Donatism) 353 · Ravenna · Ariminum, syn.359 (400 bishops from the West) · Sirmium, syn.351,357, 358,359 · Constantinopolis, 306(323)-337 Constantinus Magnus / syn.335,360,383,394; / 2nd oec.council 381(against Eunomians & Macedonians) · Hispania · Cauca, 345 Theodosius born · Pons Milvius, 312'in hoc signo vinces' · Naissus, 285 Constantinus born · Sardica, 311:Edict of Galerius & Licinius:'it is permissible to be Christians'; syn.343 · Adrianopolis, 378 Valens † · Chalcedon, 402 syn.de Quercu(ad aos) · Nicomedia, 303 beginning of the persecution · Ulisipo · Corduba, Hosius ep.†357 · Roma, syn.313,360 / 382 dispute over Altar of Victory in the Senate-house (Symmachus & Ambrosius) / 395-404 Claudius Claudianus,p. (from Paphlagonia) / 383 Augustinus at Rome · Illiberris, conc.302 (300?) · Tingis · Thessalonice, Vicariate of Illyricum (from 380 de facto under Constantinople) · Cyzicus, Eunomius (Arian) · Lampsacus, syn.364 · Nicaea, 1st oec.council 325 (against the Arians) · Ancyra, syn.314, 358 · Caesarea Cappadociae · Armenia · Ephesus · Antiochia Cariae, syn.369 · Laodicea, syn.IV cent. · Side, syn.385 · Seleucia, syn.359 · Antiochia, Asterius, sophist.†341 / Libanius / 362 Iulianus (the Apostate) / 362 Melitian schism / syn.324,330,335,341,344,351, 363,378 · Athenae, Prohaeresis (Eunapius / Iamblichus) · Halicarnassus, Iulianus ep.(Arian) · Tyrus, conc.335 · Cyprus · Syria · Caesarea, 344 syn. · Palaestina, 'holy places' 333 Itinerarium Burdigal. / 415(395?)Egeriae Peregrinat cf.Map 32 · Helena, 335 dedication of the Holy Sepulchre; syn.339 · Aelia, Bethlehem, Basilica of the Nativity · Arabia, a province in 380 · Palaestina III a, a province in 380 · Alexandria, syn.320/1:100 bishops in Egypt; / 339,362,363,369 · Nitria, Kellia, Scetis · Aegyptus · Pispir, Mons S.Antonii / Mons S.Pauli · Sinai (Mons Dei) · Tabennisi & Phov (see Map 34: Monastic Life) · Syene · Philae, cult of Isis · Himya (Yemen)

CHRISTIAN WRITERS
OF THE FOURTH CENTURY

For monastic authors see Map 34

···· Boundaries of the patriarchates in the East from 381 onwards

0   100   1 : 15 000 000   400 miles

Map 2 labels (selection):

Pictavi, Hilarius ep.†315-367 · Augustodunum, (laudes Domini);Reticius ep. · Burdigala, 333'Itinerarium(in Palaestinam)' / 353 Paulinus Nolanus born / *Ausonius,p.310-aft.393 · Mediolanum, ca.390 Prudentius (from Calagurris) p.aft.405 / Ambrosiaster ca.366-84 / Ambrosius 374-97 ep.; 386'Hymni' / Simplicianus · Aquileia, Rufinus, presbyter,†410 at Messana · Agginum, Phoebadius ep.†p.392 · Vercellae, Eusebius †371 · Brixia, Filastrius ep.†397 / Gaudentius ep.†aft.406 · Verona, Zeno ep.381 · Emona, Stridon? · Scythia minor, ca.360 Ioh.Cassianus · Civ.Convenarum, Vigilantius (404) · Arelate · Hispania, Peregrinatio Egeriae / *Iuvencus presbyter fl.p.330 / *Priscillianus(in Baetica) †385 Treveris · Stridon?(Grahovo Polje) Hieronymus born ca.347 · Novae, Laurentius ep. · Durostorum, Auxentius ep.(foll.of Wulfila) · Barcino, Pacianus ep.†aft.392 · Tarraco, Himerius ep.†ca.385 · Remesiana, Niceta ep.(Te Deum) / Wulfila Arian B.of the Goths · Roma, 354 Furius Dionysius Filocalus:calendar / 354 Hieronymus with Donatus / 350 Proba,p. / *Marius Victorinus †ca.362 / 366-84 Damasus, epitaphs in cemeteries / 378 Decretum Gratiani / 382-5 Hieronymus with Damasus(Vulgate) / ca.390 Pelagius at Rome · Sardica, Bonosus ep. · Constantinopolis, (379) Gregorius of Nazianzus,ep.381(conc.) / 397 Ioh.Chrysostomus ep.; in exile 402,404, †404 · Pontus · Nicomedia, Eusebius ep.,Arian †341 / 'Martyrologium syriacum' / Lactantius,317 departs to Aug.Treverorum · Neocaesarea · Amaseia, Asterius ep.†aft.400 · Sebasteia · Thessalonice · Nola, 409 Paulinus ep. · Nicaea, Theognis †342 · Ancyra, Marcellus ep.†374 · Caesarea Capp., Basilius †379 · Nyssa, Gregorius †394 · three Cappadocians · Nazianzus, Gregorius †390 · Sasima 371 · Samosata · Athenae, 356-357: Basilius et Gregorius · Smyrna · Corinthus, Epictetus ep. · Iconium, Amphilochius †aft.394 · Mopsuestia, Theodorus †392 · Tarsus, Diodorus ep.378-394 · Beroea, Acacius ep. · Antiochia, *Ioh.Chrysostomus presbyter 380-97 / Aetius(Arian)†360 · Edessa, Ephraem,diac. p.,306-373 · Aphrates(Persian) in Mar Mattai(Mesopotamia) · Hippo Regius, 391 Augustinus presbyter, 395 episcopus · Milev, Optatus ep.,fl.370 · Calama · Messana, Rufinus of Aquileia,†410 / Iulius Firmicus Maternus ca.336-348 · Canales, Lucifer ep.†370/1 · in Hispania: Corduba, Hosius ep.†357/8 / Elvira (Illiberris),Gregorius ep.†aft.392 / Tingis, Acta S.Marcelli Centurionis / Acta S.Felicis ep.†303? / Potamius †ca.360 (Arian) · Carthago, ca.350 Martyrologium; Aurelius ep. / Coelestius et Pelagius (post 410) / 371-383 Augustinus · Thagaste, 354 Augustinus born · in Africa: *Tyconius (exegete, Donatist) 380 his 'Liber Regularum' · Laodicea, Apollinaris ep.†390 · Gabala, Severianus · Apamea, Polychronius · Emesa, Nemesius ep.†400 · Salamis, Epiphanius ep.†403 · Syria: *Constitutiones apostolicae? ca.380 · Tyrus, Paulinus ep. · Ptolemais, Antiochus ep.ca.430 · Bostra, Titus ep.†bef.378 · Caesarea Pal., Eusebius †339(Hist.) / Acacius ep.†366 / Gelasius †395 · Aelia, Cyrillus ep.†386; 348 Catecheses / Rutinus,378-397; 416 Egeria · Bethlehem, Hieronymus 386-420 · Ptolemais, 410-14*Synesius ep.pupil of Hypatia —— (Hypatia †415 philos.) · Cyrene,370/5 Synesius born · Alexandria, *Arius presb.†336 / *Athanasius ep.295-373; 357 Vita Antonii / *Didymus †398 / Theophilus ep.385-412 · Thmuis, Serapion · Scetis, Macarius Sen. / Macarius Jun. / *Evagrius Ponticus 346-99; here 382

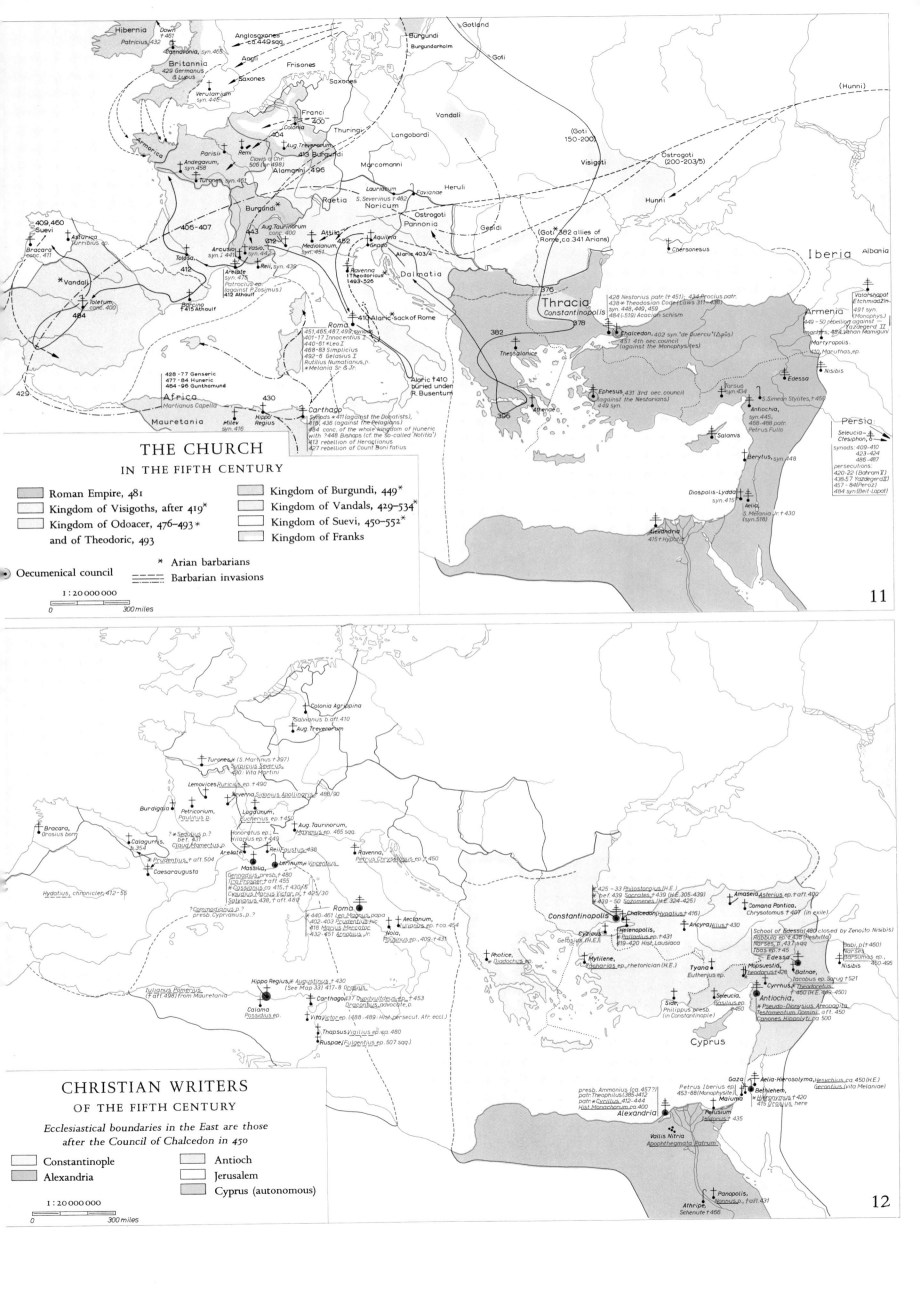

THE CHURCH IN THE FIFTH CENTURY

CHRISTIAN WRITERS OF THE FIFTH CENTURY

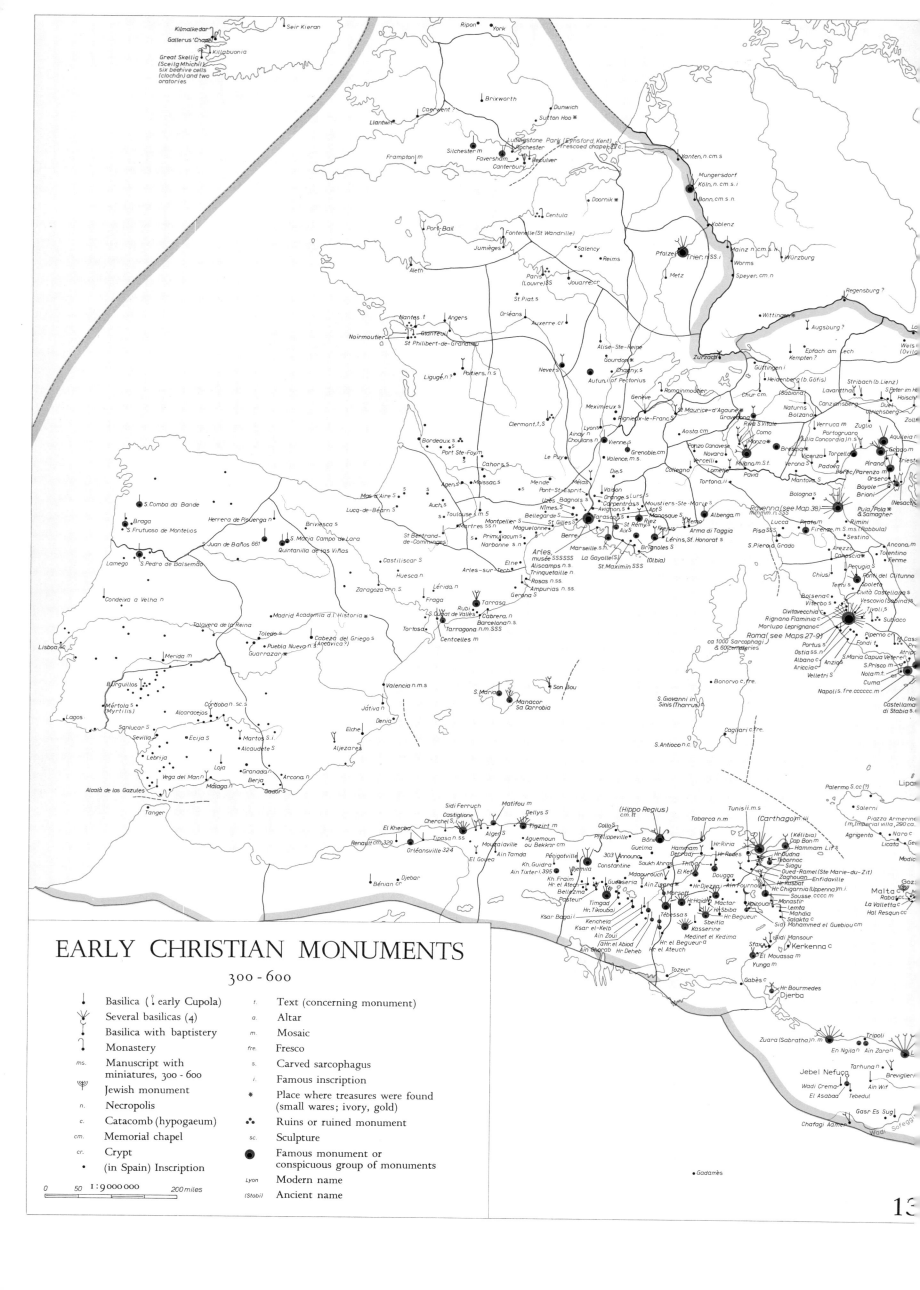

EARLY CHRISTIAN MONUMENTS

300 - 600

Basilica (early Cupola)		t.	Text (concerning monument)
Several basilicas (4)		a.	Altar
Basilica with baptistery		m.	Mosaic
Monastery		fre.	Fresco
ms.	Manuscript with miniatures, 300 - 600	s.	Carved sarcophagus
	Jewish monument	i.	Famous inscription
n.	Necropolis	*	Place where treasures were found (small wares; ivory, gold)
c.	Catacomb (hypogaeum)		Ruins or ruined monument
cm.	Memorial chapel	sc.	Sculpture
cr.	Crypt		Famous monument or conspicuous group of monuments
•	(in Spain) Inscription		
		Lyon	Modern name
		(Stobi)	Ancient name

0   50   1 : 9 000 000   200 miles

13

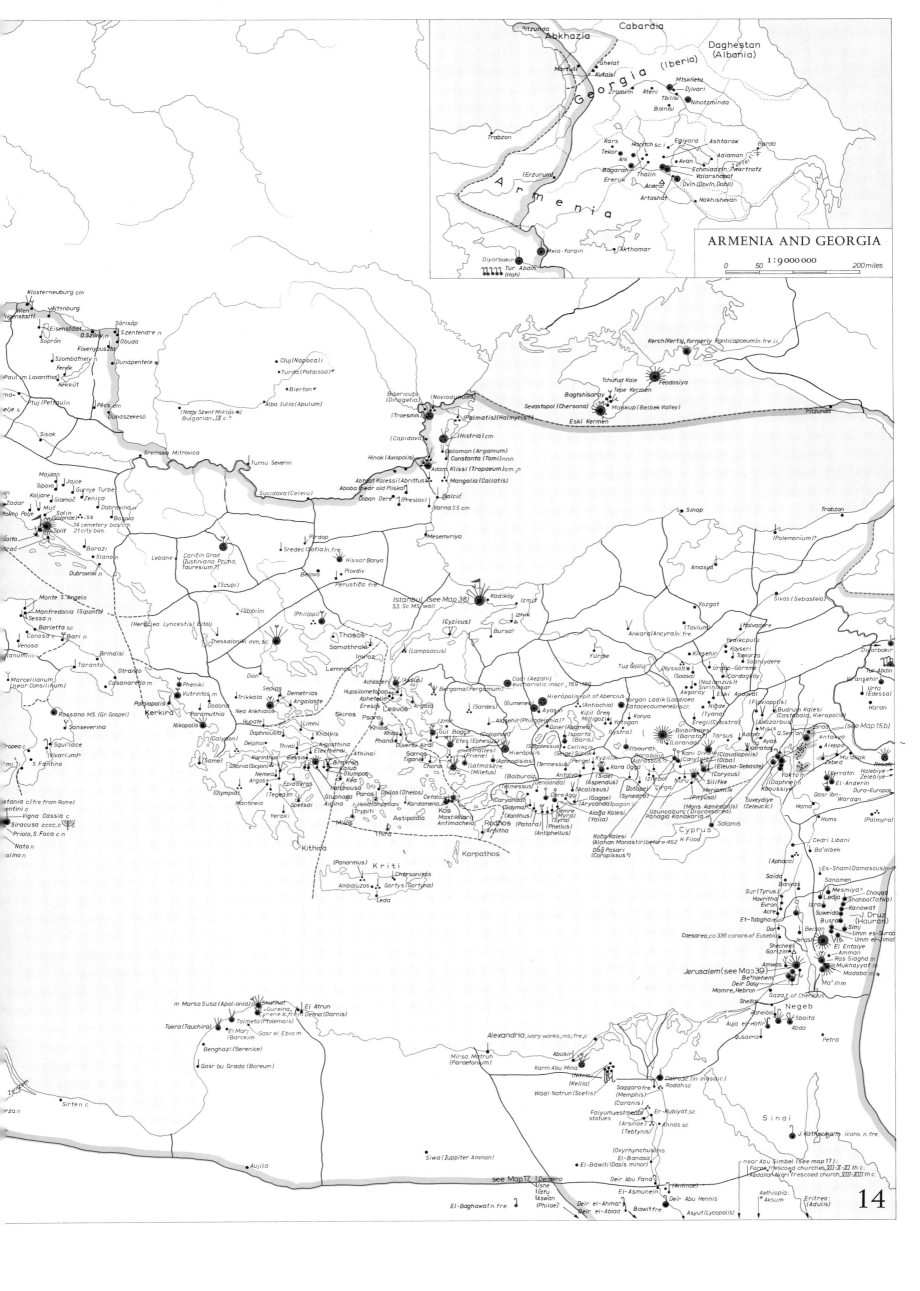

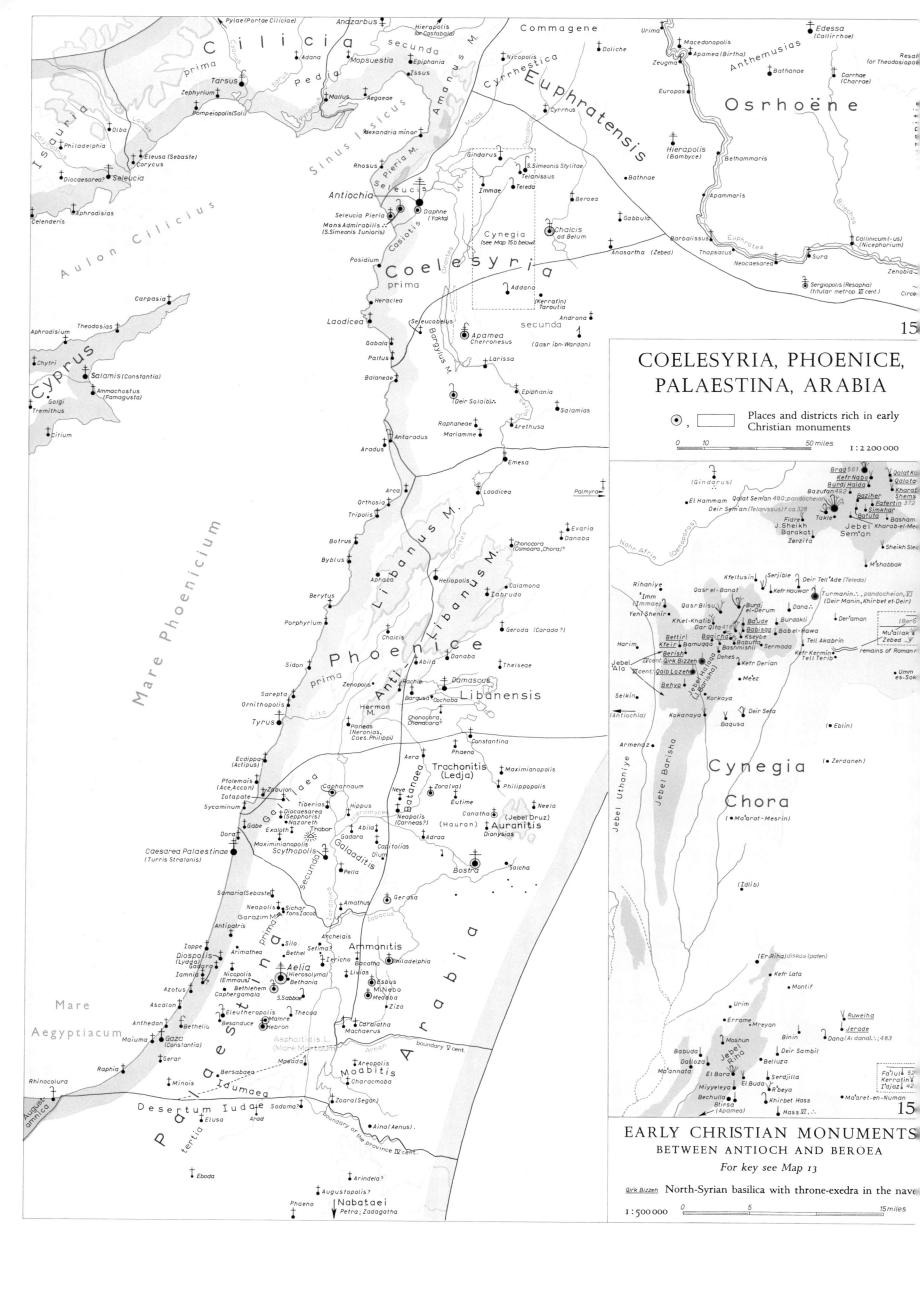

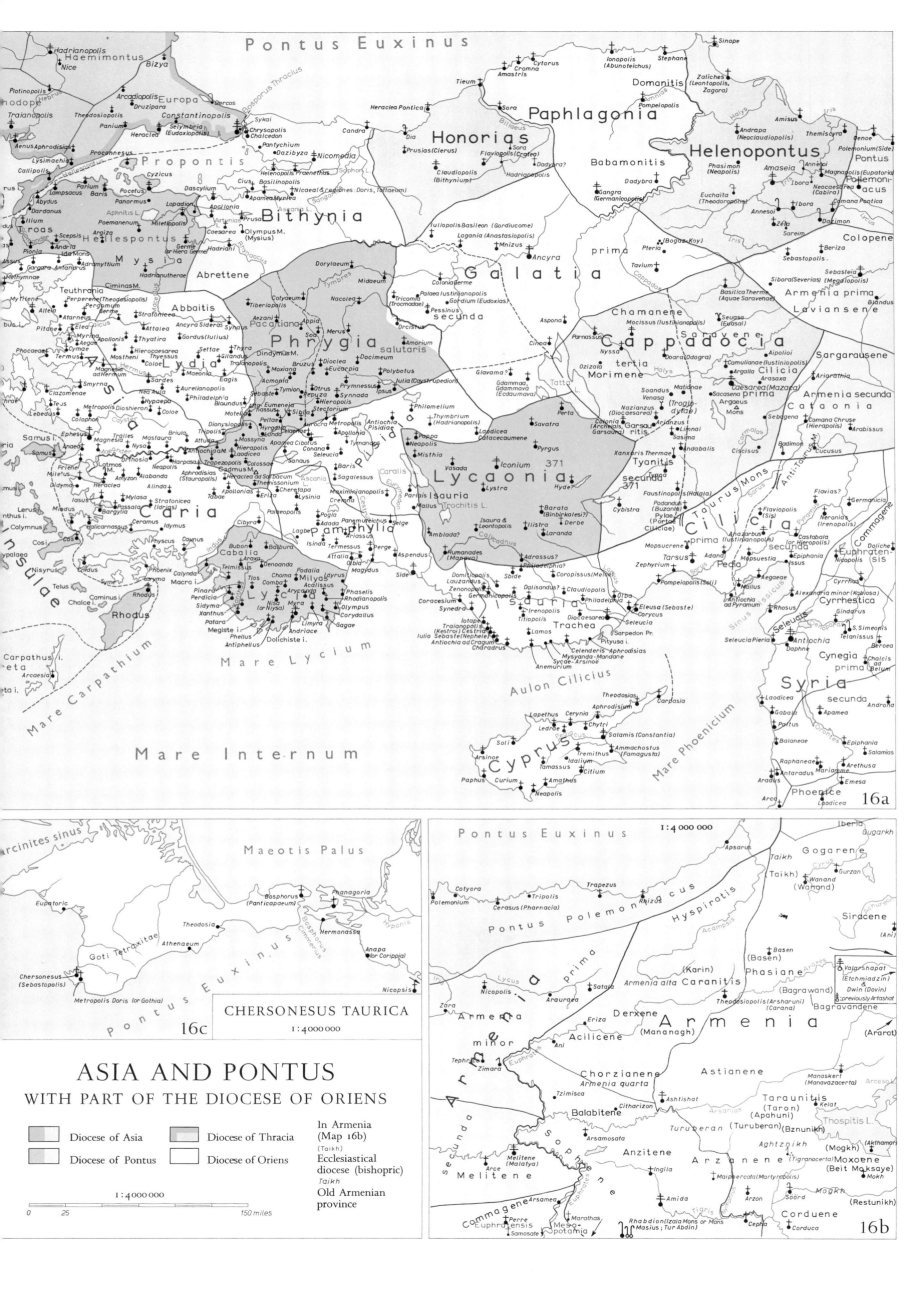

ASIA AND PONTUS

WITH PART OF THE DIOCESE OF ORIENS

▨ Diocese of Asia		▨ Diocese of Thracia	
▨ Diocese of Pontus		▢ Diocese of Oriens	

In Armenia
(Map 16b)
(Taikh)

Ecclesiastical
diocese (bishopric)

Taikh

Old Armenian
province

1:4 000 000

0   25   150 miles

16a

Pontus Euxinus

Haemimontus · Hadrianopolis · Nice · Bizya · Europa · Plotinopolis · Rhodope · Hebru · Arcadiopolis · Druzipara · Dercos · Bosporus Thracius · Sykai · Traianopolis · Theodosiopolis · Panium · Heraclea · Selymbria (Eudoxiopolis) · Constantinopolis · Chalcedon · Chrysopolis · Nicomedia · Aenus · Aphrodisias · Lysimachie · Callipolis · Procennesus · Cyzicus · Dascylium · Helenopolis · Praenetus · Sophon L. · Nicaea & regiones: Doris, Taffaeum

Abydus · Dardanus · Lampsacus · Parium · Baris · Panormus · Pocetus · Lopadion · Apollonia · Basilinopolis · Apamea Myrlea · Claudiopolis (Bithynium) · Ilium · Troas · Scepsis · Argiza · Andria · Poemanenum · Artynia L. · Prusa · Caesarea · Olympus M. (Mysius) · Iuliopolis Basileon (Gordiucome) · Lagania (Anastasiopolis)

Pontus Euxinus

Tieum · Heraclea Pontica · Dia · Prusias (Clerus) · Cytorus · Cromna · Amastris · Sora · Ionopolis (Abunoteichus) · Stephane · Sinope · Domanitis · Zaliches (Leontopolis, Zagora) · Pompeiopolis · Dadybra? · Babamonitis · Gangra (Germanicopolis) · Amisus · Themiscyra · Andrapa (Neoclaudiopolis) · Phasimon (Neapolis) · Amaseia · Annesoi · Ibora · Euchaita (Theodosiopolis) · Zela · Saneim · Comana Pontica

Paphlagonia · **Honorias** · **Helenopontus** · **Pontus Polemoniacus**

Magnopolis (Eupatoria) · Neocaesarea (Cabira) · Colopene · Beriza · Sebastopolis · Sebastea · Sibora (Severias) (Megalopolis) · Bandus · **Laviansene** · Seugsa (Eurasal) · **Armenia prima**

Galatia · Mnizus · Ancyra · Colonia Germe · Tricomia (Trocmadae) · Gordium (Eudoxias) · Pessinus · Palaea Iustinianopolis · Aspona · Cinna · **Galatia secunda** · Pteria · Bogaz-Köy · Tavium · **Chamanene** · Mocissus (Iustinianopolis) · Parnassus · Nyssa · Ozizala · Glavama? · Gdammaa, Gdammava (Ecdaumava) · Tatta L. · **Morimene** · **Cappadocia** · **tertia** · Doara (Odogra) · Soandus · Venasa · Nazianzus (Diocaesarea) · Nazianzus · Colonia (Archelais, Garsaura) ritis · Matinoe · Sacasena · Garsa · **prima** · Camulianae (Iustiniopolis) · Argala · Caesarea (Mazaca) · Argaeus Mons · Aipolioi · Arasaxa · **Armenia secunda** · Ariaratia · **Catania** · Sebagena · Comana Chruse (Hierapolis) · Arabissus · Sasima · Andabalis · Cucusus · Ciscisus · Badimon

Phrygia · **Pacatiana** · **salutaris** · Dorylaeum · Midaeum · Nacolea · Cotyaeum · Tiberiopolis · Aezani · Appia · Merus · Orcistus · Amorium · Docimeum · Abbaitis · Ancyra Sideras · Synaus · Dindymus M. · Bruzus · Dioclea · Eucarpia · Polybotus · Julia (Caystri Pedion) · Tymion · Otrus · Prymnessus · Synnada · Ipsus · Philomelium · Thymbrium (Hadrianopolis) · Savatra · Perta

Pisidia · **Lycaonia** · Iconium · 371 · Lystra · Hyde? · **Isauria** · Vasada · Derbe · Laranda · Barata (Binbirkilesi?) · Cybistra

Lydia · **Asia** · **Mysia** · Hadrianutherae · Ciminas M. · Teuthrania · Perperene (Theodosiopolis) · Pergamum · Germe · Strafonicea · Thyatira · Ancyra Sideras · Gordus (Iulius) · Settae · Silandus · Traianopolis · Acmonia · Eagis · Apollonis · Mostheni · Coloe · Maeonia · Philadelphia · Blaundus · Hierocaesarea · Thyessus · Sardes · Aureliopolis · Peltae · Hyrgaleticon · Metropolis · Antiochia Pisidiae · Apollonia · Sagalassus

Caria · Tralles · Mastaura · Nysa · Antiochia a. M. · Hierapolis · Laodicea · Mossyna · Apamea Cibotus · Conana · Seleucia · Sanaus · Baris · Maximianopolis · Cremna · Parlais · Pappa · Neapolis · Misthia · Pyrgus · Faustinopolis (Halala) · Podandus (Buzante) · Pylae (Portae Ciliciae)

Pamphylia · **Lycia** · Cibyra · Bubon · Cabalia · Balbura · Oenoanda · Araxa · Telmissus · Choma · Podalia · Lysinia · Pogla · Panemuteichus · Selge · Isaura & Leontopolis · Ilistra · Isinda · Termessus · Attalia · Olbia · Perge · Aspendus · Side · Humanades (Mapava) · Adrassus? · Sbide · Philadelphia? · Coropissus (Mela) · Claudiopolis · Philadelphia · Olba

Mare Lycium · Megiste i. · Dolichiste i.

Mare Internum

Cilicia · **prima** · Anazarbus (Iustinianopolis) · Mopsucrene · Tarsus · Adana · Mopsuestia · Aegeae · Zephyrium · Pompeiopolis (Soli) · Mallus · Antiochia ad Pyramum · Rhosus · **secunda** · Castabala (or Hierapolis) · Flaviopolis (Sis) · Epiphania · Issus · Neronias (Irenopolis) · Alexandria minor (Kabiosa) · **Commagene** · Doliche (Dolichi) · Nicopolis · **Euphraten-sis** · **Cyrrhestica** · Cyrrhus · Gindarus · S. Simeonis · Telanissus · Beroea · Seleucis · Antiochia · Daphne · **Cynegia** · **Syria** · **prima** · Chalcis ad Belum

Isauria · **Trachea** · Domitiopolis · Lauzantus · Zenonopolis · Germanicopolis · Coracesium · Synedra · Iotape (Kestroi) Cestria · Iulio Sebaste (Nephelie) · Antiochia ad Cragum · Charadrus · Anemurium · Celenderis · Aphrodisias · Mysanda-Mandane · Sycae-Arsinoe · Pityusa i. · Sarpedon Pr. · Corycus · Eleusa (Sebaste) · Seleucia · Lamos · Diocaesarea · Irenopolis · Tiopolis · Dalisandus? · **Sinus Issicus** · **Syria secunda** · Laodicea · Gabala · Paltus · Balaneae · Raphaneae · Mariamme · Arethusa · Emesa · Antaradus · Aradus · Arca · Laodicea · Epiphania · Salamias · **Phoenice**

Aulon Cilicius · **Mare Phoenicium** · Theodosias · Aphrodisium · Carpasia

Cyprus · Lapethus · Cerynia · Chytri · Ledre · Salamis (Constantia) · Soli · Ammachostus (Famagusta) · Arsinoe · Tremithus · Idalium · Tamassus · Citium · Paphus · Curium · Amathus · Neapolis

16c

Marcinites sinus · **Maeotis Palus** · Eupatoric · Phanagoria · Bosphorus (Panticapaeum) · Hermonassa · Theodosia · Goti Tetraxitae · Athenaeum · Anapa (or Corippia) · Chersonesus (Sebastopolis) · Metropolis Doris (or Gothia) · Nicopsis · **Pontus Euxinus** · **Bosphorus Cimmerius**

CHERSONESUS TAURICA

1:4 000 000

16b

1:4 000 000

Pontus Euxinus · Cotyora · Trapezus · Tripolis · Polemonium · Cerasus (Pharnacia) · Rhizus · Apsarus · **Pontus Polemoniacus** · **Hyspiratis** · **Iberia** · **Gugarkh** · **Taikh** · **Gogarene** · **Taikh** · Wanand (Wahand) · **Gurzan** · **Siracene** · (Ani)

Armenia prima · Nicopolis · Satala · Araugea · **Armenia alta** · **Caranitis** · (Karin) · Basen (Basen) · **Phasiane** · Theodosiopolis (Arsharuni) (Carana) · **Bagravandene** · Valarshapat (Etchmiadzin) & Dwin (Dovin) previously Artashat · Bagravande

Armenia minor · Zara · Tephrice · Zimara · Ani · Derxene (Mananagh) · Eriza · Acilicene · **Armenia** · (Ararat) · **Astianene**

Armenia quarta · Chorzianene · Tzimisca · Balabitene · Citharizon · Ashtishat · **Armenia secunda** · Arsamosata · Anzitene · **Sophene** · Zimara · **Turuberan** (Turuberan) · **Taraunitis** (Taron) (Apahuni) · Kelat · Manaskert (Manavazacerta) · Arceso · **Thospitis L.** · **Aghtznikh** (Mogkh) · **Akthamar** · **Moxoene** (Beit Moksaye) · **Mokh**

Melitene · Melitene (Malatya) · Arce · Ingila · Maipheracta (Martyropolis) · **Arzanene** · Tigranocerta · **Mogkh** (Restunikh) · **Corduene**

Commagene · Arsamea · Perre · **Euphratensis** · Samosate · **Mesopotamia** · Marathas · Rhabdion (Izala Mons or Mons Masius; Tur Abdin) · Amida · Arzon · Söörd · Cepha · Corduca

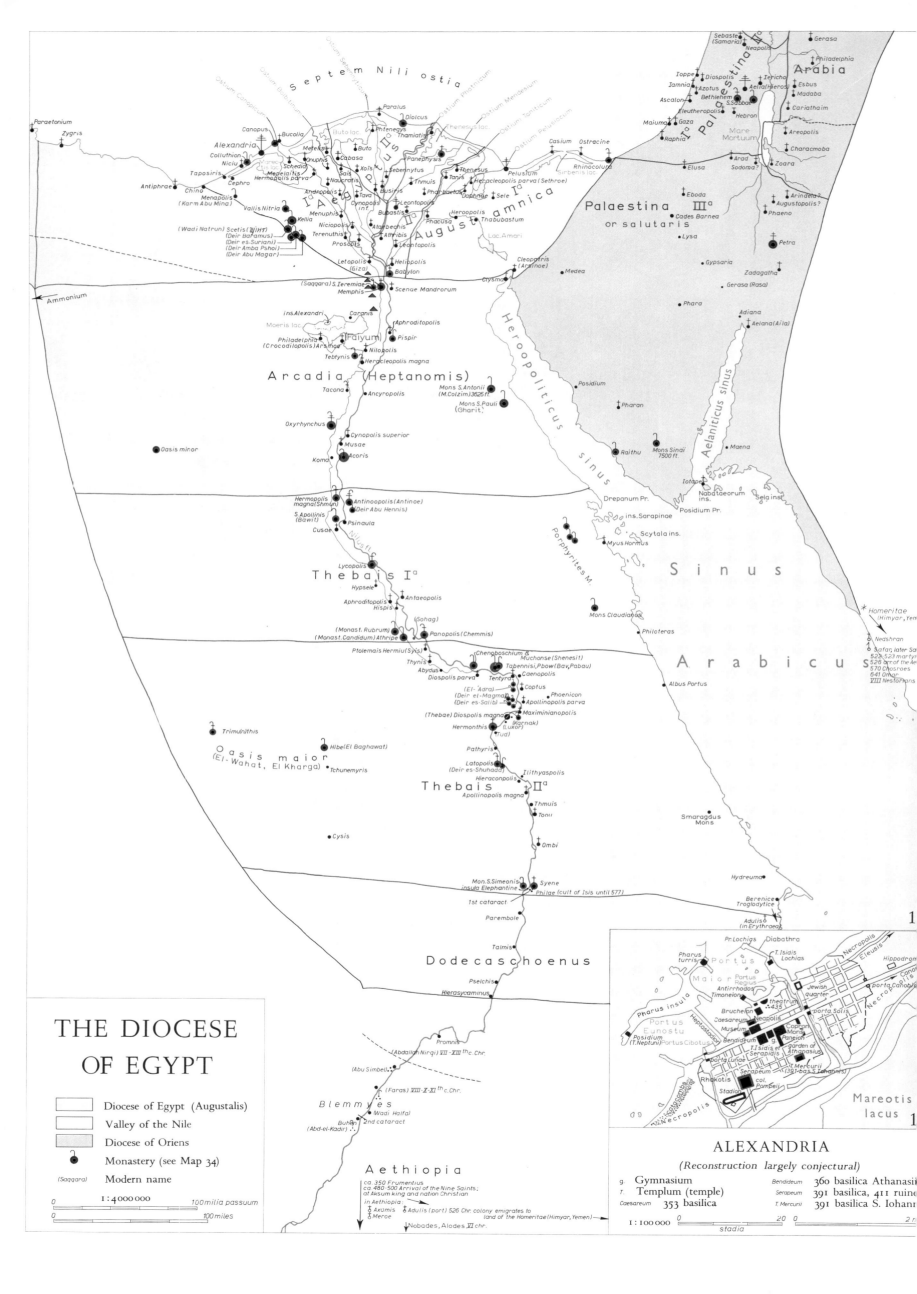

Paraetonium
Zygris

Septem Nili ostia

Paralus
Diolcus
Phtenegys
Canopus
Bucolia
Alexandria
Colluthion
Niciu
Metelis
Buto
Thmatis
Thamiatis
Taposiris
Schedia
Cabasa
Panephysis
Antiphrae
Chino
Cephro
Mepelaitis
Hermopolis parva
Naucratis
Sais
Xois
Sebennytus
Thenesus
Menapolis
(Karm Abu Mina)
Vallis Nitria
Androopolis
Tava
Busiris
Tanis
Pelusium
Casium
Ostracine
Rhinocolura
Kellia
Cynopolis inf.
Leontopolis
Heracleopolis parva (Sethroe)
(Wadi Natrun) Scetis (SIHT)
(Deir es-Baramus)
Menuphis
Nicopolis
Atarbechis
Phacusa
Thabubastum
Daphnae
Sele
(Deir es-Suriani)
Terenuthist
Athribis
Pharbaetos
(Deir Amba Pshoi)
Prosopis
Leontopolis
(Deir Abu Magar)
Letopolis
Heliopolis
Cleopatris
(Giza)
Babylon
(Arsinoe)
Clysma
(Saqqara) S. Ieremiae
Scenae Mandrorum
Memphis

Ammonium

ins. Alexandri
Moeris lac.
Carana
Aphroditopolis
(Faiyum)
Pispir
Philadelphia
(Crocodilopolis) Arsinoe
Niloopolis
Tebtynis
Heracleopolis magna

Arcadia (Heptanomis)

Tacona
Ancyropolis
Mons S.Antonii
(M.Colzim) 3625 ft.
Mons S.Pauli
(Gharit)

Oxyrhynchus
Cynopolis superior
Musae
Oasis minor
Koma
Acoris

Hermopolis
magna (Shmun)
Antinoopolis (Antinoe)
(Deir Abu Hennis)
S.Apollinis
(Bawit)
Psinaula
Cusae
Lycopolis

Thebais Iᵃ

Hypsele
Antaeopolis
Aphroditopolis
Hispis
(Sohag)
(Monast. Rubrum)
Panopolis (Chemmis)
(Monast. Candidum) Athripe
Ptolemais Hermiu (Sfis)
Chenoboschium &
Muchonse (Shenesit)
Thynis
Tabennisi, Pbow (Bau, Pabau)
Abydus
Caenopolis
Diospolis parva
Tentyra
(El-'Adra)
Coptus
(Deir el-Magma)
Phoenicon
(Deir es-Salib)
Apollinopolis parva
(Thebae) Diospolis magna
Maximinianopolis
(Karnak)
Hermonthis
(Luxor)
Tud
Trimun(th)is
Pathyris
Hibe (El Baghawat)

Oasis maior
(El-Wahat, El Kharga)
Tchunemyris
Latopolis
(Deir es-Shuhada)
Ilithyaspolis
Hieraconpolis

Thebais IIᵃ

Apollinopolis magna
Thmuis
Tonu
Cysis
Ombi

Mon.S.Simeonis
Syene
insula Elephantine
Philae (cult of Isis until 577)
1st cataract

Parembole

Talmis

Dodecaschoenus

Pselchis

Hierasycaminus

Promnis

(Abdallah Nirqi) VII-XIIIᵗʰ c. Chr.

(Abu Simbel)...

(Faras) VIII-X-XIᵗʰ c. Chr.

Blemmyes
(Buhen)
Wadi Halfa
(Abd-el-Kadir) 2nd cataract

Aethiopia
ca. 350 Frumentius
ca. 480-500 Arrival of the Nine Saints;
at Aksum king and nation Christian
in Aethiopia:
Axumis
Adulis (port) 526 Chr. colony emigrates to
Meroe   (land of the Homeritae (Himyar, Yemen)
Nobades, Alodes VI chr.

Sebaste
(Samaria)
Neapolis
Gerasa
Ioppe
Diospolis
Tericho
Philadelphia
Iamnia
Azotus
Aela (Hieros)
Ascalon
Bethlehem
S.Sabbae
Madaba
Maiuma
Gaza
Hebron
Cariathaim
Raphia
Arad
Characmoba
Sodoma?
Elusa
Zoara
Areopolis

Palaestina IIIᵃ
or salutaris
Cades Barnea
Eboda
Lysa
Gypsaria
Zadagatha
Gerasa (Rasa)
Petra
Phaeno
Augustopolis?
Arindela?
Phara
Adiana
Aelana (Aila)

Heroopoliticus sinus

Medea

Posidium

Pharan

Raithu
Mons Sinai
7500 ft.
Maena
Iotape
Nabataeorum
ins.
Sela inst

Drepanum Pr.
ins. Sarapinae
Posidium Pr.
Scytala ins.
Myus Hormus

Sinus

Mons Claudianus
Philoteras

Arabicus

Albus Portus

Homeritae
(Himyar, Yem)
Nedshran
Safar, later Sa
522-523 martyri
526 arr. of the Ae
570 Chosroes
641 Omar
VIII Nestorians

Smaragdus
Mons

Hydreuma

Berenice
Troglodytice

Adulis
(in Erythraea)

*Mareotis
lacus*

Monastery (see Map 34)

THE DIOCESE
OF EGYPT

Diocese of Egypt (Augustalis)
Valley of the Nile
Diocese of Oriens
Monastery (see Map 34)
(Saqqara)   Modern name

1 : 4 000 000
0   100 milia passuum
0   100 miles

ALEXANDRIA
(Reconstruction largely conjectural)

Pharus
turris
Portus
Maior
Pr.Lochias
Diabathra
T. Isidis
Lochias
Necropolis
Eleusis
Hippodrom
Portus
Regius
Antirrhodos
Jewish
quarter
Porta Canobi
Pharus insula
Timoneion
theatrum
+435
Brucheion
Caesareum
Museum
Neapolis
porta Solis
Portus
Eunostu
Posidium
(T.Neptuni)Portus Cibotus
Bendideum
Copron Mons
Panefon
garden of
Athanasius
T.Isidis et
Serapidis
porta Lunae
Serapeum
T.Mercurii
(391 bas. S.Iohann)
Rhakotis
col.
Pompeii
Stadia

g. Gymnasium   Bendideum   360 basilica Athanasii
T. Templum (temple) Serapeum   391 basilica, 411 ruine
Caesareum 353 basilica T.Mercurii 391 basilica S. Iohann

1 : 100 000   0   20   0
                          stadia

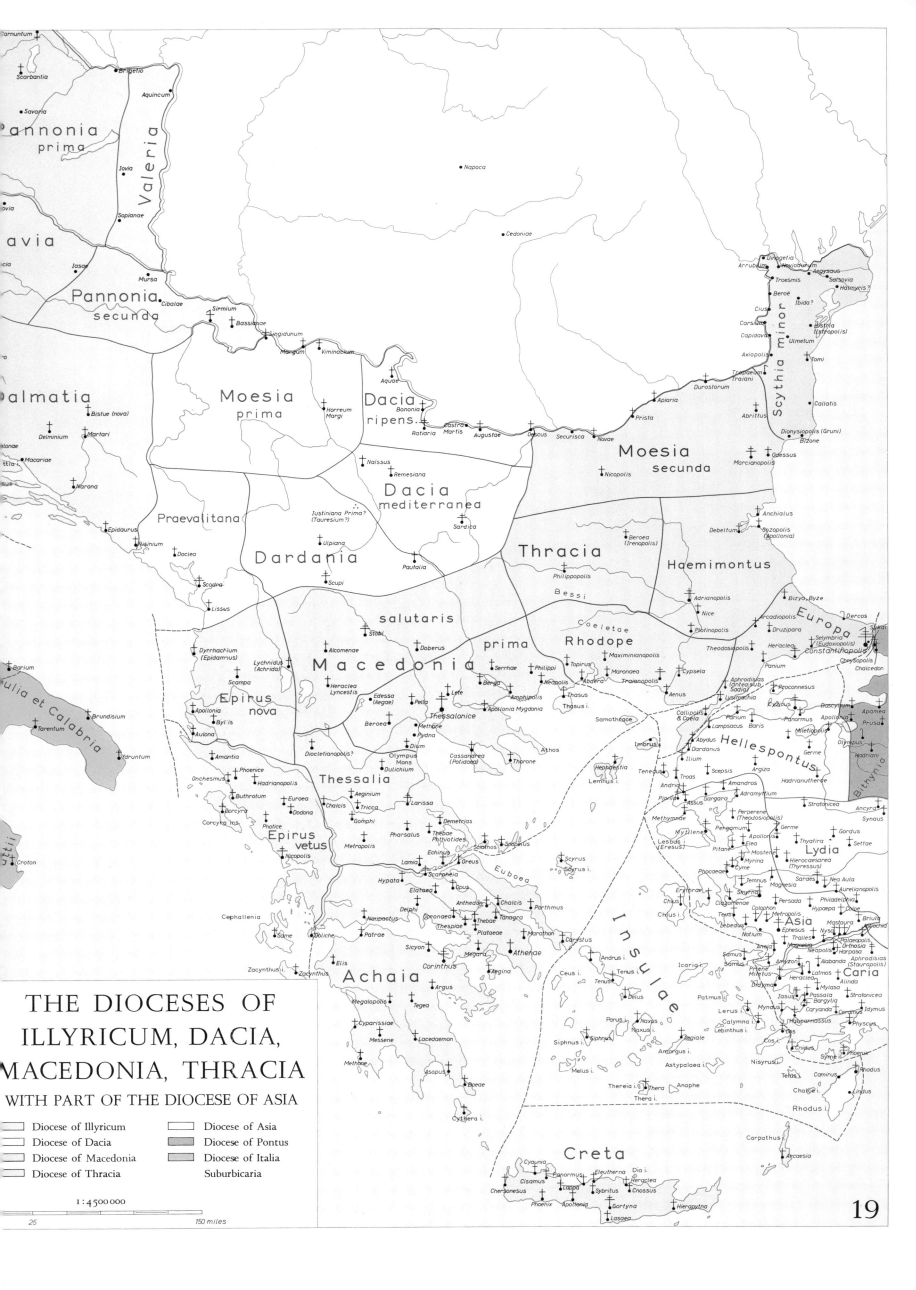

THE DIOCESES OF
ILLYRICUM, DACIA,
MACEDONIA, THRACIA
WITH PART OF THE DIOCESE OF ASIA

Diocese of Illyricum	Diocese of Asia
Diocese of Dacia	Diocese of Pontus
Diocese of Macedonia	Diocese of Italia
Diocese of Thracia	Suburbicaria

1 : 4 500 000

25   150 miles

19

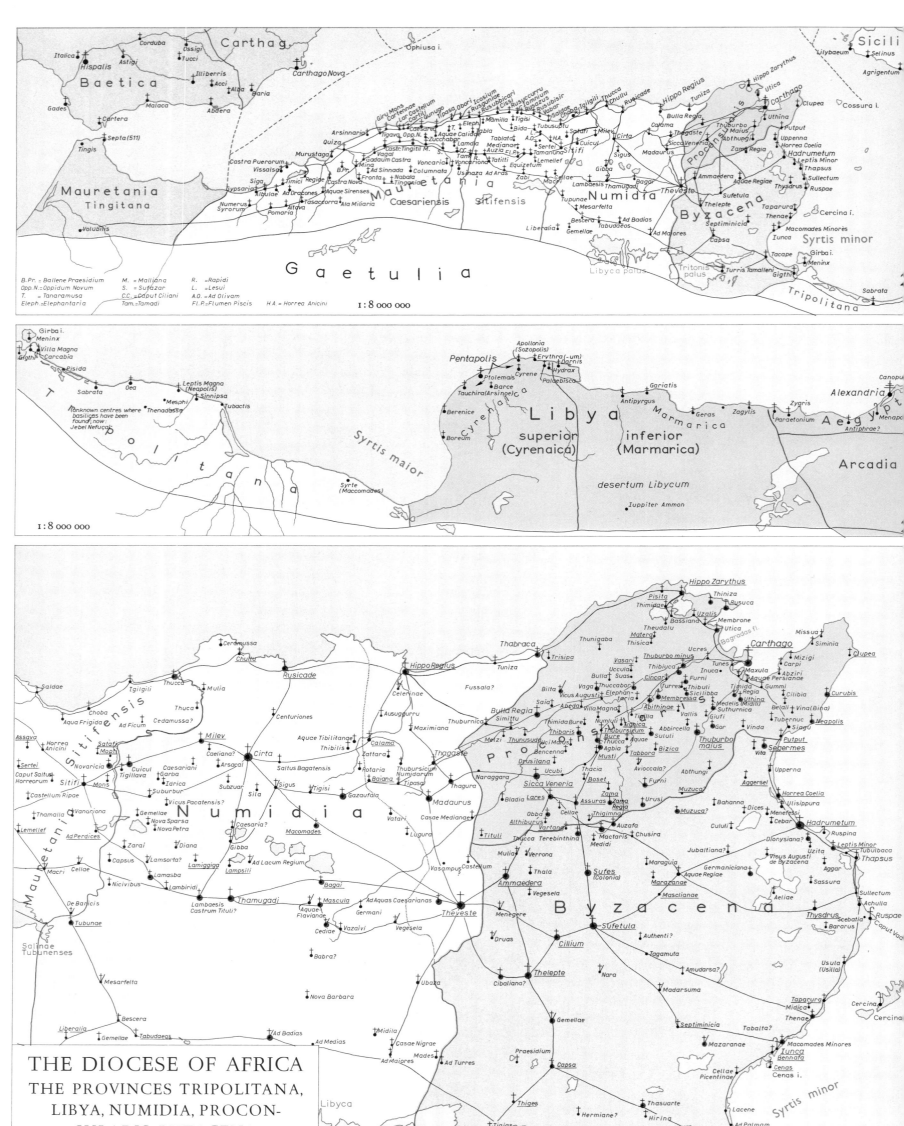

THE DIOCESE OF AFRICA

THE PROVINCES TRIPOLITANA, LIBYA, NUMIDIA, PROCONSULARIS, BYZACENA

● Churches whose bishops were present at the Synod of Carthage in 256

Thabraca = places with Catholic and Donatist See;

Thala = Donatist See; after Frend, The Donatist Church, Oxford 1952

0   25   100 miles

1 : 2 500 000

1 : 8 000 000

B.Pr. = Ballene Praesidium   M. = Malliana   R. = Rapidi
Opp.N. = Oppidum Novum   S. = Sufazar   L. = Lesui
T. = Tanaramusa   C.C. = Caput Ciliani   A.O. = Ad Olivam
Eleph. = Elephantaria   Tam. = Tamadi   Fl.P. = Flumen Piscis   H.A. = Horrea Anicini

1 : 8 000 000

THE DIOCESE
OF ITALIA
SUBURBICARIA
WITH THE CHIEF PART OF
ITALIA ANNONARIA

Diocese of Italia Suburbicaria
Diocese of Italia Annonaria
Diocese of Illyricum
Diocese of the Seven Provinces
F.P. Ferentum Polymartium
roads

1 : 3 500 000

0   25   100 miles

THE ENVIRONS
OF ROME
: 1 250 000

24

23

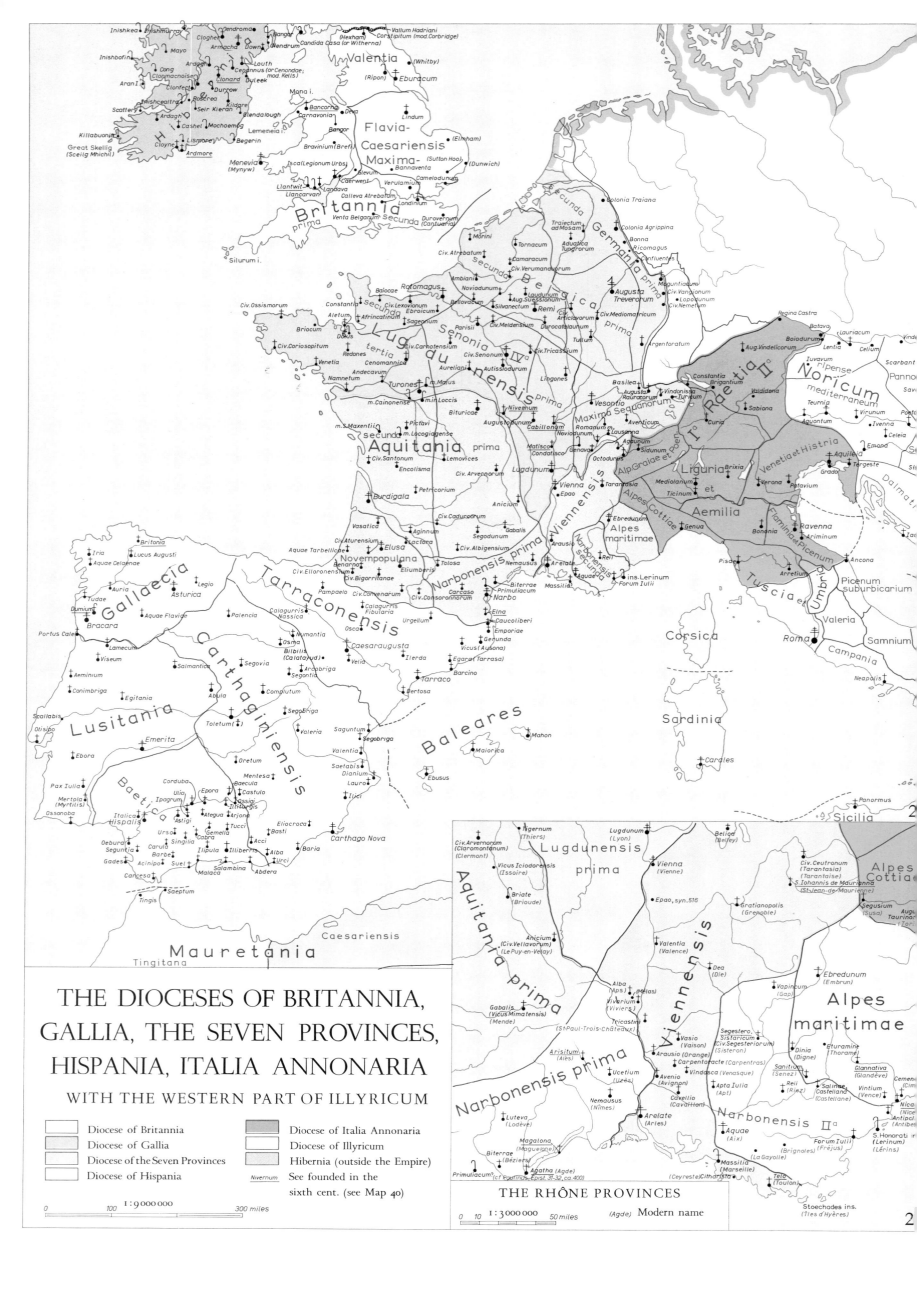

THE DIOCESES OF BRITANNIA, GALLIA, THE SEVEN PROVINCES, HISPANIA, ITALIA ANNONARIA

WITH THE WESTERN PART OF ILLYRICUM

Diocese of Britannia
Diocese of Gallia
Diocese of the Seven Provinces
Diocese of Hispania
Diocese of Italia Annonaria
Diocese of Illyricum
Hibernia (outside the Empire)
Nivernum See founded in the sixth cent. (see Map 40)

0 100 1:9 000 000 300 miles

THE RHÔNE PROVINCES

0 10 1:3 000 000 50 miles
(Agde) Modern name

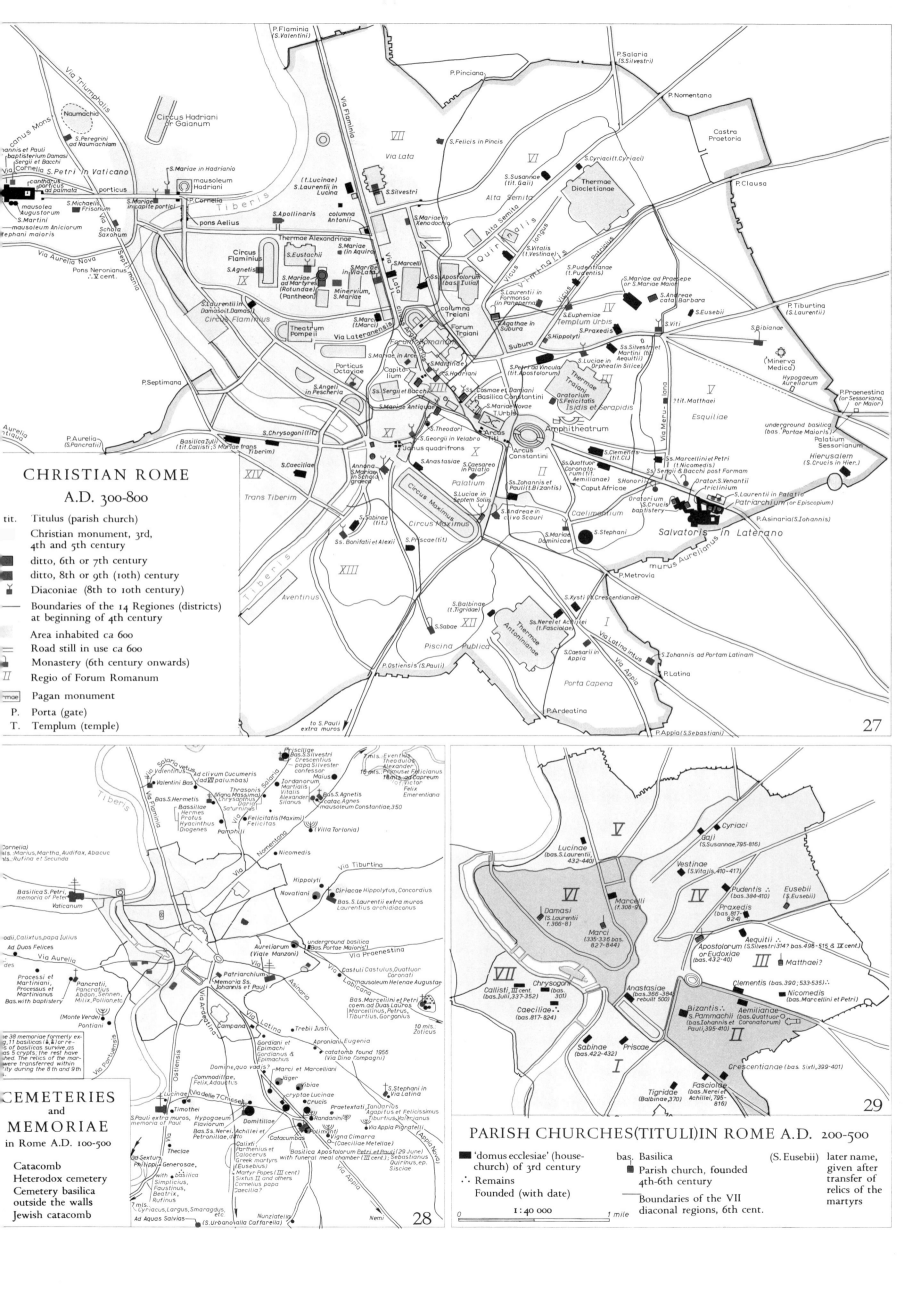

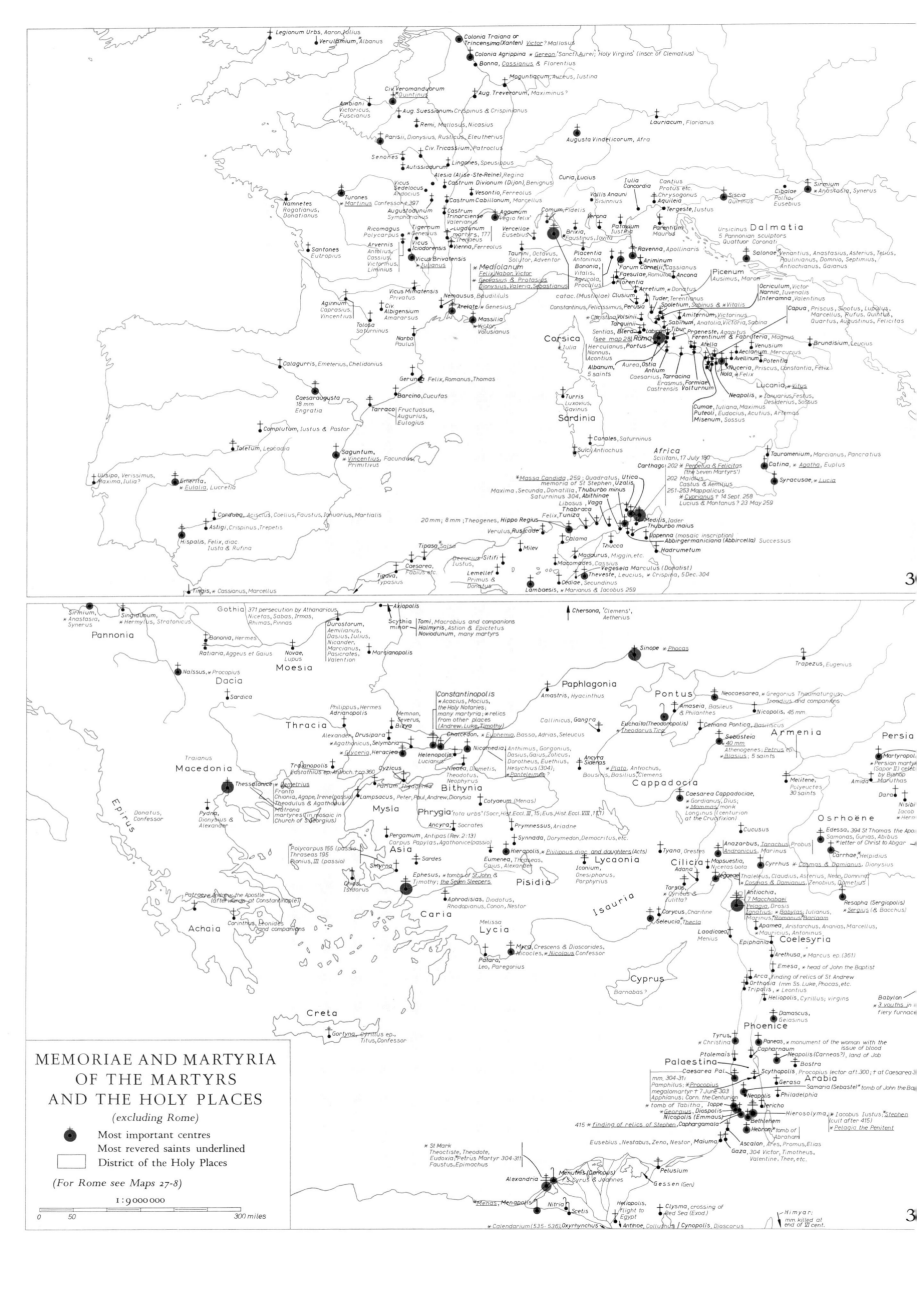

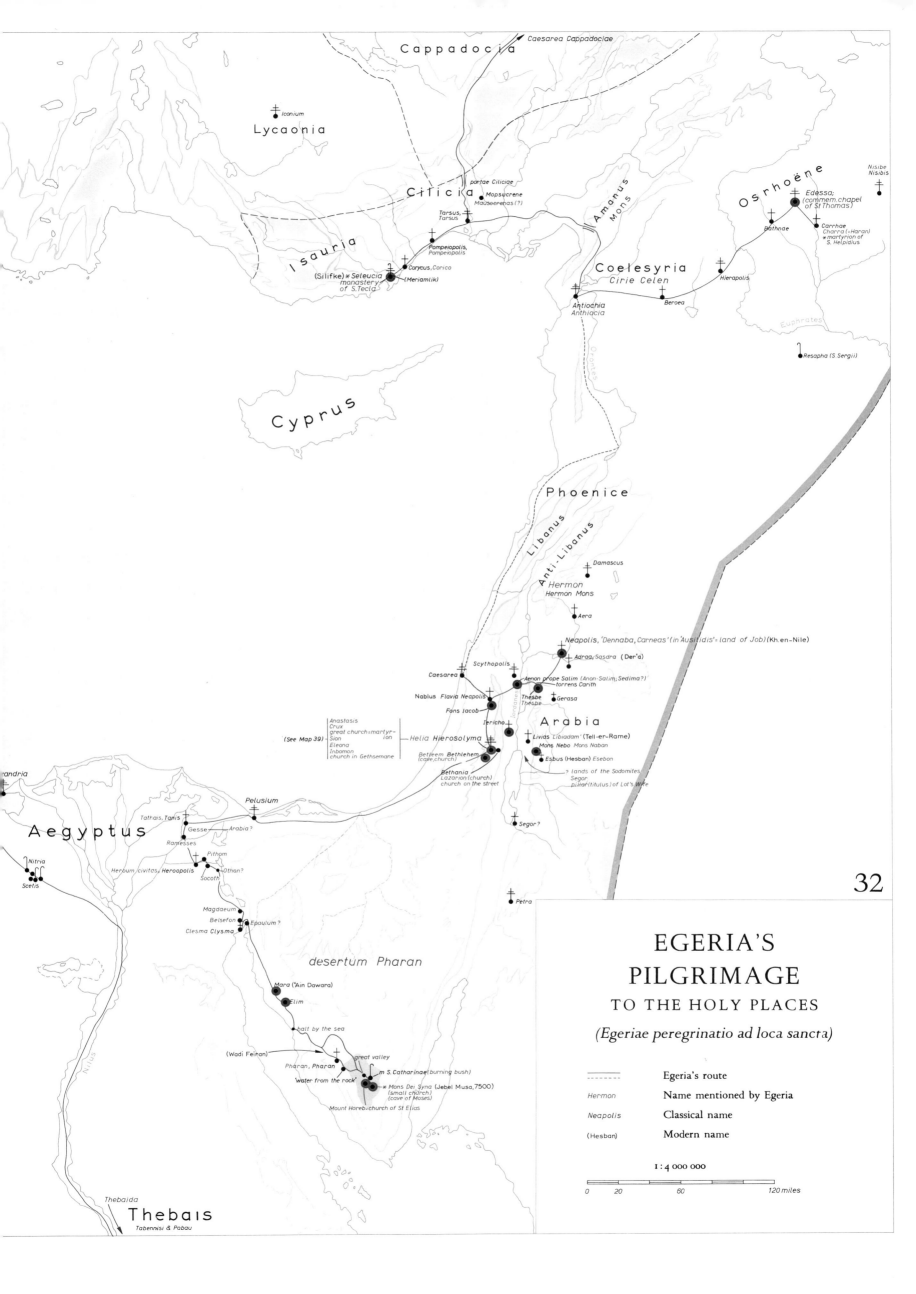

Caesarea Cappadociae

Cappadocia

✝ *Iconium*

Lycaonia

C i l i c i a

portae Ciliciae

✝ *Mopsucrene*
Mauseerenas (?)

✝ *Tarsus, Tarsus,*

I s a u r i a

✝ *Pompeiopolis, Pompeiopolis*

✝ *Corycus, Corico*

(*Silifke*) ✳ *Seleucia monastery of S.Tecla* — (*Meriamlik*)

Amanus Mons

Osrhoëne

Nisibe Nisibis ✝

✝ *Edessa; (commem.chapel of St Thomas)*

✝ *Bathnae*

✳ *Carrhae Charra (=Haran)* ✳ *martyrion of S. Helpidius*

Coelesyria
Cirie Celen

✝ *Hierapolis*

✝ *Antiochia Anthiocia*

Beroea

Orontes

Euphrates

C y p r u s

✝ *Resapha (S. Sergii)*

Phoenice

Libanus

Anti-Libanus

Hermon
Hermon Mons

Damascus

✝ *Aera*

✝ *Neapolis, 'Dennaba, Carneas' (in 'Ausitidis'= land of Job) (Kh.en-Nile)*

✝ *Adraa, Sasdra (Der'a)*

Scythopolis ✝

Caesarea

Aenon prope Salim (Anon-Salim; Sedima?)
torrens Carith

Nablus Flavia Neapolis

Thesbe
Thesbe

Gerasa

Fons Iacob

Jordanes

Arabia

Jericho, ✝

Anastasis
Crux
great church=martyr-
(See Map 39) — Sion } — *Helia Hierosolyma*
Eleona
Inbomon
church in Gethsemane

Livias Libiadam (Tell-er-Rame)

Mons Nebo Mons Naban

Betleem Bethlehem (cave,church) ✝

Esbus (Hesban) Esebon

Bethania Lazarion (church) church on the street

? *lands of the Sodomites,*
Segor
pillar (titulus) of Lot's Wife

A e g y p t u s

andria

✝ *Pelusium*

Tathais, Tanis

Gesse — *Arabia?*

Ramesses

Pithom

Herbum civitas, Heroopolis

Othan?

Socoth

Nitria ✳

Scetis

Magdaeum

Belsefon

Clesma Clysma

Epaulum?

desertum Pharan

Mara ('Ain Dawara) ✳

Elim ✳

halt by the sea

(*Wadi Feiran*)

great valley

Pharan, Pharan

✝ *m S.Catharinae (burning bush)*

'water from the rock'

✳ *Mons Dei Syna (Jebel Musa, 7500)*
(small church)
(cave of Moses)

Mount Horeb=church of St Elias

Segor? ✝

✝ *Petra*

32

Thebais

Thebaida

Tabennisi & Pabau

NILUS

EGERIA'S
PILGRIMAGE
TO THE HOLY PLACES

(Egeriae peregrinatio ad loca sancta)

– – – –	Egeria's route
Hermon	Name mentioned by Egeria
Neapolis	Classical name
(*Hesban*)	Modern name

1 : 4 000 000

0   20   60   120 miles

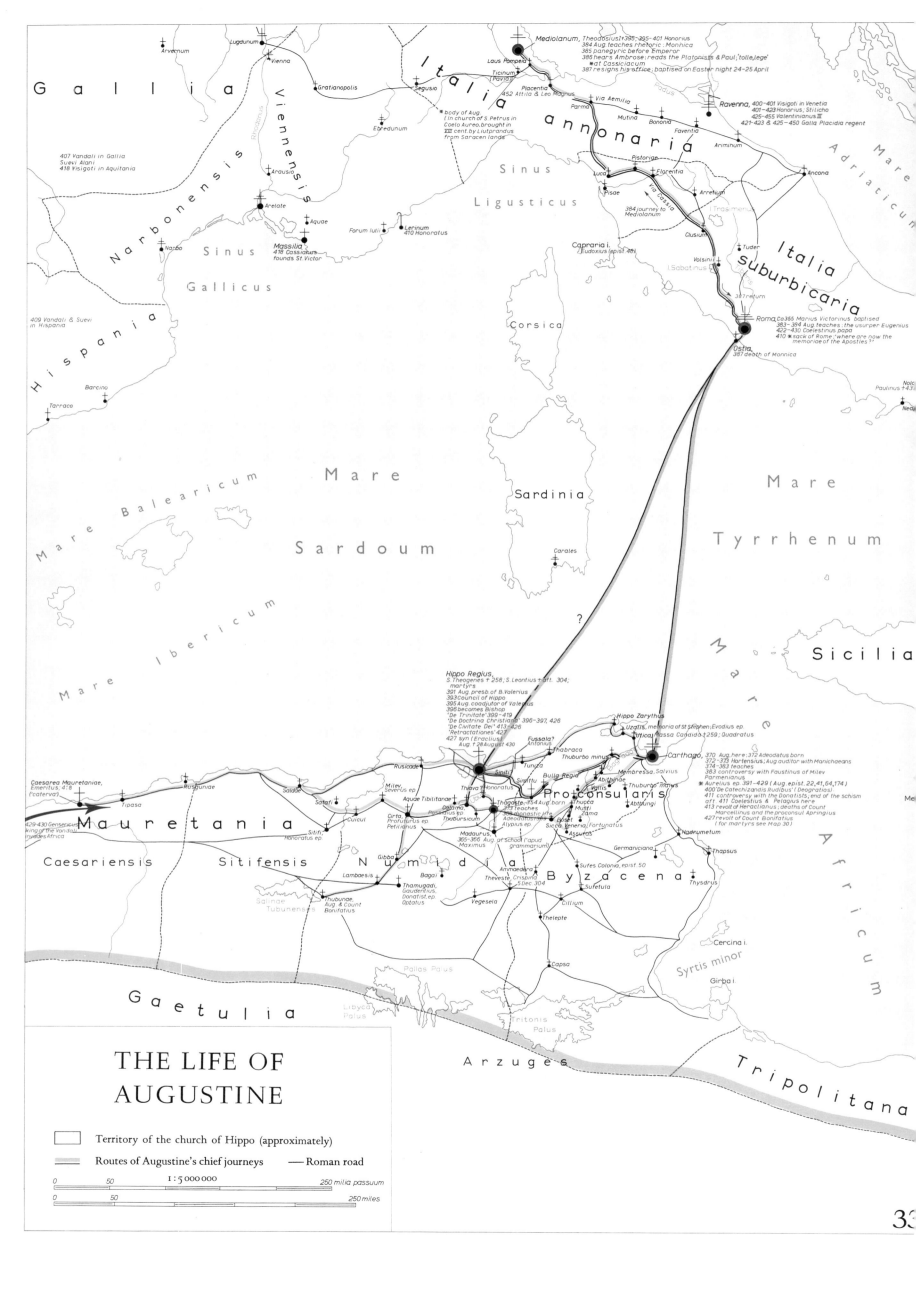

Arvernum

Lugdunum

Vienna

G a l l i a

Gratianopolis

Mediolanum, Theodosius†395; 395-401 Honorius
384 Aug. teaches rhetoric : Monnica
385 panegyric before Emperor
386 hears Ambrose; reads the Platonists & Paul; 'tolle, lege'
    at Cassiciacum
387 resigns his office; baptised on Easter night 24-25 April

I t a l i a   a n n o n a r i a

Laus Pompeia

Ticinum
(Pavia)
Segusio *Placentia*
452 Attila & Leo Magnus

Ravenna, 400-401 Visigoti in Venetia
401-423 Honorius; Stilicho
425-455 Valentinianus III
421-423 & 425-450 Galla Placidia regent

Ebredunum

Parma *Via Aemilia* *Mutina* *Bononia* *Faventia*

body of Aug.
(in church of S.Petrus in
Coelo Aureo, brought in
VIII cent. by Liutprandus
from Saracen lands

Ariminum

Adriaticum

V i e n n e n s i s

407 Vandali in Gallia
Suevi Alani
418 Visigoti in Aquitania

Arausio

S i n u s

Pistorige

L i g u s t i c u s

Luca *Florentia* *Via Cassia* *Arretium*

Ancona

Aquae
Arelate

N a r b o n e s i s

Narbo S i n u s

Forum Iulii
Lerinum
410 Honoratus

I Trasimenus

I t a l i a

Massilia
418 Cassianus
founds St.Victor

G a l l i c u s

Pisae

384 journey to
Mediolanum

Clusium

s u b u r b i c a r i a

409 Vandali & Suevi
in Hispania

Capraria i.
(Eudoxius (epist.48)

Volsinii
I.Sabatinus

Tuder

387 return

H i s p a n i a

Barcino

C o r s i c a

Roma, Co 355 Marius Victorinus baptised
383-384 Aug. teaches ; the usurper Eugenius
422-430 Coelestinus papa
410 * sack of Rome; 'where are now the
    memoriae of the Apostles?'

Tarraco

M a r e

Ostia
387 death of Monnica

Notc
Paulinus†431
Nea

M a r e   B a l e a r i c u m

S a r d i n i a

M a r e   T y r r h e n u m

M a r e
S a r d o u m

Carales

S i c i l i a

M a r e   I b e r i c u m

Hippo Regius,
S. Theogenes † 258; S. Leontius † aft. 304;
    martyrs
391 Aug. presb. of B. Valerius
393 Council of Hippo
395 Aug. coadjutor of Valerius
396 becomes Bishop
'De Trinitate' 399-419
'De Doctrina Christiana' 396-397, 426
'De Civitate Dei' 413-426
'Retractationes' 427
427 syn (Eraclius)
Aug. † 28 August 430

Hippo Zarythus

Uzalis, memoria of St Stephen; Evodius ep.
Utica, Massa Candida †259; Quadratus

Carthago, 370 Aug. here; 372 Adeodatus born
372-373 Hortensius; Aug. auditor with Manichaeans
374-383 teaches
383 controversy with Faustinus of Milev
* Aurelius ep. 391-429 (Aug epist. 22, 41, 64, 174)
400 'De Catechizandis Rudibus' (Deogratias)
411 controversy with the Donatists; end of the schism
aft. 411 Coelestius & Pelagius here
413 revolt of Heraclianus; deaths of Count
    Marcellinus and the proconsul Apringius
427 revolt of Count Bonifatius
    (for martyrs see Map 30)

Fussala?
Antonius
Thabraca
Thuburbo minus
Membressa, Salvius
Thuburbo minus

Caesarea Mauretaniae,
Emeritus; 418
('caterva')

Rusguniae

Rusicade

Sinitu

Tuniza

Bulla Regia

Vallis
Abithinae
Abithungi

Tipasa

Saldae

Milev,
Severus ep.

Thiava ? *Honoratus*

Sitiffu

Sicca Veneria, Fortunatus
Mustti
Zama

M a u r e t a n i a

429-430 Genseric
king of the Vandals
invades Africa

Satafi

Aquae Tibilitanae

Cirta,
Profuturus ep.
Petilianus

Calama,
Possidius ep.
Thubursicum

Thagaste, 354 Aug. born
monastic life
Alypius ep.
Adeodatus†389

Assuras

C a e s a r i e n s i s

S i t i f e n s i s

Sitifi,
Honoratus ep.

N u m i d i a

Madaurus,
365-366 Aug. at school ('apud
    grammaticum')
Maximus

Hucca

P r o c o n s u l a r i s

Hadrumetum

Germaniciana

Thapsus

Gibba

Lambaesis

Bagai

B y z a c e n a

Ammaedara

Sufes Colonia, epist. 50

Curcul

Salinae
Tubunenses

Thubunae,
Gaudentius,
Donatist.ep.
Optatus

Thamugadi,
Gaudentius,
Donatist.ep.
Optatus

Theveste, Crispina
5 Dec 304

Sufetula

Vegesela

Cillium

Thysdrus

Cercina i.

Thelepte

Capsa

Syrtis minor

Girba i.

Pallas Palus

G a e t u l i a

Libyca
Palus

Tritonis
Palus

A r z u g e s

T r i p o l i t a n a

M a r e
A f r i c u m

THE LIFE OF
AUGUSTINE

☐ Territory of the church of Hippo (approximately)

━━ Routes of Augustine's chief journeys   ── Roman road

0   50   1 : 5 000 000   250 milia passuum

0   50   250 miles

33

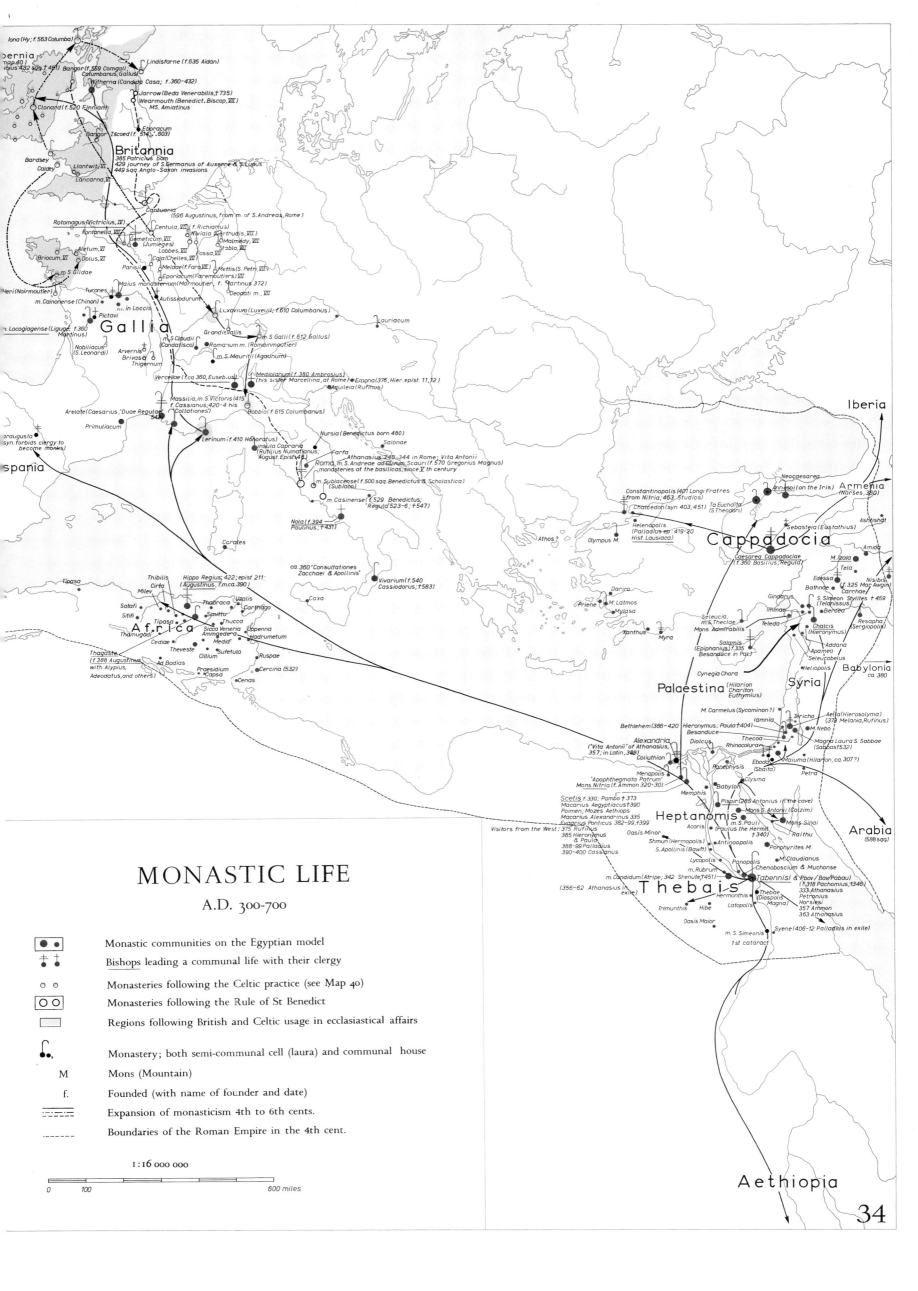

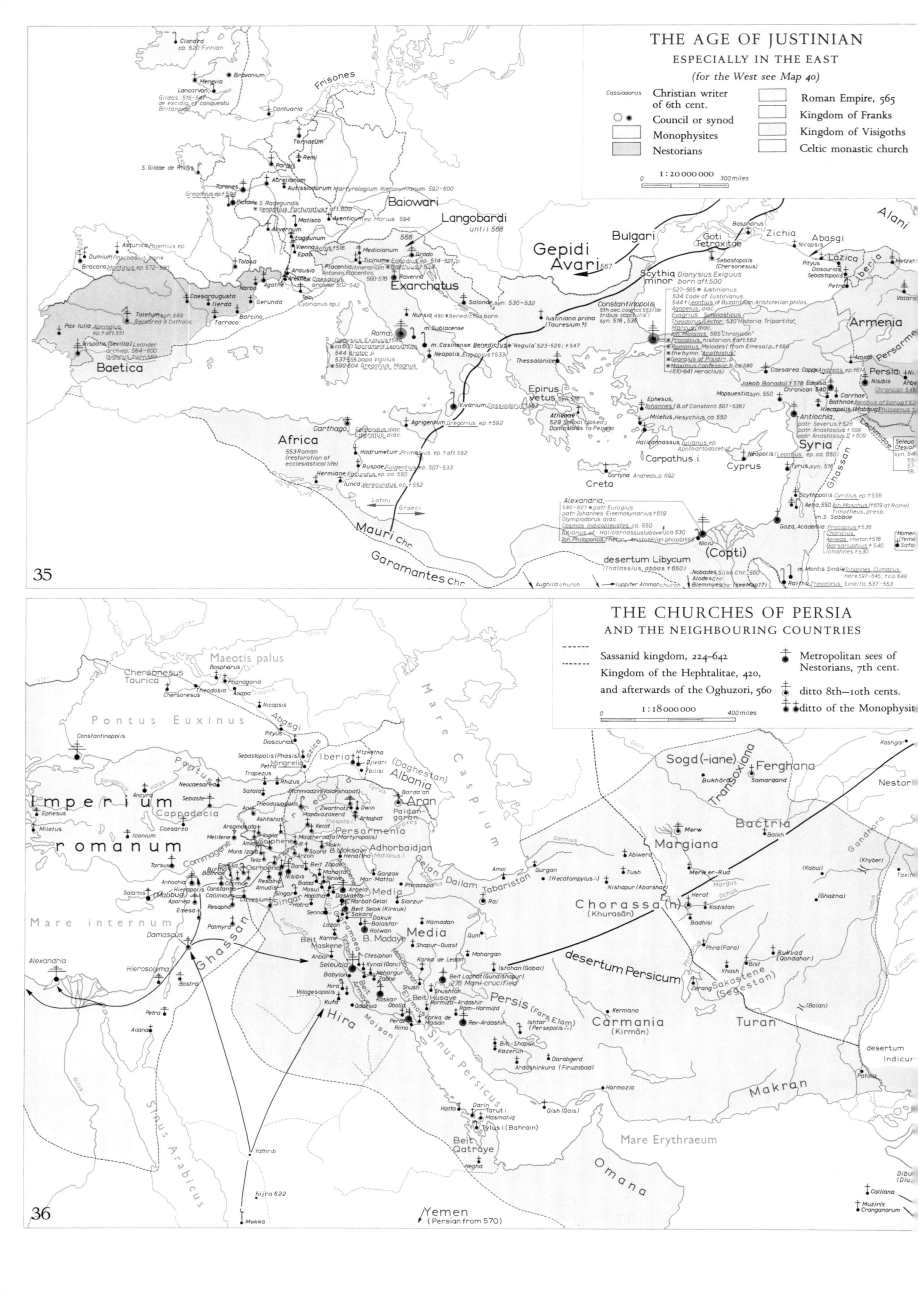

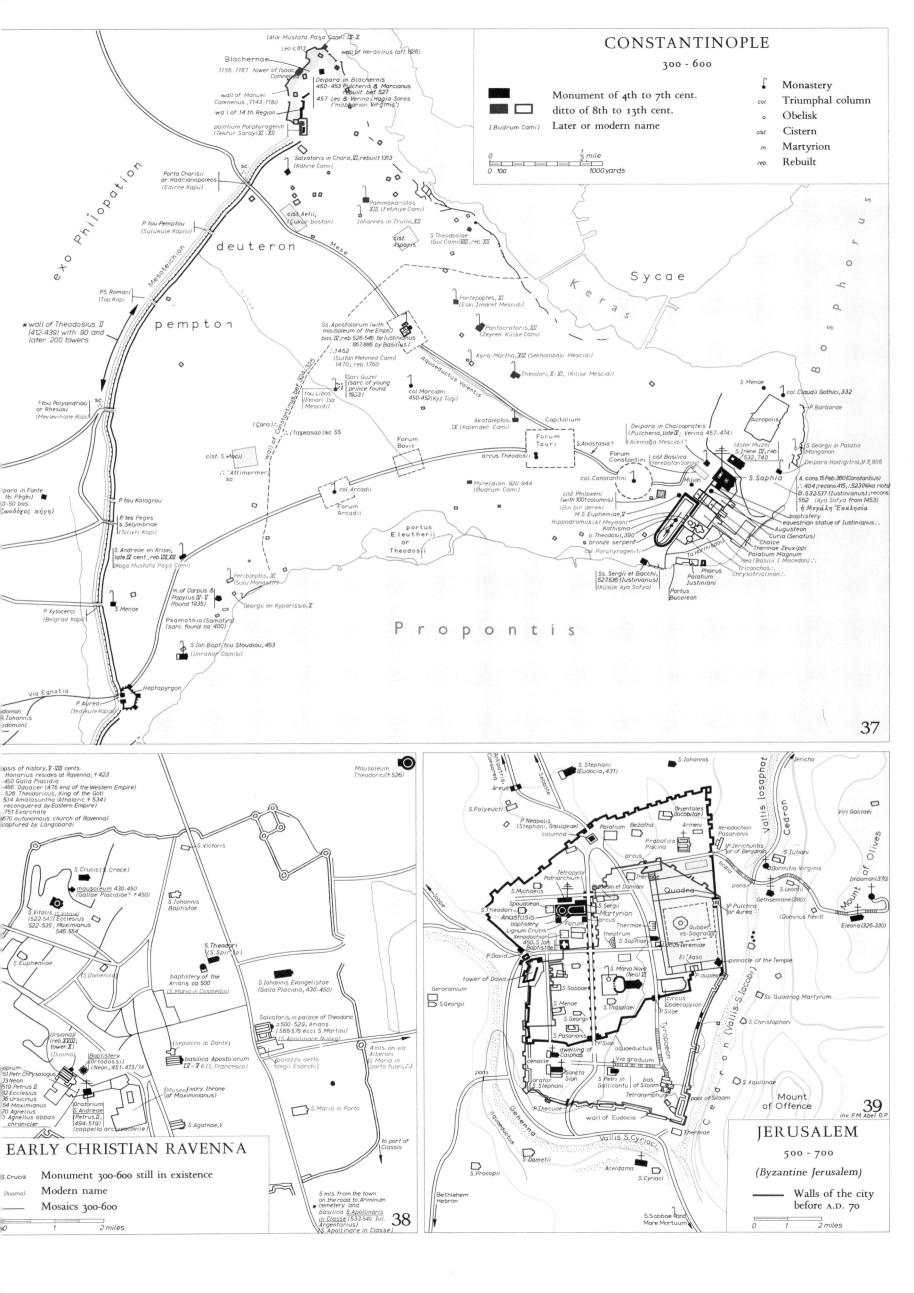

Roman Empire
Kingdom of the Visigoths
Kingdom of the Suevi (to 585)
Anglo—Saxons

Kingdom of the Franks
Kingdom of the Lombards
Celtic monastic church

Political boundaries from ca 590-600
Route of Augustine (Rome-Canterbury) 594/5
Nivernum Episcopal see founded in the 6th century
Duc. Benev.   Ducatus Beneventi

0   50   250 miles
                                    1:9 000 000

Iona (Hy, Ikolmkill)
f. 563 Columba
InberKenneth
Mull

St Brendan †577
Inishkea
Duvillaun
Mayo
Inishbhofin
Cong
Clonmacnoise
Aran I.
Seic Kieran
Scattery
Kilmalkedar
(Great Skellig)
Sceilg Mhichil
Cloyne
Begerin
Ardmore
Kilmalkedar
Lismore
Cashel
Ardagh
Mochaemog
Lemeneig
(Bardsey)

Derry
Inishmurray
Clogher
Bangor
f. 559 Comgall
Columbanus
Gallus
Down
Needrum
Armagh
Kells
Monasterboice
Clonard, ca 520 f. Finnian (†541)
Durrow
St Brigit
Kildare
Toscrea
Clonfert
Glendalough
Bangor Fawr
f. ca 560 Deiniol
Man
Mona
Bangor Iscoed
f. 514 Dunawd
.'. 603 (Ethelfrid)

Brefi
syn. 512
Mynyw
St David
519 syn.
Llantwit
Caldey ins.
St Gildas
Lancarvan
St Cadoc
Llanava

Lindisfarne (VII)
f. 635 Aidan
Bernicia
(Ruthwell)
(Bewcastle)
(Witherna)
(Jarrow)(Beda †735)
(Wearmouth)(VII)
(Whitby)
(Ripon)
Eboracum (York)
Lindum (Lincoln)
Northumbria
Mercia
East Anglia
(Brixworth)
Sutton Hoo (burial ship, 660)
Verulamium
Roffa (Rochester)
Londinium
597 Ethelbert baptised
Cantuaria
595-596
Augustinus Kent
(Stonehenge)
Crediton
Wessex
Sussex
Essex

Frisones

Morini
Tornacum, syn. 520
Tungri
(Colonia Traiana)
Colonia
Thuringia
Atrebates
Camaracum
Ambiani
Verumanduorum
Noviodunum
Laudunum
Moguntiacum
Rotomagus
Suessiones
Silvanectum
Remi
Virodunum
Treveri
Vangiones
Nemetes
Baiocae
Lexovium
Ebroicum
Bellovacum
Mettis
Constantia
Africatinum
Sagennum
Parisii
520 S. Genoveva
Meldi
Catalaunum
Tullium
(Regina Castra)
Aletum
Datus, Samson
Redones
Carnutum
Tricasses
Argentoratum
Baiowari
Ossismi
Briocum
Coriospitum
Cenomannum
Turones
*Gregorius
ept. 594
Senones
Autissiodunum
ca. 592
Martyrologium
Hieronymianum
Lingones
Luxovium (Luxeuil)
f. 610 Columbanus
Venetia
mon. S. Gildae
S. Gildas
Andecavum
Aurelianum
538, 541, 549,
syn. 511, 553
Namnetum
mon. Maius
mon. in Loccis
Bituriges
Nivernum
Vesontio
Constantia
Aventicum
mon. S. Galli, f. 612 Gallus

mon. Cainonense
S. Maxentii
Pictavi, S. Radegundis †587
Venantius Fortunatus †aft.
600
Augustodunum
Cabillonum
mon. Locogiagense
Santones
Lemovices
Matisco
syn. 581
Condatisco
Lausonna
Noviodunum
Agaunum
Sedunum
Octodurus
Curia
Sabiona
Modicia (Monza)
Theodolinde (ampullae)
Aguntum
Teurnia
Ivenna Po.
Virunum
Ducatus
Friuli

Encolisma
Petricorium
Arvernum
(Claromontanum)
syn. 535
Lugdunum
Genava
Belica
Tarantasia
Augusta
Praetoria
Mediolanum
Ticinum
Ennodius ep. †521
Verona
Tergeste
Aquileia (.:.)
Grado, syn. 579, 591

Burdigala
Cadurci
Vellavi
Vienna
Avitus †518
Epao, syn. 517
Valentia
S. Joh. de Maurianna
Sigesium
Taurini
Boethius †524
Mantua
Patavium
Parentium

Vasatica
Aquae Tarbellicae
Agennum
Ruteni
Alba
S. Joh. de Maurianna
Gratianopolis
Placentia
Cremona
Bononia
Ravenna, Theodoricus
493-526
Amalasuntha
Britonia
Iria
Lucus Augusti
Galleacia
Rufianense
Asturica, Polemius
Legio
Vasconia
Autrigonia
Elusa
Lactora
Benarno
Tolosa, syn. 589
Civ. Albigensium
Ucetium
Nemausus
Vasio
Arausio, 2nd syn. 529 (against the
Semipelagians)
Vivarium
Dea
Ebredunum
Genua
Taurini
Classis
Exarchatus
Pisae
Florentia
Ariminum
Petra Pertusa
Ancona

Tude
Dumium, Paschasius diac.
Bracara, Martinus ep. 572-580
syn. 561, 572 (capitula
Martini)
Joh. de Biclar, abbas †590
Portus Cale
Lamecum
Viseum
Aguada
Conimbriga
Asturia
Pallentia
Legio
Calafora
Pampaelo
Convenarum
Consoranni
Burdigala
Urgellum
Iustus ep.
Elena
Agatha, syn. 507
Biterrae
Narbo, King Alaric (†507)
King Amalric (526-53)
and Queen Clotilde (†531)
589 national syn.
Hierunda, syn. 517
Emporias
Magalona
Loteva
Arelate, Caesarius, †542
Aquae
Reji
Lerinum
Telo
(Cyprianus, ep.)
Tadinum
Perusia
Nursia, Benedictus b.
Spoletum
Ducatus
Spoleti
Tecte
Mon. Sublacense 500
Duc. Bene.
Mon. Casiner.
Benedictus †
Beneventum
Capua
Neapolis

Galleacia
Asturia
Numantia
Uxoma
Tirassona
Osca
Ilerda, syn. 546
Ausona
Tarrasa, syn.
Barcino, 540; King Theudis, 531-49
Tarraco, syn. 516
Lamecum
Aguada
Conimbriga
Pallentia
Septimanca
Salamantica
Secobia
Segontia
Caesaraugusta,
Braulio ep. 638
Mon. Servitanum? 570-580
Dertosa

Egitania
Caurium
Abula
Complutum
Reccopolis 578-926
Arcavica
Toletum
534 Kings here
567-586 Leovigild;
587 Reccared converted (†601)
610-612 Gondemar; Toletum a metropolis
527, 531, 589, 675, 688, 693 synods
589, 633 national conc.
654 Liber Iudiciorum
historiogr; Iulianus ep.
Segobriga
Valentia, syn. 546;
Iustinianus
Emerita
King Agila 550-4
Oretum
Scallabis
Olisipo
Ebora
Pax Iulia, Apringius ep. †aft. 551
Setobi
Dianium
Mahon
Turris
Palma
Carales
Sulcis

Martola (Myrtilis)
Nipla
Italica
Corduba
Caziona
Ilici
Bigastrium
Lacobriga
Ossonoba
Jereto
Baetica
Baetica (under the
Empire 552-629)
Astigi
Tucci
Egabro
Acci
Elberris
Lorica
Carthago Spartaria
Hispalis,
Leander †600
*Isidorus †636
syn. 590
Gades
Assidonia
Carteia
Moors 711
Septem
Tingis

Vivarium
Cassiodorus
†583
Panormus

Cartennae
Caesarea
Tipasa
Hippo Regius
Carthago Ferrandus diac.
Liberatus diac.
Anthologia latina, Luxorius 532-534
Corippus
523 syn.
635 Maximus Confessor here
Agrigentum,
Gregorius ep. 15
Syracu.

Cirta
Calama
Sicca Veneria
Ammaedera
Theveste
Hadrumetum, Primasius ep. †aft. 552
Thapsus
Ruspae, Fulgentius ep. 507-533
Cercina, f. 532
Tunca, Verecundus ep. †552
Hermiane, Facundus ep. ca. 550

501, 502 syn.
476-553 under the Goths
553-751 under the Empire
545 Dionysius Exiguus †
? ca. 600 Sacramentarium Leonianum
514 Arator, p.
Helpidius Rusticus, p.
590-604 *Gregorius Magnus, pope
595 Mission of Augustinus to Britain
(from mon. of S. Andreas in Coelio)
Roma
Ducatus
Romanus

4

THE CHURCH OF THE MARTYRS A.D. 30–313

The fullness of time

1. AUGUSTUS (27 B.C.–A.D. 14). Cameo inset in the Lotharius cross. 1st. century or, according to some, beginning of the 4th. *Treasure of the cathedral of Aachen.*

Ultima Cumaei venit iam carminis aetas,
magnus ab integro saeclorum nascitur ordo;
iam redit et virgo, redeunt Saturnia regna,
iam nova progenies caelo dimittitur alto.

Now has come the last age of the song of Cumae,
the great cycle of centuries begins anew.
Now the Virgin returns, the reign of Saturn comes again,
a new Progeny descends from heaven on high.

Virgil's lines on the golden age of peace and the renewal of the world by Augustus were regarded by the Middle Ages also as an unconscious prophecy concerning the fullness of time. They saw in them a reference to the Virgin and the Child descended from heaven and so added this mysterious prediction to the Psalms and other Messianic prophecies. Virgil and the Sybil of Cumae, all unknowing, joined their voices to the chorus of the prophets of Israel. Virgil became for Dante the 'guide through Limbo', the name given to the dwelling place of all noble souls who had lived before the coming of Christ.

"In those days a decree went out from Caesar Augustus that all the world should be enrolled. This was the first enrolment when Quirinius was governor of Syria. And all went to be enrolled, each to his own city. And Joseph also went up from Galilee . . . to Bethlehem . . . with Mary, his betrothed, who was with child. And while they were there the time came for her to be delivered. And she gave birth to her first-born son." (Luke 2:1-7)

"In the forty-third year of the reign of Augustus, Jesus Christ, the Son of God, is born in Bethlehem." (Eusebius, *Chronicle*, Augustus, 43, 4th century)

The first century

2. TIBERIUS (14-37). *Rome, Museo Capitolino.* "In the fifteenth year of the reign of Tiberius Caesar . . . the word of God came to John, the son of Zechariah, in the wilderness." (Luke 3:1-2)

The fifteenth year of Tiberius' reign is A.D. 28, the 782nd year from the founding of Rome. Jesus was about thirty years old.

"In the fifteenth year of the reign of Tiberius, John, the son of Zechariah, preaching in the wilderness near the river Jordan, bears witness that Christ the Son of God is in their midst. From here, too, the Lord Jesus Himself preaches to the peoples the way of salvation, proving by signs and wonders that what he said is true." (Eusebius, *Chronicle*, Tiberius, 15, A.D. 28)

3. CLAUDIUS (41-57). *Vatican.* "Since the Jews constantly made disturbances at the instigation of Chrestus, he [Claudius] expelled them from Rome."
(Suetonius, *Lives of the Caesars*, Claudius, **25**, 4)

Compare Acts 18:2. Aquila and Priscilla were at Corinth because they had been driven from Rome, and thus St Paul met the first members of the Christian community of Rome.

4. NERO (57-68). *Rome, Museo delle Terme.* "He caused the Christians to be put to death, a class of men adhering to a new and noxious religious sect."
(Suetonius, *Lives of the Caesars.* Nero, **16**, 3)

". . . and yet the evil rumours that the fire [which destroyed Rome] had been lighted at his [Nero's] order, could not be hushed. Therefore, in order to put an end to this talk, he designated culprits and had them punished with the utmost refinements of cruelty. And the people he chose were those whom the populace abominated an account of their vices and whom they called 'Christians'. This name goes back to Chrestus who was executed by the procurator Pontius Pilate during the reign of Tiberius. Although this execrable superstition was suppressed for a time, it reappeared later not only in Judaea, the cradle of the evil, but even in the City itself where every barbarian and shameless sect gathers from far and near to hold its conventicles. Therefore those who confessed their religion were arrested first of all; then, on their indication, great numbers were convicted who were accused not so much of fire-raising as of hatred of the human race." (Tacitus, *Annals*, **15**, 44:2-5)

". . . It was he [Nero] who began . . . to slaughter the Apostles. It is told that Paul was beheaded in Rome itself and that Peter was crucified during his reign. And this story is confirmed by the fact that their graves still bear the names of Peter and Paul." (Eusebius, *Ecclesiastical History*, **2**, 25:5)

"That both suffered martyrdom [for the faith] at the same time we know from the testimony of Dionysius, Bishop of Corinth, when he writes to the Romans: By your zealous care you bound together at Rome and Corinth the

6   7   8

plantations of Peter and Paul. For in our own city of Corinth both also planted and taught us: in like manner they also taught together in Italy and suffered martyrdom together at the same time." (Eusebius, *Ecclesiastical History*, **2**, 25: 8)

Dionysius of Corinth (see Map 6) wrote *ca* 170; Eusebius read his letter *ca* 330.

5. VESPASIAN (69-79). *Rome, Museo Capitolino.*

6. TITUS (79-81). *Rome, Museo Capitolino.* "Titus, the son of Vespasian, spoke both languages [Latin and Greek] fluently, and of such a noble character was he that when he remembered on one occasion, while sitting at table, that he had not yet done anyone a service that day, he said: Friends, today has been a wasted day for me." (Eusebius, *Chronicle*, Titus 1, A.D. 79)

"Titus conquers Judaea and lays Jerusalem waste, killing six hundred thousand people." (Eusebius, *Chronicle*, Vespasian 2, A.D. 70)

The Christian community of Jerusalem—the 'Whitsun community'— mindful of the warning of the Lord (Matt. 24), had fled in time to Pella in Transjordan (see Map 1). They formed the first nucleus of the 'Church of the Circumcision'.

7. DOMITIAN (81-96). *Rome, Museo Capitolino.* "In the fifteenth year of the reign of Domitian, Flavia Domitilla, daughter of a sister of Flavius Clemens, one of the consuls of Rome at that time, was also banished to the island of Pontia because of her testimony for Christ." (Eusebius, *Ecclesiastical History*, **3**, 18: 4)

The same historian also relates how the Emperor set out to trace Our Lord's kindred but seeing them to be such simple people let them go their way unmolested. The Apostle John, banished to Patmos (see Map 1), wrote there according to tradition the book of the Revelation (The Apocalypse).

"Domitian was the first to proclaim himself lord and god . . . Domitian was the second after Nero to persecute the Christians and during his reign the Apostle John, banished to Patmos, saw the Revelation." (Eusebius, *Chronicle*, Domitian 6, A.D. 86; 14, A.D. 94)

8. NERVA (96-8). *Rome, Museo Capitolino.* In the second year of Nerva's reign Clement, Bishop of the Church of Rome, wrote a letter to the Church of Corinth. Ever since, this letter has been held in high honour both there and elsewhere and is often read. It is mentioned by the Dionysius of Corinth referred to above and is still extant. It contains a prayer for those in authority, for the Christians attributed the persecutions and the false notions concerning their religion to the powers of evil; they did not rebel, nor were they disloyal to the emperor:

"Thou O Lord, in the unspeakable greatness of thy sovereignty hast given them the power to rule so that we, acknowledging the majesty and honour which Thou hast conferred upon them, may be subject to them without in the least opposing Thy will. Grant to them, O Lord, health, peace, concord, and the continuance of the Empire, so that they may exercise irreproachably the supreme leadership which Thou hast conferred upon them. For Thou, O Lord of the heavens and King of all ages [cf I Tim. 1:17], conferrest upon the sons of men majesty and honour and authority over the things which are upon the earth. Do Thou, O Lord, direct their will in accordance with what is good and pleasing to Thee, so that they may piously exercise in peace and gentleness the authority Thou hast granted them and thus find grace in Thy sight. For Thou alone hast the power to accomplish this and even greater good. We praise Thee therefore through the high priest and protector of our souls, Jesus Christ, through Whom

Thine be the glory and the power, now and from generation to generation, world without end." (Clement of Rome, *To the Corinthians*, 61)

The second century

The Empire reached its zenith under the Emperors of the second century (compare Map 3-4 with Maps 5 and 6). The provinces especially passed through an unprecedented period of prosperity and cultural activity. The Emperors themselves were, with few exceptions, men with a high sense of duty. Their only knowledge of the new religion, however, was based on reports (we do not know whether or not they were acquainted with the writings of the Christian apologists—see Map 6), and to officialdom Christianity remained a *religio illicita*, a non-authorised sect which constituted a danger to the State.

15 (page 36). TRAJAN (98-117). *Rome, Museo Capitolino.* "Irenaeus [Bishop of Lugdunum (Lyon), see Map 5] writes that the Apostle John lived till the time of Trajan . . . In the eleventh year of Trajan's reign Ignatius, Bishop of Antioch, is brought to Rome and thrown to the wild beasts." (Eusebius, *Chronicle*, Trajan 3, A.D. 100; 11, A.D. 108)

From 111 to 113 Pliny the Younger was Governor of Bithynia. We still possess his correspondence with Trajan. One of the letters is concerned with the Christians in his province:

"Pliny to Trajan . . . They declared that their only fault or error lay in that they were accustomed to gather together on a fixed day before sunrise and to sing in turn a hymn [*carmen*] in honour of Christ as to a god and to bind themselves on oath not to commit crime but to refrain from stealing or robbery, not to commit adultery, not to break their word, and not to default should bail be required of them. After this they usually dispersed and gathered again later for a communal and simple repast . . . [thus he unconsciously describes the Sunday services of the Word and that of the breaking of bread, or Eucharist] . . . I found myself obliged to question on the rack two slave girls, called deaconesses . . . I found nothing more than a wrong-headed and boundless superstition . . . It appears to me that the affair is worthy of consultation, especially by reason of the large numbers implicated. For many people of all ages, from every walk of life and of both sexes are endangered and will continue to be so. The contagion of this superstition has spread not only in the towns but also over villages and in the rural areas . . . It is an established fact that the temples, which had almost been deserted, are being frequented again, that long-interrupted religious services are being revived, and that meat left over from sacrifice for which up till now there had been almost no demand is everywhere reappearing on the markets. From this we can deduce what a multitude of people can be rescued from their error if their repentance be accepted." (Pliny the Younger, *Letters*, **10**, 96: 7-10)

Here follows Trajan's reply:

"My worthy Pliny, you have followed the correct line of conduct in dealing with those who were brought before you as Christians . . . They must not be hunted down; if they are denounced and convicted they must be punished, but with this reservation, that anyone who denies being a Christian and actually proves it by adoring our gods must be forgiven on the grounds of his repentance no matter how suspect his past. Nor may anonymous accusations be taken into consideration on any charge; this would set a bad example and would not be in keeping with the spirit of our times." (Pliny the Younger, *Letters*, **10**, 97: 1)

(contd. on p. 36)

MANY PEOPLES IN ONE EMPIRE (ROMANS, 9-11; PEOPLES OF THE EAST, 12-14). The framework within which the Gospel was first preached was that of an empire embracing the whole of what was then the civilised world. For two and a half centuries the peoples of both East and West, of Syria and Asia and Egypt as well as of Greece, Italy, and Spain, of Gaul, Germany, and Britain, lived side by side in peace and were sharers in the same Hellenistic-Roman culture. The only great dividing line was the linguistic frontier between the Greek-speaking East and the Latin-speaking West (see the map on the back endpaper). Only those who took no part in public life, commerce, science, or literature were ignorant of these languages and spoke only their native idiom. In the towns, however —the late-classical culture was essentially urban—everyone understood either Latin or Greek or both.

The preaching of the Gospel began in the year 30 at Jerusalem, on the fiftieth day after the Resurrection of Christ (Pentecost = fiftieth day = our Whitsuntide) with the descent of the Holy Ghost upon the Apostles and their companions and the first sermon of St Peter. It began in Jerusalem where it was heard by Jews and proselytes from all the countries of the Empire (and even beyond, from Parthia), gathered there for the Jewish feast which was celebrated on that day:

"Parthians and Medes and Elamites and residents of Mesopotamia, Judaea and Cappadocia, Pontus and Asia, Phrygia and Pamphylia, Egypt and the parts of Libya belonging to Cyrene, and visitors from Rome, both Jews and proselytes, Cretans and Arabians, we hear them telling in our own tongues the mighty works of God." (Acts 2:9-11; written in A.D. 64)

The first great Christian scholar, Origen of Alexandria, testifies in the latter half of the second century to what the Roman peace, the *pax augusta*, really meant to the Christians:

"In those days righteousness flourished and there reigned the fullness of peace [cf Ps. 72:7] which began at His birth. For God had prepared the peoples for His teaching by causing them all to be united under the power of the one Roman emperor. For otherwise, through the existence of many kingdoms, the nations would have remained strangers to each other and it would have been much more difficult for the Apostles to accomplish Jesus' command when He said: Go ye and teach all nations [Matt. 28:19]. For indeed it is generally known that Jesus was born during the reign of Augustus who, through his one Empire ... rendered the greatest number of peoples equal. The existence of many separate kingdoms would have been an obstacle to the propagation of Jesus' teaching throughout the whole civilised world not only for the reason already mentioned but also because the nations would then have been everywhere obliged to fight for their fatherland, as they had done before the time of Augustus. For how would it have been possible for the teaching of peace to have found acceptance, which does not allow a man even to repel his enemies, if the world had not everywhere become more civilised at Jesus' coming?" (Origen, *Contra Celsum*, 2, 30)

9. MARRIED COUPLE from Pompeii. (Terentius Neo and wife). Before A.D. 79. *Naples, Museo Nazionale.*

10. ROMAN WEDDING. Detail from a 2nd century sarcophagus. The married couple join their right hands (*dextrarum junctio*) above the fire of the domestic hearth. Behind them stands Concordia, symbol of conjugal unanimity. *Rome, Museo delle Terme.*

11. THE HIEROPHANT (here a priestess). Detail from a wall painting depicting the initiation into the mysteries of Dionysius; *ca* 50 B.C. *Pompeii, Villa dei misteri dionisiaci.*

12. JARHAE, aristocrat from Palmyra. Typical Semitic type; 2nd or 3rd century. *Paris, Louvre.*

13. THE GIRL TOONAH. Painted stucco from Lower Egypt; ca. 200. *New York, Metropolitan Museum.*

14. ARISTOCRATIC LADY from Palmyra; 2nd century. *Copenhagen, Ny Carlsberg Glyptotek.*

15. See page 34.

15

(contd. from p. 34)

Fully eighty years later the Carthaginian lawyer Tertullian, always rather vehement, writes in his *Apology* of 197:

"But we have discovered that no-one has any authority even to start an investigation into our affairs. For after the Younger Pliny—as governor of a province—had condemned certain Christians and persuaded others to abandon their religion, rendered hesitant none the less by their great number, he consulted the Emperor Trajan and asked what measures he should take in the future. He pointed out that, apart from their determined refusal to offer sacrifice he had found nothing else about their religious practices but that they gathered together at daybreak to sing hymns to Christ as their God and to confirm their moral code, which forbade murder, adultery, fraud, treachery, and other crimes. Then Trajan wrote back that indeed this class of people must not be hunted down but that they should be punished if accused. O marvellous decree, which cannot but be contradictory! It forbids that they should be hunted down, as though supposing them innocent and orders them to be punished as if they were guilty. It spares them and rages against them, refusing to recognise the evil but punishing none the less. O justice, why do you make difficulties for yourself? If you are ready to condemn why be chary then of hunting down? If you refuse to hunt down why do you then not grant acquittal? In every province, military detachments are selected by lot for the hunting down of highway robbers: every man takes up arms against those who violate the majesty of the Empire and against traitors; even their accomplices and confederates are hunted down. Only a Christian may not be hunted down, but he may be accused, as though the purpose of hunting down a criminal were anything other than accusation. You condemn therefore, when he has been accused, someone whom no-one desired should be hunted down. If I understand the matter rightly he is not punishable because he is guilty but because he whom it was unlawful to hunt down has nevertheless been caught." (Tertullian, *Apology* **2**, 6-9).

But the best of the martyrs viewed the matter in quite a different light: the above-mentioned Bishop of Antioch, for example, Ignatius, from whom we still possess seven letters written while he was being conveyed to Rome. In the letter addressed to the Church of Rome he writes:

"I write to all the churches and make known to all as my last wish that I desire freely to die for God, at least if you do not prevent it. I beseech you, show no misplaced sympathy on my account. Let me be a bait for the wild beasts, through which I can partake of God. Grain of God am I, ground by the teeth of the wild beasts so that I may be found as pure bread for Christ. Or rather: coax the wild beasts that they may become my tomb, leaving nothing of my body to become a burden to anyone after my death. Then shall I be a disciple of Jesus

Christ in the true sense of the word, when the world sees even my body no more. Pray for me to Christ, that by these instruments I may be found a fitting sacrifice to God. I do not command you as Peter and Paul did. They were apostles and I am a man condemned to death; they were free, while I am still a slave [cf 1 Cor. 9:1]. But once I have died a martyr's death I shall become a freedman of Jesus Christ [cf 1 Cor. 7:22] and I shall arise in Him as a free man. But now I learn as a man in my bonds, not to desire anything." (Ignatius of Antioch, *Epistle to the Romans*, 4, 1)

16. HADRIAN (117-38). *Vatican*. "In the twelfth year of his reign the Emperor Hadrian received the title of Father of the Country, and his wife that of Augusta." (Eusebius, *Chronicle*, Hadrian 12, A.D. 128)

17. ANTONINUS PIUS (138-61). *Vatican*. "In the fourth year of his reign Antoninus receives from the philosopher Justin a book in defence of our religion." (Eusebius, *Chronicle*, Antoninus Pius 4, A.D. 41)

We still possess this book; the writer died a martyr's death shortly afterwards. He was a native of Flavia Neapolis, formerly Shechem, in Samaria.

18. MARCUS AURELIUS (161-80). *Rome, Museo Capitolino*. This noble person, a Stoic upon the Imperial throne, died in his army tent near the Danube during the campaign against the Dacians. After his death a small diary was found, in which he had been accustomed to note down—in Greek—for his own satisfaction, reflections on the divine reasonableness of the cosmos and on his own ideal of human conduct. He too knew Christianity only by evil repute. He once jotted down:

"How great is the soul which is always prepared for the moment at which it must depart from the body ... whether to be extinguished, to be dispersed, or to live on. Yet this state of readiness must be founded on insight and not on pure wrong-headedness as with the Christians. It must be reasonable, serious, and worthy, without ostentation: only thus can it succeed in convincing others." (Marcus Aurelius, *Meditations*, **11**, 3:2)

During his reign, in the year 177, the death took place at Lugdunum (Lyon) of the celebrated martyrs of whose testimony and passion we are informed in the letter written by the communities of Lyon and Vienne to the churches in Asia. Everyone knows the story of the old bishop Pothinus and of the little slave Blandina. Here follows the postscript:

"They followed the example of Christ who, being in the likeness of God, thought it no robbery to be equal to God [Phil. 2:6]. For although they enjoyed such respect and had testified for their faith not once nor twice but many times, and had been taken back from the wild beasts and bore the traces of the burning irons, and scars and wounds, they neither called themselves martyrs nor allowed us to address them by this title. But if ever any one of us called them 'martyrs' in a letter or a speech they rebuked him severely. For they gladly conceded the title of martyr to Christ, the True and Veritable martyr, the Firstborn from the dead who has brought us to the life of God [cf Rev. 1:5], and they reminded us of the martyrs who had already passed away, saying: they are now martyrs whom Christ was pleased to take unto Himself by their confession. He has put a seal upon them because of the witness of their death: but we are lowly and humble confessors. And they besought the help of the brethren with tears, begging that earnest prayers might be offered that they might attain fulfilment." (Eusebius, *Ecclesiastical History*, 5, 2:2 and 3)

19. COMMODUS (180-92). Marcus' unworthy son. *Rome, Museo Capitolino*.

20 (page 37). SEPTIMIUS SEVERUS (193-211). *Rome, Museo Capitolino*. "Severus, from the province of Tripolitana, from the city of Leptis is until now the only Roman Emperor to be a native of Africa." (Eusebius, *Chronicle*, Severus 2, A.D. 194)

16   17   18   19

20   21   22   23

The third century

The decline of the Empire which began with Commodus became obvious to all after the Severi (A.D. 235), and even the courageous warrior Emperors were unable to prevent the complete collapse of the frontiers (ca 260). Valerian (253-60) died a prisoner of war in the hands of the Sassanians, and only with Aurelian (270-5), who gave Rome the famous wall (see 109), and with Diocletian do we find a precarious recovery. Yet this period of disaster for the Empire was a period of flowering for the Church. During the persecutions of both 251 and 258 the 'blood of the martyrs' proved indeed to be the 'seed of the Church', and the period 258-304 is the time of the *longa pax*, the period of peace during which house-churches were openly built and cemeteries laid out. The remains of some of these can still be seen at Dura, Rome, and Naples. It was during this period, too, that Christian scholarship began to flourish in Alexandria.

21. CARACALLA (211-7), builder of the great baths. *Rome, Museo Capitolino.*

22. HELIOGABALUS (218-22). *Rome, Museo Capitolino.*

23. ALEXANDER SEVERUS (222-35). *Rome, Museo Capitolino.* In contrast with his worthless predecessors he was a high-minded man and tolerated the Christians. Between 218 and 222 his Syrian mother Julia Mammaea attended Origen's lectures at Antioch. He himself was accustomed, on certain days

"... to perform his devotions early in the morning, in his Lararium. There he had carefully selected statues of the deified Caesars, only those of good repute, and of particularly holy spirits, including Apollonius of Tyana ... and also Christ, Abraham, and Orpheus. He had also the portraits of his ancestors."

(Lampridius, *Historia Augusta, Severus Alexander,* **29,** 2)

24. THE ENEMY. Bahram II, king of the Sassanian kingdom, 276-93. Carus (282-4) won from him Mesopotamia and Armenia. Detail from a rock relief at Shapur in south Persia.

25. GORDIAN III (238-44). *Rome, Museo delle Terme.*

26. PHILIP OF ARABIA (243-49). *Vatican.* In 248 the thousandth anniversary of the founding of Rome was celebrated: "on this occasion an enormous number of wild beasts were killed in the Circus Maximus, and for three days and nights theatrical performances were given on the Campus Martius. During all this time the people did not go to bed." (Eusebius, *Chronicle,* Philippus II, A.D. 248)

It was later said that the Emperor was a Christian. He was a native of Arabia.

27. DECIUS (249-51). *Rome, Museo Capitolino.* Among the victims of his edicts were Pope Cornelius who met his rival bishop Hippolytus in the mines of Sardinia, and died 253 at Centomcellae (Civitavecchia). During the reign of Valerian (253-60) Pope Sixtus II and his deacon, Lawrence, were put to death (see page 149).

28. GALLIENUS (260-68). He fought bravely against the barbarians who penetrated as far as Achaia. *Copenhagen, Ny Carlsberg Glyptotek.*

24

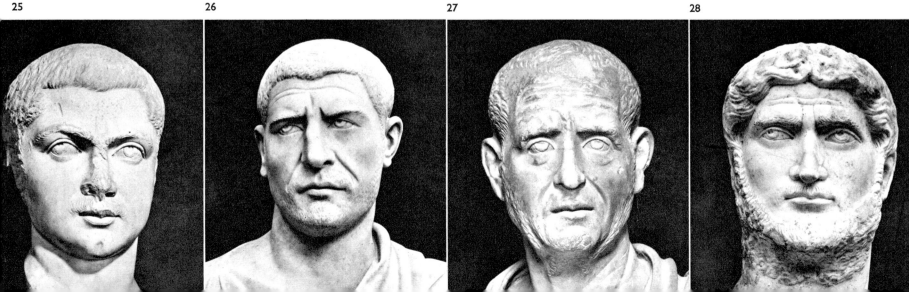

25   26   27   28

29 30

31 32

33 34

37   38

THE PAGAN RELIGIONS (29-34); THE JEWISH DIASPORA IN THE THIRD
CENTURY (35-39). The Christians held themselves strictly apart from other religions and avoided
even the slightest chance of contamination. They saw, in the outward expression of all other forms
of worship, of the ancient Roman cult and the emperor worship as much as the imported mystery
religions, deceitful and deluding practices, sustained and served by demons. For this reason, in their
own group language, they avoided, as being contaminated, any term pertaining to the pagan cults.
Yet their world of ideas and images can be described as a combination of the classical and the Biblical
views of the universe. They were divided from the Jews by their belief in Christ; they were linked
with the Jews by the Old Testament which they inherited from them, albeit in the new light of the
fulfilment. This link formed by the Jewish sacred books was broken when, even in the synagogues
of the Greek-speaking countries, the chief Rabbis ceased to recognise the Greek translation of the
Septuagint (which was used by the Church) and kept exclusively to the Hebrew text. In the second
and third centuries there arose in Galilee and later in Babylon the schools from which emerged the
Talmudic Judaism which held itself strictly apart from both the pagan and the Christian worlds.

29. MITHRAS SLAYING THE BULL. Relief from Osterburken on the German border. Mithraism was
pre-eminently a soldiers' religion. The monuments are found especially in places where frontier
troops were stationed and in the large garrison towns, including Rome. *Karlsruhe, Museum.*

30. TRIAD FROM PALMYRA. Aglibol, Baal-Shamen, Malakbel. Relief from Palmyra, middle of the
1st century; an example of the hieratic stylisation soon to become common. *Paris, Louvre.*

31. UNDERGROUND SANCTUARY of an unknown (neo-Pythagorean?) sect, near the Porta Maggiore,
Rome (Map 27). 1st century.

32. HERMES PSYCHOPOMPOS (as escort of souls). Fresco from the tomb of a child, Octavia Paulina,
ca 220. *Rome, Museo delle Terme.*

33. MITHRAEUM beneath the church of St Clement, Rome, behind the ancient house-church.

34. SARCOPHAGUS depicting the Prometheus myth (including the creation of the world and of man)
and Mercury as escort of souls; 3rd century. *Rome, Museo Capitolino.*

35. SYNAGOGUE IN CAPERNAUM, Palestine; 3rd century.

36. JEWISH SARCOPHAGUS with seven-branched candlestick; *ca* 300. *Rome, Museo delle Terme.*

37. DAGON shattered in the temple of the Philistines. Fresco in the synagogue of Dura-Europos on
the Euphrates; before 256. *Damascus, Museum.*

38. EZEKIEL'S VISION in the valley of bones, detail. Dura-Europos; before 256. *Damascus, Museum.*

39. ABRAHAM receiving the Promise. Dura-Europos; before 256. *Damascus Museum.*

39

40   41   42

THE TRUE PHILOSOPHY (40-47).

THE TRUE PHILOSOPHY (40-47). As far as the relationship between pagan and Christian intellectuals is concerned, the first contact took place not in the domain of religion but in that of philosophy, and then only in an extremely limited circle and in one city, that ancient centre of learning, Alexandria, where the great libraries and institutes of the Museion and the Serapeion were located (see Map 18).

Here they had also been familiar for a long time with the Greek translation of the old Testament (the Septuagint, or translation of the LXX), and from here it had become known to pagan thinkers. It was in Alexandria that the Jewish sage Philo had attempted his synthesis of the wisdom of the Law and that of the Ancients, principally of the Stoics and Platonists. Towards the middle of the second century there rose in Alexandria a Christian lay school of a high intellectual level. The first great writer of this circle of learned Christians—who also maintained contact with the other great ecclesiastical centre, Rome—was Clement of Alexandria.

"In its various attempts to attain to that knowledge which is closely bound up with what for us constitutes the truth, philosophy is only of remote assistance in discovering the truth. Yet to him who applies himself diligently, it is of real assistance in attaining to spiritual knowledge [*gnosis*] by the aid of reason alone. Greek truth, however, differs from our own, even though it bears the same name, by the greatness of our knowledge, imparted to us by a valid demonstration, by divine power, and through other, similar, channels. For we are pupils of God and we receive our truly sacred instruction from the Son of God. For this reason the Greeks mould minds not in the same manner as we but following another method of instruction. If now, to satisfy the critical, we must explain more fully the assertion that philosophy is none-the-less a point of departure and an aid to the understanding of truth—for is it not a searching after truth?— then we acknowledge that philosophy is a preliminary training for him who strives after spiritual knowledge. In this we do not consider as origin what is merely a secondary cause, nor do we consider as essential that which is merely an aid to knowledge. Even less do we regard philosophy as a *conditio sine qua non*. For nearly all of us, without a general academic training, without Greek philosophy, but driven by a higher power and by the help of faith, have accepted the doctrine concerning God. And thus we are pupils only of divine wisdom."

(Clement of Alexandria, *Stromata*, I, **20**, 98:3-99:2)

Thus does Clement define the difference between what, in later theology, we call supernatural knowledge concerning God, imparted by faith, and natural knowledge acquired by reason alone. There can be no doubt that the representations of the faith as the 'true philosophy' shown on the opposite page, which are found on sarcophagi carved in Rome for rich Christians of the third century, do indeed illustrate a theme of Alexandrian origin. We recognise 'the man receiving instruction from the Teacher Christ': Our Lord Himself is at this time still depicted under the veil of symbolic images—in this case under the Johannine figure of the Shepherd of souls—but the pupil clearly holds the book of the Scriptures (the Gospel, in a wider sense) in his hands.

Not every Christian held such broad-minded views concerning classical philosophy as did Clement. His somewhat younger contemporary in Carthage, the lawyer Tertullian, an intransigent spirit who later went over to Montanism (the earliest form of Christian 'enthusiasm' outside the bonds of the Church) writes:

"What have they in common, a philosopher and a Christian, a disciple of Greece and a disciple of heaven? One who seeks for glory and one who seeks salvation? One who works with words and one who works with deeds? One constructing and one destroying? A falsifier and a renewer of truth? One who obscures truth and one who conserves it? (Tertullian, *Apology*, **46**, 18)

"This truth which the philosophers, in mockery and derision, pretend to possess, whereas they are in fact the enemies of truth and debase it by their hypocrisy (since they merely seek for glory), this is the truth which the Christians seek, driven by an inward craving, and which they propagate in its full purity,

since they have their salvation at heart." (Tertullian, *Apology*, **46**, 7)

Clement found no reason for rejecting profane wisdom out of hand. In his opinion, divine Wisdom prevails everywhere and at all times. The upright pagan will also end by recognising the voice of Truth, for the divine Logos conducts an orchestra of many instruments to the ultimate harmony made manifest in the faith:

"And the union formed by the fusion of the many differing sounds into the one divine harmony becomes one symphony, following one conductor and teacher, the Word. And this comes to rest upon the motif of Truth itself, saying: Abba, Father! [cf Mark 14:36 and Rom. 8:15]. And God welcomes this voice of truth, plucking it as the first fruit of His children." (Clement of Alexandria, *Protrepticus*, **9**, 88:3)

And yet it also appeared self-evident to Clement that Christians should avoid everything that smacked even faintly of the mythology or frivolity of paganism. Thus he remarks, with reference to the decorative motifs used for everyday objects:

"Our seals must be decorated with a dove, or a fish, or a ship sailing before a stiff breeze, or a musical lyre such as that used by Polycrates, or the anchor which Seleucus had engraved upon his stone. If a fisherman be depicted thereupon, this will remind us of the apostle and of the children fished from the water. Yet beware of depicting idols, for it is unlawful even to gaze upon them. We must also avoid the sword and the bow, we who strive for peace, nor is a drinking cup suitable for those who must practise temperance." (Clement of Alexandria, *Paedagogus*, III, **11**, 59:2)

The dove was a symbol of the chosen soul and of peace; the fish of the Ichthys Christ; the fisherman, of baptism; the ship with the cross formed by yard and mast, of the Christian sign of salvation and of the voyage of life; the lyre, of the new harmony through the Word; the anchor (see **461**), of the Cross. For the fish see **56** and **57**.

40-42. The motif of the 'man of the Muses' who through meditation upon spiritual values participates in immortality; found upon profane sarcophagi.

40. PHILOSOPHER AND DISCIPLE with a sun-dial. (Simon Magus and Helena wearing the helmet? In that case a gnostic composition.) Centre relief from a sarcophagus. *Rome, Museo delle Terme.*

41. PHILOSOPHER with unrolled *volumen* (scroll) between two pupils, and two other philosophers with a learned man; right, a sun-dial; 260-75. Some have wrongly sought to identify the teacher as Plotinus, the great Neoplatonist and mystic who taught in Rome *ca* 244. *Rome, Museo Lateranense.*

42. TWO PHILOSOPHERS AND A PUPIL. Fragment of a sarcophagus. *Rome, Museo delle Terme.*

Page 41. Christian sarcophagi of the third century devoted to the theme of the true philosophy of the Logos-Shepherd of souls. The Christian soul, shown in an attitude of prayer (*orans*, Italian *orante*) is in the paradise of the Shepherd. It is surrounded by other symbols, those of baptism and of the redemption in general or of the refreshment of paradise (Jonah).

43. SARCOPHAGUS from La Gayolle: Sol (the sun), fisherman, *orans* in paradise, true philosophy, Shepherd, mountain god (a neutral cliché). *Brignoles, Séminaire.*

44. SARCOPHAGUS from the Via Salaria. Man and woman in the garb of the true philosophers, *orans*, Shepherd. Rams replace the funeral lions which often, on pagan sarcophagi, occupy the front corners. (Heads partly new.) *Rome, Museo Lateranense.*

45. SARCOPHAGUS from S. Maria Antiqua on the Forum, Rome (cf 606, left). Jonah beneath the *cucurbita* (gourd), *orans*, philosopher, Shepherd, baptism.

46. CHILD'S SARCOPHAGUS. Married couple with servant, the true philosophy (cf 40: the same grouping), paradise of the Shepherd. *Ravenna, Museum.*

47. SARCOPHAGUS. At the corners, the souls serving the Muses (with musical instruments). The Shepherd is shown twice; two Seasons (symbol of ever-returning life) flank the portrait of the deceased. *Rome, Museo Lateranense.*

48/51 49/52 50/53

CHURCH LIFE IN THE SECOND AND THIRD CENTURIES (48-108)

Baptism (48-53)

"But we small fishes, named thus after our great Ichthys, Jesus Christ, are born in water and only by remaining in water can we live." (Tertullian, *On Baptism*, **I**, 3)

48. BAPTISM. Fresco in the so-called sacrament chapel A2 in the catacomb of Calixtus, Rome. The person to be baptised was called *infans* and was therefore depicted as a child. Above him the Holy Ghost in the form of a dove.

49. BAPTISM. Crypts of Lucina in the oldest part of the Catacomb of Calixtus.

50. THE HEALED PARALYTIC who takes up his bed and walks (the forgiveness of sins = baptism). Catacomb of Calixtus, sacrament chapel A3.

51. THE LIVING WATER (the Samaritan woman beside Jacob's well). Fresco in the baptistery of the house-church at Dura; *ca* 232 (see **71-72**).

53. THE HEALED PARALYTIC (left) and (right) the Lord saving Peter from the water—*qui Petro mergenti dexteram porrexit*—words still used in the Roman Catholic rite of baptism. Fresco in the house-church at Dura, *ca* 232. *Yale, Gallery of Fine Arts.*

54. THE LIVING WATER and Christ the Teacher, cf **51**. Catacomb of Calixtus, sacrament chapel A3.

The Eucharist (54-61)

54. EPITAPH of Abercius of Hierapolis in Phrygia, dating from 216. *Rome, Museo Lateranense.* The text on the fragment (presented to Leo XIII by the Sultan) was completed with the help of a *Life* of Abercius:

"I, as citizen of a chosen city, have caused this to be made during my life-time, so that I might have here, when the time shall come, a resting place for my body. My name is Abercius. I am a disciple of the Holy Shepherd who feeds his flocks upon the mountains and in the valleys, whose great eyes are all-seeing. He taught me . . . reliable knowledge. [Here begins the fragment shown in the illustration]. He sent me to Rome to behold a kingdom and a queen robed in gold, wearing golden shoes. But there I saw a people with a radiant sign [the seal of baptism]. I also saw the plain of Syria and all the cities, Nisibis beyond the Euphrates. Everywhere I found brothers in the faith, Paul . . . and the faith was everywhere my lodestar and there was handed to me everywhere as nour-

ishment the Fish from the spring, the pure Fish of great size [Christ] caught by the chaste Virgin. And she continued to hand on this fare to the friends to eat, giving wholesome wine, offering mingled wine and water with bread [the Eucharist]. I, Abercius, have caused this to be written down in my presence, in my seventy-second year. Let every brother in the faith who reads this offer a prayer for Abercius. But let no-one lay another in my grave. Should anyone do this none the less then he must pay two thousand gold pieces to the treasure chest of Rome and a thousand gold pieces to my dear native city of Hierapolis."

55. EPITAPH of Pectorius at Autun in Gaul. Probably a fifth or sixth century copy of a second century original. Greek distichs:

"Divine race of the heavenly Fish, draw with a pure heart, ye mortals, from the immortal, divine spring water . . . Take the honey sweet fare of the Redeemer of the saints, eat, you that are hungry, holding the Fish in the palm of your hands [the communion rite prevailing at the time]. Lord, Redeemer, I pray thee, satiate [us] with the Fish! I beseech Thee, light of the dying, may my mother rest in peace. Aschandios my father, so dear to my heart, and you my beloved mother and my brothers, in the peace of the Fish, be mindful of Pectorius."

56. ICHTHYS ZŌNTŌN: Fish of the living. With fishes and anchor. (Epitaph from what was formerly the Museo Kircheriano, now the Museo Cristiano, Vatican.)

57. FISH WITH BREAD AND WINE. The Food of Life symbolised by the Eucharist and the feeding of the five thousand (John 6) with allusion to the Ichthys symbol. Crypts of Lucina, Catacomb of Calixtus. Shortly after 200.

58. THE FOOD OF LIFE. Bread and Fish on a *tripous* (small table) with *orans*. Catacomb of Calixtus, sacrament chapel A3; shortly after 200.

59. THE FOOD OF LIFE. Celestial banquet (*refrigerium*) with bread and fish: an adaptation of the ancient funeral feast. The baskets (not shown here) are an allusion to John 6. Funeral meal chamber in the catacomb of Priscilla (the so-called *cappella greca*).

60. THE FOOD OF LIFE. *Refrigerium* with bread and fish. Sacrament chapel A6.

61. THE FOOD OF LIFE. *Refrigerium* with bread and wine: right, the Shepherd and hand of an *orans* (this shows that the sarcophagus is Christian). Lid of a sarcophagus. *Rome, Museo delle Terme.*

42

62

63

64

Christ the Shepherd of Souls (62-67)

The earliest pictures of Christ, those of the Shepherd and the Teacher, are veiled, symbolic figures, only recognisable to the initiated. The outward appearance of the Shepherd is derived from an inconspicuous figure taken from the old bucolic art. He is usually shown as a young man dressed in a short tunic which leaves one shoulder bare (*tunica exomis*) and carrying a sheep on his shoulders (motif taken from St John). He is generally surrounded by his flock and stands amid the praying souls (*orantes*), quiet and gentle, in the garden of his paradise (παράδεισος originally meant a small burial garden). For the Christians such a figure was an unambiguous symbol of the peace of the redeemed, of those living in Christ even after death, which, to the baptised, meant only a transition to the rest (*quies*) and the expectation of the Resurrection in the place of refreshment, light, and peace (*locus refrigerii, lucis, et pacis*, words which are now repeated every day in the Roman Eucharistic prayer).

62. THE SHEPHERD AND THE FALL; the Fall and the Redeemer. Fresco above the font in the baptistery of the house-church of 232 at Dura, cf 71-72. The inward seal of baptism was considered as the mark of the Shepherd and the whiteness of the lambs as a symbol of the purity of those born anew. *Yale, Gallery of Fine Arts*.

63. THE SHEPHERD-TEACHER with his flock. Hypogaeum (underground burial chamber) of the Aurelii on the Viale Manzoni, Rome; a heterodox family tomb of the 3rd century (Map 28).

64. THE SHEPHERD. Sarcophagus from La Gayolle (see 43); detail. *Brignoles, Séminaire*.

65. THE SHEPHERD MILKING. Fragment of a sarcophagus. *Rome, Museo delle Terme*.

"Then I saw an immense space, a garden. And in the middle thereof sat a man with grey hair, a tall figure, dressed as a shepherd, milking the sheep. And around him stood many thousands of white-robed figures [the baptised, Rev. 6:11 and 7:9]. He lifted his head, looked at me and said: It is well that you have come

my child. Then he called me to him and gave me some of the curded milk he had by him, about a mouthful. I received this with hands folded over each other, and ate it. And all those standing by said: Amen. And at the sound of the voices I awoke with a sweet taste still lingering in my mouth." (*The Martyrdom of SS. Perpetua and Felicitas*, **4**, 8-10; A.D. 202)

The vision of paradise seen by the future martyr of Carthage (in 202) is the garden of the Shepherd and she receives the Food of Life as she received the Eucharist on earth, according to the same rite, in the hands, while all those present say: "Amen".

"Our path lay through a charming landscape with meadows and green woods with luxuriant foliage. Tall cypresses and pine trees reaching to the sky gave abundant shade and it seemed as though the whole of that place were girdled by a belt of fresh green woods. In the middle thereof was a radiant fountain, its basin running over with abundant clear water . . . Then Cyprian seized the cup which lay on the edge of the fountain, filled it like one who is parched with thirst and drained it. He filled it then anew, handed it to me and I drank eagerly. And when I said: Thanks be to God, then, so he told me, my own voice awoke me." (*The Martyrdom of SS. Marianus and Jacobus*, **6**, 12-15. Same period)

The fountain of this—related—vision of Paradise is here the symbol of the heavenly refreshment (*refrigerium*), a motif connected with the "drinking of the water struck from the rock of Christ" seen on the frescoes of the same period in the earliest Roman catacombs.

66. SARCOPHAGUS of Baebia Hertofile. On the front, *strigili* (grooves), the effigy of the deceased couple and the Shepherd, here not idealised. On the lid, Jonah's rest under the *cucurbita* and the feast of the celestial banquet, two symbols of the life hereafter awaiting the redeemed. *Rome, Museo delle Terme*.

67. SARCOPHAGUS 'of the Three Shepherds'. The sacred (?) motif light-heartedly introduced between the pagan cliché of the Bacchic vintage (with, above right, Eros and Psyche). End of the 3rd century. Period of the Tetrarchy. *Rome, Museo Lateranense*.

67

68

65   66

Christ the Teacher (68–70)

Soon after 313 the figure of Christ, the Teacher of True Wisdom, replaced that of the Shepherd. It is, however, already found in the third century and is almost certainly of Alexandrian origin. Outside the Alexandrian circle the expression 'the Teacher' occurs comparatively rarely, as in the Gospels, yet this motif does evoke St John's name of 'the Word'. The Teacher, this tranquil figure clad in the distinctive garb of an intellectual of the last centuries of antiquity, bearing a scroll and later an open codex in his hand (the other usually being raised in an attitude of speaking) is characteristic of the restricted Alexandrian Christian milieu, much given to reflection and contemplation, in which it originated. It is an intellectualistic creation, having its roots both in Early Christian theology and in the Gospels themselves, especially that of St John. It is certain that, up to 1200, this figure predominated in representations of Christ. In the East it still does; but in the West, after this date, the figure of Christ crucified begins to predominate. In the representations devoted to Our Lord's public life, however, and in abstract figuration, the late-classical Teacher survived unchanged right up to the end of the last century. Even the classical garments, the *tunica* and *pallium*, the ankle-length tunic and the cloak, continued unchanged for centuries, as did the bare head and sandalled feet. Below we see a few related motifs and a detail.

68. EZRA, as teacher, with open Torah scroll. Fresco above the niche of the Torah scrolls in the synagogue of Dura-Europos (cf 37, 38, 39). Before 256. *Damascus Museum.*

69. THE SERMON ON THE MOUNT (?) and the miracles of the curing of the woman with the issue of blood, of the paralytic, and of the man born blind. Fragment of a sarcophagus, *ca* 300. The stern philosopher's head and the naked torso do not appear again. *Rome, Museo delle Terme.*

70. THE SHEPHERD-TEACHER. Detail of 63. *Rome, Hypogaeum of the Aurelii.*

In his celebrated hymn at the end of the *Paedagogus*, Clement of Alexandria celebrates Christ as the Shepherd, the Teacher, Wisdom suckling her children, and at the same time as Fisherman, pilot Bird, and King.

Bridle of fiery horses
Wing of birds that do not stray,
Sure rudder of ships,
Shepherd of the sheep of the king;

Bring together the host
Of your pure children,
To praise devoutly
To laud sincerely
With a sinless voice
Christ the mentor of children.

King of the saints,
All-ruling Word,
Of the Father Sublime:
Prince of Wisdom,
Stay in our trouble,
Eternal joy
Of the mortal race,
Jesus the Saviour,
Shepherd and ploughman,
Rudder and bridle,
Wing towards heaven
Of the holy flock,
Fisher of men,
Of those who are saved
From the sea of sin:
Holy fishes
From an evil flood
Caught for a life of sweetness:

Lead, holy Shepherd
The spiritual sheep:
Lead, O King, your immaculate
                    children:
The footsteps of Christ
Are the pathway to heaven.

The eternal Word,
World without end,
Undying light,
Fount of mercy,·
Author of virtue,
For those who by a life of goodness
Can praise God,
Christ Jesus:

Heavenly milk
From the breasts of the bride—
The gift of your wisdom—
We children suck
With tender mouths:
We are cherished,
We are refreshed
At the pure breast
By the dew of the Spirit.

Let us all sing
Songs of praise soberly
Hymns most sincerely
For Christ the King,
As holy thanksgiving
For learning and Life:
Honouring simply
The Almighty Son.

We born, of Christ,
Chorus of peace,
A sober people,
We sing together
The God of peace.

(CLEMENT OF ALEXANDRIA,
PAEDAGOGUS III, 12, 101, 3.)

69   70

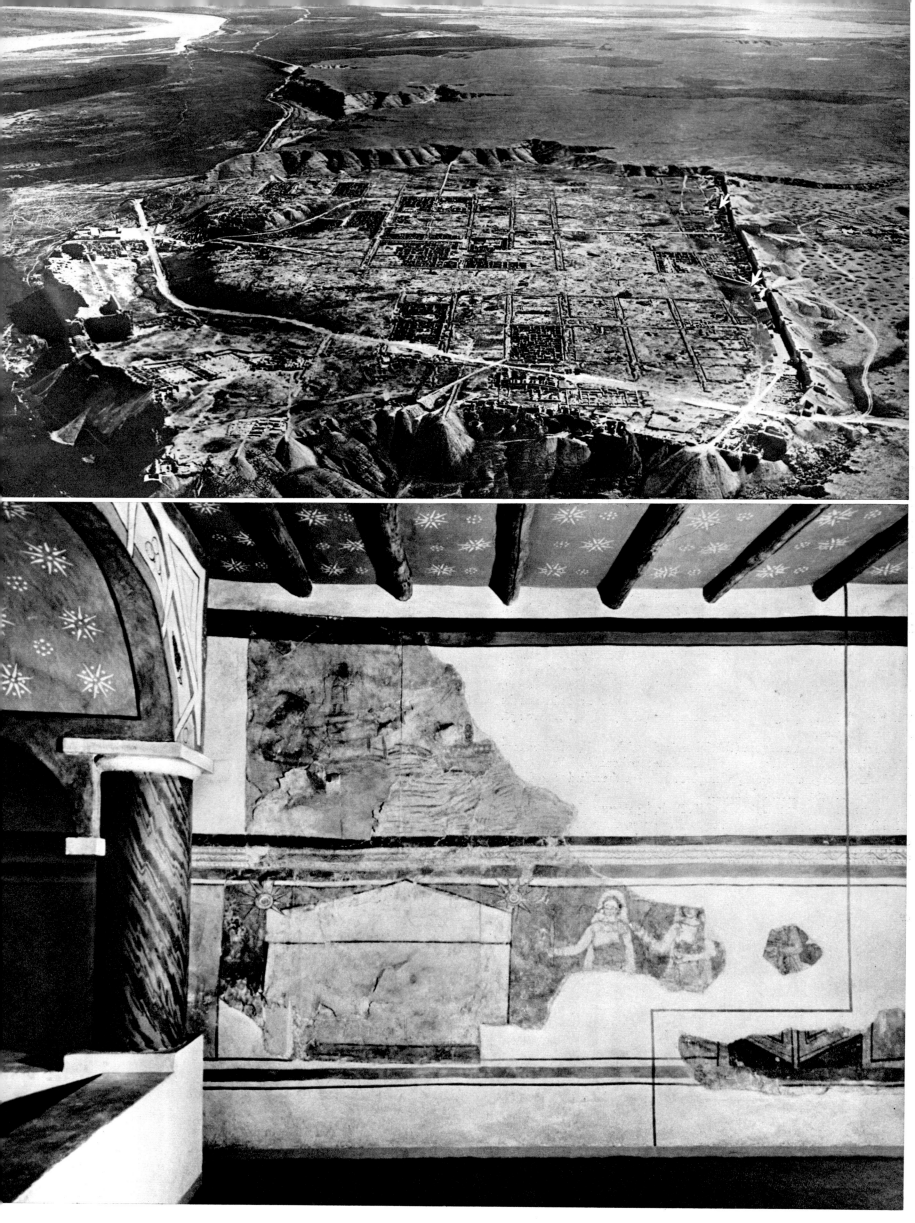

The oldest house-church (71 and 72)

71. DURA-EUROPOS, a Roman border fortress on the Euphrates, as revealed by the excavations of 1934 and following years. The upper arrow indicates the site of a Christian house-church, the lower, a large synagogue with walls completely covered with paintings (see **37, 38, 68**). Both were buried during a restoration of the city ramparts in 256 and rediscovered half intact.

72. THE BAPTISTERY in the house-church at Dura, 232-56. Left, the covered baptismal font (on the wall behind, fresco of the Shepherd and the Fall, not visible here; see **62**). On the side wall the remains of paintings. Above, the healed paralytic and Peter and Christ upon the water (see **52**). Under this, the three women at the tomb, here shown as a sarcophagus with two stars (the angels?), a reminder of the link between the Resurrection, Easter morn, and the resurrection of man born anew in baptism.

The oldest cemeteries (73-100)

Top row: from the necropolis discovered beneath St Peter's in the Vatican.

73. WALL in the burial chamber of the *Caetennii minores*. After 150. Typically elaborate *memoria* of a pagan family. A cinerary urn still stands in the main alcove and there is a little altar (*ara*) in the foreground. The decoration is in stucco on a red background.

74. CHRISTOS-HELIOS, with the Vine in the background. Mosaic vaulting in the small burial chamber M of the Julii, probably dating from the age of Constantine. The mausoleum itself is older. The owners may perhaps have later become Christians. This is the only representation of Christ as the Light of the World in the

guise of Helios driving the sun chariot. Cf text from Clemens' *Protrepticus*, p. 183.

75a and **b**. Invocations to SS. Peter and Paul scratched in the stucco of an open verandah. Here, between the years 258 and 313, Christian pilgrims held funeral feasts in honour of a *memoria* of chief Apostles. The spot, which lies *ad catacumbas* on the Via Appia (see Map 28) is under the Basilica Apostolorum, built after 320 and now known as San Sebastiano (see **130**). People gathered there on 29 June. The origin of this commemoration is not known (probably a translation of relics in 258, when the cemeteries were closed or confiscated by the edict of Valerian). **75a**. Part of the verandah wall (called *triclia*). **75b**. Fragments of plaster which have fallen from the wall.

The letters E ED PETRE P form the middle part of the invocation:
Paule ed Petre petite pro Victore. Paul and Peter, pray for Victor.

A few others: *Petro et Paulo Tomius Coelius refrigerium feci*. For Peter and Paul, I, Tomius Coelius, have held a funeral meal.

Xiiii kal. Apriles refrigeravi Parthenius in Deo et nos in Deo omnes. On the 14th day before the calends of April, I, Parthenius, held a funeral meal in God and all of us in God.

Petre et Paule subvenite Primitivo peccatori. Peter and Paul, come to the aid of Primitivus, a sinner.

Paule et Petre in mente habete Sozomenum et tu qui legis. Paul and Peter, be mindful of Sozomenus and you too who read this.

Pope Damasus likewise, who, shortly after 350, caused a monumental inscription to be set up in the Basilica Apostolorum, expresses himself in so vague a

73

74

75 b

76
77

78

79

manner as to appear no longer to know what it was that tradition placed at this spot. His famous and rather puzzling verses read as follows:

> Hic habitasse prius sanctos cognoscere debes
> nomina quisque Petri pariter Paulique requiris.
> discipulos oriens misit, quod sponte fatemur:
> sanguinis ob meritum—Christum per astra secuti
> aetherios petiere sinus regnaque piorum—
> Roma suos potius meruit defendere cives.
> Haec Damasus vestras referat nova sidera laudes.
>
> (Damasus, Epigrams, 26)

"Here the saints formerly resided. This you must know, you who here seek the names of Peter and Paul. The East sent [us] these disciples [of Christ]: to this do we gladly testify. [Here], however, by the merit of their bloody death, they followed Christ to the stars and gained the heavenly spheres and the kingdom of those who fear God. To this extent is Rome justified in calling them her citizens. May it be permitted to Damasus to offer you these words of praise, you who have newly taken up your place among the stars."

The earliest reference to the grave of St Peter on the Vatican is made by Eusebius of Caesarea in his Ecclesiastical History, written at the beginning of the fourth century:

"An ecclesiastic named Caius, who lived when Zephyrinus was Bishop of Rome [199-217] said in his 'Dialogue with Proclus', referring to the places where the remains of the said Apostles were laid to rest: 'I can show you the trophies of the Apostles. If you will go to the Vatican hill or to the Ostian Way, you will find the trophies of those who founded this Church.'" (Eusebius, Ecclesiastical History, 2, 25: 6-7)

Caius must have seen, in the Vatican necropolis, the modest memoria of Peter, —an aedicula consisting of a niche with a shelter (tugurium)—which was found during the excavations in 1945 and whose date has been fixed at ca 160.

76-79. Burial chamber of Clodius Hermes and his family and freedmen. This is a good example of a tomb of which the owners later became Christian.

76. THE SITE OF THE TOMB, in a little side road leading off the Via Appia, just below the triclia mentioned above (page 47) where the memoria of the Apostles was celebrated. Right, the inscription above the entrance. The stuccoed attica

above, with the paintings (now very faded), was introduced later by Christian owners.

77. INTERIOR OF THE BURIAL CHAMBER: decoration of vases and birds, divided up by red and green panels, with a mask on the ceiling; 2nd century. The cinerary urn and the wall tombs behind are reminders of the transition from cremation to inhumation which also occurred among pagans from the 2nd century onwards.

78. THE PAINTED ATTICA above the entrance. Left, the Shepherd with his flock; centre, the Teacher (?) in a group; right, the feeding of the five thousand (?) or else a refrigerium tableau, funeral meal, and celestial banquet at one and the same time.

79. RIGHT SIDE OF ATTICA: probably the cure of the man possessed by demons in the country of the Gerasenes, with the herd of swine into which the demons entered at the word of the Lord; 3rd century. Above, right, is the triclia. Apart from the house-church at Dura and the few wall remains of the Roman clandestine house-churches of the 3rd century (called tituli, after the name boards of the owners—see the survey map of the tituli, Map 29) no traces of ecclesiastical buildings dating from before 313 have been found. On the other hand, large cemeteries have been preserved in many places, notably the underground burial places of the community of Rome (see Map 28), and our knowledge of church life before the age of Constantine is consequently based, as far as the monuments are concerned, too largely on memorials to the dead.

In this respect most Christians clung to the ancient customs which in their eyes had become civil and neutral. These they considered to be inspired by the normal respect for the dead which also held an important place in the eyes of non-Christians and of classical humanity in general. Yet none-the-less they viewed the question in a different light. These were no shades whom they remembered with sadness and resignation. These were the ones who had gone before to the Paradise of the Shepherd, to the 'place of refreshment, light, and peace'. During the funeral meal they linked the 'refreshment' with another meal, that of the Eucharist, the Food of Life. That which served to quench their thirst was associated with the waters gushing from the springs of eternal life, the fruit of baptism. This is why, in the chamber for the funeral meal depicted on the opposite page (80) we see, on the arch above the centre couch, the picture of the meal with loaves and fishes and on the walls that of the 'deliverance' (see 86 and 88) and the 'rebirth' (see 89) from the water.

80 and **81**. Two rooms for the celebration of the funeral meal in the Roman catacombs.

80. FUNERAL MEAL CHAMBER in the catacomb of Priscilla on the Via Salaria to the north of Rome. This is the room wrongly known as the *cappella greca* on account of the Greek inscriptions. Next to it there is a small kitchen with a cistern, waste-pipe, and fireplace. The three-legged tables stood between the couches which were spread with cushions and covers on the anniversaries. It is no longer possible to determine whether the room belonged to one family or to a group. The Eucharist was certainly never celebrated there. It was celebrated on the third day in a building above ground, *sub divo*, and never here, among the dark passages.

81. FUNERAL MEAL CHAMBER in the Coemeterium Maius on the Via Nomentana (see Map 28). Here a permanent *cathedra* has been preserved, the empty seat being reserved for the deceased who, in this ancient rite of reverence for the dead, was considered as sharing the meal with those left behind. The present-day feasts of the *cathedra Petri* go back to the memorial days of the Bishops of Rome. That which is celebrated on 22 February coincides with the old Roman *parentalia* or *caristia* or *cara cognatio*. The community of Rome commemorated its spiritual pastors on the day traditionally reserved for honouring the deceased members of a family by visiting their grave and by holding a funeral feast.

The striking inscription found on a *mensa* (tombstone in the form of a table) from Satafi in Mauretania Sitifensis (Map 22, upper left corner) and dating from 299, i.e. the same period as most of the earlier catacombs, gives us some idea of the nature of the ordinary, profane funeral feast. It paints a graphic picture of these pious family reunions. The stone was erected by children for their aged mother:

> TO THE MEMORY OF AELIA SECUNDULA
> We have already spent much on mother Secundula's tomb:
> Now we have decided, at the spot where she rests,
> To place a stone funeral table
> Where, from henceforth, being gathered together,
> We shall often remember all that she did for us.

When the food is set out, the cups are filled and the cushions
Arranged round about, we, to heal the wound that pains our hearts,
Shall talk, late in the evening, eagerly and with praise
Of our worthy mother—and the good old lady will sleep.
Yes, she who once fed us is now done with food for ever.

> She lived 72 years.
> 260 Provincial era.
> Erected by Statulenia Julia.

The letters at the beginning and end of each line of the original form the words: the children, to their dearest mother.

There follows, on pages 50-3, a series of illustrations devoted to the catacombs of Rome and Naples and what remains of their decoration (**82-100**); all the monuments shown date from the third century.

The 'catacombs', so called from the use (in the fifth century) of the phrase *ad catacumbas* to denote the chambers under St Sebastian on the Via Appia—the only ones known to the Middle Ages (see page 47)—are subterranean extensions of cemeteries above ground. These cemeteries, with a few exceptions, have completely disappeared. The underground labyrinths were made possible by the nature of the soft, calcareous soil which hardens permanently on being exposed to air. We do not know what gave them their legal title but it is possible that they were always respected as *loci sacri* by the Roman legislators, with the exception of Valerian. They were public cemeteries. Even after persecution ceased they continued to be extended and used. Fully three-quarters of the area once again rendered accessible after 1590 dates from the fourth century. The oldest nuclei, however, seem to date back to the end of the second century. A few Jewish catacombs have been preserved and also a few hypogaea which, to judge by the decoration, belonged to communities that were Christian, although heterodox (see Map 28, survey). Most of the catacombs fell into disuse after the sixth century, when the Campagna di Roma became depopulated, and were subsequently blocked up and forgotten. The relics of the martyrs had already been transferred within the city walls and are still preserved there in the churches.

80

81

82-93. From the Roman catacombs.

82. BURIAL VAULT in the hypogaeum of the Flavii, the oldest part of the catacomb of Domitilla, near the entrance hall. Left and centre, tableaux illustrating the myth of Eros and Psyche; 200?

83. BURIAL VAULT in the catacomb of Calixtus, 3rd century. Examples of arched wall tombs (*arcosolia*) and left, the ordinary wall tombs (*loculi*).

84. CEILING of a burial vault (*cubiculum*) in the crypts of Lucina, in the catacomb of Calixtus; 200? In the middle, Daniel among the lions; surrounding this, masks; in the corners, two Shepherds and two *orantes*, the oldest known to us.

85. BALAAM'S PROPHECY: the star rising up from Jacob, the prophet, and the Redeemer in the arms of His Mother. Fresco in catacomb of Priscilla (near a stairway). After 200.

86. DANIEL AND THE THREE YOUTHS in the fiery furnace of Babylon, one of the classical Old Testament examples (παραδείγματα) of divine deliverance. In the *cappella greca* (see 80) in the catacomb of Priscilla, inner wall.

87. THE 'FIRST FRUITS OF THE HEATHENS', the Magi from the East offering their gifts. Catacomb of Priscilla, above the niche in the main wall (cf 80).

88. SUSANNA with the two Elders and Daniel; another example of prayer for deliverance. Susanna's prayer is heard and she is delivered from the false accusation. *Cappella greca*, catacomb of Priscilla, side wall. After 200.

89. THE LIVING WATER FROM THE ROCK, which is Christ. Symbol of baptism and of the heavenly refreshment. *Cappella greca*, catacomb of Priscilla. After 200.

90. THE JONAH TRILOGY; right, Jonah cast from the ship into the sea; centre, the sea monster (*cetus*) vomits him up; left, his rest under the *cucurbita*, 'gourd' (as found early as well as in the Authorized version), symbol of heavenly refreshment. Sacrament chapel A6 in the catacomb of Calixtus. Ca 200?

91-93. A few of the oldest inscriptions:

91. HESPEROS in the crypts of Lucina. Beginning of 3rd century.

92. RUFINA and IRENE in the crypts of Lucina. Beginning of 3rd century.

93. GERONTI VIBAS IN DEO, Gerontius, live in God (*vibas* also occurs frequently without *in deo*); an allusion to the Johannine ζωή. Origin unknown. End of 3rd century. *Rome, Museo Lateranense.*

91

92

93

94-97. The crypts of the 3rd century Popes in the catacomb of Calixtus.

94. THE PAPAL BURIAL VAULT as it was discovered by Giovanni Battista de Rossi during the excavations of 1854 and immediately visited by a greatly moved Pius IX. Fragments of the epitaphs of the martyr Popes Pontianus (†235), Anterus († 236), Fabianus († 250), Lucius († 254) and Eutychianus († 283) still lay in the original tombs, simple *loculi* in the side walls. Against the back wall still survived a piece of the magnificent memorial tablet which Pope Damasus had set up a good hundred years after their deaths, when the persecutions were already a thing of the past (lower right, behind the traces of the altar, which was added later). This tablet de Rossi succeeded in reconstructing from more than a hundred fragments, which, together with the remains of the broken epitaphs, lay scattered on the floor among the rubble (see **488** on page 147). It is a collective inscription without mention of any particular names.

> Hic congesta iacet quaeris si turba piorum,
> corpora sanctorum retinent veneranda sepulchra,
> sublimes animas rapuit sibi regia caeli.
> Hic comites Xysti, portant qui ex hoste tropaea;
> hic numerus procerum, servat qui altaria Christi;
> hic positus longa vixit qui in pace sacerdos;
> hic confessores sancti quos Graecia misit;
> hic iuvenes puerique senes castique nepotes,
> quis mage virgineum placuit retinere pudorem.
> Hic, fateor, Damasus volui mea condere membra,
> sed cineres timui sanctos vexare piorum.

(Damasus, *Epigrams*, 12)

"Here—if you would know it—there rests in crowded company a multitude of holy men. Venerable tombs contain the bodies of martyrs but the royal citadel of heaven received their lofty souls. Here lie the companions of Sixtus who overcame the enemy, here the host of princes who keep vigil before the altar of Christ; here lies the Bishop who lived during the long time of peace; here the holy confessors sent by Greece. Here lie youths and boys, old men and their chaste grandchildren who chose to preserve their chastity. Here, it must be confessed, I, Damasus, would have wished to lay my bones to rest, yet was loth to disturb the ashes of these holy ones."

The companions of Sixtus II (killed in 258 in this very cemetery of Calixtus, where he was taken prisoner with his followers) are the deacons Januarius, Magnus, Vincentius, and Stephen (Lawrence lies in the Via Tiburtina, *in agro Verano*, cf Map 28). The 'host of princes' are the Popes of the 3rd century, from 235 to 296: Pontianus († 235), Anterus († 236), Fabianus († 250), Lucius († 254), Stephen I († 257), Sixtus II († 258; he lies in a separate tomb, upon which Damasus had a separate inscription carved), Dionysius († 268), Felix († 274), Eutychianus († 283), and Gaius († 296). It is not certain whom he means by the Bishop who lived during the 'long time of peace'. The *longa pax* lasted from 258 until 304, but the Pope referred to might also be Miltiades (311-14) who lived during the period which saw the end of the persecutions and who is also buried here. Pope Cornelius, who died in exile in 253 at Centumcellae (Civitavecchia) was later transferred to the catacomb of Calixtus. He was, however, buried outside the papal tomb in a separate *arcosolium*. Damasus also devoted a monumental inscription to him. The identity of the 'Greek confessors' is equally doubtful. The names of Hippolytus, Adrias, Maria, Neon, and Paulinus from the *Martyrologium Hieronymianum* have been suggested. They lie, together with the others mentioned, outside the episcopal vault in Calixtus. Concerning the construction of the vault, Hippolytus, the rival Bishop who was later reconciled with the Pope and died a martyr's death in the mines of Sardinia, writes in his *Philosophoumena*, **9**, 12, that Pope Zephyrinus (199-217) entrusted the administration of a *coemeterium* on the Via Appia to the deacon Calixtus, who became his successor. It is this cemetery which still bears the name of Calixtus and in which he, or one of his successors, constructed the celebrated vault in which, at least from 235 onwards, the Bishops of Rome were buried.

95-97. Three of the epitaphs found.

95. PONTIANOS EPISK MR, *Pontianos episcopos martyr*, of Pope Pontianus (230-5) who died in the mines of Sardinia. The letters MR (*martyr*) were added at the end of the 3rd century.

96. ANTEROOS EPI . . . of Pope Anterus, 235-36.

97. PHABIANOS EPI MR, of Pope Fabianus, 236-50; the MR was added at the end of the 3rd century.

The original epitaphs are now in the Museo Lateranense.

94

98   99   100

The reverence with which the memory of the martyrs was surrounded also included their mortal remains. If their burial place was known—and Roman law usually allowed those who had been martyred to be buried in a fitting manner—then it was the custom to hold the annual celebrations of their glorious death near, or at the site of, their tomb. The earliest document relating to an annual memorial service at the tomb of a famous martyr dates from about 155 and concerns Bishop Polycarp of Smyrna, who in his youth had known the Apostle John. The report originates from his own Church and most probably dates from the very year of his death. Polycarp was burnt alive in the amphitheatre in the presence of the whole city and of many members of his community. After the account of his death the document continues:

"But the opponent [Satan], the wicked and evil one, the enemy of the race of the righteous, had seen the greatness of his testimony. He knew how blameless had been his life from the days of his youth; he marked how he was crowned with the wreath of immortality; how he had gained the prize which could no longer be denied him. And therefore he determined that we should not gain possession even of his mortal remains, although there were many who longed to have his holy relics among them. He therefore prompted Nicetas, father of Herodes and brother of Alce, to go to the proconsul and insist that the body should not be handed over. 'For,' he said, 'it might come about that they would abandon the Crucified One and begin to worship this man instead.' And this was done on the insistence and at the instigation of the Jews, for they also had spied on us when we had attempted to remove his body from the funeral pyre. These people do not realise that we can never abandon Christ, who suffered for the salvation of those He came to redeem, the innocent for the guilty. They do not realise that we can worship no other, for Him we adore as the Son of God, but we love the martyrs as the disciples and followers of the Lord, and rightly so, on account of their incomparable devotion to their Lord and King. May we too become their fellow disciples and sharers in their fate. When, however, the judge remarked the envy of the Jews, he declared that the body belonged to the state and had it burnt as is the custom with them. Later, however, we gathered together his bones, more precious than costly jewels and more refined than gold, and we concealed them in a fitting place. And there we shall gather together, insofar as is possible and as the Lord allows, in order to celebrate with joy and gladness the anniversary of his martyrdom, in commemoration of those who preceded us in the struggle and as an inspiration and preparation for those who are to follow after." (*The Martyrdom of St Polycarp*, **17**, **1-18**, **3**; *ca* A.D. 155-60)

Another document from a century later, dating from 258, during the time of the persecutions of Valerian, concerns the famous Bishop of Carthage, Cyprian, some of whose letters and writings we still possess.

"Thus was accomplished the martyrdom of the holy Cyprian. And, on account of the curiosity of the pagans, his body was provisionally laid to rest close by the place of his martyrdom. But it was removed from thence during the night, and with prayer, by the light of candles and torches, it was transferred as if in triumph to the burial place of procurator Macrobius Candidianus which lies close by the Mappalian Way, near to the ponds." (*Acts of Cyprian*, **5-6**; A.D. 258)

On this spot stood the *mensa Cypriani*, the stone above his grave, upon which, shortly after 313, was built the basilica bearing the same name and in which later St Augustine so often delivered the commemoration speech on the 14th of September, the anniversary of Cyprian's death. The ruins of this basilica are shown on page 116 (353). They lie close to the sea, south of the ancient, long-vanished city of Carthage.

Cemeteries dating from the third century are rare. They consist mainly of the earliest nuclei of a few catacombs on the outskirts of Rome—Domitilla, the crypts of Lucina, Priscilla, Praetextatus—and that of Januarius at Naples. Necropolises dating from the Early Christian period are found outside the walls of many cities, especially in the Greek East and in Africa. Most of the monuments which have been preserved there, however, whether under or above ground, date from the period after 313. The most important of these are grouped together on the double Map 13-14. The Roman remains are shown on Map 28.

Above, **98-100**. Remains from the oldest and largest of the catacombs at Naples, that of Januarius (S. Gennaro).

98. ENTRANCE HALL, about 200.

99. IBID., detail from a painted ceiling: the Fall. On the same ceiling, the only one in Naples dating from the third century, can be seen depicted the allegorical 'construction of the Tower of Penitence', a motif taken from the 'Shepherd' of Hermas, brother of Pius I (142-55). The 'Fall' of Naples is similar to that of Dura and the slightly later one in Rome (cf **104**). At this period the stock of motifs is still largely the same in East and West.

100. IBID., *arcosolia* and *loculi* in a disposition which differs from the Roman.

The after-life

On pages 54-5, there follow **101-108**, monuments illustrating the symbolic motifs by which Christians living before the age of Constantine gave expression to their belief in eternal life. They constitute the earliest Christian iconography of the after-life.

Although as a rule these remains do not aim at depicting the condition of the redeemed souls after death, but rather the simple fact of redemption, and although they are inspired by preaching and church linguistic usage, they are none-the-less popular creations which were conceived at first in an often surprisingly classical form in the workshops of the sculptors and painters. And yet they remain purely symbolic. It did not occur to the ancients to attempt to give concrete expression to the ineffable. These creations can all be linked up with the three famous words which are still pronounced every day before the altar in Roman Catholic churches: all those who rest in Christ are in 'the place of refreshment, light, and peace'. Of these three, the idea of 'light', as it is difficult to represent, was not attempted during the third century. The other two conceptions on the other hand, those of 'peace' and 'refreshment', give the key to nearly all the pictures.

The idea of peace is expressed by the evangelical motif of the bringing home of the lost sheep on the shoulders of the divine Shepherd. In itself this means only an abstract 'redemption through Christ', but the theme was extended into an illustration of 'the blessed soul in the peace of the paradise of the Shepherd'. The paradise is a garden with trees, and at the same time the pasture of the Shepherd in the twenty-third Psalm. The redeemed soul is shown 'in peace' (cf the epitaphs) with hands upraised in prayer to its Redeemer (*orans*), and it is difficult to determine whether it is *salvanda* or *salvata*, whether it is praying for the ultimate redemption, which includes the resurrection of the body, or whether it is sunk in peaceful prayer of thanksgiving for the redemption already granted in baptism, a redemption in no way affected by the fact of physical death: indeed the idea of death is nowhere present. And yet Christians do not avoid mentioning the day of death, as did the pagans. Bearing the anniversary celebrations in mind they always take care to mention it. We have already found these motifs in the visions of the African martyrs of 202 (texts on page 44), and they predominate in the series of magnificent sarcophagi in Rome and Arles, the oldest known to us (see **43-47** and the details shown in **101-104**). The shepherd theme is often combined with a series of tableaux illustrating the theme of 'deliverance through prayer from mortal danger', as in the deliverance of Daniel, of Jonah, of Susanna, of Noah, of Isaac, of the Three Youths of Babylon and a few others. They are

all taken from the Old Testament and are based on the readings during the preparation for baptism and, in part, on a Jewish iconography of the Diaspora (Daniel, Isaac). These are the same themes that are still heard in the twelve readings before the blessing of the baptismal font during the Easter night services and in the *Commendatio animae*, the prayer for the dying (which dates from a later period). Towards the end of the third century and the beginning of the fourth the Shepherd theme has become a cliché which visibly degenerates into a pious and sometimes fanciful pastorale (see **47, 66, 67**). This motif then disappears without trace, as does, *ca* 400, the figure of the Shepherd himself.

The second principal motif, the 'refreshment' (*refrigerium*, viz. by food, cool drink, or shadow) is usually illustrated by a banquet which, to judge by the form, is derived from the ordinary profane representations of the funeral meal. And yet the Gospel motif of the loaves and fishes—stressed by the showing of the seven baskets and by the fact of there being seven people reclining about the table—changes the funeral meal into a purely Christian conception which includes an allusion both to the celestial banquet and to the Eucharist—'the food which endures to eternal life'; cf John 6. It also embraces the prefiguration of the Eucharist, the feeding of the five thousand with the new manna by the greater Moses in the desert of life, and the meal, likewise consisting of loaves and fishes, partaken of by the seven after the Resurrection, on the shores of the Sea of Tiberias. This theme also disappears in the fourth century.

Another expression of the idea of refreshment is the shadow of the miraculous gourd (*cucurbita* in the earliest Latin translation) under which Jonah rested. Here the conception includes the idea of shade, but also that of rest, the famous *requies* of which St Augustine was so often to speak later. It is noteworthy that the Fathers never use this symbol—it is a purely popular motif and remains in vogue longer than the others.

Opposite, **101-104**. Four illustrations of the *anima in pace* theme.

101. SARCOPHAGUS of Junia Julia Juliane(te?) dedicated by her husband. Inscription:' To Junia Julia Julianete, his dearest wife, Melibius, the eighth day before the Ides of May' [= the day of death]. The deceased—obviously a portrait, with the veil indicating a married woman—is identified with Noah, saved in the Ark from the waters of death. The scene of Jonah's deliverance and the paradise of the Shepherd accompany the inscription. Julia stands, right, once more as *anima in pace*, before the funeral curtain. *Rome, Museo Lateranense.*

102. MIDDLE SECTION of the sarcophagus of the Via Lungara. *Anima in pace* in the garden of paradise; doves—symbol of souls—in the trees. At the corners of the same sarcophagus are depicted the Shepherd and the Fisher of men and, at the sides, the flock and baptism. *Rome, Museo delle Terme.*

103. ANIMA IN PACE in the garden of the Shepherd. Detail from the sarcophagus of La Gayolle, executed in Arles and probably the earliest of all Christian sarcophagi (the whole of the sarcophagus is shown on **43**). Its date is uncertain: the end of the 2nd or the beginning of the 3rd century? *Brignoles, Séminaire.*

104. SARCOPHAGUS OF VELLETRI in Latium, south of Rome. End of 3rd century. A synthesis of all the themes of salvation current at the time. The three main figures are the *anima in pace* and two shepherds; the space between them is filled in by the Fall, tableaux illustrating the theme of deliverance by divine intervention, and a few other motifs: left, Daniel, the Jonah trilogy and the True Philosophy; right, Noah and the seven baskets from the feeding of the five thousand, symbol of the Food of Life.

105. THE MEAL OF THE SEVEN with loaves and fishes and the seven baskets. In the catacomb of Calixtus, sacrament chapel A5. Shortly after 200.

106. REFRIGERIUM with bread and wine. Lid of the sarcophagus of Baebia Hertofile (cf **66**.) The representation here is still so close to the profane motif of the funeral meal that only the surrounding pictures convey the hidden significance. *Rome, Museo delle Terme.*

107. THE CELESTIAL REFRESHMENT. The prophet Jonah resting under the *cucurbita* (the gourd has been broken off). Detail from the sarcophagus in Santa Maria Antiqua on the Forum (cf **45**, the whole sarcophagus; in **606** the sarcophagus is bottom left in the side aisle). Technically, Jonah is a formal replica of the well-known figure of Endymion who, on many pagan sarcophagi, lies sleeping in the same position. The sea monster (*cetus*) is likewise a current motif. In **606** one sees the side of the case with the praying figure in the ship and, on the extreme left, the allegorical figure with the trident, symbolising the sea.

108. THE CELESTIAL REFRIGERIUM. Jonah's rest under the *cucurbita*; right, his prayer in the ship, during the storm. Detail from the lid of the sarcophagus of Baebia Hertofile (cf **66** where the whole sarcophagus is shown). *Rome, Museo delle Terme.*

105

107

109

THE AGE OF DIOCLETIAN AND THE TETRARCHY
(109-115)

109. The city wall of Rome, built between 271-80, was begun during the reign of Aurelian (270-75), the restorer of the Empire—*restitutor orbis*—and the man who met the widespread latent monotheism of his epoch by introducing the cult of the sun, the symbol of the Empire. It was he perhaps who introduced the feast of the natal day of the invincible sun—*natalis solis invicti*—thereby unconsciously determining the date for the future feast of Christmas (which originated in Rome *ca* 330 and falls on the same day, 25 December, the day of the winter solstice). "Aurelian builds a temple for Sol and surrounds Rome with stouter walls." (Eusebius, *Chronicle*, Aurelian, 4, A.D. 275)

That Rome, once taken for granted as being an open city, should have been ringed about by stout walls is a sign of the times. This enormous construction, completed by Probus (276-82), has been preserved almost intact, although it was unable to protect the city against the barbarians or against treachery.

110. COIN OF DIOCLETIAN. It was, however, Diocletian (287-305), an upstart from the army, a native of Dalmatia, and a great man, who succeeded in restoring and long maintaining order in the decayed Empire. He it was who, from

necessity, transformed the Empire, which up till then had enjoyed such flexible and enlightened rule, into a totalitarian state. Its economy was regulated down to the smallest detail, it was strongly centralised, and it was governed by a swarm of bureaucrats from a court at which, even in externals, the 'Divine Caesar' surrounded himself with a hieratic ceremonial and allowed himself to be worshipped as a god. For the first time jewels appeared on the garments and footwear of Augustus' successors. The Senate became the municipal council of Rome. After earnest consultation with conservative pagan advisers and after having consulted the oracle of Apollo at Didyma, Diocletian decided to complete the unification of the Empire by the lamentable and brutal liquidation of what appeared to him as a state within a state—the Christian church. The most terrible of the persecutions began in 304.

"In the nineteenth year of the reign of Diocletian, in the month of March, at Easter, the churches are destroyed." (Eusebius, *Chronicle*, Diocletian, 19, A.D. 304)

A contemporary eye-witness from the court capital of Nicomedia in Bithynia writes:

"A suitable and auspicious day is sought for this action and the choice falls upon the *Terminalia*, the 'festival of boundaries' celebrated on 23 February. This day seemed indicated for putting an end to this religion and was, as the poet says, 'that first day of death, that first day, the source of disasters' [Virgil, *Aeneid* IV, 169-70] which would overtake them and the world. When this day finally dawned, during the consulship of two old men, one of whom was consul for the eighth time and the other for the seventh, the prefect suddenly made his way to the church [of Nicomedia] accompanied by high-ranking army officials, officers, and civic and treasury officials. The doors are forced, the image of the god is sought for, the holy books are found and burnt. Licence is given to all to plunder and the place is robbed. Everyone is excited and runs to and fro. They [Galerius and Diocletian], however, sat watching—for the church lay on a height and was visible from the palace—and argued for a long time whether it would not be better to set the church alight. Diocletian's view, however, prevailed. He was afraid lest, in the event of a great conflagration, part of the city might also be consumed, for many large buildings surrounded the church. Praetorian guards therefore advanced in close formation with axes and other implements. They threw themselves upon the church from all sides and in a few hours razed this lofty sanctuary to the ground.

"The following day an edict was proclaimed in which it was stated that all adherents of this religion were excluded from every office and dignity, that they might be subjected to judicial torture whatever their rank or position, that any-one might bring an action against them but that they, on the other hand, might not go to law in cases of injustice, adultery or robbery. In short, that they had neither the rights of a free citizen nor freedom of speech. This edict was torn down and destroyed by a certain man. This was of course not right, but it was none-the-less a proof of great courage. And this man said, laughing, as he did so, that they had pasted up the victories over the Goths and Sarmates. He was immediately arrested and led away and was not only tortured but roasted according to the rules of cookery, and endured death by fire with great patience." (Lactantius, *On the deaths of the Persecutors*, 12 and 13).

Towards Easter the churches were everywhere destroyed. An orgy of hate followed; the Emperor, disappointed and recognising his error, retired in 305 to the colossal palace which he had had built in Dalmatia, near Salonae. Four Caesars (the Tetrarchs) succeeded him (305-*ca* 320).

111. THE TETRARCHS. Porphyry group, now on the corner of the façade of St Mark's in Venice. *Ca* 300?

112. RECONSTRUCTION OF DIOCLETIAN'S PALACE, which was at the present town of Split on the Adriatic sea in Dalmatia.

113. IBID. The mausoleum of Diocletian, now the cathedral of Split. One should note the motifs, which are shortly afterwards found again in the Christian basilicas and baptisteries: the pillars surmounted by an archivolt instead of an architrave, the façade of the propylaeum with the interrupted tympanum and the rotunda.

114. THE BATHS OF DIOCLETIAN, now the church of S. Maria degli Angeli, in Rome.

115. CUPOLA FRIEZE in the mausoleum at Split, an anticipation of the hieratic style of the 4th century.

112

113

114

110

111

115

THE CHURCH OF THE EMPIRE A.D. 313–600

Chapter II

The fourth century

THE AGE OF CONSTANTINE THE GREAT (116-144)

The Emperor and the City (116-125)

Constantine's decision to play Christianity as his trump card in his conflict with his fellow Caesar Maxentius, even before he emerged as absolute ruler from the chaos of the Tetrarchy, and to champion the cause of the persecuted Christians, constitutes one of the turning points of history and in particular of the history of the Church.

After his victory over Maxentius at the Pons Milvius, the Emperor proclaimed the celebrated Edict of Tolerance in Milan, probably in 313. This gave the churches civil status and the same privileges as the state religious institutions. Toleration, however, was soon followed by open support: the monogram of Christ appeared on the standards and upon some coins. With Constantine begins the outward Christianisation of the Empire, accompanied by state interference in ecclesiastical affairs—two developments of which the repercussions can still be felt today. Slowly but surely the Church of the Martyrs becomes, outwardly at least, the official church of the Roman Empire.

116. CONSTANTINE (306-37; sole ruler from 323). Fragment of the colossal statue in the main niche of the basilica (see **124**) on the Forum, *ca* 315. The hieratic style—frontal attitude, fixed, staring gaze, supernatural immobility—continues the Diocletian tradition. Constantine's portraits, as well as his coins and orations, convey the impression of a singular religious gravity and certainly reflect the high conception he had of his vocation. *Rome, Palazzo dei Conservatori.*

117. CONSTANTINE. Statue in the narthex of St John Lateran; 320.

118. COIN OF CONSTANTINE. After 325. One of his best portraits.

119. COIN OF FLAVIA HELENA AUGUSTA, the Empress mother, highly honoured by her son. It was she who founded the sanctuaries at the Holy Places in Jerusalem (Anastasis, Martyrion, Eleona) and in Bethlehem (the Grotto of the Nativity).

120. CONSTANTINE'S TRIUMPHAL ARCH near the Colosseum, *ca* 315. A monument to the changing times, the arch is also famous for the inscription in the middle of the *attica*. This reads:

> IMP. CAES. FL. CONSTANTINO MAXIMO
> P.F. AVGVSTO S.P.Q.R.
> QVOD INSTINCTV DIVINITATIS MENTIS
> MAGNITVDINE CVM EXERCITV SVO
> TAM DE TYRANNO QVAM DE OMNI EIVS
> FACTIONE VNO TEMPORE IVSTIS
> REMPVBLICAM VLTVS EST ARMIS
> ARCVM TRIVMPHIS INSIGNEM DICAVIT

"To the Emperor Caesar Flavius Constantine the Great
pious, happy, Augustus, since he, inspired by the Godhead
[a neutral expression acceptable to both pagans and Christians]
and by greatness of spirit, with his army,
with lawful weapons and with one blow,
avenged the State upon the enemy and upon his whole troop,
The Senate and the Roman people dedicate this arch as a sign of his triumph."

The round reliefs are *spolia* from the period of Trajan (whose head made way for that of Constantine). They form a remarkable contrast to the rest of the strongly stylised sculptures, especially the narrow friezes above the side passages. Two of these are reproduced below.

121. FRIEZE ON THE SEAWARD SIDE. The Emperor upon the rostrum of the Forum Romanum for a *congiarium* (a distribution of favours) to dignitaries and people. In the background are the buildings and columns of the Forum. The chancel of the rostrum is remarkably similar to the oldest *cancelli* (altar rails surrounding the *mensa*) of the 4th century basilicas and the composition resembles that of the contemporary Christian sarcophagi. One specimen in the Lateran Museum (see **169**) has even been taken for a product of the same workshop.

122. FRIEZE ON THE TOWN SIDE (visible on **120**, centre, right). The victory over Maxentius at the Pons Milvius to the north of Rome, 28 October 313. Eusebius of Caesarea, the historian—and the first court prelate and biographer of Constantine—compared Maxentius' destruction in the Tiber with that of Pharaoh in the Red Sea (Exod. 15). This motif appears some time later on many Christian sarcophagi (cf **402** and Eusebius, *Life of Constantine* I, 38; also **217**). Among ecclesiastical writers the crossing of the Red Sea also serves, according to the Pauline conception, as a prefiguration of baptism and of the Redemption in general.

120

121

122

123

124

123-125. Rome during the Age of Constantine. The Emperor resided most of the time in Nicomedia or in Trèves—where remains of the palace have been found—and Rome seemed destined henceforth to lie completely outside the sphere of imperial administration and to become merely a repository of the past and of tradition. Indeed, pagan opposition (to the Church) remained strong right up to 400 and the new dynasty was more interested in the new city on the Bosphorus, the new Rome which lay in the real heart of the Empire: this was Constantinople, the city of Constantine (see Map 37). And yet the City was perhaps never so impressive as at this period, around 330. We know the lay-out, the monuments, and the boundaries of the fourteen regions fairly accurately from contemporary descriptions. The number of inhabitants has been estimated at 700,000 if not more (see Map 27).

Gigantic constructions like the basilica on the Forum, begun during the reign of Maxentius and completed by Constantine (see **124**) or a gem like the interior of the mausoleum of his daughter Constantia, make it impossible for us to speak of a 'Decline and Fall' in the domain of architecture. Such monuments form rather the transition to the non-plastic, atmospheric, yet tectonic style of architecture which later, shorn of its massiveness by the Greeks, will produce the Santa Sophia and provide in the West the inspiration for the Romanesque style of architecture and, after 1400, for that of the Renaissance.

123. MAUSOLEUM of an unknown prince, in the Forum. Plain from without but elaborate within; now empty. Entrance preserved. Beginning of the 4th century.

124. BARREL VAULT of the side aisle of the Basilica Constantini on the Forum; 314-20. Span 75 feet, i.e. broader than any of the Gothic naves (Mirepoix 68 feet, Gerona 72 feet, Albi 62 feet). The cross vault of the centre aisle collapsed about 800 and the marble covering disappeared. A third of the skeleton is still standing.

125. ROME, about 330. Part of regions II, III, IV, and VIII. In the distance VI and VII. Reconstruction by Gismondi. In the foreground the temple of Claudius, to the right, the *Ludus Magnus*. In the centre, behind the Colosseum, the popular quarter of Subura; right, the baths of Trajan and to the left the *meta sudans*, the arch of Constantine, and the Templum Urbis. Behind them, the Forum Romanum with the basilica of Constantine and, still farther behind, the arch of Septimius Severus with, slightly to the left, the temples of the Capitol. Right, the imperial *fora*. Above left, the cupola of the Pantheon and the wall of the Circus Flaminius (cf Map 27). *Museo della Civiltà romana*.

The church foundations of Constantine (opposite, on page 61)

126. BASILICA OF THE REDEEMER, now St John Lateran. Interior as it was before the restoration by Borromini in 1650. Fresco by Gaspard Dughet in S. Martino al Monti. The church—as large as Amiens cathedral—had five aisles and two large *Pastophoria* (now the transept) It is considered to be the first large church to have been built after the peace. As the diocesan church of the Bishop of Rome (*ecclesia cathedralis*) it still retains, even to the present day, the title of 'mother and head of all churches in the City and in the world': *omnium ecclesiarum Urbis et Orbis mater et caput*. It was also perhaps the determining work which served as a model for the classical basilicas that began to appear all over the Empire shortly after 350. From this time onwards the Popes resided in the palace north of the church, the *domus Faustae*, presented by the Emperor to the community of Rome and later called the *Patriarchium* (see Map 27).

126
128
130

127
129
131

61

132

133

127. THE LATERAN IN 1957. The old Basilica lies between the high façade of Galilei (1735), the palace and loggia of Fontana (1586), and the new apse of Leo XIII (1885). In front, below, the baptistery of Sixtus III (432-40, cf **409**, interior) built on the site of the earlier Constantinian baptistery. The palace stands on the site of the *Patriarchium*, once the foremost *episcopium* in the world and a focal point for the history of the Middle Ages. It was irresponsibly torn down in 1586. Since 1838 the palace, rebuilt, has been arranged as a museum, and most of the Christian sarcophagi reproduced in this book are preserved there, together with countless inscriptions taken chiefly from the catacombs. The obelisk to the left, 105 feet high, was brought from Egypt by Constantine II in 357. It stood on the *spina* in the Circus Maximus and was re-erected here in 1587.

128. INTERIOR OF ST JOHN LATERAN. The four large columns are remains of the old basilica. The altar stands in the original position under the baldachin of 1367. The whole is the work of Borromini, *ca* 1650. The apse, deeper than the earlier one, dates from 1885.

129. CHURCH OF THE NATIVITY, Bethlehem. It is uncertain whether the colonnades of the five-aisled nave date from the time of Helena or from that of Justinian who restored the church in the 6th century. It was he who added the trefoil-shaped eastern part (*triconch*) which is hidden on the photo by the walls of the nave and the Greek iconostasis. The Grotto of the Nativity lies beneath the podium *(bema)*.

130. BASILICA APOSTOLORUM on the Via Appia, founded by Constantine before 356. Originally a pillar basilica with a wide gallery, it was later narrowed down to the present-day hall church of S. Sebastiano (1612). Concerning the *memoria* of the Apostles located here see page 47. The *triclia* lies to the left, under the church floor, likewise the tomb of Clodius Hermes. The gallery is now a museum.

131. BASILICA HIERUSALEM in Sessoriano, adapted *ca* 300 from the hall of a palace. The church, founded to house relics from Jerusalem—in particular a small relic of the wood of the True Cross—bore the name of the Holy City and is now known as S. Croce in Gerusalemme. The interior was rebuilt in 1743.

132-33. REMAINS of the Constantinian Basilica of S. Petri in Vaticano, the famous church where the Apostle is buried. It was ruthlessly demolished by Bramante (known to his contemporaries as *maestro ruinante*) and his successors at the command of Julius II during the gradual construction of the present-day St Peter's. One of the most beautiful and most glorious edifices of Christianity, with all its inscriptions, tombs, mosaics, and associations, it was sacrificed to the desire for renovation of the great Popes and masters of the Roman Renaissance. We know the old Basilica only from rare and always incomplete sketches dated after 1500. They show the remains of the last wall rising up in front of the lofty core of the new central structure. There also exist a few schematic views of the interior, for example the fresco in the Grotte Vaticane, 17th century (see **133**). The ground-plan, known from Alfarano's book, has now been confirmed by the excavations of 1945 and following years. It consisted of a long, five-aisled hall with a centre aisle and a transept more than 65 feet broad. In the Middle Ages an inscription, probably due to Leo the Great, was still to be seen upon the trimphal arch:

> Quod duce te mundus surrexit in astra triumphans
> hanc Constantinus victor tibi condidit aulam.

"Since under Thy leadership the Empire rose once again triumphant to the stars

Constantine the victor has founded this hall church in Thine honour." This dedication is addressed to Christ and contains an allusion to the sign XP, the monogram of Christ which, according to some, the Emperor had introduced upon the military standards before the battle of the Pons Milvius. Augustine's friend, Bishop Paulinus of Nola, incidentally describes the old Basilica of St Peter's in a letter written to his Roman friend Pammachius, on the occasion of the huge funeral banquet given by the latter to the poor of the community of Rome in 397, in honour of his deceased wife. The meal was held in the nave and in the porticoes of the atrium of the Vatican basilica. "The whole space was filled with paupers," says Paulinus:

" . . . not only the long main aisle which stretches so broad beneath the lofty ceiling in the centre and, with the shining chair of the Apostle in the distance, catches the eye of the visitor and rejoices his heart, but also the double porticoes which, beneath the one enormous roof, serve to broaden her flanks on either side [the church was five-aisled: **183**] yea, even the open inner court in front on to which the entrance hall emerges and where a round *aedicula* roofed with a bronze baldachin affords decorative shade to the fountain which gushes forth water for our hands and mouths." (Paulinus of Nola, *Letters*, **13**, 11-5)

It was of course usual to cleanse the mouth and hands with this water before entering the basilica. This is obviously the origin of the custom of signing oneself with holy water from a small font. In Syria the Moslems have adopted this old Christian usage so that we can see, in the picturesque forecourts of the mosques, the descendants of the *cantharus* (fountain) of the early Christian *atria*.

The Vatican *cantharus* is known to us from old sketches. Of the canopy, two bronze peacocks remain, and of the fountain itself the bronze pine cone which gushed forth water from between its scales. They are now housed together in the Cortile della Pigna in the Vatican, in the large recess constructed by Bramante and called Il Nicchione (see **132**).

We do not know where the altar stood in the old St Peter's. In the fourth century, on the site of the present-day *confessio* enclosing the tomb of the Apostle, there was a small *aedicula* similar to that of the Holy Sepulchre in the Anastasis in Jerusalem and surrounded by low *cancelli* (balustrades). This structure was the *memoria* proper, the real *memoria Petri*. Six pillars decorated with a motif of twisting vine tendrils supported an architrave; this colonnade shut off both the projecting rectangle of the *memoria* and the main apse of the basilica lying immediately behind it. They are depicted, together with the *memoria* itself, upon the ivory reliquary conserved in Pola in Istria (see **479**). S. Petri in Vaticano was built between 320 and 356 (it is not known for certain in what year it was begun nor when it was consecrated). It is one of the first and largest of the cemetery basilicas or *basilicae coemeteriales*. S. Salvatoris in Laterano, on the contrary, is one of the oldest and most famous of the fourth century city churches which contained no martyrs' *memoriae* but served exclusively for the ordinary liturgy and the purely ecclesiastical gatherings of the community of Rome. Both churches became prototypes of an endless series of foundations, right up to the later Middle Ages. Of the decoration, nothing remains: all we possess are the catalogues in the *Liber Pontificalis*. These lead us to surmise that everything gleamed with massive gold and silver, that curtains hung everywhere between the columns, and that the evening services were held by the light of thousands of oil lamps.

134

135

The mausoleum of Constantia at Rome (134-138)

One of the best preserved monuments of Late Antiquity is the mausoleum built (from 337 to 350) by Constantia, the daughter of Constantine, to the north of the basilica erected upon the tomb of the martyr Agnes above the catacomb on the Via Nomentana, another of her foundations. Except for the ruined walls this church has disappeared, but the mausoleum remains. The exterior is an undecorated brick rotunda with gallery and narthex, the interior is magnificently elaborate. The great porphyry sarcophagus from Egypt has long ago been transferred to the Vatican museum, but the original mosaics can still be seen in the vaulting of the gallery and in two of the wall niches. The circular colonnade of double pillars supporting the cupola is also still intact.

There is a remarkable similarity between this type of mausoleum and the baptisteries of a somewhat later period (cf 409-20). Together they make up the category of small central structures to which also belongs the special type of martyrs' mausolea called *memoriae*. Baptisteries, elaborate mausolea, and smaller – often simply rectangular – *memoriae* constituted the usual annexes of a great basilica. An important, but dilapidated, series still flanks the Basilica Apostolorum (S. Sebastiano; cf 130).

134. UNKNOWN PRINCESS of the house of Constantine. Constantia? Hair style and stylisation indicate the year of her death, 350. *Rome, Museo Torlonia.*

135. RUINS OF THE BASILICA OF ST AGNES (left), and adjoining (right), the mausoleum of the foundress. The windows in the drum of the cupola give light to the central hall. The small slit windows beneath illuminate the gallery mosaics. The old Basilica of St Agnes was a hall with pillars and a gallery, of the same type as the Basilica Apostolorum on the Via Appia (see 130). To the extreme left is the new Sant' Agnese, founded by Honorius I (625-38; cf 607 on page 179) and the medieval belfry.

136. INTERIOR of the mausoleum of Constantia following the most recent restorations. The marble revetment of the walls has disappeared and the candelabra no longer stand in the wall niches. Only the mosaic vaulting remains intact. Typical of the post-Diocletian period are the pieces of entablature between capital and archivolt. They were later replaced by the impost (see 267).

137. MOSAIC VAULTING. Motifs which hitherto had usually been found only on floors—the vintage with cupids—are here spaced out on a vault and grouped about a portrait: a sign of the transition from decorative floor mosaic to the monumental wall, vault, and apse mosaics.

138. DRAWING of part of the vanished cupola mosaic, 16th century. Other drawings give the whole composition: concentric zones divided off radially from the centre by candelabra caryatids linked by acanthus stems. The lower zone is filled with a Nile idyll; on the small scenes above one can identify: left, Tobias with his fish, the spies visiting Rahab in Jericho, Susanna vindicated by Daniel and, extreme right, Cain and Abel with the first fruits and the lamb (?). *El Escorial, near Madrid.*

136
137   138

THEODORE·FELI
DIVVANTE·DEO
OMNIPOTENTE·ET
POEMNIO·CAELITVS
DIVM·OMNIA
AFATE·FECISTI·ET
GLORIOSE·DEDICAS
TI

141   142

The church floors (139-144)

The church floors form an important category among the rare monuments which have survived from the period of Constantine. The basilicas have usually disappeared or have been restored at a later date, but the old mosaic floors were usually left undisturbed. During excavations they were often found beneath a later floor or, more or less intact, under the remains of a ruined church. The oldest floor known to us is at the same time one of the most interesting and most beautiful, and by some miracle it has been preserved relatively intact. The floor in question is that of one of the two hall churches whose foundations lie beneath the present-day cathedral of Aquileia in Venetia under the floor of a vanished fifth-century church and that of the still existing early Roman church built by Bishop Poppo (1019-42), consecrated in 1031, and restored for the last time during the Gothic period. The traces of the different periods of construction and the position of the earliest floor can be clearly seen on 143.

This earliest floor, which has been completely exposed and is only interrupted by the right-hand pillars of the nave, extends over the entire nave and the right side-aisle. It is the largest of the early Christian floors to survive. The date is established by the dedicatory inscription in the middle of the central composition of the East end. It gives the name of the founder, Theodorus, certainly Bishop of Aquileia between 314 and 320 (see 140):

143

XP	XP
THEODORE FELI(X)	Theodorus, happy one
(A)DIVVANTE DEO	with the help of God
OMNIPOTENTE ET	the Almighty and of
POEMNIO CAELITVS TIBI	the flock entrusted to thee
(CRE)DITVM OMNIA	from on high,
(B)AEATE FECISTI ET	thou hast made all felicitously
GLORIOSE DEDICAS	and hast gloriously dedicated it.
TI	

144

139-40. Details from the 'sea piece' which decorates the floor of the East end of the church of Aquileia. Here the cathedra of Theodorus and the seats of the clergy probably stood. The composition is a conglomeration of all the current motifs that could possibly be associated with water: the sailing, fishing, cupids, the Jonah trilogy, the Fisher of men, and the catch. The motif of the 'fishes born in the water' is, however, clearly the underlying theme and the fanciful combination of the mystical catch with Jonah's refreshment after his deliverance-through-water in no way detracts from the baptismal symbolism. The baptismal font stood outside the main hall of the church, as indeed was the case everywhere.

139. THE MYSTICAL CATCH represented as the profane Nile idyll (cf 138).

140. SECTION with the *clipeus* (round shield) containing the inscription. The holes which have been stopped up are the traces of the grooves for the colonnettes of the stone altar, transferred here at a later date. Its original position can still be clearly seen in the centre of the church, a little below the middle of the longitudinal axis, above the mosaic with the Eucharistic motif shown on 422.

141-42. FLOOR MOSAIC from the hall-church of Parenzo, beginning of the 4th century. It was discovered beneath the floor of the present 6th century basilica (Parenzo = Poreč, formerly Parentium in Istria). The inscription mentions the names of the founders: '[Lup]icinus and Pascasia have given four hundred feet [of this mosaic], Clamosus, the schoolmaster, and Successa, a hundred feet; Felicissimus with his family a hundred feet.' *Cathedral Museum.*

143. THE EXPOSED FLOOR of 314-20 in the cathedral, Aquileia.

144. IBID., detail. Summer garlanded with ears of corn.

145
146

148   149   150

THE AGE OF THE EPIGONES, A.D. 337-379 **(145-177)**. Throughout the whole of the fourth century many voices from within the Christian community gave utterance to the joy occasioned by the unexpected turn of events in 313. Yet this joy was not unmixed. That circumstances had changed the Church of the Martyrs into the Church of the Empire also meant that there was a danger of her becoming a State institution. There had always been differences of opinion concerning matters of doctrine or church discipline, but in the second and third centuries they had remained purely an ecclesiastical affair. They had been ultimately settled by the Bishops according to the pure principles of the faith. It was the religious faith of these often simple Bishops, their devout sense of the Apostolic tradition and, as they firmly believed, their obedience to the guidance of the Spirit which inspires the Church of Christ, that had averted the dangers of Gnosticism, Montanism, and of local stubbornness too (in such matters as the date of Easter during the time of Pope Victor and Irenaeus, 189-98). Neither the theosophists of the Gnosis nor the sectarian enthusiasts from Phrygia (later reinforced by the keen pen of Tertullian), not even Origen's genius had been able to influence the Church's tradition of faith. From the time of Constantine, however, who had wished for the one united Church within the one Empire, the Emperors had intervened whenever discord threatened. Immediately after 313 Constantine vainly tried to put an end to the Donatist schism in Africa. This movement sprang in theory from a puritanical attitude regarding the reinstatement of those who had wavered during the persecutions of 303-11, but was in reality an anti-social, anti-hierarchical popular movement among the Berbers of Numidia. It was Constantine, again, who convoked the first oecumenical council in Nicaea, in 325, in order to settle at imperial level the question of whether Christ was 'of the same substance with the Father', a dispute begun by the Presbyter Arius in Alexandria. His example was followed by his sons and successors. Like him, they attempted to force decisions and like him they failed utterly. In spite of the compulsory synods, the banishment of Bishops who had remained faithful to their duty, and the installation of imperial sympathisers in their places, the ultimate formulation of Christology—which, after all, touched the very core of the faith—remained with those Bishops who considered it their duty to obey the word of God and the guidance of the Spirit rather than the Caesars and the intuition of the gifted few. The Arian struggle especially cast a dark shadow over the Christian scene in the fourth century. Another evil was that, to use the words of St Augustine, 'an incalculable shoal

of good and bad fishes had been caught up in the nets of the Church'. For a long time the Church of the Martyrs remained an élite, while the Church of the Empire became the church of the masses.

The dynasty (145-150)

The sons of Constantine and their successors.

145. COLOSSAL HEAD OF CONSTANTIUS, part of bronze statue; *ca* 360. *Rome, Palazzo d. Conservatori*. Constantius II (337-61) ruler of the East and, after 350, of the West as well. He chose the side of the Arian court prelates and repeatedly banished the champion of orthodoxy, Bishop Athanasius of Alexandria. An historian from the circle of the traditional non-Christian intellectuals writes of him:

"He confused the plain and simple Christian religion with old wives' tales. By interfering in the controversies instead of seriously trying to settle them, he only stirred up more. As they raged thus ever more fiercely he added fuel to the fire by arguing over formulas, with the result that the continual running hither and thither of troops of bishops utilising the public transport, to what they called 'synods', where he attempted to twist the whole practice of religion to suit his own ends, threw the imperial courier service into confusion." (Ammianus Marcellinus, **21,** 16: 18)

And yet the Emperor-theologian realised, better than Ammianus, what was at stake. In his time 'the Church of the Martyrs' had still a very real meaning:

"Shapur, king of Persia, persecutes the Christians." (Eusebius-Jerome, *Chronicle*, Constantius and Constans, 7, A.D. 344)

We still possess authentic Passions of some of the countless martyrs who suffered under the Sassanian ruler Shapur II, powerfully combated by Constantius. They are evocative documents, moving and edifying.

Those within the Empire who aspired to a truly Christian 'testimony' chose another way, that of ἄσκησις, a living for God, in the desert, far from the corrupt cities with the thousands who were Christian in name alone, and from the wranglings over heresy.

"In the year 356 Antonius the monk dies in the desert in the hundred and fifth year of his age." (Eusebius-Jerome, *Chronicle*, Constantius and Constans, 19, A.D. 356)

With Antonius begins the history of the monastic way of life. The relative data, together with that referring to the spread of monasticism to the far West, to Hibernia (Ireland), are found on Map 34 and, in the text, on pages 168-72.

Ordinary church life during this period is dominated by two motifs which occur again and again in every chronicle and memoir, namely, the building of ever bigger and more splendid churches, both within the walls of the old cities and without, in the cemeteries, where the *memoriae* of the martyrs arose (see Maps 30-31); and, in the East, the translation of the martyrs' relics to within the city walls, to be interred in sanctuaries built in their honour. This idea had not yet found favour in the West:

" . . . the bones of the Apostle Andrew and of Luke the Evangelist are received into Constantinople amid great enthusiasm." (Eusebius-Jerome, *Chronicle*, Constantius and Constans, 20, A.D. 357; cf 509).

"In the year 360 the Great Church is consecrated in Constantinople." (Eusebius-Jerome, *Chronicle*, Constantius and Constans, 23, A.D. 360)

This church was consecrated to the 'Holy Wisdom', the first of the three consecutively built churches consecrated to Christ, the Son of God, as 'Hagia Sophia' (cf Map 37).

146. (?)CONSTANS (337-50), ruler in the West. *Paris, Louvre*.

147. JULIAN THE APOSTATE (361-3). recognisable by his beard, so much scoffed at by the people of Antioch. His brother, Gallus, was done to death by Constantius, their uncle, and this serious-minded man, Julian, a convert to Neo-platonism, hated the religion of his youth as much as he did his uncle. As Emperor he attempted to restore the pagan rites, to oust the 'Galileans', especially from the schools, and to emulate their charity within a pagan framework. He died an early death in 363, fighting bravely against the Persians.

148. VALENS (364-78), ruler in the East. He often intervened in favour of the Arians, but found his Athanasius in Basil the Great of Caesarea in Cappadocia. He was slain fighting the Goths near Hadrianopolis. *Florence, Uffizi*.

149. VALENTINIAN I (364-74), ruler in the West, a friend of Ambrose of Milan. *Copenhagen, Ny Carlsberg Glyptotek*.

150. (?)VALENTINIAN II (375-92). Small bust. *Lyon, Palais des Beaux-Arts*.

151-156. The calendar of 354 (the 'Roman Calendar'). Two things remained unalterably pagan, the calendar and the schools. We know parts of a calendar for the city of Rome for the year 354 which does include a short list of the anniversaries of the Popes and martyrs, but the rest of the data is entirely non-Christian: the birthdays of the Caesars, the *fasti consulares*, and a week and month calendar with the usual astrological information. The original has been lost and we possess only fragments of later copies.

151. COD. VAT. BARB. 3139, f. 1. Title page with dedication: *Valentine, floreas in Deo, vivas floreas, vivas gaudeas, lege feliciter*, the usual Christian greetings. The monogram is that of Furius Dionysius Filocalus, later the calligrapher of Pope Damasus and originator of his monumental majuscule alphabet.

152. IBID., f. 2. The city of Rome, with a Victory upon the globe of the world.

153. IBID., f. 14. Caesar Constantius Gallus as consul (354) wearing the *toga picta*.

154. IBID., f. 8. Saturday (from the week calendar) with Saturn. Subscription: "On Saturdays, in the night as well as during the day, all is sombre and difficult. Those who are born on this day have a dangerous life, the lost are not found, he who takes to his bed becomes dangerously ill and stolen property is not recovered."

155. IBID., f. 5. The city of Trèves (with a captured German barbarian). Alexandria and Constantinople are also included in the calendar.

156. IBID., f. 22. The month of November represented by a *gallus* (a priest of Isis, a eunuch) with his sistrum. The Isiaca fell in this month. Further are shown an altar of Anubis, five pomegranates, and the winter goose.

"The first day of the week is the Lord's day. The second . . . is the *secunda feria*, which the pagans call the day of Luna, Mo(o)nday. The third is the *feria tertia*, called by them the day of Mars. The fourth is the *quarta feria*, called by the pagans, and by many Christians too, the day of Mercury. But this I do not like to hear. I wish that these people would mend their ways and cease to use these words. For have they not their own expressions? Let them then make use of them . . . It is better that a Christian should follow the Christian usage. But if custom oblige a Christian to employ words of which he inwardly disapproves, let him then realise that all those who have given their names to the constellations were once mortal men and that these heavenly bodies did not appear for the first time in the firmament on the occasion of their birth." (Augustine, *Exposition of the Psalms*, **93**, 3)

Augustine means that the gods were deified heroes. But the superstition which caused the days to be judged auspicious or inauspicious according to the influence of the constellations—all gods—remained ineradicable. Most of the old names have been conserved in the Romance languages and a few in the Germanic idioms. The ecclesiastical names are preserved in the liturgy and in the Romance names for Saturday and Sunday (sabato, sábado, samedi, domenica, dimanche, domingo).

Even in the West, where the link with Hellenism was much less strong, the

151

152

153

156

157

158

159

schools continued—well into the sixth century—to follow a purely pagan programme of education. Everyone has heard of St Jerome's dream, in which he was scourged by an angel on account of his love for Cicero and for profane literature. But Cassianus, his contemporary and fellow combatant in the struggle for the integral Christian life, also writes:

"A particular impediment to my spiritual welfare is my knowledge of literature, although, indeed, I appear to have acquired it in but small measure. However, the zeal of my tutor and the effort of continual reading have rendered me so weak that now my mind, as though contaminated by the verses of the poets, even when I am at prayer, thinks constantly of the absurd fables and war-like tales with which I became familiar in my youth, in my earliest school years. And whenever I sing psalms, or pray for forgiveness of my sins, the memory of shameless verses rises to my mind and the picture of fighting heroes appears before my eyes." (Cassianus, *Collations*, **14,** 12)

The Christian family, on the contrary, (**157** and **159**) became a nursery of the faith.

The faithful (157-160; 163-6); from fourth century monuments.

157. A CHRISTIAN FAMILY GROUP. Gold glass. *Brescia, Museo Civico.*

158. EUSEBIUS. Gold glass. *Vatican, Museo Cristiano.*

159. A FAMILY. Gold glass. *Vatican, Museo Cristiano.*

160-62. Examples of pagan decoration in the houses of the rich. It remained for the most part traditional and full of neutral clichés from Antiquity.

160. WOMAN OF ROYAL BIRTH (Fausta?). Painted panel from a coffered ceiling from the imperial palace of Trèves. *Trèves, Diocesan Museum.*

162. IBID., playing cupids.

161. WINTER: detail from a floor of a villa in Daphne (Antioch). Facing, on page 69; portraits on Christian sarcophagi of the 4th century.

163. AXIA ELIANE. Sarcophagus lid. *Arles, Musée lapidaire chrétien.*

164. IMAGO CLIPEATA (portrait in a round medallion). *Rome, Museo Lateranense.*

165. ARISTOCRATIC MARRIED COUPLE; underneath, the idyll of the Shepherd. End of the 4th century. Taken from one of the mausolea near S. Sebastiano. *Rome, Museo di San Sebastiano.*

166. THE PRAEFECTUS PRAETORIO CATERUIUS AND HIS WIFE SEPTIMA SEVERINA. *Imago Clipeata*, surrounded by the monogram of Christ and the doves with the olive branch; above the heads, the wreath of victory, symbol of eternal life. The men wear the *toga trabeata* of the high officials and carry the scroll (*rotulus*) indicating a scholar. Ca 390-410. *Tolentino, Duomo.*

The Christian portraits bring to a close the long history of the Roman portrait: aristocratic, at once stylised and realistic, yet capable of depicting individual types. They form a modest introductory chapter to the history of future Christian expressionism which will gradually replace the classical idealisation especially in strictly frontal portraits. 'Expression' is, of course, least pronounced in sculpture and achieves greatest importance in the mosaics and wall paintings

160

161

162

The sarcophagi of the fourth century (167–177)

These are the best preserved monuments from the period 313–79: solid marble cases with closely crowded frieze sculptures. Most of them originate from Rome and Arles. If one includes the Theodosian sarcophagi and the fragments, there are more than a thousand altogether. The old symbols: shepherd, fisherman, banquet, have disappeared. The unveiled figure of Christ makes its appearance, mostly in the representations of the miracles of Christ, with the Old Testament prefigurations alongside. Small historical and symbolical cycles develop: the passion of Moses-Peter and the childhood of Christ. As a series, the 'deliverance' motifs hold their own the longest.

167. THE JONAH SARCOPHAGUS; early 4th century. Lazarus, living water from the rock, passion of Moses-Peter, shepherd, Jonah trilogy, Noah, fisherman. Waning of the old, first glimpse of the new. *Rome, Museo Lateranense.*

168. FRIEZE SARCOPHAGUS OF SABINUS. Water from the rock and passion of Moses-Peter, miracle at Cana, *anima in pace*, the man born blind, loaves and fishes, Lazarus. Lid: seasons and hunting scene; *ca* 320. *Rome, Museo Lateranense.*

169. THE 'DOGMATIC' two-zoned frieze sarcophagus. Perhaps from the same workshop that produced the arch of Constantine; cf **121**. Upper zone: the creation of man, the assigning of work to our first parents, portraits of the deceased, the miracle at Cana, the loaves and fishes, Lazarus. Lower zone: the first believers among the pagans (star, Magi, Balaam behind the chair), the man born blind, Daniel and Habakkuk, *Petrus in gallicantu* (Peter at cock-crow; see **173**), the passion and water from the rock of Moses-Peter. The two portrait busts remained incomplete. *Rome, Museo Lateranense.*

170. SARCOPHAGUS 'OF THE TWO BROTHERS', 330–40. Lazarus (his figure has disappeared), *Petrus in gallicantu*, the Law being delivered to Moses, the sacrifice of Isaac, Pilate washing his hands; second zone: water from the rock and passion of Moses-Peter with Daniel in between, the man born blind, loaves and fishes. *Rome, Museo Lateranense.*

171. THE CREATION OF MAN by the Three Persons. Detail from **169**. Earliest representation of the Divine Trinity.

172. THE CREATION OF MAN. Detail from the (pagan) Prometheus sarcophagus depicted on **34**. The Titan Prometheus fashions man, Minerva breathes into him his soul (or better the φρόνησις) in the shape of a butterfly; Lachesis, one of the Fates, points out on the celestial globe the star under which he will be born. Middle or end of the 3rd century. Cf **171**. *Rome, Museo Capitolino.*

173-76. Symbols of baptism and penance (the 'second forgiveness').
173. 'Before the cock crows . . .' Detail from 175 (opposite). Left side of a sarcophagus. *Rome, Museo Lateranense.*

AD GALLICINIUM

Aeterne rerum conditor,
noctem diemque qui regis
et temporum das tempora
ut alleves fastidium

praeco diei iam sonat,
noctis profundae pervigil,
nocturna lux viantibus,
a nocte noctem segregans.

Hoc excitatus lucifer
solvit polum caligine,
hoc omnis erronum chorus
vias nocendi deserit

hoc nauta vires colligit
pontique mitescunt freta,
hoc ipse petra ecclesiae
canente culpam diluit.

Surgamus ergo strenue:
gallus iacentes excitat
et somnolentos increpat
gallus negantes arguit.

Gallo canente spes redit
aegris salus refunditur,
mucro latronis conditur,
lapsis fides revertitur.

Iesu, labentes respice
et nos videndo corrige:
si respicis, lapsus cadunt
fletuque culpa solvitur.

Tu, lux, refulge sensibus
mentisque somnum discute:
te nostra vox primum sonet
et ora solvamus tibi.

Ambrose, *Hymn* I, A.D. 388; cf *In Hexaemeron*, 5, 24, 88;
and Augustine, *Retractationes*, **I, 20**: 1

The cock was considered of old to be a bird of light which scattered the demons at break of day with its clear cry. Since it is inseparably bound up with Peter's fall and repentance St Ambrose has linked both motifs in his morning hymn. The Rock who tottered, the cock which breaks the demonic spell, the fresh

opportunities brought by each new day and by conversion, Christ's gaze which comforts the fallen (*lapsi*), the tears of repentance—all these are contained in this simple hymn that is still sung today, a striking accompaniment to the countless scenes to be found on sarcophagi and small objects. These scenes are all identical. We see Our Lord predicting to the ashamed Peter his three-fold denial (Peter puts his hand to his mouth in the classical gesture of confusion). The cock stands on the ground or else, as here, on a pillar, with one or more churches in the background. This may be intended to represent the pillar-with-cock and the small commemorative church of S. Petri in Gallicantu, outside the south wall of Jerusalem (see Map 39). It is almost certainly a symbol of repentance and in particular the repentance of those who had denied their faith during the persecutions of 304-11 (the *lapsi*). It later came to represent ordinary church penance.

174. ILLUMINATION, the opening of the eyes of the man born blind, a symbol of baptism which was also called φωτισμός, illuminatio. Also, the raising of Lazarus from the dead, likewise a symbol of resurrection through baptism. Detail from a sarcophagus; ca 330. Rome, Museo delle Terme.

175. 'BEFORE THE COCK CROWS . . .' Left side of a sarcophagus. This relief is famous on account of the accurate depiction of, left, a baptistery (cf 418), a basilica with memoria behind a city wall, and right, a basilica outside the walls; perhaps the Anastasis and Martyrion of Jerusalem with S. Petri in Gallicantu outside the south wall (see Map 39). The baptistery recalls the forgiveness of sins (=baptism) motif. Rome, Museo Lateranense.

176. IBID. Right side. The water from the rock (= baptism), and the woman troubled by an issue of blood, symbol of the Church of the Gentiles, who 'had spent all her living upon physicians' (i.e. upon the pagan philosophers). The buildings depicted here have not been identified.

177. SARCOPHAGUS from Salonae (Dalmatia); beginning of the 4th century. Shepherd, with Mother Church (?) and teacher (?). The motifs have not yet been satisfactorily explained. Split, Museum.

AT THE CROWING OF THE COCK

Maker of all, eternal Lord,
O Thou who rulest night and day
and sendest changing seasons round
to temper time's monotony:

Now cries the herald of the morn
who watches in the depths of night,
dividing off each passing hour,
the travellers' nocturnal light.

At this the early morning star
dispels the universal gloom,
at this the roving demon bands
affrighted, leave their work of doom.

At this the sailor gathers heart
and calmer grow the boiling waves,
at this the Church's Rock himself
in bitter tears his treason laves.

Come, let us with fresh courage rise,
the cock wakes those who sleeping lie,
and chides the drowsy lie-a-beds;
the cock convicts those who deny.

The cock crows, and fresh hope returns,
all those who suffer are made well,
the robber sheathes his evil blade
and faith returns to those who fell.

O Jesu, see us tottering here
and seeing us, become our stay:
then will our many failings fall,
our guilt in tears be washed away.

Shine Thou as light upon our hearts,
rouse up our slothful souls again:
may first our voices sing to Thee,
those praises which are truly Thine.

175

176

177

(178-205) is the decisive phase in the Christianisation of the Empire and at the same time a period of flowering in Christian art and literature. It is, indeed, known nowadays as the 'Theodosian renaissance'. It had its centre in the court capital of Milan.

The dynasty (178-182)

178. THEODOSIUS (379-95). Detail from a silver *missorium* (an ornamental shield sent as a gift) of 388. Cf **180**. The Emperor sits enthroned between his two sons Honorius and Arcadius, in the attitude of the later Byzantine rulers, later to become the attitude of the enthroned Christ. He is robed in the imperial purple *chlamys*, crowned with the jewelled diadem, and his head is encircled by a halo (the halo is derived from the court iconography and is given to the Emperor before being transferred to Christ and His saints). *Madrid, Real Academía de la Historia.*

Theodosius was the last great absolute ruler to govern both parts of the Empire. An upright, anti-Arian, orthodox Christian, he abolished the budget for the pagan religious services (not, however, that for the popular feasts and games which traditionally accompanied the temple feasts) and began the codification of Roman Law. The *codex Theodosianus* (of Theodosius II, 438) also includes his laws (*novellae*) which signal the abolition of official paganism and the definitive Christianisation of public life. Shortly after his death St Augustine sketched his portrait and the spiritual climate of his times:

"Theodosius thus not only remained loyal to Gratian while he lived [Gratian had been his fellow Emperor in the first years of his reign] but after his death, like a good Christian, he received into his territory his younger brother Valentinian, who had been banished by his [Valentinian's] brother's murderers. He treated him as his ward and protected him with fatherly love. And yet, had his desire to extend his power been greater than his will to do good, it would have been easy for him to thrust the boy aside, since he was entirely without resources. This love of doing good, however, prompted him rather to take the boy into his household, allow him to retain his imperial dignity, and offer him the consolation of his kindness and patronage.

"Furthermore, when success made of Maximus a formidable opponent, he did not, under the burden of his cares, have resort to unlawful pagan superstitious practices, but sought the advice of John, a servant of God who lived in the desert of Egypt. Popular opinion had it, and he had also heard, that this man possessed the gift of prophecy. He was assured by him of certain victory. When, a short while after this, he had rid himself of the tyrant Maximus, he restored the young Valentinian to his proper dignity in that part of the Empire from which he had been driven. This was a deed of charitable piety. But, shortly afterwards, when Valentinian had lost his life in an attack or in some other manner, or perhaps as the result of an accident, he defeated another tyrant, Eugenius, who had unlawfully succeeded him. This also he did relying upon a prophecy. Against the mighty army of his opponent he fought more with prayers than with arms . . . Yet when he had gained the victory, as he had confidently expected and predicted, he tore down the statues of Jupiter which had been 'consecrated', as it is called—I know not by what rites—and placed upon the Alps to oppose him. When his couriers, in righteous joy at the victory, jestingly remarked that they would gladly be struck by the golden thunderbolts of these statues, he presented them to them in a gesture of jovial good-will. In addition to all this he never ceased, from the beginning of his reign, to support the Church in her trials by passing just and temperate laws against the unorthodox. For the Church had indeed suffered much from the heretical Valens [see **148**] who favoured the Arians. It was a greater source of joy to the Emperor to be a member of the Church than to be sole ruler on earth. Everywhere he caused the statues of the pagan gods to be pulled down [in the East this was done by force, but in the West the temples were closed and turned into museums, or the famous statues were removed to the open air], fully realising that earthly favours are not dependent upon demons but on the one true God. And can one imagine anything more admirable than the humility of his faith? Incited by a handful of his immediate entourage, he had been persuaded to punish in a cruel manner a serious offence of the Thessalonians [their rebellion, in 390]·although he had at first promised the Bishops when they had intervened that he would be lenient. When, then, he was punished under ecclesiastical disciplinary laws, he did penance in such a way that the people, who were praying for him, wept more to see the Emperor's majesty so humbly prostrated than they had feared his wrath after the transgression. These and other good works, all of which I cannot mention here, he took with him from out of the mist that veils every pinnacle of human existence. The reward of these works is the eternal bliss which God grants only to the truly pious." (Augustine, *The City of God*, 5, 26)

It was Ambrose, Bishop of the court capital, who, after the mass murder in

178

179

Thessalonica (the troops slaughtered the people indiscriminately in the amphitheatre during a performance) found the courage to refuse the Emperor the Sacraments and to impose penance. It was told that, when the Emperor asked: Did not David also sin? the Bishop replied: Whom you have imitated in sinning, imitate also in doing penance. We do not know the real circumstances. The inhabitants of the punished city did not see the Emperor's act of penance, but, like all the world, they heard of it. Theodosius' penance has remained the symbol of the moral courage of a Christian ruler; Ambrose's action that of the inflexibility of a Bishop faithful to his duty. Augustine's portrait tallies with the opinion of his contemporaries and provided the 'mirror of princes' for Charlemagne and other rulers.

179. THE EMPEROR with courtiers and bodyguard in the grand box (*kathisma*) of the hippodrome in Constantinople. Obelisk of Theodosius, postament, north side; *ca* 390. The obelisk, like the 'serpent's column' from Delphi, still stands in its original position: the *spina* of the great circus. The hippodrome itself has disappeared, and on the site of the *kathisma* and the great palace stands the mosque of Sultan Ahmed. The hieratic group sit and stand behind a balustrade with trellis work framed by herms. Cf Map 37. *Istanbul, At Meydan.*

180. ARCADIUS (395-408), as hereditary prince in 388. Figure on the right side of the *missorium* of Theodosius (see 178). He succeeded his father in the Eastern half of the Empire after the division of 395.

181. HONORIUS, ruler of the Western half of the Empire from 395 to 402; Constantius III, second husband of Honorius' sister Galla Placidia, and Galla's young son Valentinian III who ruled from 425 till 455, his mother being regent until 437. Under increased pressure from the Goths, Honorius transferred the capital from Milan to Ravenna, impregnable behind the barrier of the coastal marshes (cf Maps 23 and 38). Sardonyx (of Romulus, who is mentioned in the inscription); *ca* 423. *Leningrad, Hermitage.*

182. COLUMN OF ARCADIUS, Constantinople, erected 402-21, after the campaign against Gainas. South side of the postament. A few weather-beaten remains can still be seen on Avret Pazari in Istanbul. Like Trajan's column in Rome, the shaft was decorated with an upward spiralling frieze. Upon the friezes of the base: above, weapons, trophies, *labara*; below them, the monogram of Christ between trophies; below these again, Arcadius and Honorius with court and bodyguard; and, last row, the tribute of seven provinces from East and West and prisoners in chains. Drawing of 1572-78 in the Freshfield collection. *Cambridge, Trinity College.*

Monuments of the Theodosian renaissance (183-205)

Until 1823 Rome possessed one of the great foundations of Theodosius, the new tomb basilica of St Paul outside the city walls on the road to Ostia, where from the time of Constantine had stood only a modest *memoria*. The new church equalled S. Petri in Vaticano in size and splendour. On the triumphal arch was written:

> *Theodosius coepit, perfecit Honorius aulam*
> *doctoris mundi sacratam corpore Pauli*

"Theodosius began, Honorius completed this church, consecrated by the body of Paul, teacher of the world." As appears from a later inscription, the large, and now so distorted, mosaic of the triumphal arch—with the adoration of the twenty-four elders offering their wreaths—was founded by Honorius' sister Galla Placidia under Pope Leo the Great (440-60):

> *Placidiae pia mens operis decus omne paterni*
> *gaudet pontificis studio splendere Leonis*

"The devout soul of Placidia rejoices to see this foundation of her father radiant in splendour through the devotion of Bishop Leo."

183. ST-PAUL-WITHOUT-THE-WALLS (S. Paolo fuori le mura), begun after 385, completed after 400. Interior as it was at the end of the 18th century, before the fire of 1823. Etching by Giovanni Battista Piranesi. Jacob Burckhardt recounts (*Der Cicerone*, 3rd ed., 1874, vol. I, p. 81) that those who had seen the four original colonnades before the fire assured him that this spectacle of ancient splendour was unequalled throughout the world. Certainly, until 1823, St Paul's was the most impressive late-Roman interior in the world and perhaps the best preserved. A great poet of *ca* 400 said of it:

"Yonder, where Tiber's stream embraces the grassland to your left, the Ostian Way keeps watch o'er Paul's domain. It shines in imperial splendour. The Good Prince founded this holy citadel and adorned it round about with fanciful and costly array. Beam and joist he covered with gold leaf, that there but purely golden light should shine as of the morning sun. The ceiling of fair gold he propped with marble pillars: here and there they stand spaced out in double row. All the arches above are covered with colourful marbles: thus do meadows bloom when spring comes with her flowers." (Prudentius, *Peristephanon*, **12**, 45-54)

180

181

182

The gilded coffered ceiling and marble incrustations had disappeared by Piranesi's time. He was, however, still able to see the Old and New Testament cycles, the life of Paul, and the *imagines clipeatae* with the portraits of the Popes, begun under Leo the Great *ca* 450 and which for centuries provided one of the main sources for Western iconography. The cycle was restored by Pietro Cavallini shortly before 1300 (on the walls of the nave, above right). The pillars are the originals, not spoils from the temples but made especially for the church.

184. ST PAUL-WITHOUT-THE-WALLS after the fire (1823). Drawing by Pinelli. The transept and apse were spared; the rest was pulled down and rebuilt on classical lines after the old model.

185. ST PAUL-WITHOUT-THE-WALLS as it is today. The architects of 1824-54 restored the coffered ceiling, halved the number of clerestory windows, replaced the fluted pillars by smooth, polished ones, and made the floor appear smaller by using too large a design. A few medieval remains—the apse mosaic of 1218 and the altar ciborium of Arnolfo di Cambio—were spared, but the old mosaic was completely ruined. The two large statues and the wall revetment behind them and also the excessively colourful decoration continue to disturb the harmony of this interior; but in spite of everything, it still retains something of its ancient grandeur.

186. THEODOSIAN SARCOPHAGUS from the court capital: the largest and most beautiful (cf 527, front). It is now beneath the ambo of S. Ambrogio, Milan. Left side (380-90): the sacrifice of Abraham, an unknown prophet, a high official, and the pinnacles of the heavenly city, continued from the front. On the lid: *chrismon* (monogram XP) in the wreath of victory, with soul-doves.

187. ST PAUL-WITHOUT-THE-WALLS. Façade and atrium in the 18th century. Etching by Piranesi. Campanile and gable are medieval, the seven arcades later than 1723. Right: part of the wall of the old atrium; upper walls intact (400).

Now follow (188-94), monuments from northern Italy. The greatest of these is the colossal octagonal rotunda, begun *ca* 380 under St Ambrose in Milan and completely rebuilt during the early years of the Renaissance, *ca* 1500. It is now S. Lorenzo Maggiore (188-90 and 192). The adjacent chapels date from 380-400. In that of S. Aquilino (189-90) two mosaics have been preserved in the half-domes of niches, and others have recently been discovered in the short narthex in front (189). 191. Chiusi, the old Clusium; cathedral. Reconstructed basilica of *ca* 400, drastically restored during the last century. 193-4. Spoleto, San Salvatore-without-the-walls. 193. Interior and presbyterium. 194. Main door in the West front. It is not known whether the church dates from the 5th century or was built in the 8th, the age of the Dukes of Spoleto, from 5th century materials. This puzzling construction remains unique.

By far the most attractive remains of the Theodosian renaissance are the north Italian ivories. They are mostly consular or liturgical diptychs, small pyxides and reliquaries in the form of a box with lid and lock. Some of them are true masterpieces, for example the 'Adam, king of creation' depicted on page 79, upper centre (196a).

185

186

187

188   189

190
191

192
193
194

195

196a

196b

197

198

188. S. LORENZO MAGGIORE, Milan, seen through the colonnade of one of the main streets of the Roman period. The cupola dates from *ca* 1500.

189. IBID., the atrium of S. Aquilino. Patriarch, a tableau taken from Genesis; 380.

190. S. AQUILINO, eight-niched rotunda (*memoria*?) near S. Lorenzo, with remains of mosaics. Shortly after 400. Photograph taken after the restorations of 1946.

191. CHIUSI (prov. Siena); cathedral. Basilica dates from 400, restored during the 19th century.

192. S. LORENZO MAGGIORE. Restored section of the gallery above the ambulatory, with painted decoration imitating marble intarsia.

193-4. S. SALVATORE, Spoleto. Nave, presbyterium, and main door; 400? 750?

195. EASTER MORNING. Leaf of a diptych; 380-400. The Sepulchre represented as a mausoleum. *Milan, Castello Sforzesca.*

196ab. ADAM, KING OF CREATION (here, of the animals); St Paul on the island of Malta; Paul as teacher; he shakes the serpent from his arm into the wood fire, to the amazement of the Maltese. They bring to him the sick: the wasted man is perhaps the father of Publius who 'lay sick with fever and dysentery'. The so-called Carrand diptych; *ca* 380-400. *Florence, Bargello.*

197. EASTER MORNING and the Ascension; 400. Note the tomb mausoleum and the 'assumption into glory'. *Munich, Bayerisches Nationalmuseum.*

198. PASSION CYCLE. Lid of a *lipsanotheca* (shrine for relics). Agony in the garden, the arrest, the denial of Peter, Our Lord before Caiaphas, Pilate washing his hands; 370? *Brescia, Museo Civico.*

79

The fifth century

It is a period of disaster, especially in the West, the fifth century. In 404 the Rhine frontier collapses, Trèves burns, and endless hordes swarm into the defenceless provinces of Gaul, overwhelming the towns and *latifundia*. They penetrate even as far as Spain. Bypassing Ravenna, where Honorius keeps his court between the coastal marshes and the port of Classis (see **233**), Alaric reaches Rome. After eight centuries the mistress of the world is plundered: 'it seemed as though the world were decapitated'. Alaric, having made off with the booty, perished in Calabria; but all knew that the old order had vanished for ever. Struck by this sudden proof of the finiteness of the 'eternal' city, Augustine began his *City of God*. Fifty years later Africa and Gaul were occupied by the Franks, Visigoths and Vandals. They took over the Roman administration but, being Arians, they persecuted the Catholics, especially in Africa. The Catholics then began to pin their hopes upon the East Roman Emperor, and 'catholic' became synonymous with *romanitas*.

Milan and north Italy (199-205)

In other regions and especially in north Italy, everything seemed to have returned to normal after the incursions, except that illusions had vanished for ever. In the many minor works of art produced in Milan and north Italy we find no trace of the troubles of the times, nor do we find reference to them in the brilliant panegyrics delivered by the court orators: on the Emperor, on the Empire, on Rome, on the past.

199. HONORIUS (395-423), 'pale flower of the women's quarters' (Duchesne), who was in Ravenna from 402 onwards. Diptych of Probus, consul in 406. On the *labarum*: 'may you always conquer in Christ's name'. *Aosta, Cathedral.*

200. STILICHO(?) with his wife Serena and his son; *ca* 396. The Vandal who, as supreme commander, long defended Italy, he was to all intents and purposes ruler, but was put out of the way by court intrigues. *Monza, Cathedral.*

201. LUDI CIRCENSES. Chariot racing in a hippodrome. Diptych of the Lampadii. The giver of the games, a consul, sits in the box; *ca* 425. The theatres, amphitheatres (where the *venationes*, combats between wild beasts, replaced the forbidden gladiatorial games), and above all the circuses, were always crammed with citizens, who had absolutely no say in politics. They were more interested in betting on the 'green' or 'blue' than in the invasions. *Brescia, Museo Civico.* "He who said: I do not want you to be partners with demons (1 Cor. 10:20) meant by this that they [the faithful] should follow a different way of life from those who serve the demons. The demons take pleasure in frivolous songs, they rejoice in idle spectacles, in the multifarious immorality of the theatres, in the folly of the circus, in the cruelty of the amphitheatre, in the heated quarrels of those who, in debating and squabbling over corrupt people, become each other's enemies: for a mime, a player, a pantomime, a jockey, a fighter of wild beasts . . . they burn incense to the demons on the altar of their hearts." (Augustine, *Sermon* **198**, 3; delivered at Carthage)

202-3. FIVE-PART DIPTYCH, a panel of a binding for a copy of the Gospels; A.D. 402. Facing: the lamb in the wreath of victory over death, *victoria agni*; the Gospels of Matthew and Luke (man and bull); the Annunciation, the Nativity, Mary and the star (?), the Magi, the Child in the Temple, the baptism, the Entry into Jerusalem, the massacre of the Innocents with Herod; two evangelists. Below: the Cross upon the hill of Paradise with the four streams, the Gospels of Mark and John (lion and eagle), the Adoration of the Magi, the blind men of Jericho, the paralytic, Lazarus, the loaves and fishes (Our Lord enthroned upon the globe of the universe), the Last Supper, the widow's mite, the miracle of Cana, the evangelists Mark and John. *Milan, Cathedral.*

204. The woman with the issue of blood. *Paris, Louvre.*

205. The man possessed by demons in the country of the Gerasenes, with the herd of swine. Right-hand panel of a five-part triptych. *Paris, Louvre.*

203

204/205

213

Rome in the fifth century (206-217)

The shock of the sack of Rome in 410 (although Alaric, an Arian, respected the right of sanctuary and the church treasures) was so great that the people cursed the times and cast up the past to their Bishops as a challenge to Christ. This spirit prevailed even in Africa:

"Peter's body lies in Rome—they say—and those of Paul, of Lawrence and of other holy martyrs. Yet, in spite of this, Rome has fallen on evil days. Rome is laid under contribution, is ravaged, crushed and burned to the ground. Death strikes there in so many different ways: by hunger, by sickness, by force of arms. Of what use are the graves of the Apostles now?" (Augustine, *Sermons*, Morin, Bibl. Casin. I, 133 : 6)

"I have for a long time been conscious of what you are murmuring to yourself: 'see, in Christian times, Rome is being laid waste, or rather, has already been laid waste and been set aflame. Why does this happen in Christian times?' Who are you who say this? 'A Christian'. But if you are a Christian find the answer then yourself: because God has willed it so. 'But what must I say to a pagan? He taunts me'. But what does he say? With what does he taunt you? 'See, while we still offered sacrifice to our gods, Rome remained standing, but today, now that the service of your God has prevailed . . . now that the sacrifices to our gods have been restricted and even forbidden, just see how it fares with Rome'. Give him a short answer in order to be rid of him. But other thoughts must occupy *your* mind, for you have been called, not to set your heart on earthly things but in order to gain heaven . . . not to earthly but to heavenly bliss. Yet answer quickly none-the-less this lover of bodily joy, this one who rails against the living God and wishes to serve pagan gods of wood and stone. According to what is written in their history, this is the third fire of Rome . . . The city which has now been consumed once during the sacrifices of the Christians had already been burned twice during that time when sacrifice was offered to the pagan gods . . . why do you wish to protest against God for the sake of a city that is wont to be consumed by fire?" (Augustine, *Sermons*, ibid., 9)

Here the Bishop's rhetoric has rather run away with him. Rome was indeed plundered but she was neither ravaged nor burned to the ground. The walls were left intact and normal life was resumed sooner than might have been expected. And the buildings founded after 410 (see Map 27) are among the most beautiful in the city, even though less grandiose than those built after the Edict of Milan in 313.

206. TITULUS OF AEMILIANA (Parish church of Aemiliana; now SS. Quattro Coronati; 401-7), founded under Pope Innocent I. The church was later reduced in size but the original apse still stands.

207. TITULUS OF SABINA (S. Sabina, 422-32), founded under Pope Celestine; front and narthex.

208. TITULUS OF THE APOSTLES OR EUDOXIA (S. Pietro in Vincoli), founded by the Empress Eudoxia and later enriched with relics of St Peter's chains (432-40).

209. S. STEPHANI IN COELIO (S. Stefano Rotondo; 468-83), founded under Simplicius. A large round *memoria* with two ambulatories. The outer colonnade was later walled up and the sumptuous ceilings have disappeared. The church has the same dimensions as the Anastasis (Church of the Holy Sepulchre) in Jerusalem, and the roofing was once cruciform.

210, 212. TWO PANELS from the main door of S. Sabina. Shortly after 430. Left: *Gloria Christi*: the Lord in the glory of victory (wreath) surrounded by the Four Living Creatures above the firmament, and the Church of Rome crowned by SS. Peter and Paul with the monogram of Christ. Right: a prince and an angel before a sanctuary. Unexplained scene famous on account of the building with two towers, the oldest that we know.

211. MARBLE INCRUSTATIONS in the narthex of the Lateran baptistery (cf 127); 432-40, in the time of Sixtus III, who enlarged the older baptistery.

213. TITULUS OF SABINA (S. Sabina; 422-32). The church lies high on the Aventine in what was then a fashionable residential quarter full of gardens and palaces. Above the main door, inside, between the life-size figures of the 'Church of the Circumcision' and the 'Church of the Gentiles' (cf 451 ab) the dedicatory inscription is introduced in gold mosaic on a blue ground. According to this the basilica dates from the time of Celestine I and was founded by a priest, a native of Illyricum (the apsidal windows are a non-Roman motif which does, however, occur in Illyricum). The inscription measures 43 by 13 feet and reads:

"When Celestine occupied the Apostolic Chair and shone as the first bishop in the whole [Roman] world, a priest of the City founded this [edifice] which you admire now: Peter, a native of Illyricum, and worthy of so great a name. Nourished in the church of Christ from his earliest youth, he was rich for the poor and poor for himself, and since he scorned the benefits of this world, he may expect the blessings of the world to come."

The basilica was restored by Muñoz; window fillings, chancel, and ceiling

being modelled on early medieval remains. The columns and the marble incrustations above date from the fifth century.

214-17. S. Mariae Maior (or: ad Praesepe; S. Maria Maggiore) on the Esquiline. The first church in Rome to be dedicated to the Virgin, founded by Sixtus III, 430-40. It is almost certain that the foundation inscription was situated under the apse mosaic (which has disappeared, being replaced by the present one in 1296). The inscription was seen as late as 1500 and describes the disposition of the vanished central mosaic: five martyrs with the instruments of torture at their feet, together with Sixtus himself, grouped about the Mother of God:

> *Virgo Maria tibi Xystus nova tecta dicavi*
> *digna salutifero munera ventri tuo*
> *tu genitrix ignara viri te denique foeta*
> *visceribus salvis edita nostra salus.*
> *ecce tui testes uteri tibi praemia portant*
> *sub pedibusque iacet passio cuique sua:*
> *ferrum, flamma, ferae, fluvius saevumque venenum*
> *tot tamen has mortes una corona manet.*
> (Inscriptiones Christianae Urbis Romae, **2**, 1, p. 71, 98, 139)

> "Mary Virgin, to thee I, Sixtus, dedicate this new abode:
> a fitting offering to thy womb, the bearer of salvation.
> Thou, O Mother, knowing no man yet bearing fruit
> brought from thy chaste womb the Saviour of us all.
> Behold, the witnesses of thy fruitfulness bring thee wreaths,
> at each one's feet the instruments of his passion:
> sword and fire and water, wild beasts and bitter poison
> yet the one crown awaits these several deaths."

The composition on the triumphal arch has been preserved. It was inspired by the theology of Ephesus (the Council of 431 which Sixtus' legate attended). Here the mystery of the Word made Flesh is linked with the confession of the Church of Rome. The founders of the Roman *ecclesia*, Peter and Paul, flank the Throne with the *insignia Christi*; the temple in which Christ is recognised by Simeon is the *Templum Urbis* (see Map 27), recognisable by the *dea Roma* on the tympanum, and Simeon's features are those of Peter and perhaps of Sixtus (see **216**). The Childhood of Christ is depicted in the court style, with thrones, guards, and retinue. We see His Epiphany in Jerusalem-Rome, in Bethlehem (the Magi), and in Egypt (following an apocryphal gospel: **215**) The whole may be inspired by Sixtus' archdeacon, the future Leo the Great.

214. CEILING of 1492. Half of the windows have been walled up. The nave has been restored several times (the last being in 1750 by Ferdinando Fuga) yet the original disposition of this splendid *aula Dei* (Hall of God) has been preserved. The colonnade, the small mosaics devoted to scenes from the Old Testament (above the architraves: one of the panels is shown on **217**), the disposition of the wall bays and the triumphal arch also date from the time of Sixtus.

215. CHRIST received in the city of Sotinen in Egypt. Governor Aphrodisias and his philosopher and people acknowledge the infant Logos. Detail from the second zone of the mosaic on the triumphal arch.

216. SIMEON recognises the Divine Child in the Temple—here the *Templum Urbis*. He has the same cast of feature as St Peter and it is perhaps a portrait of Sixtus. Detail from the upper zone of the triumphal arch. After 431. The mosaics of S. Maria Maggiore form not only a culminating point in the history of early Christian art but are an impressive document of late-classical illusionism.

217. MOSES striking the waters of the Red Sea. Detail from the 'Passage of the children of Israel and the destruction of Pharaoh'. Nave mosaic from S. Maria Maggiore, founded 430–40 under Sixtus III; cf **402**.

Ravenna in the fifth century (218-236)

Official court residence from 402 onwards, in the first place of the last Western Roman rulers, then of Theodoric, king of the Goths, Ravenna, after 540, was again in the hands of the Eastern Roman Emperors and was from 568 till 751 the seat of their exarchate. It has since then been but a dead city. This has ensured that some of the monuments have been preserved; they are now being restored with the utmost care to their original condition (see Map 38).

218. COIN OF GALLA PLACIDIA, regent of Valentinian III, 423–50. She was the half-sister of Honorius and a pious, courageous woman.

219. SO-CALLED MAUSOLEUM of Galla Placidia; 430–50. It stood at the end of the narthex of the basilica; more probably a *memoria* of St Lawrence.

220. THEODOSIUS II (408–50), ruler in the East; *ca* 400. *Paris, Louvre.*

221. BASILICA OF JOHN THE EVANGELIST, Ravenna. Founded by Galla.

222. IBID. The interior. The windows in the apse and the imposts on the capitals are Eastern features. In 1945 the church was again brought into use.

223. INTERIOR of the so-called mausoleum of Galla Placidia (cf **219**). One of the most beautiful interiors of Late Antiquity, preserved almost intact. The walls are covered with marble and the vaults with mosaic, here once again on a blue ground. In the small cupola is depicted the 'Glory of the Cross' (see **468**) and in the side lunettes the 'Water of Life' (see **394**). In the lunette of the end wall is the martyr Lawrence (see **490**), and above the door (facing, not visible here), the Good Shepherd (see **519**). We do not know whose remains the sarcophagi contained. The interior is illuminated by four small windows in the lunettes.

218

220

219

221

222

223

224/226   225/227

224. THE BAPTISTERY of Bishop Neon (451-73), or 'of the Orthodox' (i.e. of the Catholics as contrasted with that of the Arians). It is next to the Ursiana, the five-aisled cathedral basilica founded by Bishop Ursus at the beginning of the 5th century. It is now the cathedral (cf Map 38). To the left of the cathedral apse projects the chapel of the *episcopium*, an oratorium on the first floor with an antechamber, both decorated with mosaics (see 230). The cathedral itself, together with the cupola, was rebuilt in the 18th century. To the right of it is the baptistery, which has now sunk several feet into the ground. It is a small, octagonal building with three side niches. Above, is the round tower, one of the oldest in Europe, dating from the 10th century (cf Map 38).

225. DETAIL from the wall incrustations (in variegated marble including thin discs of porphyry from sawn columns) and from the arch mosaic of the baptistery. The upper zone, between the windows, is decorated with stucco reliefs. For the whole interior 'one of the most splendid pictorial compositions in the world' (Burckhardt), see 410.

226-33. Monuments from the time of King Theodoric, 493-529.

226. MAUSOLEUM OF THEODORIC outside the city walls (see Map 38). The mausoleum, in the form of a ἡρῷον, has a second storey above the burial chamber which contained the sarcophagus (now disappeared); it has an enormous monolithic cupola, the handles of which are still intact, and is decorated with a remarkable geometric frieze.

227. THE PALATINE CHURCH of Theodoric, at the same time basilica of the Arians, dedicated to Christ the Saviour (now S. Apollinare Nuovo); *ca* 500-29. The tower dates from the 10th century, the apse from a recent restoration; the cloisters are medieval. The purpose of the building in the right foreground (palazzo degli Esarchi) is not known.

228. THE PALATINE CHURCH of Theodoric (S. Apollinare Nuovo); present-day façade. The narthex dates from the 16th and the tower from the 10th century.

229. CLASSIS, the port of Ravenna. Detail from a mosaic in S. Apollinare Nuovo dating from before 529 (the upper part has been restored).

230. ORATORY OF S. ANDREAS in the *episcopium* (*cappella arcivescovile*) built by Bishop Peter II (494-519/20) on the first floor of his residence. In the vaulting four angels in the attitude of the profane Victories hold aloft a medallion with the monogram of Christ. In the intervening fields are the Four Living Creatures. On the intrados of the arches are *clipei* (medallions) with portraits of Christ, the Apostles, and some of the martyrs (see 502-7): the Carthaginian martyrs Perpetua and Felicitas are to the left. The chapel has been very much restored.

231. THE PALATINE CHURCH of Theodoric after the restorations of 1945-56 (S. Apollinare Nuovo). The 18th century rococo apse has been pulled down and the old apse with the three windows rebuilt on the foundations of the original. What remained of the *cancelli* and the four columns of the *ciborium* has been erected there but not according to the original disposition, since there is no *cathedra*. The nave, with the exception of the ceiling, was in a good state of preservation and was restored after the bombardments of 1914-18 and 1944. The columns, capitals, and imposts, like the walls, date from 500-20, as do the upper zones of the mosaics. Above the windows on either side are thirteen scenes representing Our Lord's public life and thirteen devoted to the Passion and the Apparitions. They show no evidence of a typically Arian iconography: there was, apparently, no such thing. Examples are shown in 234-36. Between the windows are the authors of the sacred books, prophets, and Apostles on a gold ground. The lower frieze was executed between 566 and 570, after Justinian's armies had conquered Ravenna. The extremities on both sides, however, date from the time of the Goths (see 229, 232). We do not know how the intervening spaces were formerly filled in; now they contain the processions of the martyrs illustrated in 501 and 508, with details in 492 and 493. After 566 the church was consecrated anew and dedicated to St Martin. It was given the name S. *Martini in coelo aureo*. It was only in the 9th century that the relics of the city's patron, the martyr Apollinaris, were transferred here from the cemetery basilica in Classis (265-6, 268-70), and since 959 the church has been known as S. Apollinare Nuovo. Right, next to the wall, are the remains of the old 6th century ambo.

237
238

239
240
241

242
243
244

Church Foundations at Constantinople: the age of Justinian (245-53)

245-6. MARTYRION of Sergius and Bacchus; 527-36. *Istanbul, Kusük aya Sofya.*
Cf S. Vitale, Ravenna, 258-61, dating from 522-47.

247. CISTERN OF PHILOXENUS (see Map 37; same as Binbirderek, 'of the 1001
columns'). One of the underground water reservoirs of Istanbul.

248. THE CHURCH OF THE APOSTLES. Miniature in 12th century MS. It was
cruciform and had five cupolas and celebrated mosaics (one of them is represented
on the miniature). *Paris, Bibliothèque Nationale*, MS. gr. 1208.

249. THE MARTYRION OF CYRUS (with the dream of the hymnographer
Romanus). Miniature in the Menologion of Basil II; 11th century. *Vatican,*
MS. gr. 1613.

250-3. SANTA SOPHIA, the cathedral dedicated to Christ as 'Divine Wisdom',
built 532-7 after the Nika riots, consecrated in 562. Architects: Anthemius of
Tralles and Isidore of Miletus, both from Asia. Dimensions: 243 feet by 201
feet; cupola 179 feet high, 101 feet across. 250. Apse. 251. Interior, looking
towards the narthex (drawing by Fossati, 1847-9). 252. Apse mosaic, *ca* 859,
restored 14th century. 253. Women's gallery.

MONUMENTS OF EARLY OR PROTO-BYZANTINE ART FROM THE PERIOD 500–729 (254–287; cf Map 36)

254. MASK. Detail from a floor mosaic in the Great Palace at Constantinople; *ca 500*. The classical motifs survive to a large extent.

255. THE TRANSFIGURATION (Metamorphosis) upon the Mount. Mosaic in the apse of the monastery church of St Catherine on Mount Sinai. Shortly after 550. Above: (not visible) the handing of the Law to Moses on Mount Sinai—the local *memoria*; the Apparition itself with the Law and the Prophets bowing down before Grace: Moses and Elijah before Christ; below, the three disciples. In the *clipei*, portraits of the Apostles and martyrs; above, portraits of Justinian and Theodora.

256. THE ANNUNCIATION. Byzantine silk. From the Papal chapel *Sancta Sanctorum* near the Lateran; now in the Museo Cristiano, Vatican; 7th century.

257. BYZANTINE SILK CLOTH with Sassanian animal motifs. *Ravenna, Museo.*

Ravenna in the sixth century (258–270)

258–61. MARTYRION OF VITALIS (S. Vitale). Begun 522, consecrated 547 by Bishop Maximianus (for his portrait see **455-6**); it is a foundation of Justinian and Theodora. Bishop Ecclesius (522-32) met them on a journey to the capital with Pope John I, and they took over the construction of the church planned by him in 522. This is why his successor introduced Ecclesius' portrait in the apse (see **491**) and portraits of Justinian and Theodora in the world famous foundation mosaics underneath, to the side of the *cathedra*.

258. THE APSE, with the *pastophoria* or side apses, later called *diaconicon* (for the sacred vessels, books, and vestments), and the *prothesis* (for the preparation of the bread and wine and the forming of the procession for the Great Entrance). The liturgy of Ravenna was, however, purely Latin, thus there was no Entrance; it seems in fact to have been only introduced later in Constantinople.

259. S. VITALE from the air. It is an octagonal building with an ambulatory and gallery (for the emperor and court); below, the three apses. The tower and claustrum are post-medieval; the narthex, at the front, is not visible.

260. INTERIOR, from the ambulatory. Note the capitals with the imposts above:

a free, imaginative creation deliberately replacing the Corinthian leaf capital. The altar stands on a podium (*bema*) consisting of two steps: the chancel (the balustrade which always enclosed the sanctuary) has disappeared. In the somewhat lower niche of the apse stands the *cathedra*, between the benches for the priests. Next to the windows are the mosaics with the sovereign, court, and clergy and above them the apse mosaic (see **491**). The decoration of the cupola dates from the baroque period. The original floor level has been carefully restored.

261. VIEW FROM THE AMBULATORY; in the foreground, above the capitals—free variations on the composite capital—are the original vine tendrils in stucco; in the background is the gallery above the ambulatory.

262. DETAIL FROM A TRANSENNA (open-work balustrade slab before a tomb or in the chancel). Peacocks (immortality) with the 'life-giving Cross' and vine tendrils springing from a vase (the 'Draught of Life'). *Ravenna, S. Apollinare Nuovo.*

263. THE 'SOURCE OF LIFE' (the same motifs as in **262**; the vine is possibly an allusion to the Eucharist). Floor mosaic from Classis. *Ravenna, Accademia delle Belle Arti.*

264. DETAIL FROM A TRANSENNA, as above, **262**. *S. Apollinare Nuovo.*

In the light of these specimens of an already mature and original style, we can define this style as a system which, both in decoration and in the architecture itself, deliberately sacrifices the plastic values of classical architecture for the sake of certain three-dimensional and visual effects. What distinguishes both decoration and architecture from the Ancient Greek style is above all the systematic use of arch and vaulting, a heritage of the Roman engineering genius. The true Hellenic manner is, however, apparent in the un-Roman, refined, completely Greek, lightness of frame and logic of structure. The decoration, on the other hand, which obtains its effect from an inter-relation of colour, light, and shadow, can be considered as a renaissance of the visual values in a late-classical setting. Not sculptures, nor heavily framed walls, nor deeply coffered ceilings, but abstract figures against a gold ground (in the mosaics) and abstract ornamentation, as smooth as a piece of embroidery (see **267**) dominate the interior which, to the smallest detail, is calculated to the human scale and to which the sober exterior is completely sacrificed.

271

265-66, 268-70. The *memoria* of Apollinaris in the cemetery of Ravenna, near Classis. Cf Map 38. Ravenna was rich in *memoriae*—commemorative churches—of martyrs from other places, yet honoured only one of her own martyrs for the faith, the priest Apollinaris. The basilica upon his tomb rises solitary in the flat countryside.

265. MEMORIA of Apollinaris on the road to Ariminum (Rimini) to the south of the city. The narthex originally housed the sarcophagi of Ravenna's Bishops (269-70) which now stand in the side aisles. The church was founded by Julius Argentarius, a banker, who also collaborated on Ecclesius' foundation, S. Vitale. Begun under Bishop Ursicinus, 533-6, it was consecrated by Maximianus in 549, a year before his death. The decoration was evidently never completed. Apart from the decorated apse and the magnificent colonnade, the interior makes a very sober impression. *S. Apollinare in Classe*.

266. S. APOLLINARE IN CLASSE viewed from the East. The side walls, constructed in thin bricks with thick mortar between, show for the first time the flat pilasters, linked at the top by arcaded string courses. Next to the polygonal, windowed apse are the small side apses of the *pastophoria*. The tower is medieval.

267. CAPITAL with an impost; stuccoed coffers in the intrados of the archivolt. Before 547. Example of the new style. *Ravenna, S. Vitale*.

268. COLUMN, capital, impost, arcade, and pilaster capital in S. Apollinare in Classe. Behind, part of the triumphal arch with a mosaic of the archangel Gabriel wearing a *chlamys* (with inserted pieces, like a courtier) and a *labarum*. Extreme left, a fragment of the abstract apse mosaic representing the Transfiguration as lambs looking up at a glorified Cross (cf **470**). The capital is a variant of the composite capital with a decoration of drill-holes on the stylised leaves.

269. FIFTH CENTURY SARCOPHAGUS. On the front, a remarkable variant of the usual Roman 'Delivering of the Law to Peter'. Our Lord hands the Law, not to Peter (who is carrying a cross) but to Paul. This may be an expression of anti-Roman feeling dating from the time when the rulers of the Exarchate were in conflict with the Apostolic See of Rome. Cf **530-3**. *S. Apollinare in Classe*.

270. SARCOPHAGUS ('of Bishop Theodorus' † 688); end of 5th century. The lid is decorated with three monograms of Christ within the wreath of immortality, the front by the motifs of the peacocks flanking the *chrismon*. *S. Apollinare*

in Classe. The tranquil, spacious composition, the high, curved lids, and especially the preponderance of a purely symbolic decoration, mark the fifty Ravenna sarcophagi as a distinct group; they are, moreover, later than the more numerous and more varied Roman group.

Istria (271-77)

The sixth century monuments in Istria are related to those of Ravenna.

271. THE EUPHRASIANA, the basilica founded (535-43) by Bishop Euphrasius at Parentium on the western coast of Istria, now Poreč (in Yugoslavia, formerly the Italian Parenzo). View after the recent restorations. The Euphrasiana is one of the most beautiful and best preserved of the early Christian churches. The apse mosaics (with the portrait of the founders and the earliest representations in the West of the Mother of God, in the centre of the apse) the apse wall decorated with mother of pearl and multi-coloured marble incrustations, the *cathedra*, parts of the *cancelli*, a section of the mosaics on the triumphal arch, both side apses (invisible here), and the magnificent colonnade—all these date from the time of the foundation. The altar, on the other hand, dates from the Renaissance and the baldachin from the thirteenth century.

272. EUPHRASIANA, Poreč. Atrium, 535-43. One of the few well-preserved basilical atria. Remains of the mosaics on the façade: between the windows, the flames of the seven lampstands from Revelation 1. Note the horse-shoe arches and the embroidery-like pattern on the capitals.

Grado (273-77)

Monuments from the small lagoon city of Grado, successor to Aquileia, which was destroyed by Attila and his Huns in 452 (see Map 23). The main church, dedicated to St Euphemia of Chalcedon (275, 277), the baptistery (411, 415), and the church of S. Maria delle Grazie (274, 276) form one of the most impressive complexes of the sixth century. They were founded (571-88) by the Patriarch Elias when the Lombards occupied Aquileia, obliging him to transfer the see permanently to Grado. The cathedral floor (273), five feet higher than that of the older church of which remains have also been found, contains the inscriptions of the donors. Among them were five *lectors*, four *notarii*, two deacons, three soldiers, an actuary, a *primicerius*, two skippers, a shoemaker, a palace official, and a *vir clarissimus*.

97

272 273

274

275

273. GRADO, cathedral. Floor dating from the 5th and 6th centuries. Above right, the inscription of the founder, the Bishop-Patriarch Elias: "This hall which you see before you, enriched with adornment of many kinds, had grown dark with great age—vile earth lies hidden beneath this marble mosaic floor—but the old has vanished and the new shines honourably forth through the devotion by the blessed Bishop Elias. This is from henceforth the house dedicated to the fear [of God]". Beneath this is the inscription of a deacon: "The servant of Christ, Lawrence, a deacon, has here fulfilled his vow." Above left, that of a married couple who offered twenty-five feet of mosaic; below, that of Probina with her son Thoma the *notarius* (short-hand writer); beneath this is that of the skipper Stephen and lastly the inscription of Paul, Diugenia, and their family. Just as in the Middle Ages people offered windows and later altar panels and retables, so in this century did people offer to their favourite church pieces of mosaic so many feet long.

274. GRADO, S. Maria delle Grazie; 6th century.

275. GRADO, cathedral. Chancel and presbytery. The ambo is a medieval composition, a new pulpit on old colonnettes; the canopy dates from after 1100.

276. GRADO, S. Maria delle Grazie (cf 274). The space before the altar with the chancel screen and the *regula*, the architrave on four columns which stressed the railing off of the sanctuary from the rest of the church. It is wrong to use the expression '*iconostasis*' in this connection. It was only very much later that icons appeared on the *regula*, at which time curtains were also hung over the openings, as is done today in the Orthodox churches. Traces of the older altar space with the grooves made by the altar and the substructure of the *cathedra* can still be seen below, between the apse wall and the podium.

277. GRADO, cathedral. The basilica of Grado with the floor of Bishop Elias is one of the most beautiful and best preserved that we possess. It has recently been restored.

Monuments from Greece and Asia (278-287)

278. RECONSTRUCTION of a 5th century *bema*. *Athens, Byzantine Museum.*

279. RECONSTRUCTION of a *bema* typical of the 10th century (cf 278). *Athens, Byzantine Museum.*

280. BASILICA at Philippi in Macedonia (cf 281).

281. TWO BASILICAS near the forum of Philippi in Macedonia; with annexes and atria.

282. THE CHURCH OF OUR LADY in Ephesus, where the Council of 431 met.

276 277

285   286   287

283. THESSALONICA in Macedonia. Martyrion and basilica of Demetrius, the city's patron saint. This enormous basilica, slightly cruciform, with galleries above the side aisles and the entrance, was built in the 5th century. During the 6th and 7th centuries it was filled with votive mosaics, fragments of which were found under the plaster of the mosque into which the church had been converted. The greater part of these was lost, however, in the fire of 1921, together with a section of the church. After 1922 the church was thoroughly examined by the Greeks, rebuilt, and returned to the Orthodox cult. It is one of the greatest martyria of the 5th century, in the first see of Christian Illyricum, although the city, as far as civil status is concerned, was superseded by Sirmium which lay closer to the frontier, on the Danube (modern Mitrovica).

284. REMAINS OF A MARTYRION near basilica D in Nea Anchialos, the early Christian Thebae Phthiotides (near Volos) where many ruins have been discovered.

285. MOSAIC FLOOR, *ibid.*, with geometrical design.

286. THE MARTYR DEMETRIUS (Dmitri) of Thessalonica. Detail from one of the votive mosaics; he is wearing the military chlamys. This is a typically hagiographical portrait.

287. THE NATIVITY; above, remains of a 'Journey to Bethlehem'; 5th century. *Athens, Byzantine Museum.*

In the small Early Christian towns of Greece and the Archipelago remarkably little sculpture has been found, apart from such pieces as the ambo of Thessalonica with the Adoration of the Magi, and the intact staircase, now in the Ottoman Museum, Istanbul. On the other hand, many mosaic floors have been discovered, and such clear traces of the wall foundations and interior disposition that it has been possible to reconstruct the ground-plan of more than a hundred-and-twenty basilicas with their annexes (cf 280, 281). It was in Greece that the

altar was first placed closer to the *cathedra* and the priests' benches sometimes stood on either side. This disposition, as far as concerns the position of the altar, is to characterise Byzantine church interiors from this time onwards (see 278).

The outer provinces of the Empire

A completely distinct category is formed by the monuments of those regions lying on the outer fringes of the Roman Empire. They are admittedly influenced by the motifs current in the capitals and in the lands lying nearer to the Empire's heart, yet are at the same time remarkable for, on the one hand, very archaic, and on the other, extremely original features. These are the provinces which, one after another, were lost to the Empire; first the western regions, through the barbarian invasions, then Syria and Egypt, engulfed by the sudden onslaught of Islam after 630.

In the matter of churches, Syria could be proud of her past, for she was the cradle of the faith. In Palestine multitudes flocked to venerate the Holy Places and to witness the liturgy of Jerusalem which gave rise to many a striking motif, artistic and otherwise. Egypt was the cradle and home of monasticism: anyone wishing to visit its original source journeyed to the desert on either side of the Nile. In Africa Christian Latin literature had its first flowering. It was a land made holy by the *memoriae* of countless martyrs (see Maps 30, 31) and there, about the year 400, shone the light of St Augustine. Yet all this venerable and fertile ground, once harvested, was lost wholly or in part both to the Empire and to Christianity.

SYRIA (288-314)

288-93. Antioch (Antakya), the city where the name *christianoi* first came into use, where St Paul began his journeys, and where an uninterrupted line of great bishops, exegetes, poets, and scholars had made the name of Christian renowned. Now, however, having suffered the onslaught of Persians, Arabs, Crusaders, Turks and, above all, earthquakes, it lies buried beneath an insignificant Turkish vilayet and is as though vanished from the face of the earth. Excavations in the district have been in progress since 1930, outside the Turkish city and especially in the former suburban residential districts of Daphne (**290**) and Yakto (**291, 292, 293**), where a great many mosaic villa floors have been discovered, dating from the first to the fifth century. Many of these floors have found their way to Paris and to the United States.

288. THE ORONTES, flowing through the laurel wood of Daphne, south of Antioch. Here a famous temple of Apollo stood. The Emperor Julian the Apostate found here only one solitary priest who had nothing to sacrifice but a single goose. He ordered the temple to be restored and he himself offered rich sacrifices. Shortly afterwards the temple was burned to the ground. The Emperor then ordered the relics of the martyr Babylas, which 'polluted the sacred precinct of Apollo', to be removed. The people of Antioch, bearing their beloved saint in triumph to the city, sang beneath the imperial windows the verses from Psalm 115: 'Let them that make idols become like unto them and all such as trust in them'. (Ps. 115:8, LXX 113:16).

289. ANTAKYA (Antioch). From the ruins of the medieval citadel. The ancient city lay on the same site, on either side of the Orontes; it is estimated to have contained about 200,000 inhabitants *ca* 380, half of them Christian. In the background the Mons Pieria, merging left into the Amanus which divides Cilicia from Coelesyria (see Map 15).

290. THE PHOENIX. Detail from a floor mosaic in a country villa in Daphne, 6th century. The floor, bordered by a frieze of rams' heads, has a yellow-white background filled with rosebuds. The bird's head is encircled by the aureole of the sun. The phoenix which, according to the legend, rises anew from its ashes every five hundred years, was considered as a symbol of the Resurrection of Christ. We possess a rather long-winded poem, possibly by Lactantius, *On the Phoenix*, in which the phoenix builds its tomb-nest in a palm tree in Syria, a motif which recurs in Roman monuments of the same period (380-450; see the *Dominus legem dat* in **551, 496**), and on ivories and gold glasses. *Paris, Louvre.*

291, 292. TWO DETAILS from a topographical border frieze in mosaic from a villa floor in Yakto, near Antioch. In the upper illustration, extreme right, one sees the octagonal silhouette of the Great Church of Antioch, a rotunda with a gilded cupola, dating from the 4th century. On the lower is a street scene with inn and bridge. Probably end of the 5th century.

293. BORDER FRIEZE from a floor mosaic in a house at Yakto. Beginning of the 4th century (cf Aquileia, **139, 143**). *Worcester Art Museum, U.S.A.*

Two martyria found near Antioch, one, 4th century, on the far side of the Orontes, at Kaoussiye and another, 6th century, near the port of Seleucia Pieria, are depicted in **307-310**. The first, dated 387, is probably that of the above–mentioned Babylas.

288

289

291

292

293

297/299   298/300

The Early Christian monuments of Syria are not to be found in Antioch, nor in the episcopal towns on the coast or in the valleys of the Orontes and the Leontes, destroyed and rebuilt time and again. They are found, remarkably enough, in the hinterland, and there in great number. They lie close together in three compact groups: (1) Between Antioch and Aleppo (Beroea, see Map 15b) on a chalk plateau; (2) Eastwards, stretching to the Euphrates, on the fringe of the desert; (3) In the basalt mountain range of the Hauran, the Ledja, and in the region of Bostra in Transjordan. These are all outlying districts full of villages, monasteries, and small rural episcopal towns (see Map 15) built entirely of stone. A few of them have been damaged by earthquakes and the depredations of stone-stealing Bedouin. They were abandoned suddenly after 630-50, rediscovered in 1862 by de Vogüé and sketched by Duthoit (295, 303, 313). Since then they have been examined by the expedition of Butler and by Krencker, Lassus, Tchalenko and others. The most impressive of these monuments is undoubtedly Qalat Sem'an.

Qalat Sem'an (294-300 and 587-90)

Here was the pilgrimage centre built *ca* 480 around the pillar upon which Simeon Stylites the Elder († 459), the first and most famous of the pillar saints, had lived for thirty years. He was the counsellor of countless pilgrims, Arabs from the desert as well as those from the Syrian towns.

294. QALAT SEM'AN, general view. Left, the apses of the basilica and in front of them the three three-aisled exedrae grouped about the octagon within which

is the base of the pillar. The hills are those of the Jebel Sem'an.

295. THE OCTAGON in 1862, drawing by Duthoit. It is uncertain whether the central space was ever covered over but it seems unlikely.

296. THE RUINS in 1862, drawing by Duthoit. Left, the basilica; in the middle, the octagon, in front, one of the exedrae, behind, the storeyed building of the monastery or *pandocheion* (guesthouse; cf 587). Duthoit omits to show the rubble near the pillar.

297-9. QALAT SEM'AN in 1954.

297. APSE of the basilica.

298. NARTHEX of the basilica; tri-partite. The roof has disappeared.

299. FAÇADE of the basilica. Note the non-classical proportions, the pure tectonic structure, the local and probably Antiochian decorative motifs such as the continuous profile above the clerestory windows.

300. DÉCOR of arcades and pilaster capitals to the right of the main apse. Refined, stylised variations on the Corinthian capital, the Ionic cyma, ovolo, and leaf friezes. (Duthoit, 1862)

One of Simeon's contemporaries, Bishop Theodoret the historian, from the neighbouring town of Cyrrhus (see Map 15a) was often an eye-witness of what took place there before 459:

"From that time onwards until the present day—twenty-eight years have elapsed since then—he passes the forty days of Lent without taking any nourishment at all. Time and practice have made the ordeal lighter. For he was notably accustomed to stand during the first few days and loudly to sing God's praises.

301

304

302

305

303

306

After this, when, through lack of food, he no longer had the strength to stand, he sat, and thus accomplished his holy task. During the last few days he also leaned. And as his strength gradually diminished and declined he was obliged to lie down half dead. But once he had taken up his place upon the pillar he did not wish to descend again and therefore invented a way by which he could remain standing in another manner. He installed a beam on the pillar and bound himself to it with ropes and thus he spent the forty days. Later, however, when he had received more strength of grace from above he no longer needed this aid and now he stands throughout the whole forty days. He takes no food but derives his strength from his own will and from the grace of God." (Theodoret of Cyrrhus, *Phil. Hist.*, 24)

What impresses the modern reader more than the self discipline of the great saint, reminiscent of that of the Indian ascetic, is the boundless love of this holy man, accessible to all and always filled with joy. He was the 'peacemaker of the desert' and the distant forefather of the Russian *startsi*.

301. DER TURMANIN. 6th century basilica as it was in 1862 (Duthoit); the apse between the *pastophoria*; left, the famous tower façade with loggia. As a result of stone theft the church has now practically disappeared.

304. QALB-LOZEH. Basilica, 6th century. Above the short piers with broad arcade the corbels for the colonnettes which once supported the roof. In Syria the altar stood in the apse; the *cathedra* was on a separate podium (*bema*) in the nave (see 442), sometimes next to a *cathedra* throne for the Holy Scriptures.

302. QALB-LOZEH. The basilica in 1862: remains of the tower front with loggia above the narthex (cf 302).

303. DER SETA, Hexagonal baptistery, 6th century.

305. GOLD ENKOLPION (medallion worn on the breast), *ca* 600, from Adana in Cilicia. The Annunciation, the Visitation, the Nativity, The Flight, the Adoration of the Magi. *Istanbul, Musée Ottoman.*

306. SILVER VASE FROM EMESA (Homs) with *clipei* of Christ, Peter, and Paul. End of 5th century. *Paris, Louvre.*

307. MARTYRION OF BABYLAS, in the shape of a cross, at Kaoussiye, near Antioch, dating from 387. In the centre of the four exedrae lies the *memoria* proper, with the tombs of St Babylas and Bishop Meletius of Antioch. Not only martyria but also large churches were built in the unusual cruciform style, for example the Churches of the Apostles in Constantinople and Milan (see 248). For the latter St Ambrose composed an inscription explaining the motif:

> This church is in the shape of a cross: the church is dedicated
> to Christ's triumphs, and the sign of victory seals the place.
> *Inscriptiones Christianae Urbis Romae*, **2**, 1, p. 162

308. MARTYRION (6th century) at Seleucia Pieria, the port of Antioch: a cloverleaf-shaped central building (*quadriconchos*) with a broad ambulatory. In the centre is the *bema* for the *synthronos* (seats for the Bishop and priests) and the honorary cathedra for the Holy Scriptures (cf 307). Right, the traces of the altar and the remains of two of the piers which supported the cupola; the cupola was perhaps made of wood.

309. IBID., detail from the floor mosaics in the gallery. 6th century.

310. KAOUSSIYE. Mosaic inscription in the *pistikon*, the room adjoining the baptismal recess, used perhaps for the anointing with myron (our chrism) or the taking of the baptismal vows. It dates from the year 412 and is in the martyrion shown in 307.

The Holy Places

For the travel-minded Christian of the fourth and fifth centuries Syria was, above all, the land of the Holy Places. The whole coastal stretch, from Egypt through Palestine to Antioch, was dotted with visible reminders of the story of salvation, both from the Old Testament and from the New. As a sample of the writings of travellers to these holy places we give here a passage from one of Jerome's letters and three extracts from the famous *Peregrinatio ad Loca Sancta*. This latter was written by the *sanctimonialis* (nun) Egeria, probably a native of northern Spain, a woman of noble birth and perhaps of very high senatorial ancestry. Jerome's letter tells of Paula's journey to Bethlehem (see Map 15a):

"I do not speak of her journey through Coelesyria and Phoenicia, for it is not my intention to write a travel report. I shall name only those places which occur in the Holy Scriptures. Having left behind Berytus [Beirut], a Roman colony, and the ancient city of Sidon, she visited the upper room of Elijah on the coast of Sarepta and having prayed there to Our Lord and Saviour she came, by way of the beach of Tyre, where Paul once knelt, to the city of Acco, now called Ptolemais ['Akka]. By way of Megiddo, which saw the death of Josiah, she reached the land of the Philistines. After she had admired the ruins of Dor [Dura] once a mighty city, she proceeded to the 'tower of Strato', named Caesarea [Kaisariye] by Herod, king of Judaea, in honour of Caesar Augustus. There she saw the house of Cornelius and the little house of Philip and also the chamber of the four virgins who were prophetesses. From thence she made her way to Antipatris [Ras-el-'Ain], a half-ruined town which Herod had named after his father, then to Lydda [Ludd] in the neighbourhood of Diospolis, famous because Aeneas was cured there and Dorcas raised to life. And not far from thence she came to Arimathaea, the hamlet of Joseph who buried Our Saviour, and to Nob, once a priestly city but now merely a burial ground for its murdered inhabitants. She also visited Joppe [Jaffa, Tel-Aviv] the port from which Jonah fled and also—to touch in passing upon one of the tales of the poets —the place that beheld Andromeda chained to the rock. After this, returning [from the coast] she came to Nicopolis formerly called Emmaus [Amwas] where the Lord was recognised in the breaking of bread and where He marked out the house of Cleopas as a church . . . After leaving at her left the sepulchral monument of Helena, queen of Adiabene, who had succoured the people with corn during a famine, she arrived in Jerusalem, the city of three names—Jebus, Salem,

307
308

309
310

311 312/313 314

Jerusalem—which was later rebuilt by Aelius Hadrianus from the ruins and ashes of the former city and received the name Aelia [see Map 39]. But although the governor of Palestine, who knew her [Paula's] family well, had sent his servants and had given orders that his official residence should be made ready for her, she preferred to lodge in a humble cell. She showed such interest in visiting the Holy Places that she only quitted one in order to hasten to another. Casting herself down before the Cross [the staurotheca, south of the Anastasis, with the relic of the True Cross, cf 320] she prayed as though she saw the Lord hanging there. When she had entered the Tomb in the Anastasis [see 321] she kissed the stone which the angel had rolled away from the entrance and with the ardour of true faith touched with her mouth the place where Our Lord had lain, as a thirsty man approaches the water he so ardently desires. The whole of Jerusalem is witness to the floods of tears she shed and the grievous sighs she uttered there. When she had left the church of the Holy Sepulchre she went up to Zion, which is rendered as 'citadel' or 'eminence'. This city was once conquered and built by David . . . There she was shown the pillar at which Our Lord is said to have been scourged and which is spattered with the blood of the Lord. She was also shown the place where the Holy Ghost descended upon the hundred and twenty souls so that the prophecy of Joel might be fulfilled. After this, having distributed money among the poor and among her fellow religious in so far as her modest means would permit she journeyed to Bethlehem and on

* * *

311. SMALL OCTAGON AT BINBIRKALESI ('Thousand and one Churches') in Lycaonia. About thirty ruins, mostly *memoriae* and basilicas, lie here abandoned among the hills, at the spot where the episcopal city of Barata is thought to have stood (see Map 16). No good pictures exist of these monuments which have attracted few visitors (Miss Bell, Strzygowski). The one reproduced here is taken from a travel book by the Comte de Laborde, 1834. The date of these monuments is uncertain but is thought to be somewhere between the 5th and 7th centuries.

312. RESAFE (Sergiopolis), the city of St Sergius. Churches and walls have remained as ruins in the middle of the desert. North gate of the city, 6th century.

313. GRANITE BASILICA with stone vaulting on transverse semi-circular arches and galleries in the side aisles at Shaqqa (Maximinianopolis) in the Hauran (see Maps 14, 15a) one of the oldest churches in Syria, 4th century. There is no wood in this region.

314. KOCA-KALESI or ALAHAN MONASTIR in Isauria. One of the earliest cupola basilicas, *ca* 500. The cupola—which has disappeared—was supported by small squinches. For all the monuments shown, see the large Map 13-14 and Map 36.

the right-hand side of the road she halted by Rachel's grave . . . After this she entered the Grotto of the Saviour. Having gazed her fill upon the Virgin's refuge and the stall in which the ox recognised its owner and the ass the manger of its Lord [Cf Isaiah 1:3: the origin of the ox and the ass in the representations of the Nativity, see 321 and 287] so that the words of the same prophet might be fulfilled: 'Happy are you who sow beside all waters, who let the feet of the ox and the ass range free' [Isa. 32:20]. Then she swore—as I myself have heard —that with the eyes of faith she beheld the Child, wrapped in swaddling clothes and crying in the manger, the Magi adoring God, the star that shone above, the Mother who was a Virgin, the revered foster-father and the shepherds who came in the night to see the Word which had come to pass." (Jerome, *Letters*, 108, 8-10)

St Paula died in January 404 and this letter—her epitaph—was written in the spring or summer of the same year.

Egeria's book describes a journey made during the years 415-16 or, according to others, a few years before 400. The part which has been preserved is devoted to Egypt, Sinai, Jerusalem and the Holy Week liturgy, and also Horeb, the land of Job, Edessa and, on the road to Constantinople over the Cilician passes, the martyrion of St Tecla at Seleucia in Cilicia (see Map 32, on which the journey has been reconstructed as far as possible). Here follow the passages on Edessa and Sinai. The translation naturally cannot hope to recapture Egeria's more or less affected Latin, a queer mixture of popular elements and Biblical unction. It does, however, give some idea of the vitality, erudition and keenness of eye of this 'grande dame' who moves everywhere with the ease of a princess.

"That mountain [Sinai] appears from a distance to form one solid bloc, but one penetrates into it, one sees that it is composed of several mountains, although the whole is called the mountain of God. That mountain, however, upon whose summit the majesty of God descended, as it is written, lies in the centre of them all. And whereas all these mountains around are higher than any I have ever seen, yet the middle one, upon which the majesty of God descended, is so much higher than all the rest that when we had climbed to the top, all those other mountains which had appeared to us so lofty lay as far beneath us as though they were but little hummocks . . .

"And then, according to the will of Christ, our God, and aided by the prayers of the holy men who were our companions, I set out with great effort, since I was obliged to accomplish the ascent on foot (for it was impossible to gain the summit in a carrying chair). Yet the effort was not so great after all, and the reason for this was that I saw that the desire which I cherished was about to be fulfilled by the grace of God. At ten in the morning then, we arrived at the sum-

318/319

mit of the holy mountain of God, Sinai, where the Law was handed over, that is to say, at the place where the majesty of God descended upon the day on which the mountains gave forth smoke. There is now a church on this spot, not a big one, since that place, that is, the summit of the mountain, is not very large, yet the church is extremely pleasing. [The foundations have been identified, see Map 32.] When, then, by the will of God, we had climbed to the top and had reached the door of the church, a priest came to meet us there, coming from his cell. This priest served the church, an upright old man who had been a monk from the time of his youth and was, as they say here, an ascetic, and . . . what shall I say more? A man worthy to be in such a place. Other priests also came to meet us and all the monks who lived there by the mountain, that is to say, all those who were not prevented by weakness or old age. On the actual summit of this central mountain, however, nobody lives, for there is nothing but the church and the cave where the holy Moses dwelt. After we had read the entire passage from the book of Moses and the oblation had been made according to the rite and we had all communicated, we left the church. And then the priests gave us souvenirs (*eulogia*) of this place, apples which grow on the mountain.

"And departing again from thence [from Bathnae = Batanae = Sarug, modern Sürüç] we came, in the name of Christ Our God, to Edessa [Urfa]. And when we arrived there we went immediately to the church and memorial chapel of the holy Thomas. And when we had offered up our prayers there according to custom, and had done all those things which we were wont to do at the holy places, we read something there about the saintly Thomas [the *Acta Thomae*?]. Now the church there is very large, very beautiful, and built in a new style; it is a worthy house of God. And since there were many things I wished to see, I was obliged to remain there for three days. Thus I saw in that city several commemorative chapels [*memoriae*] and also holy monks, of whom some live near the chapels and others have their hermitages farther from the city, in more isolated places. The Bishop of the city, a truly pious man, a monk and confessor, received me warmly and said to me: 'Since I see, my daughter, that from a spirit of religion you have gone to such great pains to journey hither from distant places, we shall, if you desire it, show to you here all those places which Christians like to see'. Then I thanked first of all God and afterwards him and eagerly besought him to make good his promise. Then he brought me first to the palace of King Abgar and there showed me a statue of this man, a very good likeness, it is said. It was made of marble, shining like pearls. And one could clearly see from Abgar's face that he was an exceedingly wise and honourable man. Then

the venerable Bishop said to me: 'This now is King Abgar who, before he had seen the Lord, already believed that the Lord was truly the Son of God.' Next to this stood another statue of the same kind of marble and this, as he told me, represented Abgar's son Magnus [Ma'nu]. His face too had something attractive in it. After this we entered the palace. There were fountains full of fish such as I had never seen before, that is to say, they were so large and their water was so clear and delicious to taste. The city has now absolutely no other water than that which flows from the palace like a great silver stream. And then the reverend Bishop told me the following story about the water. Shortly after Abgar had written to the Lord and the Lord had sent Abgar a letter in return by the courier Ananias, as is written in the letter, it happened that the Persians came and surrounded the city. But immediately Abgar took the Lord's letter to the city gate and prayed in the open with all his army. And after this he said: 'Lord Jesus, hast thou not promised us that no enemy should enter this city and behold, the Persians are attacking us'. When the king had uttered these words holding the open letter in his upraised hands, it suddenly became dark, that is, only outside the city before the eyes of the Persians who had already approached so close to the town that they had reached the third milestone. But they were so suddenly overcome by the darkness that only with difficulty could they strike camp . . ." Egeria, *Pilgrimage to the Holy Places* **2,** 5-7; **3,** 2-6; **19,** 2-9)

The legend narrated to Egeria in 416 was imputed to Abgar V Ukkama, a contemporary of Christ (king of Osrhoene, 4 B.C. to A.D. 7 and 13-50). In actual fact Abgar IX (179-216), an ally of the Romans from 195 onwards, was the first Christian ruler (cf Map 5). A later legend replaces the letter by an icon 'made by no human hands' imprinted upon a cloth.

PALESTINE (315-326)

315. ALEXANDRIA. Detail from a topographical mosaic, A.D. 500. Church of St John in Gerasa (Jerash) in Transjordan.

316. CANOPUS (Aboukir) near Alexandria, with the martyrion of SS. John and Cyrus (Apa Kyr); detail from the same mosaic at Gerasa.

317. NICOPOLIS (Amwas). Topographical mosaic in Ma'in (Transjordan); inscription: Νηκωπολεὶς; 6th century; detail from a schematic monument map.

318. GERASA; the three churches of SS. John the Baptist, Cosmas, and Georgios, which lie close together. End of the 5th century. Gerasa possesses more Early Christian monuments than any other city in Palestine. Eighteen large and small basilicas have been identified there, among them the grandiose cathedral with the piscina credited with healing powers and the monumental *propylaea*.

319. THE BASILICA with Abraham's tomb, within the *temenos* of Herod (1st

107

320

321

century) at Hebron (El Khalil), formerly a pilgrimage centre for Jews, Christians, and Moslems. Here lies the man who is the 'Father of the Faithful' in the eyes of all who profess the three great monotheistic religions. Christians are no longer admitted.

The Holy Places in Jerusalem (320-26)

320. THE EARTHLY JERUSALEM *ca* 400, image of the heavenly city. Background of the apse mosaic in the *titulus Pudentis* (*ecclesia Pudentiana*, now S. Pudenziana) in Rome. From left to right; the rotunda of the Anastasis, the staurotheca (containing the relic of the True Cross) on Golgotha, behind this the Martyrion with, to the right, the Imbomon with the open *oculus* in the roof, upon the Mount of Olives, at the place of the Ascension. Christ the Teacher is depicted between SS. Peter and Paul, wreathed by the Churches of the Circumcision (Peter right), and of the Gentiles (Paul, left) and surrounded by symbols from Revelation 4 and 5 (the Four Living Creatures, the Heavenly City; the Lamb was formerly beneath the throne). In the book: 'the Lord is the preserver of Pudens' church'.

321. LID of a small wooden reliquary with souvenirs from Palestine; *ca* 580-600. From the private chapel of the Popes, Sancta Sanctorum, now in the Museo Cristiano, Vatican. It is thought that the five tableaux reflect the Palestinian iconography (perhaps the mosaics at the Holy Places themselves?). Above, left, the Women at the Tomb: this is the *aedicula* beneath the cupola of the Anastasis described by Egeria and others. Right, the Ascension, already the classical Byzantine composition. Centre, the Crucifixion with Longinus the centurion who wounded Christ on the Cross, named from Gr. λόγχη (lance) and Stephaton carrying the sponge on the hyssop rod, also Mary and John (the Church and the Faithful). Below, the Nativity in the Cave of Bethlehem with the ox and the ass mentioned in Isa. 1:3. Right, the Baptism in the Jordan: already the classic composition of Byzantine art.

322-3. TWO OF THE AMPULLAE from the cathedral of Monza; *ca* 600. Presented by Gregory the Great to Queen Theodolinda of the Langobards. They contain oil from lamps burning in the Holy Places. They come from Jerusalem and it is thought that they reproduce schematically the iconography of the sanctuaries there (compare with 321). On 322 at the top, can be seen: the Ascension, below this, left, the Annunciation, right, the Visitation, then the Nativity with, below, left, the Baptism; right, the Crucifixion with the three crosses and below, the Three Women at the Tomb (μυρροφόραι).

323. ADORATION OF THE MAGI and the shepherds. Above, the star, below, the flock. Legend: 'Emmanouel, God with us' and 'Olive oil from the Tree of Life from the Holy Places of Christ'.

324-5. THE TOPOGRAPHICAL MOSAIC from the basilica of Madaba in Transjordan; 6th century. This floor mosaic, which had been preserved almost intact, was carelessly damaged during the rebuilding of the (Greek) church during the last century (cf Maps 15a and 17). Above, Characmoba; below this, in the centre, the Dead Sea; left, the Jordan and, under this, Jericho; beneath the gap at the left side, the 'holy city of Hierosolyma' (reproduction below). Further, Bethlehem-Ephrata, Nicopolis; lower fragment, Ascalon; right, the 'tribe of Simeon'; lower right, Gaza; extreme right, the Nile Delta with Tanis, Sais and other episcopal towns in the Delta which can easily be found on Map 17.

326. Jerusalem, detail from 324-5. In the centre, the main colonnaded street (*cardo maximus*); below, in the centre, the Anastasis and the Martyrion; right, the baptistery; see also Map 39 (which corresponds with the mosaic plan).

322   323

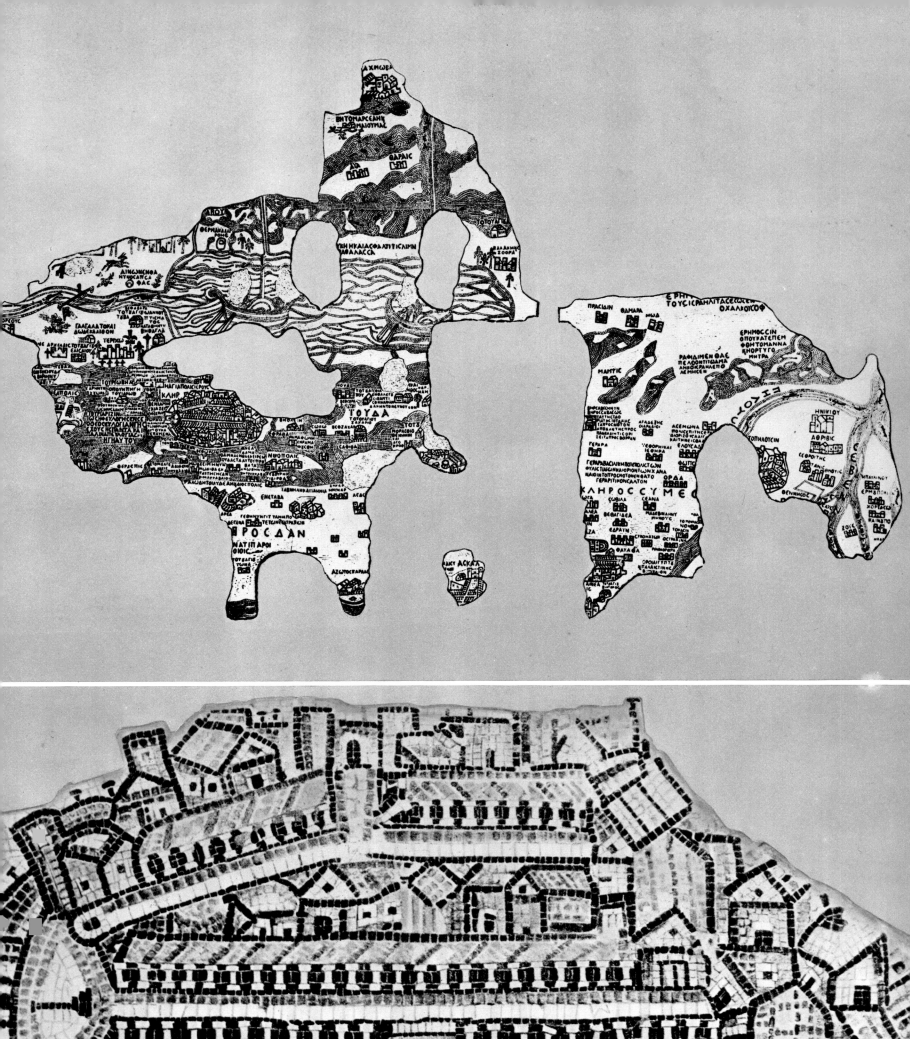
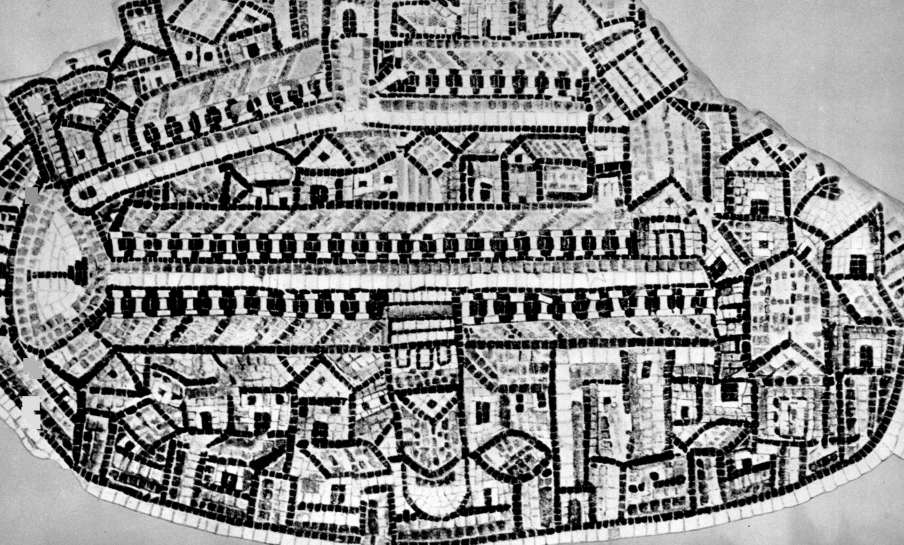

EGYPT (327-347). In this ancient land, already considered by Herodotus as an archaic treasure-house of unsuspected wisdom, the old religion had continued to live on under the Ptolemies and the Romans. It was only superseded by the coming of Christianity and Isaiah's prophecy was fulfilled:

'Behold the Lord is riding on a swift cloud

and comes to Egypt; [also taken as an allusion to the Flight into Egypt]

and the idols of Egypt will tremble at his presence,

and the heart of the Egyptians will melt within them'. (Isa. 19:1)

Outwardly the land had remained unchanged during the time of the Caesars. The Nile still flowed past the immemorial sanctuaries consecrated to the ancient gods—although they had sometimes acquired Greek names. The cult of the sacred animals, the care for the bodies of the dead, all this remained unaltered.

327-8. EGYPT in the 2nd century; details from the floor mosaic of the Palazzo Barberini, Palestrina. Left, pylon temple; next to the *aedicula*, the 'barker Anubis', *latrator Anubis*; right, hippopotami and crocodiles.

329-33. Early Christian remains from Alexandria, the Hellenistic metropolis on the fringe of an Egyptian, Coptic-speaking nation.

329. ALEXANDRIAN MINIATURE: the third day of Creation. The Logos, the Three Days, and the creation of the plants. Copy from the so-called Cotton Bible, burnt in 1731; from a drawing by Peiresc. One can see precisely the same composition in a 13th century mosaic in the narthex of San Marco. *London, British Museum.*

330. ALEXANDRIAN TEXTILE. Daniel and Habakkuk and a frieze with martyria, among others, that of SS. Michael and Stephen; also a 'Great Church'. *Berlin, Kunstgewerbemuseum.*

331-33. Three details from the Alexandrian(?) ivory *cathedra* of Bishop Maximianus (546-54) of Ravenna. *Ravenna, Archbishopric.*

331. THE FRONT OF THE SEAT: St John the Baptist and the Evangelists; monogram of Maximianus.

332. SIDE: Joseph sold to Potiphar and tempted by his wife (note the local colour in theme, scenery, and dress).

333. INNER SIDE OF THE BACK-REST: the test with the bitter water which Our Lord's mother was compelled to drink in order to prove her innocence: a motif taken from one of the apocryphal gospels.

The polished products of the workshops of the great city of Alexandria, a centre of learning for pagan and Christian alike, form part of the cosmopolitan imperial art. They differ noticeably from anything produced by the population of the interior—including an incalculable host of monks—whose language was Coptic.

Here follow, **334-47**, examples of the 'Coptic art'. The unmistakable local style does not rule out the possibility that some of these were produced in the capital.

334. PANEL OF A DIPTYCH from Murano. Teacher with Cross trophy, blind man, man possessed by a devil (demon, bound), Lazarus, the paralytic, the Three Youths in the Furnace, Jonah. *Ravenna, Museo.*

335. COPTIC CENSER with Baptism, Entry into Jerusalem, Crucifixion. *Berlin, Museum.*

336. ADORATION OF THE MAGI and Nativity. *London, British Museum.*

337. CHRIST AND THE DEAD MAN. 5th century tombstone. *Copenhagen, Ny Carlsberg Glyptotek.*

338. CHRIST with diptych and bread baskets. Example of popular regression in style. *Hanover, Kestner Museum.*

339. THE PATRIARCH THEOPHILUS (Cyril's uncle) standing on the ruins of the Serapeion, 397. Miniature from the Alexandrian World Chronicle, *ca* 400.

340. ASCENSION, lower part; apse fresco in a chapel of the Apollo monastery at Bawit; 6th century.

341. COPTIC TUNIC with *clavi* (vertical embroidered or woven strips) and other ornamentations, from a tomb in Akhmim (Panopolis; see Map 17). *Berlin, Museum.*

342. THE ANNUNCIATION. Textile from a tomb in Akhmim; 5th century. *London, Victoria and Albert M.*

343. DETAIL from a *clavus*; cf **341**. *Berlin, Museum.*

344. FRAGMENT from a decorative frieze showing the typically Coptic, dead-sharp, stylisation which gives an incomparably smooth black-and-white effect. *Cairo, Coptic Museum.*

345

346

347

345-7. Cupola frescoes from burial chapels at El Baghawat (Hibe), in the Great Oasis west of Diospolis (Thebes) (see Map 17).

345. CUPOLA FRESCO. From left to right, beginning at the bottom: Daniel and Habakkuk, εἰρήνη (Peace) with the Sign of Life (ankh = Cross), the sacrifice of Isaac, the Fall, Paul and Thecla, Mary, Noah in the Ark, Isaiah, εὐχή (Prayer), and δικαιοσύνη (Justice). The date is uncertain, perhaps 5th century.

346-7. Details from the cupola of the so-called Exodus chapel, number 80.

346. NORTHEAST SIDE: the Jews with Moses, shepherd, Thecla in the fire, Abraham and Isaac, the wise and foolish virgins with their lamps, the Fall.

347. WEST SIDE: the Egyptians pursuing the Jews, Jonah, Rebekah and Eliezer, the martyrdom of Isaiah (he is sawn in two), the Three Youths in the furnace, Daniel in the lions' den; above, the Magi.

For the monasteries and the earliest icons from Egypt see 581-2 and 552, 554-6.

AFRICA (348–61; see Maps 22 and 34). In the Africa which bloomed of old, a land sown with hundreds of small bishoprics both Catholic and Donatist, the foundations of hundreds of basilicas, baptisteries, annexes, and chapels have been unearthed. In the necropolises, sarcophagi, *mensae* (tombstones, mostly in mosaic), and even the remains of reliquaries have been found, not only in the towns but in the country as well.

348. TIPASA in Mauretania Caesariensis. Basilica of S. Salsa.

349. IBID. Christian necropolis *sub divo* (in the open air, not underground); catacombs have been found only at Hadrumetum (Sousse), near the sea.

350-1. CUICUL (Djemila) in Numidia.

350. CHRISTIAN CITY CENTRE: two basilicas and behind them the round baptistery.

351. The baptistery with annexes (cf 407).

352. THE LARGE BASILICA at Theveste (Tébessa) in Numidia. It was built in the 4th century and enlarged in the 6th. Left, the apse in front of which can be seen traces of the tribunes above the side aisles. In the middle, behind, a baptistery and a *cella trichora* (a cloverleaf-shaped chapel); right, the square atrium with porticos; the annexes and circular wall belong to a large monastery which was later joined on to the Basilica. St Crispina the martyr was venerated here. It is the best preserved of the African basilicas.

349

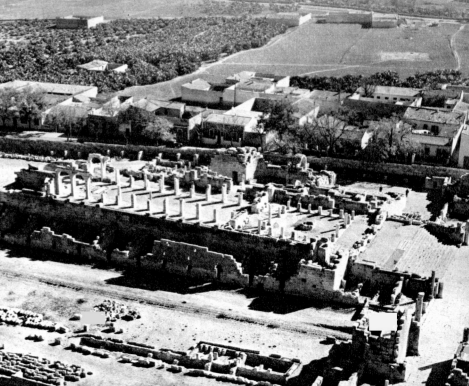

353

354

353. BASILICA at Carthago, perhaps the MENSA CYPRIANI, the memorial church of Bishop Cyprian († 258). The seven-aisled basilica lay outside Carthage by the sea. Above: the narthex; in the middle of the nave, the altar; on the apsidal podium stood the *cathedra* where St Augustine preached; at the side are the *secretaria* (sacristies).

"He [Cyprian] administered the church of Carthage during his lifetime and honoured it by his death. There he exercised his episcopal office and there his martyrdom was accomplished. Upon that spot, where he laid aside his mortal shell, where at that time a raging crowd had gathered who, out of hatred for Christ, wished to shed the blood of Cyprian, there, on this day [the nineteenth of September] a multitude flocks to do him honour and on his anniversary to drink the blood of Christ. And the blood of Christ is drunk at that spot, upon the anniversary of Cyprian's death, with all the greater love, since there the blood of Cyprian was shed with such great devotion. Those of you who know Carthage [Augustine is speaking here in Hippo] know that a *mensa*, a table of sacrifice to God, has been erected upon that spot. And yet people speak of the table of Cyprian. Not because Cyprian ever ate there, but because he was sacrificed there and because by that sacrifice he prepared this table. Not so that he might give or receive food there, but that upon that table sacrifice might be offered to God, to whom he himself had been offered. But the reason why this table of sacrifice, which belongs to God, is also called the table of Cyprian, is this: Cyprian was surrounded by persecutors so that this table might now be surrounded by his followers. Where now this table is venerated by praying friends, there was Cyprian once taunted by roaring enemies. And finally: where this table of sacrifice now stands, there was he smitten to the ground." (Augustine, *Sermon* **310**, 2:2)

354. CHERCHEL (Caesarea in Mauretania Caesariensis), museum. *Mensa* (Christian tombstone) with the symbols of eternal life.

355. TIPASA, in Mauretania Caesariensis. *Mensa*. Inscription: 'Memorial table of Avianus and Bavaria XP, A-Ω'. The sigma form, traditional for a dining room table, reminds us of its origin: the funeral meal on the tomb.

356. SILVER RELIQUARY from 'Ain Zirara in central Numidia. On the lid, a martyr with wreath in the *locus lucis* (the candlesticks); see **485**. On the box, the hart by the paradisal springs of Christ (Psalm 42; LXX, 41); 5th century. *Vatican, Museo Cristiano*.

357. TÉBESSA (Theveste). Apse of the great basilica (cf **352**).

358. SABRATHA in Tripolitana. Basilica south of the forum; altar in the middle of the nave; left, baptistery.

359. IBID Piscina in the shape of a cross, in the baptistery.

360-1. SABRATHA. Basilica of Justinian; 6th century: mosaic floor; ambo with steps; *cancelli*; baldachin above the altar. *Museo Sabratense*.

357

358

359

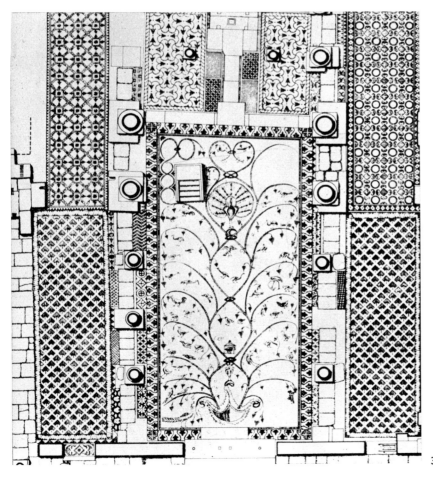

360 361

GAUL, which as early as the 2nd century saw the flowering of glorious churches in Lyon, Vienne, and Trèves, is not now especially rich in Early Christian remains. In the more southern provinces, however, in Novempopulana, Aquitania, and above all Narbonensis (see Map 25) a few cemeteries have been preserved, and, most important, about a hundred sarcophagi. The earliest and most richly decorated specimens were produced in the workshops of Arles, the later ones (Aquitanian) originated elsewhere, perhaps in Toulouse and Bordeaux. These form the transition to the Merovingian models. The Arles sarcophagi of the fourth century resemble the Roman, the later ones the Theodosian sarcophagi of Milan. The La Gayolle sarcophagus, *ca* 200, is perhaps the earliest that we know (see 43) and belongs to the period when veiled symbols were still common.

362. A DEAD MAN being conducted into the Heavenly City where the Apostles are enthroned. Detail from the sarcophagus of Concordius (see 528). End of the 4th century. *Arles, Musée lapidaire chrétien.*

Page 118 (inset). SILVER FLAGON from Traprain Law, Scotland; parcel-gilt, decorated in repoussé; end of 4th century. *Edinburgh, National Museum of Antiquities.*

363. APOSTLE crowned with a wreath acclaiming the Cross elevated to the stars. Detail from a sarcophagus, middle of the 4th century. *Arles, Musée lapidaire chrétien.*

364. CHRIST AND PETER. Detail from a 'tree sarcophagus'; 350. *Arles, Musée lapidaire chrétien.*

365. APOSTLES enthroned with Christ. Detail from the sarcophagus of Concordius (see 362 and 528); John the Evangelist has his name written in his book.

366. ALISCAMPS, the early Christian cemetery of Arelate (Arles) with the later church of St Honorat. Many undecorated sarcophagi still stand, with their high lids, beneath the ancient trees.

367. SARCOPHAGUS from Le Mas d'Aire (on the Adour, in Landes; for the distribution and localisation of the sarcophagi see Map 13-14); *ca* 300. Lazarus, Daniel (not naked = Eastern formula) among the lions, dead soul (a little girl) with the Shepherd, a woman, the Fall, Adam receiving the Spirit of Life; on the lid, the sacrifice of Isaac, the paralytic carrying his bed, Jonah, Tobias with the fish.

368. VIENNE. St-Pierre, 5th cent. pier basilica, later rebuilt (Roman tribunes, right); now at Musée lapidaire.

369. BAPTISTERY of Aquae Sextiae (Aix-en-Provence), next to the cathedral; 5th century. Remains of the piscina can still be seen between the eight pillars of the colonnade; the cupola was later rebuilt.

370. BAPTISTERY of Forum Julii (Fréjus), in front of the cathedral; 5th century. A well-preserved niche rotunda with remains of the piscina; the cupola was restored by Formigé. Other Provençal baptisteries, Venasque, Vaison, Riez—date from a later period, yet retain the early form. The foundations of one dating from the 6th century were recently discovered beneath the cathedral of Nevers.

368

369

370

366

367

SPAIN (371-75), the birthplace of Trajan, the Emperor Theodosius, the poets Damasus and Prudentius, still possesses the remains of a few basilicas and baptisteries, a group of sarcophagi related to those in Gaul, and fragments of church sculpture from both the Roman and Visigothic periods. The most important necropolis is that of Tarraco (Tarragona). Baetica (Andalusia) had the most bishoprics (cf Map 25).

Shortly after 400, the barbarians burst upon this peaceful land which had been entirely converted to Christianity; the Vandals passed through, burning and pillaging, on their way to defenceless Africa (in 429, with the permission of the Count Boniface and in spite of the protests of his friend Augustine). After 419 the Visigoths coming from Gaul occupied the entire country, with the exception of Gallaecia, which was occupied by the Suevi. A hundred years later Justinian's generals conquered Baetica which remained part of the East Roman Empire until after 711, when the Arabs forced the pillars of Hercules and founded the (later) Caliphate of Córdoba. The famous mosque there (La Mezquita) was built with the - much too short - pillar stumps and capitals of the old basilicas. Now Christians disappear before the conquerors. They were able to hold out in the extreme north, in the region of the present-day Oviedo and there they made ready for the Reconquista and the freeing from foreign domination of their brothers in the faith (the Mozárabes).

371. SARCOPHAGUS from Berja (Almeria). Peter and Paul before Nero; 350

372. FRONT OF A SARCOPHAGUS from Ecija (Astigi), S. Cruz. The sacrifice of Isaac, the Shepherd, Daniel in the lions' den. First half of the 5th century. The composition and Greek inscriptions and also the fact that Daniel is clothed, point to an Eastern model.

373. TOMB MOSAIC of Optimus; 4th century. From the necropolis of Tarraco The dead man is wearing the *toga contabulata* and carries the *rotulus* in his hand cf **166.** *Tarragona, Museo Paleocristiano.*

374. CANCELLI with Visigothic ornamentation; *ca* 600? Pola de Lena, in Asturias; incorporated in a later Asturian church.

375. CÓRDOBA. Great mosque (now the cathedral). Altar pedestal, taken from a Visigothic church; probably 6th century. In manuscripts as late as the 10th and 11th centuries we find pictures of altars resting upon a single pedestal (*stipes*) like the one depicted here.

371

372

374

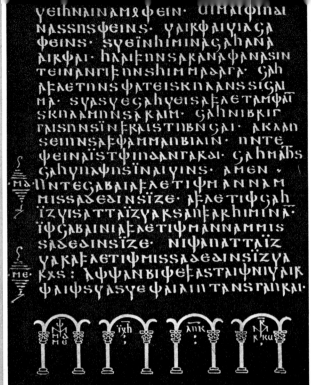

379

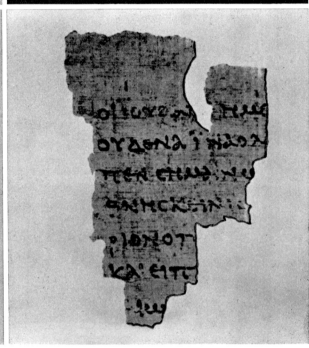

Church life from the fourth to the seventh century

HOLY SCRIPTURE (376-93). The Early Church lived from the Scriptures. At every religious service the faithful listened to extracts from the Sacred Books, as, for that matter, did the non-Christians and catechumens who were admitted to the 'service of catechumens'. They sang the Psalms and frequently knew both them and the Gospels by heart. The bishop's preaching generally consisted of a commentary upon that part of the Scriptures which had been read aloud (homily). It was only in the fourth century that the panegyrics delivered after 313 in the martyrs' *memoriae*, notably in the East, and the custom of singing metrical hymns (St Ambrose set the example in Milan) began to penetrate into the strictly Scriptural liturgy. They had not found acceptance before, even though they breathed the same spirit and were for the most part based upon motifs taken from the Word of God. We are justified in assuming that the ubiquitous sacred books of this period had a decisive influence on the transition, in the fourth century, from the scroll (*volumen, rotulus*), to the book (*codex*). We know how carefully and sometimes magnificently these sacred books were copied and ornamented, yet the chief concern of all was for the text:

"You now, who excel by your knowledge of sacred and profane literature and who possess the knowledge necessary to determine what departs from common linguistic usage, must examine the sacred texts in the following manner. For this must always be done by a limited number of scholars, fully conscious that thus the way is paved for the generality of simpler, less educated people. For this reason you must begin by becoming fully acquainted with the texts and only then correct the copyists' mistakes in such a way that you yourself cannot be found guilty of error in attempting to correct others over zealously. This sort of textual criticism is, in my opinion, a splendid work and a glorious task for

scholars. First of all, you must not obscure the distinctive, scriptural modes of expression through self-conceit. You must also beware of profaning the purity of the word of God in a desire to render the texts understandable to all: may this idea remain far from you! 'Expressions' of God's law is the term employed for those turns of speech which, so far as we know, are not found in general linguistic usage, as for example: 'according to the innocence of my hands' [Ps. 7:9, after the Roman Psalter used by Cassiodorus] . . . That expression which, so far as we know, has been found pleasing to God, must everywhere be preserved intact, so that it shines with its own radiance and is not subjected to the caprice of human taste." (Cassiodorus, *De institutione divinarum litterarum*, 15; 6th century.)

376. PAGE FROM THE OLD TESTAMENT in Greek (1 Kings 14:26-15:16). The text is in three columns without spacing or punctuation. This meant that the readers (*lectores*, ἀναγνῶσται) had to be practised in declaiming aloud. Even at home people usually read in this manner. MS Vaticana, gr. 1209, the famous Vaticanus B, one of the very earliest MSS, from the 4th century.

377. THE LORD'S PRAYER in Gothic. Page from the 6th century *Codex Argenteus*; translation by Bishop Ulfilas; *ca* 360. Gold and silver writing upon a purple painted parchment. *Uppsala, University Library.*

378. TWO PAGES of a papyrus codex from Egypt, the so-called Egerton papyrus, with fragments from an unknown Gospel. First half of the 2nd century. *London, British Museum.*

379. PAPYRUS FRAGMENT (recto) from the Gospel of St John, before 150; this is the earliest New Testament fragment we possess. The text is John, 18:31-33, *Manchester, John Rylands Library.*

380

381

382 383

380–82. THREE MINIATURES from the Vienna Genesis, a purple codex of the 6th century from Constantinople or Asia. The Greek text is incomplete, the illustration unsymbolic, almost profane-bucolic. It may have been a present for a young prince. The codex, now in the National Library in Vienna, is the earliest illustrated Genesis. **380.** Fol. 7r: Rebekah and Eliezer. For the highly stylised picture of the town, cf **315**; spring with a nymph; milestones along the side of the road. **381.** Fol. 15v; Joseph takes leave of Benjamin and meets the man in the field. *Clavi* and *orbiculi* (round ornaments) on the tunics, pillar along the roadside. **382.** Fol. 17v: Pharaoh's butler restored to favour and the baker hanged on a tree. Picture of an ancient classical banquet: sigma-shaped table with plate-like indentations, couches, orchestra of women with flute and percussion instruments, servants with cooler and pouring can.

383. GOSPEL CODEX from Rossano; 6th century. The earliest illuminated book of Gospels. Page of text in two columns. Greek text of Matt. 6:23 "...(ΦΩΤΙ) ΝΟΝ ΕΣΤΑΙ ΕΑΝ / ΔΕ Ο ΟΦΘΑΛΜΟΣ / ΣΟΥ ΠΟΝΗΡΟΣ / Η ΟΛΟΝ ΤΟ ΣΩ / ΜΑ ΣΟΥ ΣΚΟΤΙ / ΝΟΝ ΕΣΤΑΙ... (...'but if your eye is not sound, your whole body will be full of darkness...'). Silver writing on red. *Rossano, Archbishopric.*

384. ASCENSION. Codex of Rabbula (586), from the monastery of Zagba in Mesopotamia. The Lord ascends upon the throne-chariot with the tetramorph (the Four Living Creatures) of Ezekiel 1:5: a vision read in Syria on Ascension Day. Mary, in prayer, as the personification of the Church. *Florence, Laurenziana.*

385. CANON TABLE (of Eusebius, concordance of the four Gospels), *ibid.*, with marginal illustrations: Salomon enthroned, Baptism, Nativity, Massacre of the Innocents, David. Syriac script of the 6th century. The canon tables, which came into being around 330, accompany all *evangeliaria* until late into the Middle Ages.

386–88. THREE MINIATURES from the codex of Rossano (see **383**). **386.** The man born blind washing himself in the pool of Siloam, symbol of baptism. **387.** The Agony in the Garden. **388.** Christ and Barabbas. On the covering of Pilate's table and behind his chair, icons of the Caesars. The officials are wearing early Byzantine robes of office.

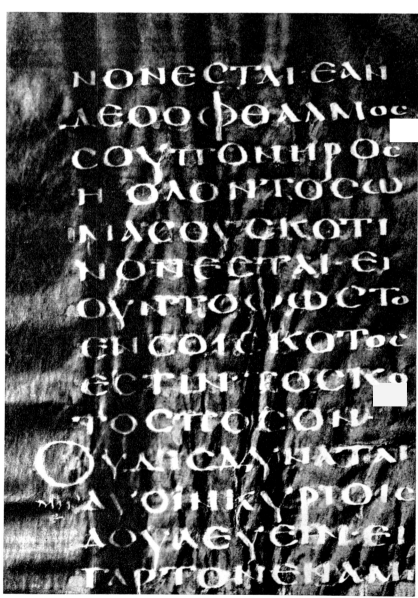

386

387

388

389-93. Latin codices.

398. WRITING TOOLS, codex, a red leather box (*scrinium*) for scrolls, with label, Matthew with the symbol of his Gospel. One of the four evangelists portraits in the bema of San Vitale, Ravenna (547). Scrolls disappear almost entirely after 400.

390. CUPBOARD (*armarium*) with the four Gospels. These cupboards stood in the sacristy adjoining the apse of the basilica. Detail from a mosaic in the so-called mausoleum of Galla Placidia, Ravenna; *ca* 450 (cf 490).

391. Ezra copying the Law. In the background a cupboard with the nine codices of the Old Testament. Codex Amiatinus, Fol. 5r. Copy, executed at Jarrow in Northumbria, before 700, after an Italian model of 550, probably originating from the monastery of Vivarium in Calabria where Cassiodorus died in 583. This monastery possessed an Old Testament in nine volumes. *Florence, Laurenziana.*

392. PASSION CYCLE (from the entry into Jerusalem to the carrying of the cross); miniature in a 7th century Gospel codex. According to the testimony of the Venerable Bede, Benedict Biscop brought back similar books to Jarrow from his journeys to Rome. *Cambridge, Corpus Christi College.*

393. MINUSCULE WRITING; 6th century. Codex of Victor of Capua, *ca* 547. It was in the possession of St Boniface and is preserved at Fulda. Text: Acts 28:20-22 (St Paul at Rome; from the address to the Jewish leaders after his arrival):

"... *propter spem enim Israhel catena hac circumdatus sum. At illi dixerunt ad eum: nos neque litteras accepimus de te a Judaea, neque adveniens aliquis fratrum nuntiavit aut locutus est quid de te malum. Rogamus autem a te audire quae sentis. Nam de secta hac notum est ...*"

"... since it is because of the hope of Israel that I am bound with this chain. And they said to him: We have received no letters from Judaea about you and none of the brethren coming here has reported or spoken any evil about you. But we desire to hear from you what your views are, for with regard to this sect we know that [everywhere it is spoken against]".

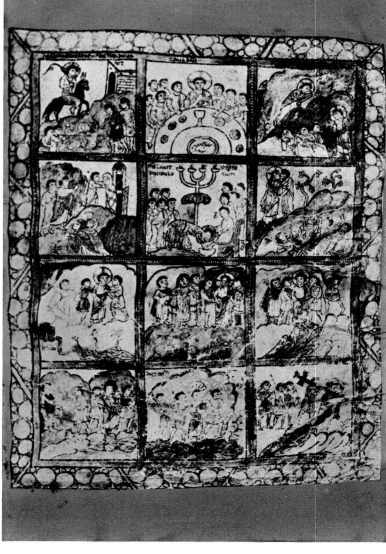

393

PROPTERSPEMENIM
heLcatenabacciro
datussum. Atilli
runtadeum. nos
Litterasaccepim
texJudaea. Neqa
niensaLiquisfrat
nuntiauitautLocu
estquiddetemalu
Rogamusautemate
requaesentis.
desectahacnotum

394

BAPTISM (394-420). **Rite and symbols.** Here follow a few illustrations of the rite and of the symbols of this first of the sacraments. They are to be found everywhere in sermon literature and in the iconography. One should compare them with those prior to 313 (see **48-53**).

394-5: Motif taken from Psalm 42 (LXX 41)

> sicut cervus desiderat ad fontes aquarum
> ita desiderat anima mea ad te ...

> As a hart longs for flowing streams,
> so longs my soul for thee, O God.
> My soul thirsts for God,
> for the living God.
> When shall I come and behold
> the face of God? ...
> how I went with the throng,
> in procession to the house of God,
> with glad shouts and songs of thanksgiving.
> a multitude keeping festival ...

Throughout the whole of Christendom the candidates for baptism, *competentes*, sang these verses during the procession to the baptistery on Easter night, in the midst of the host of the faithful who kept the vigil of the feast in the basilica.

394. MOSAIC from a lunette in the so-called mausoleum of Galla Placidia, Ravenna (450); Psalm 42:1 (LXX 41:2).

395. MOSAIC from baptistery of Salonae in Dalmatia. Floor mosaic near the entrance to the baptistery, with a text from Ps. 42 (LXX 41); 5th century.

The deer are often replaced by lambs and the Shepherd also appears in a field of flowers, as, for example, in the baptistery of Naples, *ca* 400 (cf the baptismal chamber in the house-church at Dura). For it was also the custom to sing Psalm 23 (LXX 22):

> The Lord is my Shepherd, I shall not want;
> he makes me lie down in green pastures.
> He leads me beside still waters;
> he restores my soul ...
> Thou preparest a table before me ...

The last line was taken to refer to the Eucharist which followed, amongst the faithful, immediately after the anointing, and concluded the *initiatio christiana*.

395

The newly baptised, in their snow-white linen garments (without a single animal thread) and marked with the Cross, the sign of the Shepherd's flock, were seen as lambs about the Lamb (cf the vision of the multitude in Revelation), an increase of his flock, like 'new lambs come to the source' (*fons* = font), 'come to the peace' (the unity of all within the Church), 'filled with light' (for baptism was called an 'illumination' an 'opening of the eyes' as of the man born blind). The words 'refreshment' and *in pace* were synonymous with 'eternal life', the life in Christ which in those days was considered as beginning with baptism and which was not interrupted by the fact of the body's death.

396-7. Two of the rare representations of the rite, from the 4th century. In both, the person to be baptised is a child. Those who were born anew to the life of the spirit were called *infans*, 'newly born child' and were thus depicted as children. The water flows from above, from the mouth of the dove of the Spirit, for in the baptisteries too, the water flowed from above, from the mouth of a lion or hart, into the font. The Bishop held the head and shoulders of the person receiving baptism under the stream as the latter stood in the living, i.e. flowing, waters of the piscina, completely naked, without rings or bracelets and with loosened hair. The Holy Spirit was invoked above the baptismal water, which was considered as the mother womb of the Church, made fruitful by the Holy Ghost. These ideas are resumed in the diptychs of the Lateran font (see 409).

396. BAPTISM. Burial chamber in the catacomb of Petrus and Marcellinus, 4th century. Water from the mouth of the dove of the Spirit.

397. BAPTISM. Tombstone of a nameless child; *ca* 400. The Holy Ghost descends from a starry sky and from his mouth the water spills on to the *infans*. The minister holds him and a saint stands by. Inscription:
To the innocent spirit whom the Lord has chosen. He rests [here] in peace [baptised] in the faith. On the tenth day before the calends of September" (= date of death; the child was probably baptised immediately after birth). *Aquileia, Museum.*

398. ILLUMINATIO, the opening of the eyes, the 'enlightenment', symbol of baptism. The man born blind. Detail from a sarcophagus; 4th century. *Rome, Museo delle Terme.*

399. THE FISHER OF SOULS AND THE SHEPHERD, two allusions to baptism. Detail from the great 'Jonah' sarcophagus (see 167); *ca* 300. *Rome, Museo Lateranense.*

400. THE EIGHT SOULS saved from the waters in the Ark of Noah (cf 1 Peter 3:20), one of the Biblical symbols for baptism. Sarcophagus from the Constantinian period, from the court capital of Trèves. *Trèves, Rheinisches Landesmuseum.*

401. WATER FROM THE ROCK and the penitents gathered about the Teacher. Front of the Jairus sarcophagus. Beginning of the 4th century. Probably illustrates the idea of conversion through baptism or, according to others, 'both the first and the second forgiveness', i.e. baptism as penance. *Arles, Musée lapidaire chrétien.*

402. THE CROSSING OF THE RED SEA. Following 1 Cor. 10:1-2: 'All were under the cloud, and all passed through the sea and all were baptised into Moses in the cloud and in the sea . . .' the classical prefiguration of baptism. Front of a sarco-

phagus from Salonae in Dalmatia; *ca* 340. Right: Miriam with the timbrels, the children of Israel with the booty of the pagans, Moses with the rod, the destruction of Pharaoh (symbol of the powers of evil). *Split, Museum.*

"That the Red Sea is a prefiguration of this baptism is stated by the Apostle with the words: 'our fathers were all baptised in the cloud and in the sea' and he adds: 'all this, however, was to them as a prefiguration' (1 Cor. 10:11). Prefiguration for them, but reality for us . . . Moses held his rod on high and led the Jewish people: at night by the pillar of light, by day following the pillar of cloud. What is light but truth, since this gives forth a clear and certain light? What is the pillar of light other than Christ the Lord who has banished the darkness of unbelief and has filled the hearts of the people with the light of truth and of spiritual grace? But the pillar of cloud is the Holy Ghost. The people were in the sea and the pillar of light preceded them, and after followed the pillar of cloud as the foreshadowing of the Holy Ghost. Thus you see that the prefiguration of baptism is shown to us by the Holy Ghost and the water." (Ambrose, *The Sacraments,* **I,** 6: 20 and 22)

Compare this passage from an instruction on baptism with one written two hundred years earlier:

"When the people, liberated from Egypt, crossed the waters and thus escaped from the might of the Egyptian king, the waters overwhelmed the king himself with all his troops. What image could be more clear in the sacrament of baptism?

The pagans are liberated from the world through water and leave behind them their former master, the devil, overwhelmed by the water . . . This is the water which flowed down to the people from the rock going with them [cf 401]: if the rock indeed be Christ then we see that without doubt, the immersion is sanctified through the water in Christ." (Tertullian, *Baptism,* **9,** 1 and 3)

Baptismal fonts (403-8)

403. FONT in the baptismal recess in the house-church at Dura (cf **72**), the earliest known (232-56).

404. FONT at Thamugadi (Timgad) in Numidia; octagonal. The eight pillars have disappeared but the grooves for the bases of these pillars can still be seen. Three steps; 5th century.

405. ROUND FONT in the baptistery at Nocera Superiore (near Capua); cf **413**. Three steps; 6th century.

406. HEXAGONAL FONT in the baptistery at Poitiers; 4th century. It underwent alterations in the 7th century together with the baptistery itself which was rebuilt and so preserved.

407. SQUARE FONT with baldachin. Curtains hung between the pillars. Cuicul (Djemila) in Numidia; cf **351** and **420**.

408. CRUCIFORM PISCINA in the baptistery of the northern Basilica of Sbaita in the Negeb (south of Beersheba, Palestine III, see Map 14).

Baptisteries (409-20)

409. BAPTISTERY of the Lateran in Rome, rebuilt by Sixtus III, 432-40, on the foundations of its Constantinian predecessor. The octagonal piscina has disappeared. On the architrave above the eight surrounding pillars are graved the eight famous distichs which resume the entire baptismal theology of the time; lines 11 and 12 can be seen in the picture:

> *fons hic est vitae qui totum diluit orbem*
> *sumens de Christi vulnere principium*

To judge by style and content they may be attributed to Sixtus' archdeacon and successor, later Leo the Great. The whole reads as follows:

> A heaven-destined race is quickened here from holy seed:
>   begotten by the Spirit that upon the waters moved.
> Plunge sinner then, who would be pure, into the sacred streams;
>   whom the flood old receives, return to life renewed.
> No difference divides the newly born, united by
>   one source, one Spirit, and a common faith.
> What children of God's Spirit she receives as virgin progeny
>   does Mother Church bear here from out this stream.
> Would'st thou be sinless? cleanse thyself beneath the show'ring flood,
>   by thine own sins or by thy fathers' guilt oppressed.
> Here springs the fount of life by which th'entire earth is laved (11)
>   since from Christ's wound it takes its origin and source. (12)
> Await the heavenly kingdom, who are reborn in this font:
>   eternal life does not accept those who are born but once.
> Though his sins be many or grievous, let none draw back afraid;
>   reborn from out this stream, a Christian he shall be.
>
> (*Inscriptiones Christianae Urbis Romae*, **2**, **1**, p. 424)

The 'wound' is the wound in the side of the crucified Christ from which blood and water flowed, i.e. the sacraments of baptism and the Eucharist which together edify and perpetuate the Church.

410. BAPTISTERY of the Orthodox at Ravenna, built by bishop Neon, *ca* 450. It is octagonal with three niches. The floor is raised up a few feet and the piscina is medieval. Apart from the lower walls, the whole of the decoration has been preserved: vine tendrils in mosaic on the arcades, stucco reliefs between and above the windows, and a mosaic frieze showing the four Gospels open upon the altars – an allusion to the *traditio evangeliorum* (explanation of the Gospel symbols) customary at baptism; the great cupola mosaic shows the baptism of Our Lord and the Apostles (cf 443).

Both fonts and baptisteries can be round, cruciform, or square, but by far the greater number are octagonal. Like the eight pillars surrounding the piscina, this basic shape was connected with the mystical meaning of the number eight. Six was the number of Creation, after the number of the days of Creation, seven that of the rest of God and of the present aeon; eight was the number which marked the beginning of the new Creation. The eighth day was that of the Resurrection, the Lord's day, of the future aeon and of eternal life. Eight became the symbol of all that was permanent, abiding, and eternal and also of the life which blossomed in the font. For the baptistery near the Tecla basilica (a little in front of the present cathedral) St Ambrose composed by way of inscription:

> Eight-niched soars this church destined for sacred rites,
>   eight corners has its font, the which befits its gift.
> Meet it was thus to build this fair baptismal hall
>   about this sacred eight: here is our race reborn.

The baptistery in **410** is octagonal with four niches; that of Milan must have had a ring of eight lower niches supporting a central cupola.

409

410

411

413

414

411. BAPTISTERY adjoining the cathedral at Grado in Istria, 6th century. It is octagonal, like the piscina. Fragments of the eight pillars have been preserved (1956).

412. BAPTISTERY of the Arians, Ravenna (later called S. Maria in Cosmedin). In the small octagonal rotunda only the cupola mosaic has been preserved, a modest imitation of that of the Orthodox (see 410); 520-26. In the centre is the baptism of Christ: John holds the shepherd's staff in his hand. On the bank sits the river god of the Jordan with his lobsters' claws, his reed, and his flowing pitcher; round about are the Apostles who bear their wreaths of victory to the victor, Christ, here represented under the sign of the life-giving Cross, enthroned upon the throne of the Second Coming; cf Ps. 9:7.

413. BAPTISTERY at Nocera Superiore near Capua; 6th century. Octagonal piscina, round within, with round steps; double ambulatory. The church itself is round.

414. MOSAIC in the intrados of an arch—visible in 419, in the centre—in the baptistery of Albenga in Liguria (see Map 23), ancient Albingaunum. Doves, symbol of souls, about the three-fold monogram of Christ, an allusion perhaps to the triple immersion in the three-fold name of Father, Son, and Holy

Ghost. End of the 5th century or beginning of the 6th. Blue background.

415. BAPTISTERY of Grado (cf 411); 6th century.

416. BAPTISTERY of Albenga; 6th century, with an ambulatory and small apsidal niches.

417. BAPTISTERY of Fréjus; 5th century, in front of the cathedral, cf 370.

418. BAPTISTERY, ca 350. Relief from a famous sarcophagus in the Museo Lateranense, Rome (cf 175). This is the best preserved picture of a baptistery to survive from Antiquity: acroterion with XP; tiled roof, windows filled in with pierced wooden frames containing translucent selenite, bronze doors with lions' heads and rosettes, surmounted by an open trellis work and the inevitable *vela* (curtains) which the Italian churches have retained up to the present day and which no church of that period was without. The baptisteries were always open and a lamp burned above the font; the faithful used to enter and recall their own baptism and—as St Augustine tells us in the *City of God*, 22, 8—to make vows.

419. BAPTISTERY at Albenga (cf 416); end of the 5th century or beginning of 6th. Niche rotunda with remains of an octagonal piscina; in the middle, the arch with the mosaic shown in 414. The niches served perhaps as robing rooms.

420. BAPTISTERY of Cuicul (Djemila) in Numidia (cf 407). Ambulatory with robing niches. At the adult baptismal ceremony the men were attended by deacons and the women by deaconesses. The sacred act itself took place behind drawn curtains while the oil lamps burned in the canopy above the font.

The numerous processions of lambs on the mosaics and sarcophagi of Rome, Ravenna and Gaul are a direct allusion to the joyful entry of the 'newly enlightened' (called also *neophytes*, or newly born). They were the *candida grex*, the white flock.

> Then, fatherlike, the Bishop leads himself his children forth
> from the baptismal house, pure white in body, heart, and robe,
> and, round the festal altar herding the still timid lambs,
> he feeds them, fasting, with the Bread of Life.
> Then does the older host approve the younger with its cries,
> and 'Alleluia', bleats the flock amid the new-formed choir.
>
> (Paulinus of Nola, *Letters*, **32**, 5)

THE EUCHARIST (421-29).
This mystery, always mentioned with reserve and celebrated with sobriety—*observatione castissima*—says St Augustine, was deliberately explained, from the fourth century onwards, in 'mystagogical' instruction given, at their first communion, to the newly baptised who stood near the altar in their white robes and beheld the eucharistic act for the first time. They themselves, could now take part in it and thus their initiation was complete.

"You have approached the altar and the Lord Jesus calls you, or else your soul, or the Church, saying: Let him kiss me with the kisses of his mouth [Song of Solomon, 1:1]. Would you apply that to Christ? Nothing is more delightful. Would you apply this to your soul? Nothing gives more joy. Let him kiss me. He sees that you are now cleansed of every sin, because your sins have been washed away. For this reason does he consider you worthy of the heavenly sacraments and therefore does he invite you to the heavenly banquet. Let him kiss me with the kisses of his mouth. But, for the rest, it is your soul, or the human race, or the Church which, certain of having been cleansed of every sin and of being worthy to approach the altar of Christ—for what is the altar but the image of Christ's body?—sees the admirable sacrament and says: Let him kiss me with the kisses of his mouth, which is to say: That Christ would give me a kiss." (Ambrose, *The Sacraments*, **5**, 2:5-7).

A confidence and fervour like that of St Ambrose is, however, rare; in Greek Christendom the spirit of awe soon prevails:

"Let us not be ungrateful towards our benefactor, but let us all offer him everything, as far as lies in our power: faith, hope, love, temperance, charity, and hospitality. And now I repeat what I have already said to you, nor shall I cease in the future to impress that same upon your hearts again and again. And what is that? When you draw near to that divine and awful table and approach these holy mysteries, do so with fear and awe, with a clear conscience, with fasting and prayer." (John Chrysostom, *In Diem Nativitatis Iesu Christi*, 7).

During the first centuries everyone who had been baptised participated in the Eucharist; the ecclesiastical penance for the baptised consisted in 'exclusion from the mysteries'. And yet, already at the end of the 5th century and in the sixth, many who considered themselves unworthy refrained from approaching the sacred table and receiving the sacrament. Throughout the whole of the fourth and fifth centuries the Eucharist remained a closely guarded mystery, revealed only to the initiated. After the service for the catechumens, they, together with the non-believers, were solemnly sent away with bread and salt and prayer. The guardians made fast the doors with bolts, the candelabra full of oil lamps were lighted, the curtains between the columns were drawn, the faithful left the exedra and congregated in the nave, about the chancel of the altar, and the Bishop, together with the clergy and acolytes, 'descended to the place of prayer' (St Augustine). Then, in seclusion, amid a deep silence broken only by the short acclamations responding to the exhortations of the Bishop and the vigorous 'Amen' at the end of the Eucharistic prayer, the baptised *fideles* celebrated the 'sacrament of the altar', also called simply *sacrificium* or *oblatio*.

415   416   417

423

424a

424b

421. THE SOURCE OF LIFE. Relief from a chancel slab; 6th century. On the altar, the motifs of the vine tendrils rising from the *cantharus* (chalice), together with the monogram of Christ and the peacocks of immortality, form an allegory of the sacrament of the altar which the Greeks, thinking of John 6 ("I am the bread of life..... he who eats this bread will live for ever."), called: φάρμακον ἀθανασίας, the 'medicament for immortality'. *Ravenna, S. Apollinare Nuovo.*

422. VICTORIA CHRISTI. Mosaic on the site of the wooden, movable altar in the church of Bishop Theodorus in Aquileia (cf 143 and text); 314-20. The grooves are those made by the supports of an altar from the later, 5th century, church. A *Victoria*, with victory wreath and palm branch and the eucharistic elements: a basket with bread and a cup with wine (only the foot remains). Small figures on the side panels bring bread and garlands of flowers. We do not know what this is intended to represent (Lietzmann wrongly assumed it to be a direct representation of the offertory procession to the altar). The central motif, typical of the Constantinian period with its improvisations, undoubtedly means that here, in this sacrament, the Lord conquers sin and death and grants eternal life. Compare, on the communion bread of the modern Greek Church, the motif: IC XC NIKA: Jesus Christ is victorious.

423. LOAVES AND FISHES, the age-old prefiguration of the Eucharist (cf 56-61 and text), derived from the symbol of the feeding of the five thousand. Columnar sarcophagus, 350-80. *Arles, Musée lapidaire chrétien.*

424 ab. IBID., details: loaves and fishes.

425. BREAD AND WINE. Ever recurring symbols of the eucharistic offerings: the seven (!) wine jars of Cana, the seven baskets of the five thousand, the new wine and the new manna. Christ's staff recalls the 'sign' Panel from the door of S. Sabina, Rome; 422-30.

425

Cups with wine do not always figure, even in the historical representations of the Last Supper; loaves and fishes, on the contrary, invariably have a place on the Lord's table. This ancient prefigurative symbol provides a link between the earliest symbolic representations and the later historical ones (right up to 1200: they can still be seen on the oldest window in Chartres cathedral, *ca* 1180-1194).

426. THE LAST SUPPER. Codex of Rossano, 6th century. Sigma-shaped table, loaves and fishes. *Rossano in Calabria, Archbishopric.*

427. IBID. Mosaic; before 529. Note the cloth covering the sigma-shaped table. It displays the decoration customary on the altars of that time (cf **446**). Seven loaves, two fishes. *Ravenna, S. Apollinare Nuovo.*

428-9. THE COMMUNION RITE: the communion of the Apostles in the codex of Rossano (see above, **426**). **428**: Communion in the form of bread, with hands crossed. **429.** Communion in the form of wine.

"Stepping forward, you must approach, not with outstretched hands, nor with fingers spread wide apart, but let your left hand make a throne for your right, as if to receive your king, and, forming a hollow in the palm of your hand, you must receive the body of Christ, saying: Amen. Sanctify first your eyes by touching them carefully with Christ's body, then eat, taking care that no part of it be lost." (Cyril of Jerusalem, *Catechetical mysteries*, **5**, 21)

After this, the communicants took a small sip from the chalice, again answering: 'Amen'. The bishop or priest said: 'Body of Christ' and 'Blood of Christ' and each one answered: 'Amen'. The women usually covered their hand with a linen cloth. Before 313 the faithful took a small portion of the bread home with them in a *theca* (small shrine or pyx) so that, if no synaxis were held, they might be able to communicate at home during the week, together with their wives and baptised children. This custom persisted until the fourth century in Cappadocia. The bread which remained on the altar was consumed by priests, deacons, and 'innocent children'. A small portion was reserved for the sick, as Holy Viaticum.

426

427

428

429

430

THE ELEMENTS OF THE BASILICA (430-50).

THE ELEMENTS OF THE BASILICA (430-50). The basilica, the most impressive and, for a thousand years to come, the decisive creation of the Christian (imperial?) architects of the fourth century, is a house for public worship. In Syria, for example, its country of origin, it is visibly a development of the house-church common there before 313. It lies about an inner court, the entrances are at the side and, together with the annexes, it forms a rather unimposing complex. The earliest example is found at Qirk Bizzeh (see **442**, Map 15b) and has recently (after 1945) been thoroughly examined.

The basilica contained no new architectural elements since, by its very nature, its form was determined not by technical considerations, but by the very simplest, self-evident, and purely functional synthesis of the five basic requirements arising from the nature of Christian worship. These were: (1) the large assembly room destined to hold the entire community, disposed according to a hierarchy and therefore designed about an axis; (2) the *cathedra* of the presiding Bishop, placed upon a podium and, in the case of a very large hall, in an apse or *exedra* similar in every way to the pagan *exedrae*; (3) the pulpit—*ambo, pulpitum*—for the reading of the Holy Scriptures; from here too the singing of the Psalms was conducted; (4) the baptismal font which, in view of the character of the baptismal rite, stood outside the assembly place; (5) the table for the Eucharist, serving both as a table and as an altar for the eucharistic celebration.

The place of assembly and the pulpit were inherited from the synagogue; even the word *ecclesia* (Greek ἐκκλησία), which means assembly, is synonymous with συναγωγή. It first means 'assembly', then, 'place of assembly'; in the Romance languages it still denotes the actual church building. The ritual bath and, in a certain sense, even the *cathedra*, belong to the synagogue; the latter stood beside the Torah shrine. The table for the 'bloodless mysteries', however, distinguishes every Christian church, house-church (*domus ecclesiae* or κυριακόν), and basilica from the synagogue, and from the halls for pagan rites.

The surprising uniformity of the basilica in all the countries of the Empire *ca* A.D. 400, at a time when the differentiating process in the liturgy had already begun, must not, however, make us forget that this uniform type did not come into existence immediately after 313; there was first an experimental period. We have found scarcely any traces of the very earliest dispositions after 313.

Only in the conservative outer fringes of the Empire, in Syria and in Africa, has excavation brought to light traces of this early disposition, and it is precisely there that we notice considerable variations. In Syria the altar stands in the apse, while the *cathedra* and pulpit are often found in the nave. In Africa, the altar seems always to have stood in the middle of the nave, right up to the time of the Byzantine restoration in the sixth century. In Rome, on the contrary, it was placed under the triumphal arch; in a few cases, in the very large churches, it was separated from the apse podium by a wide transept. The history of these dispositions, however, has still to be written.

The original, extremely simple, arrangement was later slightly modified as a result of the complications brought about by the growing complexity of the religious service. This modification occurred first of all in those basilicas which contained a *memoria*. In the beginning, this *memoria* stood apart from the main building, as in the case of the Anastasis, situated to the west of the Martyrion, the normal church of the Jerusalem community. Yet already in S. Petri in Vaticano, the *memoria* was incorporated into the basilica itself; we do not even know where the altar stood. For centuries *martyria* and *memoriae* were constructed along the side walls of the basilicas or at the side of the apse; even in the West this custom prevailed right up to the Carolingian period, and these *memoriae* or *martyria* were surrounded in their turn by the ordinary mausolea of rich and devout citizens. Another complication was the combination of martyr's tomb and altar. This was an obvious development in the cemetery *memoria* outside the city walls, but it became general everywhere when the relics of the martyrs, whether from a spirit of piety, or for reasons of safety, began to be transferred inside the city walls and lodged within the churches. A third complication was the presence of permanent seats for the growing host of *continentes* or monks who daily sang the Psalms in their church; this was the *chorus psallentium*.

430. S. CLEMENTE, Rome. This illustration shows how the earlier disposition has been modified. Here a 5th century church was rebuilt in the 11th century above the old. Remains of the earlier *cancelli* were utilised and the original disposition is still recognisable, yet it shows today no 'typically Early Christian disposition' but a purely medieval Romanesque rearrangement. It contains a *confessio* (*memoria*, after that of St Peter) underneath the altar, connected with the

135

431

432/433

434/435

436

cathedra podium following a pattern introduced by Pelagius II and Gregory the
Great in St Peter's, ca 590, two ambones (unheard of before 1000) with the candlestick for the paschal candle, and stalls for the chorus psallentium inside the cancelli
which formerly surrounded only the altar. It is not the Roman churches, however, which can throw light upon the earliest synthesis, but ruins in deserted
districts.

The cathedra (431-36)

This throne embodies the weight of apostolic authority. From it the Bishop, and
only he, presided over the assembly and from this seat (ex cathedra) he pronounced
the authoritative commentary upon the Holy Scriptures. Very few cathedrae
dating from the first centuries of Christianity have been preserved.

431. DISPOSITION of the cathedra and seats for the presbyters (subsellia) in
S. Clemente, Rome. The disposition is 5th century but the church itself is 11th

432. IVORY CATHEDRA of Bishop Maximianus, Ravenna (cf 331-3); middle of
the 6th century. Probably of Alexandrian workmanship.

433. CATHEDRA of Gregory the Great: an antique Roman chair in S. Greg-
orio Magno on the Celio in Rome. There is no doubt that spoils were utilised

434. CATHEDRA, cathedral of Vasio (Vaison) in Provence; 6th century.

435. CATHEDRA from Egypt; 6th or 7th century? It reached St Mark's in
Venice by way of Grado and is known as the cattedra di San Marco. Its shape is not
unlike that of the large Coptic thrones. Neither the decoration (cherubs, Tree of
life, Cross) nor the inscription has been satisfactorily explained.

436. APSE PODIUM with seats for the presbyters in the Great Church (basilica
maior or pacis) at Hippo Regius. Of St Augustine's cathedra only the opening for
the steps has been preserved. According to him it was customary to place a piece
of tapestry or a cushion on the seat (cathedra velata).

The ambo (437-42)

The ambo embodies the motif of the χήρυγμα, the preaching, the propagation of the Word of God. In large edifices built after 313 it was a lofty and sometimes rather grand pulpit with steps and a marble stand upon which to rest the codices. The singing of the Psalms was also conducted from here and the long, triumphant alleluias. Later, the Bishop himself sometimes mounted the *ambo* in order, as Chrysostom says, 'the better to be heard'. From the *ambo* (from ἀναβαίνειν, to climb up, go up), are derived the later Italian *pergamo* and *cantoria*, the medieval jube or choir screen with organ loft, and even the modern pulpit as it is used in Western churches from the 15th century onwards. Now that the sounding board has become superfluous, the original form has once again returned to favour. Note, however, that the homily must be associated with the *cathedra* (Fr. *chaire*) and the reading of the Scriptural lessons with the *ambo*.

437. AMBO from Leptis Magna (Tripolitana), a 6th century basilica near the Forum of Severus. The upper part is a capital taken from a civil building.

438. AMBO of the type common in the 6th century, re-assembled in the 11th from old material. The modern location is arbitrary. *Castel Sant' Elia, near Nepi.*

439. UPPER PART of an *ambo*; 596; *Ravenna, S S. Giovanni e Paolo.*

440. AMBO, 6th century, reconstructed without steps and placed in a completely arbitrary spot in the nave. *Ravenna, S. Apollinare Nuovo.*

441-2. SYRIAN AMBOS upon a bema (podium) in the nave. 441: at Resafe (Sergiopolis, cf 312) in the 6th century cathedral. 442: in the 4th century house-church of Qirk Bizzeh, with *cancelli*, stalls, and honorary *cathedra* (extreme left), for the books of the Holy Scriptures; cf also 308.

437

438

439

440

441

442

451a   452   451b

The altar (443-50)

This is always and everywhere in the form of a table, in deliberate contrast to the massive block (cf 73) of the pagan altar. It was called either 'table' (τράπεζα, Lat. *mensa*), or 'altar' (θυσιαστήριον, Lat. *altare*), two words which were used in the Old Testament translations to denote the altar of the true God; the strictly pagan terms such as Greek βωμός and Latin *ara* were carefully avoided. In these two names, the word 'altar' stresses the element of sacrifice, and 'table' that of the mystical banquet, as well as the actual shape. We find the sigma-shaped tables of the classical dining-room (*triclinia*) in the representations of the Last Supper (see 426-7), in the shape of the *mensa* above the tombs (354-5), and also in the stone altar-tables of the Coptic churches. The platelike indentations around the edge of the table remained common until well into the Middle Ages (cf the main altar of Cluny, now in the Musée Ochier). The wooden altar was soon replaced by one of stone.

443. ALTAR in an *exedra*. Detail from the cupola mosaic, Baptistery of the Orthodox, Ravenna; *ca* 450 (cf 410).

444. ALTAR and bema screen; end of the 6th century. *Diskos* (paten, dish for the bread) of silver gilt from Riha in Syria, 9½ inches across. In the 'communion of the Apostles' we see the ordinary communion rite depicted: left, veiled hands for the chalice, right, crossed hands for receiving the bread. The inscription gives the names of the founders: 'For the repose of the soul of Sergia, Joannes, Theodosius and the redemption of Megalus and Nonnus and their children'. *Dumbarton Oaks Collection, U.S.A.*

445. COVERED ALTAR with *velum*, common in the Greek East; 6th century miniature from the Vienna Genesis, Fol. 4r. The sacrifice of Melchizedek: bread and wine.

446-7. THE THREE SACRIFICES of Abel, Abraham, and Melchizedek, from the Latin Eucharistic prayer *Supra quae*:

"Deign to regard them with a favourable and gracious countenance and to accept them as thou didst graciously deign to accept the offerings of Thy just servant Abel, and the sacrifice of our father Abraham, and that which Thy high priest Melchizedek sacrificed to Thee, a holy offering, a victim without blemish."

446. 6th century altar (530-47), decked with the altar cloths, the round twisted loaves, and the chalice with handles (*cantharus, calix*). 447. The 6th century idea of an altar for burnt sacrifice; in contrast, an ordinary table, in the

'hospitality of Abraham and the three angels'. Mosaics in the bema, on either side of the altar. *Ravenna, S. Vitale.*

448. ARA (pagan altar) from Ostia. Garlands and bacchantes beside another ara; 2nd century. *Rome, Museo delle Terme.*

449-50. EXAMPLES of the combination of tomb with relics and table altar. The reliquarium becomes a preliminary stage of the *stipes* (massive pedestal or support). 449. S. Apollinare in Classe; ciborium of 807-12. 450. Euphrasiana, Parenzo.

MATER ECCLESIA (451ab-454)

The Church is represented as a veiled, maternal figure, majestic, clad in dark robes, and holding a book in her hand.

"In this consists the purity of the holy Church: she is untouched, having no intercourse, yet fruitful, since she bears. She is virgin by her chastity, mother by her children. We are born to a maid with child, not of man, but of the Spirit. We are born to a maid, not amid physical pangs, but amid the joy of the angels. We are fed by a maid, not with the milk of her body, but with that of the Apostle, with which he fed the tender youth of the growing Christian people [cf I Cor. 3:2]. What married woman has more children than the holy Church, a virgin in the sacrament [of baptism] yet a mother through her children in the Church, and to whose fruitfulness even the Holy Scriptures bear witness, saying: 'for the children of the desolate one will be more than the children of her that is married' [Isa. 54:1]. Our mother has no husband but she has a bridegroom, so that both the Church in her faithful and the soul in the individual may be united with the Word of God as with her eternal bridegroom, without any violation of chastity, impervious to injury but fruitful for spiritual experience." (Ambrose, *On Virgins*, I, 6:31).

451ab. THE 'CHURCH OF THE CIRCUMCISION' (Judaism) and the 'Church of the Gentiles'. Mosaic in S. Sabina, 422-30 (right, with *mappula* (napkin) in the hand).

452. THE 'CHURCH OF THE GENTILES' crowning St Paul. Detail from the apse mosaic in S. Pudenziana, Rome; shortly after 400.

453. ECCLESIA MATER, the basilica as a symbol of the Church. Tomb mosaic of Valentia; *ca* 400, from Thabraca. *Tunis, Musée du Bardo.*

454. ECCLESIA? OR ROME? Middle section of a Christian sarcophagus from Tébessa; *ca* 400. *Algiers, Museum.*

453   454

THE BISHOPS AND THE CLERGY (455-60).

455. TWO DEACONS with *evangeliarium* and censer and their Bishop, Maximianus
of Ravenna. Above their tunics the deacons are wearing the *tunica dalmatica*
with wide sleeves and dark ornamental strips or *clavi*, just as they are worn
today. In addition they wear the tonsure and the usual black half-boots worn
by all people of consequence. Over the dalmatic the Bishop wears the wide
chasuble (Gk. φελόνιον), and over this, the *pallium*, the ecclesiastical counter-
part of the *toga contabulata*. On a 5th century mosaic from Syria a deacon is
shown for the first time wearing the *orarion* (diaconal stole, but worn in the
manner of the Greek Church at the present day). Detail from a mosaic in the
bema. *Ravenna, S. Vitale.*

456. MAXIMIANUS with portable cross (which could be laid upon the altar).
It did not 'stand' but was held aloft for veneration. Detail from a mosaic.
Ravenna, S. Vitale.

457-60. FOUR BISHOPS of Ravenna, portrayed in mosaic above the *cathedra*
in the apse of S. Apollinare in Classe, Ravenna; 6th century. They are, from
left to right: 457, Ursus, founder of the main church; 458, Severus; 459, Ecclesius, the founder of S. Vitale (522-32); 460, Ursicinus (533-36). All are wearing *pallium*, chasuble, dalmatic, black boots, and the tonsure, and each has a
Gospel codex in his hand. A pagan author writes of the Bishops of the large
towns in the 6th century:

"... they are well off, for they grow rich on the gifts of noble ladies. They
ride in carriages, dressed in exquisite robes. They give such sumptuous dinners
that their banquets rival those of kings. And yet they could be really 'reverend'
if they would only learn to despise the size of their city, which they are accustomed to give as excuse for their vices, and would imitate the manner of
life of certain provincial bishops who, by their extreme moderation in eating
and drinking, their sober dress and their eyes fixed always upon the ground,
delight the Eternal Godhead and His true worshippers as pure and venerable
people." (Ammianus Marcellinus, 27, 3:14-15)

Yet those who occupied an exalted position did not always live in great style.
The example set by Eusebius of Vercellae, who lived with his priests and deacons
in a strict monastic house-community, was followed immediately by the
great St Ambrose, then by St Augustine in Hippo, and was soon adopted by
countless others. In East and West, more and more monks were chosen as
Bishops. Their great reputation for impartiality, selflessness, and devotion appears from the fact that when, during the reign of Constantine, the bishops
received the *privilegium fori*, the power to administer justice even in civil matters, Christians and non-Christians alike deserted the civil tribunals and flocked
to the ecclesiastical. Some Bishops, on the other hand, were national leaders,
and not always imperialistically minded—the Alexandrian *papae*, for example
who relied particularly upon the monks for support. In the West it was the
Bishops who were the real *defensores civitatis* against the barbarian rulers and
championed their town and people in everything. Pope Leo, journeying to
meet Attila, and forcing him to a compromise, Gregory the Great, and so many
others, these were the last representatives of *romanitas*, and shining examples
to the centuries to come.

Here we have Jerome's portrait of the dedicated pastor of a small church:
"He [Nepotianus] took care that the altar shone, that the walls were never
covered with soot, that the mosaic floor was swept, that the door keeper was
at his post and the curtains were drawn across the door openings, that the sacristy
was clean and the vessels were polished until they shone ... and he decorated
the church basilicas and, on the anniversaries, the commemorative chapels, with
a variety of flowers and green branches and vine tendrils. In this way, everything
in the church that was remarkable for its tasteful arrangement testified to the
work and zeal of its priest." (Jerome, *Letters*, 60, 12:2 and 4, to Heliodorus)

Heliodorus was Bishop of Altinum in Venetia (see Map 23) and Nepotianus
was his nephew. He served his uncle's church, concealed his erudition, lived as a
monk and died young. Jerome makes of his letter of condolence a long eulogy.

THE SIGN OF THE CROSS (461-78). On 461-63, early cryptograms;
464-65. monograms after 313.

461. ANCHOR. *Rome, Museo Lateranense*; cf. 56 and 91.

462. AXE, upon a pagan sarcophagus, the sign used for the Pythagorean
symbol Y, applied by Irenaeus to the Cross. *Arles, Aliscamps.*

463. THE CROSS (the palm is an allusion to the name of the deceased, Victoria).
Roman catacombs.

464. CROSS; from the *labarum* of Constantine, with *alpha* and *omega*. *Arles,
Aliscamps.*

465. THE CROSS as the monogram of Christ (*chrismon*) in a *clipeus*. *Ibid.*

From the very beginning the Cross was the distinguishing mark of the

467

Christian. The sign worn by the elect upon their foreheads as a seal and stamp was taken by the Christians to be the sign of the Cross. The first thing a catechumen received from the Church was that sign, traced with the fingers upon his forehead.

"He [Christ] wished to die for us, but with this we have not said enough. He wished to be crucified, becoming obedient unto death, even unto death on a cross [Phil. 2:8]. He chose the most terrible and ignominious form of death, He, who was to destroy death in all its forms. By this most ignominious death He killed all death. It was the most ignominious form of death to the Jews, who did not understand it; for this death was chosen by the Lord. He was, indeed, to make the Cross His sign, and to that Cross, as a trophy won from the devil, He would give a place upon the foreheads of the faithful. And thus could the Apostle say: But far be it from me to glory except in the cross of our Lord Jesus Christ, by which the world has been crucified to me and I to the world [Gal. 6:14]." (Augustine, *Tractatus in Evangelium Joannis*, **36**, 4)

"What is the sign of the Cross that all men know, other than the Cross of Christ? If this Cross be not traced upon the foreheads of the faithful, or over the water from which we are born anew, or over the oil with which we are anointed, or over the sacrifice with which we are fed, then none of these acts is accomplished according to the rite." (Augustine, *Ibid.* **118**, 5)

The converted Greeks, sensitive, as all peoples of the Ancient world, to the evocative power of a symbol and ever seeking after the reality which this symbol could represent, saw the Cross everywhere and were struck first of all by its 'extensive' function. They called the Cross the 'sign of extension', for of its very nature it designates the axes of the cosmos and draws everything from the four corners of the earth towards its own centre. They understood why the Lord had said: 'when I am lifted up from the earth I will draw all men to myself' (John 12:32). We sometimes come across this idea in sermons, in, for example, the anonymous homily delivered on Easter night. It dates perhaps from after 313, but is based on motifs current *ca* 220, and is perhaps by Hippolytus of Rome.

"And when the cosmic struggle was ended, and He had withstood all, victor on every front, neither exalting himself as God nor defeated as man, then He tarried there, immobile on the frontier of the universe, a trophy of victory, all alone, triumphant over the enemy. And the universe was appalled at His steadfastness in suffering: then the heavens shook, the Powers, the supernatural Thrones and Dominations trembled: when they saw the commander of the heavenly host hanging upon the cross, the stars of the heavens all but fell, when they saw Him outstretched, He who is before the morning star [Ps. 109:3, Vulg.]. Almost was the fire of the sun extinguished when it saw that the great Light of the world [John 8:12] was dimmed. Then the rocks of the earth split asunder, proclaiming aloud the folly of Israel: you have not recognised here the supernatural Rock which followed you and from which you have drunk [1 Cor. 10:4]. And the veil of the temple was rent, suffering with Him and proclaiming the true, heavenly High Priest. And almost would the whole world have fallen apart and collapsed in dismay at the Passion, had not the great Jesus breathed the divine spirit over it saying: 'Father, into thy hands I commit my spirit' [Luke, 23:46]. For the universe was in a state of turmoil and confusion, in a trembling of fear. All was convulsed. Yet when the divine spirit ascended again to heaven, the universe grew calm once more as though reanimated, awakened to a new life and to a lasting peace." (*Paschal Homilies* 1, ed. Nautin, 55)

In this cosmic vision of the Passion and of the death which conquered death, we also find the motif of the Cross as 'trophy' of the victory. It was this motif that artists liked most to represent.

During the time of the persecutions the Christians traced their symbol under the guise of some inconspicuous figure; the yard which formed a cross with the mast of a ship, a ship's anchor (see the text of St Clement, page 40). It even seems that Irenaeus of Lyon proposed to the faithful the forked cross of the Pythagoreans, the Y, which the pagans depicted in the form of an axe (*ascia*, see **462**), as a cryptogram of the Cross of Christ. The yard on the mast is never missing in Jonah's ship, and the anchor is often accompanied by the fish, the *Ichthys*, Christ (see **56**).

After 313 all this is changed. The cryptogram becomes a monogram, at the same time Cross and monogram of Christ (for both forms see **464** and **465**), and from then onwards it is found everywhere. It appears on shields, on furniture, on the roofs and gables of basilicas and baptisteries (see **418**), on epitaphs and sacred vessels. The monogram is encircled by the laurel wreath of victory and this gives rise to the classical *victoria Christi*. Roman sculptors go even further and transform the *chrismon* into a trophy, the *trophaeum crucis*.

466. THE TROPHY OF THE CROSS. Central motif of a sarcophagus in the Museo Lateranense and illustrated above (**467**). Left, Simon of Cyrene carrying the Cross and the 'crowning' of Our Lord with the wreath of victory; the crown of thorns is replaced by one of laurel. In the central niche the focal point is the cross-monogram of Christ; the wreath hangs from the beak of an eagle. It forms at the same time the crowning of a trophy which consists of an upright cross flanked by the abashed soldiers who were on guard at the Tomb. They are sitting in the traditional posture of the defeated barbarians who were usually depicted at the side of the imperial trophies. This central motif has rightly been called '*Anastasis*', the Resurrection. The Cross Trophy is here the symbol of the victory over death won by the death on the Cross. Right, another subtle allusion to the Passion; Christ, as Teacher, calmly conversing with the ashamed Pilate who turns away, making the traditional gesture of confusion, the hand raised to the cheek, while the servant stands ready with the basin in which he will wash his hands in innocence. The sarcophagus dates from about 350. The motif of the 'Trophy of the Cross' was adopted into the liturgy and also into the preaching (Pope Leo the Great, Sermons, **59**, 4; **82**, 5). It is still heard during Holy Week in the hymns of Venantius Fortunatus on the Cross (the *Vexilla regis* and *Pange lingua gloriosi proelium certaminis*). In place of these very well known hymns we give here another by the same author, who was Bishop of Poitiers in the 6th century. With him, the 'trophy' has become the 'Tree of life':

UPON THE CROSS OF THE LORD

It shines, the blessed Cross, where, flesh, our Saviour hung
and with His precious Blood once washed our wounds;
where once the sacred Lamb, in kindly love for us
a gentle victim, drew His sheep from wolfish jaws;
where with His piercèd hands redeemed the world from sin,
and by His cruel death sealed off the path of death.
Here once, with bloody nails transfixèd, hung that hand
which snatched Paul back from sin, Peter from death.
Be mighty by thy fruit, O sweet and noble Tree,
since that upon thy boughs thou bearest fruits so new,
at whose fresh scent dead bodies rise again
and those return to life who fled the light of day.
Beneath thy spreading boughs shall none more suffer heat,
neither the moon by night, nor sun by light of day [Ps. 121:6].
Thou shinest, planted firm, hard by the running streams,
and spreadest forth thy leaves, decked out with budding blooms;
and in thy branches twined hangs that same Vine, whence flows
abundance of sweet wine—red with the red of blood.

(Venantius Fortunatus, *Hymns*, **2**, 1)

The Cross as the new 'Tree of life' planted upon the hill of paradise restored from which the four streams flow anew (Gen. 2) is also a fourth century motif

477

478

(cf **203**), originating perhaps from the liturgy at the *staurotheca* in Jerusalem:

"Your life-giving side, gushing forth like the streams of paradise, has drenched your Church, O Christ, like a spiritual Eden. From thence dividing into streams, into four Gospels, it waters the cosmos . . ."

468-71. GLORIA CRUCIS, symbols of the exaltation of the Cross.

468. THE CROSS AMID THE STARS, symbol of Christ's assumption into glory; this is why His sign is surrounded by the Four Living Creatures which bear His throne (Rev. 4, cf Ezek. 1). Cupola mosaic in the so-called mausoleum of Galla Placidia; *ca* 450.

469. THE CROSS AMID THE STARS, surrounded by ethereal light. Mosaic in the cupola of a small 6th century *memoria* at Casanarello in southern Italy (Map 14).

470. SALUS MUNDI. The Cross as the sign of salvation. A reproduction of the *staurotheca* of Jerusalem, which is set with precious stones. In the centre, a portrait icon of Christ; a crown of gems frames the sphere within which the Cross is elevated to the stars. The Cross is the central motif of a symbolic representation of the Transfiguration of Our Lord upon the mountain, in which the Apostles are depicted as lambs, whereas Moses and Elijah are in human form. It fills the gigantic apse of S. Apollinare in Classe (532-6).

471. THE CHRISMON CROSS crowned by the Hand of the Father in the starry sphere. A symbolic representation of the glory of the Lord, *gloria Christi*. Above the Hand, in the surrounding frieze, the phoenix of immortality (cf **290**). Baptistery of Soter, beside the cathedral of Naples; *ca* 400.

472-74. THE CROSS as the Tree of life in the Paradise restored.

472. THE TREE OF LIFE; inscription: Jesus Christ is victorious. Central panel of an ivory triptych from Constantinople; 10th century. *Paris, Louvre.*

473. THE LAMB upon the Tree of life (cf Venantius Fortunatus: *agnus in crucis levatur immolandus stipite*: the lamb is raised to the Cross as a sacrifice). Golden votive cross commissioned by the Emperor Justinus II and his consort (565-78). On the arms of the Cross the branches of the tree of life; above and below two icons of Our Lord; the augusti in the attitude of prayer. *Rome, Treasure Chamber of St Peter's.*

474. THE TREE OF LIFE. Apse mosaic from the upper church of S. Clemente in Rome. This 11th century composition reproduces 5th century motifs (from the

abandoned lower church); the hill of Paradise with the four streams and the drinking hart, the tendrils of the Tree of life, which is the Cross. The Lamb upon the mountain underneath is an allegorical repetition of this motif. The Crucified figure and the two others date from the 13th century; the doves and the Hand date back to the old model. As in Venantius, the Tree is at the same time the Vine.

475-78. THE EARLIEST REPRESENTATIONS of a more or less historically conceived Crucifixion. It is seldom found in the 5th century and the definitive composition originates in the 6th, perhaps in Jerusalem. The 5th century efforts are shapeless and distasteful; it is only later that a worthy form is achieved.

475. DETAIL FROM AN IVORY CASKET from northern Italy; *ca* 400. Judas' end; Mary, John, Our Lord, and the centurion confessing his faith. One of the other sides shows the tomb and the sleeping soldiers. *London, British Museum.*

476. PANEL from the wooden door of S. Sabina, Rome; *ca* 422-30. The woodcarver was ignorant of the manner of execution common in the early Imperial period and no longer in use at this time.

477. THE CRUCIFIXION. Upper part of a full page miniature in the Syrian Codex of Rabbula, from Zagba in Mesopotamia, dated 586. The oldest of the classical compositions. Our Lord is wearing a long tunic with golden *clavi* (this garment was called the *colobium*). The soldiers are casting lots for the outer garment; left, Mary and John; right, the other women. Above the lance-bearer the name Longinus (from λόγχη = lance) is written in Greek. To the right, the man carrying the sponge soaked in gall upon the hyssop rod. Above the mountains the moon is covered over and the sun is red as blood, cf Hab. 3, 11.

478. THE CRUCIFIXION. Fresco in the *memoria* of Quiricus and Julitta in Santa Maria Antiqua on the Forum; beginning of the 8th century. The church belonged to monks who had fled from the iconoclastic Eastern Roman Empire. The fresco reproduces the Crucifixion motifs which will remain constant from now on. Our Lord is shown wearing the *colobium* and fastened to the Cross by four nails; the inscription is written above in Greek; Mary stands by the side in which the wound is opened by Longinus and from which the blood and water flow, symbol of the sacraments; the man carries the sponge and John the beloved disciple stands by. The Crucified figure, life size, and sculptured in the round, is a 10th century creation which most probably originated in the Rhineland.

479/480

THE MEMORIAE OF THE MARTYRS (479-513). The most popular Christian devotion after 313 was the veneration of the martyrs. The sanctuaries in which their relics were venerated were called in the East *martyria*, and in the West *memoriae*. Nearly every city possessed a few, usually erected in a cemetery, either beside or above the grave. Later, when the relics began to be divided up and transferred, *memoriae* were also built within the city walls. Some became world famous pilgrimage centres (see Map 30/31). Most of them disappeared during the time of the troubles, together with the cemeteries; the relics, however, were saved, and were transferred within the city walls. The names of the early martyrs, preserved in the *martyrologia* (calendars giving the dates of death), have never been forgotten and are borne by millions.

482

483

481 484

146

485   486

488

487   489a   489b

479. THE MEMORIA PETRI IN VATICANO; cf page 62. Ivory casket from Samagher, near Pola; *ca* 400. Formerly *Pola, Museo Civico*; now in Rome.

480. THE FAITHFUL before the doors of a *memoria*. Ivory casket from Pola. *Rome, Museo Civico*.

481. MEMORIA of St Alexander on the Via Nomentana near Rome; end of the 4th century (the broken columns have been wrongly replaced).

482. EPITAPH OF THE APOSTLE PAUL; 4th century, beneath the altar of the basilica on the Via Ostiensis. The holes are for the depositing of souvenirs (*brandea*), mostly small pieces of costly material which touched the bottom of the sepulchral cavity (*confessio*). The inscription was later completed into: PAULO APOSTOLO MARTYRI.

483. TOMB OF POPE CORNELIUS † 253 at Centumcellae (Civitavecchia). The inscription reads: CORNELIVS MARTYR, with EP(*iscopus*) added later. Above, remains of the inscription placed there by Pope Damasus in the 4th century; the fresco dates from the 6th. Catacomb of Calixtus, near the tomb of Caecilia.

484. TOMB OF ST LAWRENCE, deacon of Sixtus II († 258), under the floor of S. Lorenzo-fuori-le-mura. The pillars and disposition of the Constantinian *memoria* have been preserved; it was rebuilt in the 6th century (see 605).

485. MARTYR WEARING HIS WREATH in the 'place of light'. Reliquary from 'Ain Zirara in Numidia, lid (cf 356); 4th century. *Vatican, Museo Cristiano*.

486. SVSTVS and TIMOTEVS crowned by Christ. Gold glass; 4th century. They are Popes Sixtus II (in the catacomb of Calixtus) and Timotheus (in a small catacomb on the Via Ostiensis). *Vatican, Museo Cristiano*.

487. VENERATION OF A MARTYR. Fresco in the house-church beneath SS. Giovanni e Paolo on the Celio; Rome, 4th century.

488. EPITAPH by Pope Damasus on the martyrs in the catacomb of Calixtus, in the crypt of the Popes (see 94). The translation is given on page 52.

489a. EPITAPH on SS. Nereus and Achilleus by Damasus, *ca* 366, executed in the alphabet of Furius Dionysius Filocalus (the same as in 151) in their *memoria* built in the catacomb of Domitilla in the 4th century. The text of this epitaph reads:

"They had entered military service and both practised their cruel trade, carrying out the commands of the tyrant, prepared, out of fear, to accomplish his orders. Then behold! a visible miracle; suddenly they lay their savage nature aside, they turn about and depart, leaving behind the barracks of the godless commander. They throw away their shields, badges, and bloody javelins and, as a profession of faith, they joyfully wear Christ's sign of victory. Believe from Damasus what the glory of Christ has power to accomplish." (Damasus, *Epigrams*, 8)

489b. THE ORIGINAL EPITAPH of the martyrs Simplicius and Faustinus in a small cemetery on the road to Portus, close by the Tiber. The inscription is touchingly simple: "XP. The martyrs Simplicius and Faustinus who suffered death in the river Tiber and are laid to rest in the cemetery of Generosa 'super Philippi'" (see Map 28).

Rome was surrounded by a ring of *memoriae* unrivalled throughout the whole Christian world (see Map 28, survey). Thirty-eight large and small basilicas arose in the cemeteries (eleven of them still remain, either as ruins or rebuilt). On the tombs of the principal saints in the catacombs, Pope Damasus had magnificent epitaphs carved in marble (see 488, 489a). Yet people still came to Rome chiefly to visit the graves of Peter, Paul, and Lawrence; even today, every pilgrim visiting Rome begins with a journey *ad limina*, that is, 'to the thresholds of the Apostles' that is, of their *memoriae* on the Vatican and on the Via Ostiensis.

490. LAWRENCE, the 'Roman Stephen', deacon of Pope Sixtus II, died on August 10th, 258, under Valerian, three days after Sixtus. Lunette in the so-called mausoleum of Galla Placidia at Ravenna (cf 390). The peculiar composition is explained by the position of the window. The grid and fire are allusions to Lawrence's (legendary) passion; the cupboard with the Gospel books (see 390) and the Codex in his hand to his diaconate, for the deacons had the care of the sacred books and vessels and read the Gospel during the service. The cross is a reminder of Christ's triumph in this martyr. It is not known for certain whether or not the mausoleum was formerly a *memoria*.

UPON THE FEASTDAY OF THE HOLY MARTYR LAWRENCE

Apostolorum supparem
Laurentium archidiaconum
pari corona martyrum
Romana sacravit fides.

A truly Roman faith once crowned
with equal wealth of martyrs' fame,
Lawrence, who with the Holy Pair
wellnigh equality might claim.

Xystum sequens hic martyrem
responsa vatis retulit:
maerere, fili, desine,
sequere me post triduum.

While following in Sixtus' train
his fate was told in prophecy;
the martyr spoke: Grieve not, my son,
in three days you will follow me.

Nec territus poenae metu
heres futurus sanguinis
spectavit obtentu pio
quod ipse mox persolveret.

No fear of torment made him quail,
soon to become an heir in blood,
disguised, the deacon saw the pains
soon by himself to be withstood.

Iam tunc in illo martyre
egit triumphum martyris
successor aequus, syngraphum
vocis tenens et sanguinis.

Already in this martyr's death
he gained his own martyr's reward,
a worthy successor, who held
the covenant of his blood and word.

Post triduum iussus tamen
census sacratos prodere,
spondet pie nec abnuit
addens dolum victoriae.

Three days had passed when order came
the church's treasures to display,
he, adding guile to victory,
shrinks not, but hastens to obey.

Spectaculum pulcherrimum:
egena cogit agmina
inopesque monstrans praedicat:
hi sunt opes ecclesiae.

O see, what wondrous sight is this!
the poor he brings from far and near,
cries, pointing to their piteous band
these are the church's treasures here.

Verae piorum perpetes
inopes perfecto sunt opes:
avarus illusus dolet,
flammae et ultrices parat.

The pious, as abiding wealth
the treasureless his treasure claims:
the miser, cheated, mad with grief,
makes ready the avenging flames.

Fugit perustus carnifex
suisque cedit ignibus:
versate me, martyr vocat,
vorate, si coctum est, iubet.

The torturer recoils afraid,
draws back before the scorching heat,
come turn me now, the martyr cries,
and when the meal is cooked, then eat!

(Ambrosian hymn, shortly after A.D. 400)

For the legend and history see Ambrose, *De officiis ministrorum*, I, 41 : 204; Prudentius, *Peristephanon* 2, 28 : 120; Maximus of Turin, *Homily* 74.

491. VITALIS conducted into Paradise and presenting his wreath to Christ. Apse mosaic in his *memoria* (530-47). The Lord sits enthroned upon the orb of the world and holds in His hand the book sealed with seven seals (Rev. 4); under the throne are the four streams of Paradise. Right, Bishop Ecclesius of Ravenna (cf 459), with the model of the church he founded. *Ravenna, S. Vitale.*

492. AGNES OF ROME, Agatha of Catania, Pelagia of Antioch, Euphemia of Chalcedon, with the wreath of the virgin martyrs. Detail from the processional mosaic in S. Apollinare Nuovo, Ravenna (see 501).

493. VINCENT OF CAESARAUGUSTA (Zaragoza), Pancratius of Rome, Chrysogonus of Aquileia, Protus of Rome. *Ravenna, S. Apollinare Nuovo.*

494-5. THE MARTYRS of Salonae in Dalmatia. Mosaics in their *memoria* near the baptistery of the Lateran in Rome, where their relics were transferred by Pope John IV (640-2), himself a Dalmatian, after the invasion of Dalmatia by the Avars. The officers Paulinianus and Felius, the monk Asterius, the layman Anastasius; Bishop Maurus, Deacon Septimus, the officers Antiochianus and Gaianus. The patron saint, Bishop Venantius (the chapel is called S. Venanzio), is not depicted here.

492

493

494

495

499 a/b

500

496. COSMAS AND DAMIAN, the Persian physicians, being conducted into Paradise by SS. Peter and Paul, bringing Christ their wreaths. Mosaic in the apse of their *memoria*, founded by Pope Felix IV, 526-30, in two buildings on the Forum, rebuilt as one small basilica (cf **123**: the rotunda forms the entrance). The church is disfigured by a second floor at mid height and, as a result, the mosaic, the most beautiful in Rome, cannot be properly seen. The Lord, coming with the red clouds of the *Parousia*, above the stream of Paradise marked IORDANES, is crowned by the Hand of the Father. In the paradisal palms sits the bird of Paradise, the Phoenix, symbol of immortality. Left, the founder, Damian, and Paul; right, Peter, Cosmas, and the martyr Theodorus Tiro, the soldier. Theodorus' tomb was venerated at Ta Euchaita in Pontus, that of the 'silverless' ('Ανάργυροι, because they refused to accept money for their medical services) Cosmas and Damian, at Cyrrhus, in Syria Euphratensis (see Map 30/31). From Rome they have become universally venerated as the patrons of the medical profession.

497. MARTYR WITH HIS WREATH. Mosaic in the baptistery of Soter, beside the cathedral of Naples; *ca 400*. He is wearing white garments: one of the 'white host'.

498. PETER AND COSMAS (with his doctor's bag under the chasuble). Detail from **496**.

499ab, 500. THE MARTYRS OF MILAN. 499a: Felix. 499b. Nabor. 500. Victor. Two wall mosaics and the cupola mosaic in the *memoria* of Victor, now S. Vittore in ciel d'oro near S. Ambrogio in Milan; *ca 400*. The *memoria* was originally in a cemetery outside the wall on the southwest side of the city. The names on the monogram which Victor is holding are probably those of the founders. The saints were natives of Mauretania, suffered martyrdom at Laus Pompeia (Lodi) south of Milan, and are buried in Milan. On the mosaic they are not represented either as Moors or as soldiers.

Victor, Nabor, Felix, pii	Victor, Nabor, Felix, pious
Mediolani martyres,	martyrs of our town Milan,
solo hospites, Mauri genus,	of foreign birth and Moorish race,
terrisque nostris advenae.	they came as strangers to our land.
Torrens arena quos dedit,	They came from lands of burning sun,
anhela solis aestibus	the scorching desert gave them birth,
extrema terrae finium	beyond the confines of our Realm,
exsulque nostri nominis.	the very outposts of the earth.
Suscepit hospites Padus	Exacting payment of much blood
mercede magna sanguinis,	the Padus was their cruel host,
sancto replevit spiritu	the faith of Holy Mother Church
almae fides ecclesiae	infused them with the Holy Ghost
et se coronavit trium	and crowned herself with holy blood
cruore sacro martyrum	of three who shared a martyr's fate,
castrisque raptis impiis	snatched from the camps of pagan hosts,
Christo sacravit milites.	Christ's warriors now consecrate.
Profecit ad fidem labor:	Proficient in the arts of war
armisque docti bellicis	they learn to combat for the faith:
pro rege vitam ponere,	once for the king, but now, for Christ,
decere pro Christo pati.	they see 'tis meet to suffer death.
Non tela quaerunt ferrea	Christ's soldiers seek no iron spears,
non arma Christi milites:	no flashing arms by them are found:
munitus armis ambulat	sufficient armour hath that man
veram fidem qui possidet.	whose faith encompasseth him round.
Scutum viro suo est fides .	A shield to him is his true faith,
et mors triumphus. Quem invidens	a triumph, death. Malevolent,
nobis tyrannus ad oppidum	the jealous tyrant, seeing this,
Laudense misit martyres.	to Lodi our fair martyrs sent.
Sed reddiderunt hostias:	But soon the offer was returned
raptis quadrigis corpora	as on the triumphal car of state
revecti in ora principum	Four-spanned, the martyrs' bodies rode
plaustri triumphalis modo.	Back through th'imperial city gate.

(Ambrose)

The 'imperial city' is the court capital, Milan. For the triumphal reception of martyrs' relics (*translatio* and *depositio*) see **509**: here too, in Constantinople, the entry takes place in a triumphal chariot and in the presence of the Emperor.

With Nabor and Felix the usual martyrs' wreath is replaced by a Gospel codex. St Ambrose was perhaps responsible for this change. The crown of victory belongs, not to the individual, but to Him by whose power alone they were able to confront the enemy and to face death; to their Lord Jesus Christ. This is also the reason why, in the apse mosaics, they are shown as offering their crowns to the Lord (and not, as is usually said, receiving them from Him). They approach Him as their sovereign, with their hands covered in the conventional way (see **491, 496**):

"Christ alone wears the wreath of glory with which He was crowned by the Church. In this wreath are contained all others, since glory is no part of one wreath, but the reward of all." (Ambrose, *In Psalmum CXVIII expositio*, **15**, 11)

The restraint of the Bishops of Rome, who refused to touch the relics contained in their city's *memoriae*, contrasts sharply with the freedom with which the Greeks transferred the relics of their martyrs to other places, thus propagating the veneration of their martyrs for the faith throughout the whole of Christendom. Gregory the Great refused to send relics of the Apostles to the Greek Empress; he sent her instead pieces of material which had been laid upon the *confessio*. Nor did the Romans encourage the legends which were everywhere woven about the deaths of martyrs, of whom, according to the same Pope, nothing but the name was to be found in the archives. These legends, in the sixth and seventh centuries particularly, degenerated into fanciful, albeit pious, works of fiction. It is only after 600, too, that these works cease to contain any notion of historical criticism. In the time of Augustine and Ambrose, the authentic acta, whenever these were available, were read in the *memoriae* in both Africa and Milan upon the various anniversaries.

151

501

502   504   506

503   505   507

Here, facing and above, **501** and **508**, are the processions of martyrs introduced between 566 and 578 in the Palatine Church, now S. Apollinare Nuovo, in Ravenna, in place of the mosaics dating from the reign of King Theodoric (before 529), of which no trace remains. The other mosaics, the Life of Christ above the windows, and the prophets and Apostles in between, form part of the decoration executed in Theodoric's time.

Both series, taken together, constitute an iconographical calendar of the martyrs venerated in northern Italy at that time (cf Maps 30 and 31).

501. THE FEMALE MARTYRS bringing their wreaths to the Lord who, seated upon His Mother's lap, receives the gifts of the Magi. They are: Euphemia of Chalcedon, Pelagia of Antioch, Agatha of Catania, Agnes of Rome, Eulalia of Emerita (Mérida in Spain), Caecilia of Rome, Lucia of Syracuse, Crispina of Theveste in Africa, Valeria (of Milan?), Vincentia, Perpetua, and Felicitas of Carthage, Justina of Patavium (Padua), Anastasia of Sirmium in Pannonia, Daria of Rome (Via Salaria), Emerentiana of Rome (Via Nomentana), Paulina, Victoria, and Anatolia from the land of the Sabines, Cristina of Tyre (or perhaps of Bolsena?), Savina of Vindena, and Eugenia of Rome (Via Latina).

508. THE MARTYRS bearing their wreaths to Christ, enthroned and surrounded by a guard of angels. They are: Stephen of Jerusalem (disappeared after 1857), Martin, Bishop of Turones (Tours, †397), the only non-martyr or *confessor*, placed here as the new Catholic patron of the reconstructed church, the Popes Clement and Sixtus II with Lawrence the deacon, Hippolytus, the anti-pope who, converted, died, in Sardinia with Pope Cornelius, all of Rome; Cyprian, Bishop of Carthage († 258), Cassian, the schoolmaster of Forum Cornelii (Imola), John and Paul of Rome, Vitalis of Bononia (Bologna), Gervasius and Protasius of Mediolanum (Milan), Ursicinus from Illyricum, Nabor and Felix of Milan (see **499ab**), Apollinaris, the patron saint of Ravenna itself, Sebastian of Rome, Demetrius of Thessalonica (see **286**), Polycarp, Bishop of Smyrna († 155/6), Vincent of Caesaraugusta (Zaragoza), Pancratius of Rome,

Chrysogonus of Aquileia (venerated in Rome), Proteus and Hyacinthus of Rome, and Sabinus of Spoleto. All walk between the palm trees of Paradise from which red fruits hang against an abstract golden background. They are wrapped, the men in white, the women in golden stoles, and are veiled in white:

"There now, is the glorious choir of the Apostles . . . there the innumerable host of martyrs, crowned by virtue of the glory of their combat and passion and of their victory, there the triumphant virgins." (Cyprian of Carthage, *On Mortality*; 26)

502-7. IMAGINES CLIPEATAE. Round mosaic portraits in the shape of shields on the intrados of the apsidal arch in the chapel of the *episcopium* at Ravenna (see **230**); shortly after 494. They represent Christ, the Apostles, Gervasius and Protasius of Milan, and some of the virgin martyrs.

502. ANDREW, the 'first-called', venerated near his tomb at Patrae in Achaia; already a fixed type, with his head of thick, grey, tangled hair. **503.** Philip. **504.** Thaddaeus. **505.** Simon the Canaanite. **506.** Lucia of Syracuse. **507.** Caecilia of Rome.

509-13 on page 154. The veneration of martyrs in the Greek East.

509. TRANSLATION OF RELICS at Constantinople: ivory, 6th century. Two metropolitans, wearing the *pallium*, bear upon the triumphal chariot the *theca* containing the relics. They are preceded by the Emperor and court carrying torches. To the right is the *martyrion*, next to a basilica. The emperor hands his torch to the martyr (the woman with the Cross, = Euphemia?). Above the city gate is an icon of Christ; in the windows above the colonnade the faithful are swinging censers. *Trèves, Cathedral Treasure.*

510. MENAS, the national desert saint of Egypt, in his *martyrion* south of Alexandria; 11th century copy of an Alexandrian ivory of *ca* 600, at Grado; *Milan, Castello Sforzesco.* Images like this one have been found in many countries. He is wearing the tunic and *chlamys* of a soldier.

511. MARTYRION of the Apostle John at Ephesus in the province of Asia. Floor mosaic from the 5th century church, later covered by the cruciform, domed church of Justinian, which resembled the Apostoleion at Constantinople.

512. TOMB OF THE APOSTLE JOHN 'the Theologian' at Ephesus. Excavations reveal that a *memoria* existed here in the 3rd century; it lies between the later, 5th century basilica (see 511) and that built in the 6th, and lay outside the old city. The site was called Ayasuluk (ὁ ἅγιος Θεολόγος), since 1914 Selçuk. For the legends about the tomb and the 'manna' (dust taken by pilgrims from the opening), see Augustine, *The City of God*, 22, 8.

513. RUINS of Justinian's Church of St John at Ephesus.

THE SACRED IMAGES (514-556). The images of Christ, of His Mother, of the Apostles and Prophets, and also of the martyrs, made their appearance quite simply; first in disguised form, as symbols, and then, after 313, with obvious historical intent, as 'portraits'. Up to the end of the 6th century there was no question of such icons being venerated, although they were regarded with reverence—the same reverence as was given to images of the Emperor and of ancestors. Time and again voices were raised in protest against this 'portraiture'; Tertullian, *ca* 200, even objects to pictures of the Shepherd (on the chalices) and after 313, chiefly in the Syrian hinterland, it was the turn of the monks. A famous incident is that of Bishop Epiphanius of Salamis in Cyprus who, in Anablatha—a village in Palestine—tore down from a church door a curtain into which was woven a medallion portrait of Christ; he was obliged to pay for the damage. Protest was heard too among some semi-Arian prelates, including the church historian Eusebius, who wrote to Constantia, daughter of Constantine: no portraits, 'so that we may not give the appearance of carrying our God about with us in the form of an image, as do the idolaters'. (Eusebius, *Letter to Constantia*, 17)

Yet the images, reminders of the historicity of the Revelation and of the truth of the Incarnation, remained undisturbed until the crisis precipitated by the iconoclasm suddenly decreed in 726 by an Emperor of Byzantium. This crisis was resolved by the oecumenical episcopate with the pronouncement that: 'the sacred icons might receive the same degree of reverence as the Cross and the codices of the Holy Gospels'. (Second Council of Nicaea, A.D. 787)

Christ (514-540). The Shepherd in the 4th century, 514-518.

514. STATUETTE. *Rome, Museo delle Terme.*

515. PANEL in the mosaic floor of Aquileia (see **143**; *ca* 314-20). He is carrying a syrinx (shepherd's pipe) and wears a *clavicula* (shoulder cloak).

516. STATUETTE. *Rome, Museo Lateranense.*

517. STATUETTE from Old Corinth. *Athens, Byzantine Museum.*

518. SARCOPHAGUS, with sheepcotes and flock. *Pisa, Camposanto;* Christian or pagan?

After 400 the Shepherd disappears. The famous Ravenna mosaic which follows (see **519**) can be considered as a farewell. The quiet, bucolic, figure has become a divine Prince, who in a beautiful Hellenic attitude, his head encircled by golden ethereal light, clasps his jewel-studded cross. He plays the shepherd for the last time in the dim mausoleum,

517

8

glittering with gold mosaic, built in the corner of a court capital which soon, like a dead city, solitary and forgotten, will preserve this last splendour of classical Christian Antiquity.

Here follow, page 156, the last Shepherds.

519. LUNETTE above the door in the so-called mausoleum of Galla Placidia, Ravenna; 450. See page 63.

520. FOUR PORTRAITS OF CHRIST. Front of the *lipsanotheca* (shrine for relics) in the Museo Civico in Brescia; *ca* 370 (?). On the lid, the young, idealised figure of Christ between Peter, Paul, and two other Apostles. Also: Christ speaking to the woman with the issue of blood, lecturing as Teacher in a public building, and, in the same teacher's dress, defending the sheep-fold against the wolf while the hireling flees.

Below: Christ the Teacher and heavenly King.

521. THE TEACHER in the celestial city, enthroned amid the Twelve; the new, bearded figure, of which the origin is unknown, but which appears here for the first time in a work of the Theodosian renaissance. Sarcophagus of Concordius (see **528**), central figure. *Arles, Musée lapidaire chrétien.*

522. THE TEACHER enthroned above the heavens (upon the celestial veil of Coelus), handing the Law to Peter; left, Paul. Upper central niche, sarcophagus of the city prefect of Rome, Junius Bassus, who was baptised and died in 358. The inscription reads: *neofitus iit ad Deum*, 'newly baptised, he went to God'.

523. STATUETTE, *ca* 350, the Teacher (cf **529**). *Rome, Museo delle Terme.*

524. THE TEACHER. Ivory pyx; *ca* 400. Syro-Egyptian? The throne and pose elevate this symbolic portrait to something more than the classical cliché of the school of rhetoric or philosophers' dispute. *Berlin, Staatliche Museen.*

525. THE TEACHER ENTHRONED in the heavenly Jerusalem. From the apse mosaic of S. Pudenziana, Rome, shortly after 400. Golden light plays about the head—here Semitic, bearded—and there is a purple *velum* over the back of the jewelled throne. The neck and breast, and the left side of the throne, have been very much restored.

526. THE TEACHER with the Twelve Apostles. Ivory, *ca* 400, from northern Italy. The Cross appears here in the aureole about the head; the beginning of the 'cross halo'. The leather cylinder for the scrolls stands in the middle of the circle of the disciples. *Dijon, Musée.*

The Theodosian period, however, brings forth three compositions in which Christ the Teacher is no longer depicted as a sage among his disciples in an auditorium, but amid supernatural surroundings: the heavenly city, or else the Paradise restored where flow the new streams of life. The two finest follow here: the Thirteen Thrones, and the *Dominus legem dat* (pp. 158, 159).

In the sermon literature of this period we also find the theme of Christ the heavenly king, sometimes a warlike king:

"We beseech Thee, O Lord, our God, Spirit eternal, and Christ, our Lord and King, hold Thy mighty hands protectingly above Thy holy Church, and above Thy holy people that are always Thine. Guard and protect them, fight and wage war for them, subdue all their enemies, conquering with invisible power those who set themselves up against Thee. And, since Thou hast also defeated our enemies, set up now Thyself for us the trophies of victory, and grant that we may sing with Moses the song of victory: for Thine is the power and the glory, for ever and ever, Amen." (*Paschal Homilies*, I, 63, ed. Nautin)

The warrior against the forces of evil, against Satan, the opponent of God, did not, however, inspire in the plastic arts any image other than that of the Lord crushing the adder and the basilisk and treading upon the lion and the serpent (that is: hell and death), the motif of Ps. 91 (LXX 90).

BEATI AECIDII
SEPVLCHRVM

527. THE TEACHER ENTHRONED amidst the enthroned Twelve in the heavenly city of Jerusalem. Theodosian sarcophagus; *ca* 380. At the Lord's feet stands the Lamb, venerated by the deceased man and his wife. On the lid, surrounding the portrait of the couple, are the Three Youths refusing to adore the statue of Nebuchadnezzar and, as a pendant, the Three Wise Men, in the same Chaldaean costume, performing the true act of adoration before the Child in Bethlehem. *Milan, S. Ambrogio* (under the ambo, difficult to see).

528. THE TEACHER in the Heavenly City. Sarcophagus of Concordius; *ca* 390. Here, the deceased couple, named in the inscription on the lid, are conducted into Paradise by a male and female saint, and they approach their sovereign with hands covered. Four of the Apostles are holding books; it was only very much later that the names of the evangelists were inscribed upon them. Upon the lid are scenes which have not yet been deciphered; perhaps a gathering of ecclesiastical writers. *Arles, Musée lapidaire chrétien.*

529. THE TEACHER ENTHRONED upon the arch of heaven, between the Church and the Apostles. Sarcophagus; *ca* 360. One of the finest of the 4th century sarcophagi, with magnificent heads and a majestic *Mater Ecclesia*. *Perugia, San Bernadino.*

530-33. Specimens of the composition *Dominus legem dat*, which most probably originated in Rome as an apse motif but which is also found in Milan and the surrounding district. Standing upon the new Sinai, upon the hill of Paradise, between the celestial palms with the Phoenix, Our Lord transmits the New Law of the New Testament to the New Moses, Peter (but cf 269). The Prince of the Apostles is always recognisable by his cast of feature and by the Cross predicted to him by Our Lord himself (John 21), the sign of his passion at Rome:

"You [Peter] have carried the trophy of the Cross of Christ within the ramparts of the city of Rome, whither, according to divine decree, both the honour of governmental power and the glory of the passion had preceded you." (Leo the Great, '*Homily on the Apostles*', *Sermons*, **82**, 5)

530. DOMINUS LEGEM DAT PETRO, here, however, enthroned upon the arch of heaven spanned by Coelus and surrounded by a prefiguration and evocation of the Passion: the sacrifice of Isaac and the confusion of Pilate. Sarcophagus with the famous side panels shown in 175-6. *Rome, Museo Lateranense.*

531. DOMINUS LEGEM DAT PETRO. Sarcophagus of Gorgonius; *ca* 380. The deceased clasp Christ's feet as suppliants. The hill of the transmission of the Law is surrounded, not by the trees of Paradise, but by the celestial city. *Ancona, Cathedral.*

532. DOMINUS LEGEM DAT PETRO. Lid of an ivory casket. North Italian; *ca* 440. Below, the lamb allegory which here, as well as in later copies found in the vicinity of Rome, repeats the main composition. The Lamb stands upon the hill, and from the sheepcotes (which represent the Churches of the Circumcision and of the Gentiles), the twelve lambs hurry towards it, to drink from the four streams. Formerly *Pola, Museo Civico.*

533. DOMINUS LEGEM DAT PETRO. Mosaic in the cupola of the baptistery of Soter at Naples; *ca* 400. Here the Lord stands among the palms of Paradise, upon the orb of the world.

534   535   536

Christ's facial type (534-40).

Towards the end of the 4th century, alongside the youthful, idealised type common up till now, a type which, technically, owes much to stereotypes like Eros and the young Bacchus, although often presenting a distinctive hair style there unexpectedly appears a bearded face, sometimes Semitic, sometimes resembling that of Aesculapius. This finally develops into a clearly defined facial type, influenced perhaps by legends concerning the 'images made by no human hands'. Yet, even around 400, St Augustine writes decisively and positively: 'We do not know His face, any more than that of His Mother'. Until late in the Romanesque Middle Ages, the youthful and bearded types continue to exist side by side. In the Greek East, on the contrary, after 500, in scenes devoted to His public life, Passion and glorification, Our Lord is always bearded and depicted according to a carefully defined set of rules.

534. SARCOPHAGUS; *ca* 350-60. *Rome, Museo Lateranense, No. 138.*

535. CHRIST AT CANA. Sarcophagus; *ca* 320. *Rome, Museo Lateranense, No. 122*

536. SARCOPHAGUS (see **530**); *ca* 350. *Rome, Museo Lateranense No. 174.*

537. NAVE MOSAIC in S. Apollinare Nuovo, Ravenna. Cross in the aureole, long hair, youthful features; before 529.

538. CHAPEL OF S. PRISCO near S. Maria Capua Vetere in Campania; 5th century mosaic-lunette. The new type: portrait in the form of a *clipeus*. Typical Christ icon prior to the Iconoclasm.

539. THE HEALING of the two blind men. Detail from a miniature in the *evangeliarium* from Sinope in Pontus. Severe, expressive head (here very much enlarged) only conceivable in a miniature accompanying a narrative text. *Paris, Bibliothèque nationale.*

540. IMAGO CLIPEATA of Christ in the centre of the Cross shown in **470**. Apse mosaic in S. Apollinare in Classe; 532-6.

537
538   539   540

The Mother of God (541-546)

Images of the Virgin begin to attract our attention after the Council of Ephesus in 431, at which the Church Fathers declared her *Theotokos*, the 'God-bearing'. In the years that follow, she is seen in Rome as a queen, *domina*, wearing the purple *palla*, white veil of byssus, with pendants in her ears and glittering with precious stones. Yet her definitive portrait emerges from the East, perhaps from Palestine or from Constantinople. There she is a tranquil, mature, figure, wrapped from head to foot in a dark blue mantle and veil (*maphorion*, later a relic venerated in the church of the Blachernae at Constantinople) with shoes upon her feet and a *sudarium* loose upon her girdle. She is always shown in one of three positions: standing (see 544); frontally enthroned with her Child upon her knee (see 542, 546); or else alone, standing in an attitude of prayer, with outstretched arms, a symbol of the Church, ever persevering in prayer. This last image is first found in pictures of the Ascension (cf 384), where she clearly represents the Church left behind, persisting in faith and prayer, amid the troubled Apostles (cf Acts 1:14). Examples from Palestine: 321-23; from Constantinople: 252, 542.

Constantinople was known as 'her own city'. Thence originate the names for the three classical types: the enthroned *Nikopoia*, the standing *Hodigitria*, and the praying *Blachernitissa* (in other words, that of the 'Bringer of Victory', of 'Conductress of the blind' and that 'of the church of the Blachernae'; cf Map 37 where the three sanctuaries are marked).

541. THE ANNUNCIATION. Mosaic from the triumphal arch of S. Maria Maggiore, Rome. After 431. The queen; she is spinning purple in the Temple.

542. THE GREEK TYPE, enthroned. Ivory; 6th century. Sun and moon above; one of the angels holds the celestial globe. A preparatory phase of the *Nikopoia*.

543. THE PRESENTATION in the Temple; as 541. The queen. S. Maria Maggiore.

544. SYRIAC CODEX of Rabbula, Fol. 89; *ca* 586. Type of the later *Hodigitria*. Florence, Laurenziana.

545. APSE MOSAIC in Santa Sophia, detail (see 252). *Nikopoia*; 859, restored 14th c.

546. VOTIVE FRESCO OF TURTURA in the catacomb of Commodilla, Rome; 6th century. The Mother of God enthroned between the martyrs Felix and Adauctus who lie buried there. Turtura, the donor, offers wax tapers, with covered hands. Everywhere in the 7th century one notices the pleated white cap under Mary's dark head veil.

541

542

543

544

545

546

551

Peter and Paul (547-551)

From 313 onwards we find, everywhere recognisable, the conventional portrait heads of Peter and Paul, which probably originated in Rome.

547. PETER (= Moses) taken prisoner. Sarcophagus; *ca* 350. Rome, *Museo Lateranense*.

548. PETER AND PAUL with XP monogram. Bronze coin; 4th century. *Vatican, Museo Cristiano*.

549. ROUGH RELIEF in the museum of Aquileia. Left, Peter; right, Paul.

550. PETER (this type, with beard and fringe of hair encircling the head, persists). Sarcophagus, right corner niche; 4th century. *Rome, Museo Lateranense*.

551. DOMINUS LEGEM DAT PETRO; the transmission of the Law to the new Moses in the heavenly city upon the hill of Paradise; *ca* 380. Sarcophagus. For the composition, cf above, page 159. *Arles, Musée lapidaire chrétien*.

For early Christendom, the splendour of Christian Rome was almost exclusively bound up with the graves of Peter and Paul. Rome was the 'Apostolic See' par excellence, more than Ephesus, more than Antioch. Even in the Greek East they were familiar with the passage from the letter written by Clement of Rome, *ca* 96:

"Yet let us speak no more now of the old models [from the Old Testament] but turn to the fighters who are nearest to our times. Let us take the noblest models for our generation. Through jealousy and envy even the greatest and most righteous pillars of our faith were persecuted and were obliged to struggle unto death. Let us turn in thought to the brave Apostles. Peter, who, the victim of unjust envy, had to withstand not one or two, but many trials and so, after having borne testimony [for the faith] departed hence to the place of glory which he had merited. Paul too, as a result of envy, was able to show the victory of patience. After having been seven times in chains, after having been banished and stoned, and after having been the herald of the faith in East and West, he entered upon the true glory of his faith. After having preached justice throughout the whole world, even going to the far West [Spain?], after having testified before those in authority, he left this world and went to the heavenly place—after having been the greatest model of patience." (Clement, *To the Corinthians*, 5)

On the 29th of June Rome was black with pilgrims come to visit the Apostles' tombs, for that day was considered of old as the day of their death. People travelled to the basilica on the Vatican, to the basilica on the Via Ostiensis, and to that on the Via Appia (cf page 47):

> Since then fair Roman glory shines
> In godliness eclipsing all,
> Founded anew by Holy blood [allusion to Romulus and Remus]
> By Peter noble and by Paul.
>
> Throughout th'entire city crowd
> The multitudes in close array,
> On three of Rome's immortal roads [Viae Cornelia, Ostiensis, Appia]
> The martyrs' people feast this day.
>
> The world seems gathered here today;
> In concourse all the faithful come
> To her who is all peoples' head,
> Seat of all peoples' master - Rome.
>
> (Ambrose (?), *On the Feast of the Apostles*)

The first icons (552-556)

The oldest icons that we possess date from the end of the fifth and from the sixth century and are found only in or around Egypt, notably in that safe, secluded spot, Sinai. They form the earliest examples of small, portable portraits of holy persons and are painted in wax colours upon carefully prepared wood. From the point of view of art history, they link up with the later imperial portraits and, more immediately, with the family portraits which in Egypt were painted upon small pieces of wood and affixed to the outer shroud of the mummies of the deceased. (A remarkable series of such portraits has been discovered in the region of Lake Moeris, modern Faiyum in Egypt, left of the Nile valley.)

The mosaics high up in the apsidal arches or upon the clerestory walls were naturally not the object of a special cult, nor were the frescoes beneath the porticoes ever venerated. They formed merely an impressive, instructive, and edifying scheme of decoration. The small icons, however, placed at eye level in the churches, forming a sufficiently evident contrast with the plastic portrait busts of pagan Antiquity and made vivid by that typically Christian innovation —the wide, intense gaze, testifying to a profound inner life—became, we know not where or when, something more than mementos. They were considered as a symbolic evocation, and even representation, of the individual venerated and, given the already established invocation of the saints, became objects before which people came to pray. Face to face with the intense features of the icons, which were decorated (as of old were portraits of the Emperor and kinsmen) with candles and costly fabrics, people prayed to the saints whom they portrayed. By the seventh century this practice was general throughout the Eastern Roman Empire. In the hinterlands, on the contrary, people still clung to the old, abstract symbols—the monogram of the Lord and, above all, the Cross. The Nestorians continued to do so and also, for a long time, the Christians living in Armenia and Georgia.

552. THE MOTHER OF GOD enthroned with two martyrs. Encaustic icon (painted in wax colour) from the monastery of St Catherine at Sinai. Both the angels in the background have been restored.

553. THE MOTHER OF GOD. Remains of an encaustic icon recently discovered beneath later coats of paint on an icon in S. Maria Nova (S. Francesca Romana on the Forum), Rome; 7th century, origin unknown.

554. THE APOSTLE PETER holding the keys of the Kingdom and the cross of his martyrdom. In the background, an *exedra*. Above; the *clipei* of Moses, Christ, and the Mother of God. From the monastery on Sinai; 7th century. The facial type does not differ from the Roman. This well-preserved icon, one of the most beautiful of Antiquity, is of Egyptian origin.

555. THE MARTYRS SERGIUS AND BACCHUS, with a small *clipeus* of Christ. An Egyptian icon, discovered on Mount Sinai by Bishop Porfirii Uspensky and now in the museum of what was formerly the Ecclesiastical Academy, Kiev; 6th century. Both saints, officers, died during the reign of Diocletian, in Coelesyria. The sanctuary of Sergius, in the desert city of Resafe (see 441), also called Sergiopolis, was known throughout the Christian world. Justinian built a large church in their honour in the capital. Each has a golden *manakion* about his neck – insignia of officers of the Guard. In the East, from now on, martyrs will no longer be depicted upon the icons as wearing a wreath, but as holding a stylised Cross. This feature will persist for centuries on the Russian icons.

556. CHRIST AND MENAS. Painting in tempera on wood, from the inland monastery of Apollo at Bawit in the Nile Valley. Example of Coptic popular monastic art. *Paris, Louvre.*

ΑΓΙΟC ΘΕΟCΕΒΗC
ΕΥΤΡΟΠΟC ΕΝΙ ΡΗΝΗ
ΥΙΟC ΕΠΟΙΗCΕΝ Κ ΠΙ Κ CΕΠ

THE CEMETERIES AND THE EPITAPHS (557-568). Nearly all the Christian necropolises of which some trace remains date, in all ancient lands from after 313. So do four-fifths of the Roman catacombs. The later cemeteries naturally lack the moving atmosphere of the earlier which date from the times of persecution; they are just ordinary cemeteries. The places where the martyrs rested were made accessible to all and decorated in a fitting manner. Thousands bought themselves a grave near the *memoriae* and especially near those above ground; for everyone wished to rest *ad sanctos*, 'near the saints'. 'If this can incite visitors to prayer, then it is good', wrote St Augustine, 'otherwise it is vain.' The Roman catacombs were famous, and became the goal of pilgrims and tourists.

"When I lived in Rome as a young boy and went to school there, I used to wander about the tombs of the Apostles with a few companions from the same class, and often descended in particular into the burial corridors hollowed out deep under the ground. On entering, one finds the walls on both sides of the corridors filled with tombs and it is so dark that one almost imagines the words of the Psalmist to have been fulfilled: Let them go down to Sheol alive [Ps. 55:15]. Only here and there does one catch a gleam of light which mitigates the icy darkness so faintly that one imagines, not a window, but rather light filtering through some chink, and amid the pitch darkness the line of Virgil rises to one's mind: 'Cold terror bears you on: the very silence is full of horror' [*Aeneid* 2, 755]." (Jerome, *On Ezechiel* 12, 40, A.D. 354-60)

557. CATACOMB of the Jordani; corridor; 4th century. Frescoes: left, a section of the Teacher amidst the Apostles, Jonah in the place of refreshment, Daniel, the sacrifice of Isaac; the old scenes of deliverance.

558. IBID. Frescoes: Lazarus, Shepherd, *anima in pace*.

559. TOMB OF THE SCULPTOR EUTROPOS, *ca* 300. Left: the toast to the departed during the funeral meal (πίε, ζήσης! drink, live!), father and son working with the drill; right, sarcophagus with the inscription: Eutropos. Epitaph: 'the holy and pious Eutropos, in peace. His son made this. The laying to rest [Κατάθεσις] took place on the tenth day before the calends of September.' *Urbino, Museo*.

560. WALL PAINTING, 4th century, catacomb of Thraso (or, of Maximus, see Map 28). Upper row: water from the rock, the Lord with seven bread baskets, the Adoration of the Magi, the deceased (a mother with two boys, hence the three *loculi*), Noah in the Ark. Second zone: Daniel, Tobias with the fish, and the angel accompanying Tobias on his journey, Job in wretchedness; between, Lazarus. The fresco was later broken through to make room for the large *loculus* and for the lamp niche.

Facing: epitaphs after 313, from the Roman catacombs.

561. SEMNE, ORA PRO TOUOS. (Name is Latin, invocation is Latin with Greek characters): Holy One, pray for your own.

562. 'DEMETRIS and LEONTIA to their daughter Sirica, the well-deserving. Be mindful, Lord Jesus, of our child.' (Half Latin, half Greek.) Beginning of the 4th century.

563. 'VI[C]TOR[I]A IN PEACE'.

564. 'KALIMERUS (or -A), may God refresh your spirit, together with that of your sister Hilara.'

565. '[OUR] DEAR TYCHE'. She lived one year, ten months, and fifteen days. She was baptised on the eighth day before the calends of ... She died on the following day.' Child baptism on the death-bed, practised everywhere at this time.

566. 'ROMULIESIA erected this; the mother for her dear son who departed in peace, an innocent child; laid to rest the ninth day before the calends of August. [Received] by God [into paradise? Cf symbols]'.

567. 'HE DIED as a little boy, his name was Dulcisus. He lived five years and six months.'

568. 'FATHER OF ALL, thou hast taken unto thyself those whom thou didst create: Irene, Zoe, and Marcellus. To you be honour in Christ.' (Greek) They probably passed away together as the result of an accident or in an epidemic.

A few other epitaphs, not illustrated, from the same period:

'Wife, who now enjoy eternal peace, you were fearful of the suffering of this world and hastened therefore to the abodes of light. There, as one of the elect, you now receive your merited reward. But by this separation you have hurt us cruelly, now that the children can no longer see you. Lighten, therefore, we pray you, our grief, now that you have entered upon your heavenly reward, admitted to the holy places, every time that you address your prayers to Christ.' (Epitaph upon a mother, Diehl, *Inscriptiones Latinae Christianae veteres*, 2, 3348)

'Here lie I, a child. I have had no part in life. The firstborn of a dear father and a beautiful mother, two years old, beloved of God, a sunny darling, bringing grief to my good and worthy parents.' Upon a child's tomb. *Villa Giustiniani, Rome*.

'Anatolis, our firstborn, given to us for but a short time, pray for us.' Upon a child's tomb in Velletri (Cardinali, 145).

> Many marbles are mute, they close a silent
> tomb, and only show their number infinite.
> (Prudentius [on the catacombs], *Peristephanon* 11, 9-10)

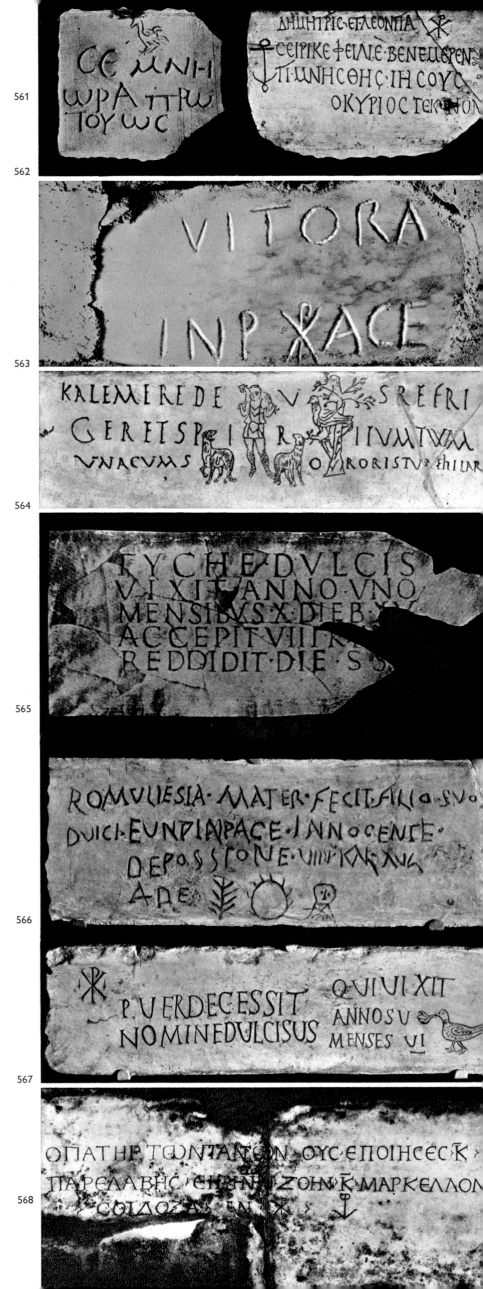

561

562

563

564

565

566

567

568

THE AFTER-LIFE (569-580). Of the subtle, veiled motifs of the time of the persecutions—the 'soul in peace' in the Paradise garden of the Shepherd, the meal of the Seven with loaves and fishes, the refreshment symbolised by the shadow of the *cucurbita* above the sleeping Jonah—only one element remains after 313: the *anima in pace*. The praying figure (with hands upraised, formerly called 'orans'), changes into a portrait which becomes increasingly clear. Often it stands between lighted candelabra, the first expression of the *locus lucis*, the place of light.

569. GOLD GLASS (the bottom of a drinking cup, used at the funeral meal and as a memento). *Anima in pace* in the garden of Paradise. Inscription: ZESES VIVAS DVLCIS ANIMA MARA = 'Live [Greek], live [Latin], sweet soul. Mara [Maria?]'. *Vatican, Museo Cristiano.*

570. GRAFFITO upon a tombstone from the catacombs. Doves with the olive branch, *anima in pace*: a portrait. *Rome, Museo Lateranense.*

571. GOLD GLASS. *Anima in pace.* From the inscription AGNE one can perhaps assume that it is a memento from Agnes' *memoria*. *Vatican, Museo Cristiano.*

572. MOTHER AND CHILD. Fresco on an *arcosolium* lunette. *Coemeterium Maius* on the Via Nomentana, near Rome; 4th century. The twice repeated monogram XP above the praying figure of the woman makes it impossible to suppose that this famous fresco represents the Mother of Christ. The intense, spiritual gaze is, from the very beginning, the hallmark of the Christian figures; in this respect this fresco deserves the reputation it enjoys.

573. ANIMA IN PACE in the Shepherd's garden of Paradise; left, the Shepherd milking. Beginning of the 4th century; a reminder of the 3rd.

574-576. From the catacomb of Januarius at Naples. All after 400.

574. THEOTECNUS, Ilarias, and their daughter of almost three, Nonnosa. The burning torches indicate the *locus lucis*. The inscription on the arch gives the dates of death, the three other dates give the ages of the departed.

575. PROCULUS in the *locus lucis*. Inscription: HIC REQVIISCET PROCVLVS: Here lies Proculus.

576. VITALIA with the codices of the four Gospels (the book markers are hanging out), and the monogram of Christ. BITALIA IN PACE. Beginning of the 5th century.

577/579   578/580

A new motif—after *ca* 360—is the conducting of the deceased into the heaven-ly city (see 577 and 578) by an angel or saint.

577. CONCORDIUS conducted into the heavenly Jerusalem by an unknown saint. The twelve Apostles sit enthroned with the Teacher, Christ. The deceased approaches his heavenly king with hands covered. Sarcophagus of Concordius (see **528**). *Arles, Musée lapidaire chrétien.*

578. VENERANDA conducted into the garden of Paradise by the martyr Petronella, near whose grave she rests. Fresco upon a tomb in the catacomb of Domitilla, behind the basilica where Petronella is venerated, together with Nereus and Achilleus. The deceased woman is veiled and her hands are raised in prayer. Left, the garden of Paradise. The saint points to the scrolls of the Holy Scripture in the leather cylinder; above, a codex. Beside the deceased: 'Vene-randa, laid to rest the eighth day before the Ides of January'; beside the saint: 'Petronella martyr'. The deceased is wearing the dalmatic, the saint the palla.

579. THE REFRESHMENT: Jonah in the shadow of the *cucurbita*. From the floor mosaic in the cathedral of Aquileia, 314-20. The 3rd century motif.

580. CEILING FRESCO in a burial chamber of the *Coemeterium Maius*, Rome. Beginning of the 4th century. The surrounding motifs are also the ones well-known from before 313.

MONASTIC LIFE (581–592ab; cf Map 34.)

When the really ardent Christians could no longer testify with their blood, and the crowds of opportunists and conformists had begun to fill the basilicas, many of the best among the faithful sought a new means of testifying (*martyr-ium*), no longer by a bloody death, but by a life that bore testimony to Christ. Thus did the spiritual life, *vita spiritalis*, originate as a mode of existence. It began as a separation from the world, in the Egyptian desert, for the spiritual man was, after all, a solitary (*monachus*). The man who laid the foundations of monastic life, first as a hermit, then as guide and teacher of great multitudes of like-minded Christians, so becoming the distant forefather of the later monas-ticism, was Anthony.

"Anthony was an Egyptian by birth, the son of a well-to-do family. His parents lacked for nothing, and, as Christians, they gave him a Christian educa-tion.... After the death of his parents he remained alone with a little sister. He was then about eighteen or twenty years of age and had the care of the house and of his sister. Not six months had passed after his parents' death when, while going to church as was his custom, he started to ponder on the way upon how the Apostles, leaving all, had followed the Saviour, and how others, according to the Acts of the Apostles, had sold all their possessions and had laid the proceeds at the feet of the Apostles to be distributed among the poor. And he reflected upon the reward awaiting such men in heaven. Filled with this idea he entered the church. And it happened that just at that moment, that part of the Gospel was being read in which he heard the Lord say to the rich man: If you would be perfect, go, sell what you possess and give to the poor, and you will have treas-ure in heaven; and come, follow me [Matt. 19:21]. And Anthony, as though he had received this admonition of the saintly writers from God himself, and as though it had been read especially for him, left the church and gave the property which he had inherited from his parents to the villagers—it consisted of three hundred plots of good and fertile land—so that neither he nor his sister should be troubled with it further. He sold all his goods, and having received a great deal of money for them, he distributed this money among the poor, keeping a little of it for his sister." (Athanasius, *Life of Anthony*, 1-2)

168

581

582

583

He then retired into a rock tomb where he 'fought against the demons'. He was unlettered and spoke only Coptic. Later he went to live in the desert east of the Nile, and his fame was so great that he was consulted in the struggle against the Arian heresy and the Emperor wrote to him. He died, a centenarian, about 356. Athanasius' *Life of Anthony* had already been translated into Latin in 388, by Evagrius of Antioch. In 386 Augustine heard in Milan how officials of the court of Trèves had retired from the world after having read the Greek *Life*. Anthony was the founder of the μονή, the dwelling (in the desert) of anchorites living alone in caves and cells and only coming together for the religious services. The founder of the 'communal life' (κοινός βίος), the coenobitic monasticism proper, was another Egyptian, Pachomius. First a soldier, then baptised, and the disciple of an anchorite, he founded the first walled 'cloister' (walled place) at Tabennisi opposite Dendera in 320 (see Map 34). When he died, in 346, thousands were living in monasteries. Economically speaking, these were collective enterprises (basket weaving, agriculture) but what really filled the lives of the monks was prayer, the reading of the Scriptures, and the practice of 'asceticism', that is, bodily mortification through vigil and fasting. From this time onwards 'the deserts on either side of the Nile re-echoed to the singing of the Psalms'.

581-2. DEIR EL-MEDINAH ('the monastery of the city') near Luxor. A Ptolemaic temple later converted into a monastery with encircling wall and storehouses.

583. TÉBESSA IN NUMIDIA. Monastery, founded in the 6th century, near the 4th century basilica (rebuilt in the 6th). Cf 352.

584. SBAITA, IN THE NEGEB (the desert south of Judaea). 6th century monastery church. The rest of the complex still exists as a ruin.

584

169

"Letter from our father Pachomius to all the monasteries. All heads of houses and directors of monasteries must assemble in the monastery called Bav [Pbov] on the twentieth day of the month, which among the Egyptians is called Mesore, so that the remission of all sins and deeds may be accomplished according to the rite. The time approaches when you must all come together according to an old custom, according to ancient usage, so that the remission of all may take place according to the rite; so that you may all forgive one another and that each one, according to the evangelical command, may forgive the trespasses of his brother and the quarrels and feuds. And if there be any dispute, this must be settled by the company of holy men. Each one must free his heart in the fear of God, falsehood must be banished and truth reign. Conflicts must be brought to an end and the calm of peace return, and in this peace you must be able to walk before the face of God and man. You must love all men equally, serve God in harmony, and not be slaves to changing desires, to the roving of the eyes, to the deceits of puffed-up knowledge and the sins of the flesh. For these give rise to disruption: contempt for the law of God, quarrels, evil thoughts which, bubbling upon the fire of the passions, boil over like water and are spattered like foam in the lusts of the flesh. For this was the law of God written, that the law and rights of the flesh might be abolished, that they who walk in concupiscence might be ashamed and return to God in the end; so that, despising the temporal, they might seek the eternal, preparing themselves thus for the inheritance of the saints, who counted our present life as but little and kept their minds fixed upon the world to come, putting their hope in good rather than in evil, in peace and harmony rather than in dissension and discord, in the service of God rather than in the works of the flesh. You must strive after that which is pleasing to God, surmounting the temptations of the flesh. For it is written: For if you forgive men their trespasses, your heavenly Father will also forgive you [Matt. 6:14] . . . .

Let us then reflect, dearly beloved brethren, with how much testimony [of the Scriptures] the believer is hemmed about by God, so that he may not sin, if he will but listen to His law and lend an ear to His precepts, keep his eyes open and so direct his heart that he is able to accomplish what is required of him. For there are many who wish to do good, who seek God with tears, sighing night and day, yet who, deluded by the desires of the eyes and overcome by the pricking of the flesh, depart this life amid sighs and anguish of heart because they could not remain master of their bodies, nor curb the promptings of their unruly thoughts. And thus they strive after vain and fleeting things instead of what is permanent and lasting . . . . They see where the truth lies, but are overcome by falsehood.

And therefore they sigh, according to the sayings of the Prophets, and vacillate in continual fear until they yield and languish in the path they have chosen, and pass away in torment. But they who are truly just, and walk in peace, enjoy eternal bliss." (Pachomius, *Letters*, 7; Jerome's translation)

585. MAR SABA on the Wadi en-Nar, southeast of Jerusalem, the famous 'Grand Laura' (*laura*: a colony of anchorites under an abbot) founded by S. Sabbas († 532) in 492. He was a disciple of Euthymius the Great who introduced Egyptian monasticism into Palestine. Cyril of Scythopolis and John of Damascus, the 8th century Church Father, later lived here.

586. ANCHORITES' DWELLINGS (μοναί) on the eastern flank of the Jebel Beqa' (Lebanon) in the south of Phoenice Libanensis (see Map 15a).

Immediately after it had come into being monasticism spread from Egypt over the whole of the Christian East: to Syria, Palestine, Cappadocia, Mesopotamia, and Armenia. From this time onwards the East, already the land of the Holy Places, attracted all those pilgrims who sought the 'spiritual life' and wished to see the great models. They went first of all to Tabennisi and Pbov, and, somewhat later, especially to the Scetis, the communities living in the Natron valley south of Alexandria (Wadi Natrun). But they also went to the desert near Chalcis in Syria; even in the Holy Places they found ascetics of the same kind. Before long these ascetics began to dominate Church life, at least in the East. For whole multitudes, in a society which, while possessing compulsory magistrature and military service, allowed the ordinary citizen no say at all in political affairs, sought in the monasteries as much the opportunity to give free development to their personality as to adopt a radically Christian way of life. No emperor succeeded, either by law or by any other means, in stemming this exodus of the best members of the community.

For it was precisely the best who could not resist the attraction of this new way of life. They all received their schooling from the monks: the two Gregories, Eustathius, and Basil. It was Basil who made the Egyptian ideal practicable for cultured Greeks: his Rule is still followed by the Greek monks. But the same was true of the Westerners: Jerome journeyed to the East and remained there as a monk in Bethlehem, with his friends the aristocratic Roman ladies who also became *moniales* (nuns). Ambrose and Augustine introduced the monastic way of life into their own episcopal houses; Cassian brought it to Marseille, Honoratus to the isle of Lerins, unknown monks to Britain, and Patrick to Ireland. The movement aroused opposition: the pagans hated the 'obscurantist rabble' who always lent a helping hand in demolishing temples in the East, and even Christian Rome refused the ascetics admittance. Jerome was obliged to leave 'Babylon' disappointed.

The man who rendered possible for the Latins the sober ideal of the desert fathers, in a land where there were no deserts at an hour's distance from the towns, and no Egyptian sun, this man was, in the beginning of the sixth century, the young Roman nobleman, Benedict of Nursia. His wise *Regula*, intended for the needs of a retiring community who wished to live the *vita spiritalis* in an impoverished land during a period of catastrophe, became the abiding code for those communities which, in still more difficult times and in isolated countries, ensured the continuity of Early Christian culture and made possible the culture of the Middle Ages.

587-90. THE MONASTIC SANCTUARY of Qalat Sem'an (cf **294-300**). **587.** Storeyed construction (monastery or guest-house). **588.** Base of the pillar of St Simeon. **589.** The monastery church. **590.** The octagon surrounding the pillar.

587/589

588/590

591

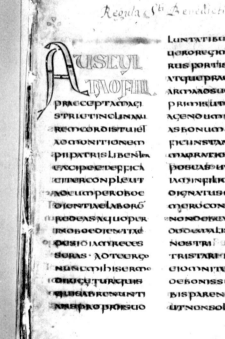

592 a

592 b

"Listen, my son, to the precepts of the master and incline the ear of your heart. Accept willingly the exhortations of a loving father and fulfil them with care so that, in the effort of obedience, you may find the way back to Him from whom you had strayed through the weakness of disobedience. My words are directed to you, whoever you may be, who, renouncing your own will in order to serve Christ the Lord, the true king, take up the mighty and glorious weapons of obedience. First of all: whatever good work you may undertake, beseech Him, in ardent prayer, that He may bring it to a good end, so that He, who already looks upon us as His sons, need never be afflicted by our evil deeds. For, with the gifts He has given us, we must always obey Him in such a manner that not only/will He not disinherit us like an outraged father his sons, but also that He will not, like a dreaded master, be driven by our sins to cast us into everlasting punishment, as wicked servants who would not follow Him to glory." (*The Rule of St Benedict*, Beginning of the Prologue)

"We intend thus to found a school to train men in the service of the Lord. And in founding it we hope that we shall not lay down any rules which will be too strict or too heavy to bear. Yet if, prompted by righteous reflection, for the correction of faults or the conservation of love, we show a certain severity, you must not immediately take fright and flee the path of salvation, the entrance to which must of necessity be narrow. For when you progress in the monastic life and in the faith, the heart expands: with the ineffable sweetness of love it speeds along the path of God's commandments. And thus may we, never departing from that which He has taught us, persevering unto death in His way in the monastery, by our patience become sharers in the sufferings of Christ and so merit also to become sharers in His kingdom. Amen." (*Rule of St Benedict*, End of the Prologue)

591. MONTE CASSINO, the monastery upon the mountain near Casinum where Benedict and his sister, the *sanctimonialis* Scholastica, lie buried.

592a. REGULA S. BENEDICTI, the earliest manuscript, dating from *ca* 700, in the Bodleian at Oxford, Hatton 48. Fol. 1: beginning of the Prologue. The translation is given above (the Latin text on Fol. 1 goes as far as the sign /).

592b. REGULA S. BENEDICTI, codex in Monte Cassino (Cod. Cass. 175), Fol. 2: Benedict hands a writing tablet (the symbol of the Rule) to Abbot John of Monte Cassino. The abbot wears the square portrait frame—the sign of the living—about his head and St Benedict the halo of the dead and of the saints; an angel whispers his thoughts to him. Although dating from a much later period, the miniature gives some idea of the original habit of the monks: a tunic, a short scapular with *cuculla* (hood). Here they are not wearing cloaks. The ornamentations on scapular and *cuculla* go back to those of the Eastern monks who had introduced them into southern Italy at the period when this miniature was painted.

593. (See opposite page.) GREEK AND LATIN FATHERS: from left to right: the Latins Gregory, Augustine, and Silvester; the Greeks Basil, John Chrysostom (the 'golden-mouthed'), and Gregory the Theologian (of Nazianzus). Mosaics in the choir of the cathedral of Cefalù on the island of Sicily. Shortly after 1148.

Chapter III

THE FATHERS OF THE CHURCH AND EARLY CHRISTIAN LITERATURE

The group of documents which we are accustomed to class together as 'Early Christian literature' is made up of many different sorts of writings of which only comparatively few can be described as 'literature', in the modern sense of the term. They have, however, this in common: all are concerned, in some way or other, with the typically Christian life and thought of the first centuries. They constitute in various forms a documentation of the Christian faith, life, and struggle. In this heterogenous collection, of which the greater part was not intended as literature, the writers have none-the-less followed those traditional rules of style which in ancient times served to make of every written document a work of art to a certain degree. It is only very slowly that a typically Christian style develops, and in this respect the West proves more creative than the East. Before seeking a distinctive style, however, it was necessary to tackle the problem of language.

Language. One of the first practical problems facing those whose task it was to propagate the Gospel was that of language. The account, in Acts 2, of the preaching on Whit Sunday, gives us a clear, though rather unintentional, picture of this problem. On this one occasion it found a solution in the linguistic charism, but it was not thereby resolved. It is above all St Paul—the type of the hellenised Jew—who in his preaching lays the foundations for what we term Early Christian Greek. The basis and point of departure of this idiom is the Hellenistic κοινή, the general Greek language of communication of this time. It was not only spoken in the East but was also very widespread in the large cosmopolitan cities of the West. In addition to this, in St Paul and in Early Christian Greek in general, the influence of the Jewish-Hellenistic linguistic usage can be felt, an influence which remained active through the Alexandrian Bible translation, the Septuagint. For centuries the Greek language, including the κοινή, had borne the stamp of the classical culture, of Greek thought in all its forms. It had the suppleness of a language which for centuries had been the instrument of a pre-eminently abstract culture. From the elements of this language, combined with those of the Jewish tradition (while carefully avoiding words too laden with pagan significance) was formed the new language of the Christian message, used both in speech and in writing. This Greek, which develops extremely rapidly under the breath of the Spirit, became the oecumenical language of the earliest preaching and of the earliest Christian literature in both East and West.

It is only about the year 150 that Latin gradually becomes the common language of the Christian communities in the West. Soon they too undertake the translation of parts of the Scriptures into Latin. Slowly but surely Latin becomes the official language of the Western church. This process, however, reaches its conclusion only in the fourth century, with the Latinisation of the eucharistic liturgy, although the second century sees the beginnings of Early Christian Latin. This Latin was to continue throughout the centuries to testify to the older oecumenical Greek by the presence of countless Greek loanwords, and it preferred at the outset the freedom and creativity of the popular idiom to the strict conservatism of the cultural language. This Christian Latin, with the straightforward conservatism which remains one of the characteristics of Western Christianity, was to maintain its position for centuries as a group language of a very distinctive character.

At about the same time as Latin, Syriac also begins to evolve as a Christian medium of communication, to be followed somewhat later by Coptic and then by Armenian. Before this linguistic differentiation was complete, however, there already existed a Greek Christian linguistic unity which not only facilitated the propagation of the faith, but also fostered the unity of doctrine and the uniformity of the κήρυγμα (preaching) in a very providential manner.

I. THE CHURCH OF THE MARTYRS

Thus it comes about that the earliest documents of the post-Apostolic period—the writings of those whom we call the Apostolic Fathers—are all written in Greek. Although very different in kind, they all breathe the same spirit. The expectation of the second coming of Christ still gives a distinctive stamp to spiritual and temporal life. Christ is always close at hand, and the *maran atha* of the liturgy of the *Didache* (which probably originated in Syria before 150) voices the mood and expectation of these times. IGNATIUS OF ANTIOCH († *ca* 110) constantly gives utterance in his letters to the ardent desire for a martyr's death which will enable him to 'partake of Christ' (see page 36). This is not only an expression of typically Ignatian mysticism, but the reflection in an ardent soul of the mood that possessed many at this time. The letter of Bishop CLEMENT OF ROME (*ca* 96) to the church of Corinth is couched in less ecstatic and more sober terms. The beautiful prayer at the end (see page 34) gives proof of moderation in his attitude towards the temporal powers.

Popular literature. To this early period belong also the earliest Christian pseudepigrapha and apocrypha which, continuing a Jewish tradition, were woven about both the Old and New Testament. These writings, often of Gnostic origin, give us an idea of the popular literature which was growing up about the fringes of official Christianity. The *Shepherd of Hermas*, usually included among the works of the Apostolic Fathers, belongs in fact to these apocryphal apocalypses. It is a typical expression of popular devotion—a summons to conversion and penance.

The Apologists. Around the year 150 a form of literature begins to develop which concerns itself more with the world, i.e. literature addressed to the non-Christian. The consciousness that Christians must perforce live in this world—albeit as exiles—and that the Church must maintain her position against hostile forces, calls into being an apologetic literature. The Church is defended against both the State and the Gnostic heresy which is developing into a powerful movement; the recent discoveries of Nag-Hammadi give some idea of the extent of this Gnostic crisis. The Christians are also becoming increasingly aware of their own importance in the world. They are the Third Race—along with the pagans and the Jews—and, according to the treatise *To Diognetus*, the Christian must be to the world what the soul is to the body. The philosophers especially take upon themselves the task of defending the Church against the persecuting State. Aristides, a philosopher of Athens, stresses, as did the anonymous author of *To Diognetus*, the irreproachable morality of the Christians. JUSTIN, a native of Shechem († ca 165), 'philosopher and martyr', as Tertullian calls him, follows the tradition of the pagan philosophers in both theory and practice. Robed in the *pallium*, the garb of the old Greek philosophers, he journeys like the Cynic popular preacher from city to city. In Rome he founds a school where TATIAN, later apologist and author of a Gospel Harmony, is among his pupils. For Justin, Christianity is the true philosophy. ATHENAGORAS too, who addressed himself in his Apology to the Emperor Marcus Aurelius, and THEOPHILUS OF ANTIOCH follow in the footsteps of the apologists.

At this period the struggle against the Gnosis is carried on by IRENAEUS, a native of Asia, and from 177 onwards Bishop of Lyon. His *Against Heresies* is a valuable source of knowledge concerning this heresy. Irenaeus occupies an important place in the history of theology both by his recapitulation theory and by his theories on ecclesiastical tradition and original sin.

The third century: the first centres. After 200 a new age dawns: the mobility of the first centuries, fostered by the Greek linguistic unity, gives place to an intellectual and eventually theological concentration in certain centres, in Antioch and Alexandria in the East and in the West in Carthage and in Rome. The Latinisation of the Western Church which now begins and which finds its first literary expression in the brilliant figure of Tertullian, severs the old Greek unity. East and West each finds its own distinctive modes of expression which are essentially determined by the ancient tradition of each hemisphere.

Alexandria. In the East, Alexandria becomes the centre of a more or less humanistically oriented Christianity. Taking as their model the classical philosophical and philological tradition and at the same time the Jewish Hellenism of a writer like Philo, the Christians endeavour here to achieve a theological *approfondissement* of the elements of religion. What Justin had attempted, namely the reconciliation of profane philosophy with Christian doctrine, is carried on by CLEMENT OF ALEXANDRIA on a wider basis. Clement, an Athenian by birth, a citizen of the world by his travels, becomes in Alexandria a pupil of Pantaenus and, after the latter's death (ca 200), the leader of the so-called Alexandrian school of catechesis—a Christian school modelled upon those of the old Greek

philosophers. After a few years he was banished during the persecution of Septimius Severus and died in Asia (before 215). In his trilogy *Protrepticus*, *Paedagogus*, and *Stromata*, an extremely ambitious undertaking which exceeded his capacities and which, in the third part especially, was really never more than a rough draft, he attempts to find a synthesis of faith and philosophy. For Clement, the faith is the true philosophy in the full sense of the word, the sublimation and crowning of the work of the Ancients (see page 40). His mystically inclined spirituality is more intellectual than that of an Ignatius, yet is by no means devoid of Biblical inspiration. In his language, which in the lyrical sections (see page 45) shows certain traces of Gnostic influence, he likewise seeks a synthesis of profane philosophical and Biblical tradition.

Clement is overshadowed by the brilliance of his successor ORIGEN (born ca 185), who at an early age was appointed by Bishop Demetrius to succeed Clement as head of the school (202/3). He was dismissed in 230, as not being lawfully ordained, and retired to Caesarea in Palestine where he founded a school. Gregory Thaumaturgus, the apostle of Cappadocia, was among his pupils (he outlines Origen's method of teaching in his *Panegyric*). Origen died at the age of seventy, apparently from the effects of torture undergone during the persecution of Decius (253/4).

No theologian of Antiquity has aroused more controversy than he. As a result of the later dispute over his work and the condemnation of certain elements of his doctrine in 563, only a limited part of his immense work has been preserved in Greek: most of it we possess in not always reliable translation by Hilary, Jerome, Rufinus, and others. To his Biblical studies belongs that remarkable work of textual criticism, the *Hexapla*, used later by Jerome. Following the example of the Alexandrian philologists, he wrote *scholia* upon the Scriptures and also Bible commentaries and exegetical homilies. His spiritual, allegorical Bible exegesis (on the threefold meaning of the Scriptures), although it aroused controversy, found countless imitators in East and West. His apologetical works are the *Against Celsus* and the *On Fundamentals*, which latter can be considered as an early form of dogmatic handbook. Origen is notably the first to view theology as a whole, although always in the light of the Scriptures. The beautiful dissertation on prayer, and his 'Exhortation to martyrdom', are basically ascetic. As a mystic he exercised a great influence upon monasticism.

One of Origen's opponents was METHODIUS OF OLYMPUS († 311 as a martyr; see Map 8) who wrote in the form of the Platonic dialogue. The only work of his that has been preserved in its entirety, the *Symposium*, a dialogue of ten virgins singing the praises of chastity, shows how much he was under the spell of the profane past.

The earliest writings of the school of Antioch have been lost.

594. THE GREEK FATHERS: Athanasius, Basil, John Chrysostom, Gregory the Theologian (of Nazianzus), Cyril of Alexandria. Greek icon; 16th century: the liturgical dress is also 16th century. *Rome, Pinacoteca Vaticana*.

595. EASTER TABLE engraved upon the seat of the statue of Hippolytus († 235); discovered in 1551. *Rome, Museo Lateranense*.

North Africa: Carthage. Carthage was the first place in which the Latinisation of the Church led to a flourishing literature. It begins with a short *acta*, the *Acta of the Scilitani martyrs* (180). A good twenty years later appeared the *Martyrdom of S. Perpetua and Felicitas*, extremely interesting for the spirituality of the martyrs and attributed by many, probably erroneously, to Tertullian (see page 44). We do not know whether the celebrated and rather over-rated dialogue of MINUCIUS FELIX, the *Octavius* (the author, according to Fronto, was a native of Africa) was written before or after Tertullian's *Apology*. This short work imitates the Platonic dialogue after the manner of Methodius of Olympus; the form is elegant but the content poor. Tertullian is, in any case, the first African Christian of whom an extensive work has been preserved.

Like Clement in the East he is a pioneer, yet one can imagine no greater contrast than Clement, the philosophically-minded mystical humanist, and the stern rigorist Tertullian who found his inspiration more in Roman law than in philosophy. In his dynamic style he does not scruple to introduce the new elements in the Christian language which Minucius so conscientiously avoids. He undoubtedly contributed to the development of Christian Latin, which he helped to make into a literary language, yet one cannot consider him—as some tend to do—as the creator of Christian Latinity. A rebellious, puritanical spirit, obstinate and intransigent, he came into conflict with the ecclesiastical authorities, went over to the Montanists, broke in turn with them, and founded his own sect. His work, the greater part of which has been preserved, bears the stamp of his distinctive personality. Although he borrows freely from his Greek predecessors he always succeeds in adding some individual touch, often in the typically

Roman style, to the traditional elements. Thus, in his *Apology*, he assimilates the apologetic elements into a simulated juridical plea full of the artifices of the age-old Roman legal practice. He adopts the same process in his dogmatic polemical work *On the Proscription of Heretics*, where he succeeds in introducing a new and again juridical element to the doctrine of 'tradition' already dealt with by Irenaeus. In his earliest practical-ascetical writings, especially in the trilogy *Baptism, Prayer, Penance*, he is still comparatively moderate in tone, but his later works breathe a spirit of intransigence almost without equal in the Early Church and which is wrongly considered by some as characteristic of the first centuries (see page 40). His dogmatic works are nearly all polemical: against the Jews, against the Gnostic sect of the Valentinians, against the Marcionites and others. The dogmatic-polemical treatise *Against Praxeas*, written in his ultra–Montanist period, proves that he is not always the lawyer, stern preacher of penance and criticaster, but is also really capable of theological thought. In his exposition on the Trinity he often seems on the point of anticipating the formulas of the later Council of Nicaea (325).

The second great figure in Africa is the former rhetorician CYPRIAN (born in Carthage *ca* 200). He was converted to Christianity in 246 and in 248/9 became Bishop of his native city. From his extensive works emerges for the first time from the age of persecution the picture of the spiritual pastor. His writings owe

596ab. JOHN CHRYSOSTOM AND BASIL. Mosaics of *ca* 1148, showing the conventionalised, unchanging style of portrait head. *Palermo, Cappella Palatina.*

596a

596b

597

598/599

a great deal to Tertullian, although one can imagine few greater contrasts than Cyprian the churchman and Tertullian the spiritual freelance. Having the unity of the Church very much at heart, severe but just in disciplinary matters, as in the treatment of the *lapsi* (the Christians who had 'lapsed' during the persecutions), adopting a sober and sensible attitude towards child baptism, he is the prototype of the spiritual leader of the flock, devoted, but inexorable on matters of principle. His correspondence—for us the most interesting part of his work—gives an impressive picture of the *grandeur et misère* of an average community under the pressure of the persecutions. His martyrdom (in 258) is soberly described in the *Acts of Cyprian*, but his *Life*, written by his deacon Pontius, is not very reliable.

Rome. Although Tertullian in Carthage wrote in a Christian Latin that had already reached an advanced stage of development, HIPPOLYTUS, a native of the East, was still writing in Greek in the Rome of *ca* 200. A rigorist like Tertullian, he came into conflict with Pope Callistus; he allowed himself to be chosen as anti-Pope but finally died in exile in 235, reconciled to the Church (see 595). He was later venerated as a martyr. In the West he and his works soon passed into oblivion, but in the East some of his writings were preserved and were gradually brought to light in the nineteenth century. His *Commentary on Daniel* is one of the oldest Bible commentaries to survive; his *Philosophoumena* is a mediocre anti-heretical work. His *Chronicle*, from the Creation to A.D. 234, was intended to prove that the expectation of the Millennium still cherished in Christian circles was utter foolishness. His *Apostolic Tradition* has been preserved only in translation, but even so it is a valuable source of knowledge for the organisation and liturgy of the community of Rome shortly after 200.

NOVATIAN is the first theologian to use Latin in Rome. He too became the leader of a rigorist group and allowed himself to be consecrated anti-Pope (in 251, against Cornelius); his schism persisted for centuries. His main work is *Of the Trinity*; written in an elegant, rhythmical prose, it resumes the then prevailing doctrine concerning the Trinity.

The final period before the Peace of the Church produces only second-rate writers. In Sicca, in Africa, ARNOBIUS the rhetorician is converted as the result of a dream and in order to demonstrate the seriousness of his conversion writes an apologetic work, *Against the Pagans*, from which it is obvious that even the elementary truths of the faith have escaped him. The curious late-classical syncretism which he attempts to pass off as Christianity is also reflected in his language.

Arnobius' disciple and compatriot LACTANTIUS, appointed as rhetorician in Nicomedia by the Emperor Diocletian and there becoming a convert (before 303), sees as his mission the creation of a Christian literature that would closely follow the classical tradition in language and style. In his opinion the simple and exotic language of the early Bible translations and the Christian Latin of a writer like Cyprian repel intellectuals who would otherwise be converted.

597. THE EARLIEST PORTRAIT of St Augustine. Fresco in the Papal library of the Lateran, *ca* 600.

598. BAPTISTERY OF THE GREAT CHURCH at Hippo Regius: *piscina* dating from the time of Augustine.

599. APSE PODIUM with the spot where Augustine's *cathedra* stood, in the Great Church at Hippo Regius.

In his *Divine Institutes*, the first attempt to resume the essentials of faith and doctrine in Latin, he aims at winning over the men of letters by the polish of his style. His thought and language show the influence of the Stoic philosophy, and in his dogma he repeatedly strays from the path of orthodoxy. He did, however, correct himself here and there in his *Epitome*, an abridgement of his large work. The authenticity of the *On the deaths of the Persecutors* (cf page 57) attributed to him, has often been contested but seems now to have been definitely established. In this work, the ultra–civilised humanist shows that he too possesses something of the fire of a Tertullian. Whether the poem *On the Phoenix* (see page 101) may be attributed to him remains an open question.

On the frontier between two periods—the age of persecution and the Peace of the Church—stands EUSEBIUS of Caesarea in Palestine. Born around 263 in Caesarea where he was a pupil in the school founded by Origen, he became Bishop of his native city *ca* 313. He was an able politician and obtained a great influence over Constantine, but his rather unprincipled attitude during the Arian struggle and his eulogies addressed to the Emperor mark him as a man of weak and vacillating character. A man of wide learning but no theologian, his claim to fame rests chiefly on his merits as the historian of the earliest Christian Church. His *Chronicle*, short synchronistic tables dealing with the history of the people of the Ancient World, dominated the chronology and historiography of the Middle Ages in the translation and continuation of St Jerome (see pages 33 ff.). The same is true of his *Ecclesiastical History* in ten books (up to 324) written with apologetic intent and important as a collection of sources although by no means a well constructed historical work. His task was carried on by Socrates (for the years 305-439), Sozomen (324-425), and others; and in Latin by Rufinus and Cassiodorus.

II. THE CHURCH OF THE EMPIRE

The measures adopted by Constantine and his successors, which eventually resulted in the Church becoming the Church of the Empire, also left their mark upon the literature of the period. Within a short space of time a many-sided literature develops, embracing every aspect of Church life. The period between the Councils of Nicaea and Chalcedon (325-451) becomes in East and West the flowering time of Early Christian letters. A new style of life emerges in the Imperial Church; the outside world pierces through the old barriers, and at the same time begins the exodus to the desert where many seek to recapture the old ideals. This 'return to the sources' finds expression even in the language of the monks, who give new meanings to the old words and symbols. Thus for example does *frater*, the 'brother Christian' of the times of persecution become 'the brother monk' within the community; *miles Christi*, the 'soldier of Christ', becomes the monk fighting against the devil. Even outside ascetic circles the Church experiences a great devotional revival, nurtured by meditation upon the heroic past and joy at present liberty. The sanctuaries which arise everywhere upon the Holy Places and above the graves of the martyrs set in motion a busy pilgrimage traffic. Constantine's attempt to make Jerusalem the devotional centre for the whole of Christendom seems at the beginning to have succeeded. The pilgrimage literature like the *Pilgrimage to the Holy Places*

600. AMBROSE. Mosaic portrait in S. Vittore in ciel d'oro, Milan; shortly after 400.
601. THE BASILICA MAIOR or Great Church of Hippo Regius, looking towards the apse.
602. AUGUSTINE'S TOMB; 15th century. *Pavia, S. Pietro in ciel d'oro.*

601

written by the Spanish (or perhaps southern French) *sanctimonialis* (nun) Egeria, and travel records like those of Jerome give us an impressive picture of this new form of Christian devotion. We find the literary repercussion of the veneration of the martyrs in the rapidly flourishing epigrammatic poetry like that of Damasus (366-84; see pages 48, 147). The old series of sober *Acta* are also enriched at this time by more or less legendary 'passions', by the martyr ballads of Prudentius (*Peristephanon*; see page 149), and by the anniversary hymns (*Natalicia*) of Paulinus of Nola (cf pages 62 and 131). On the other hand, the rapid growth of the Church stimulates the desire to penetrate and formulate clearly those dogmas which have been handed down. This is not accomplished without a fierce struggle, especially in the East, where the Christians were superior not only in numbers, a struggle rendered more bitter and more confused by the intervention of the State. This, too, finds an echo in the extensive polemical theological literature.

The great interest in the Scriptures which finds its expression in the pilgrimages to Palestine also gives rise to a flourishing exegetical literature concentrated in the East in Alexandria and Antioch. Both these centres exercised a decisive influence upon the Western exegetes.

Alexandria. In the East the great figure of ATHANASIUS, Bishop of Alexandria (295-373), dominates the beginning of this period. He was the opponent of Arianism and the defender of the faith of Nicaea. Between 335 and 366 he was banished five times. The greater part of his work is devoted to the struggle against the Arians and to the scientific formulation of the dogmas concerning the Trinity and the Logos; his principal work is the *Orations against the Arians*. Like nearly all the Greek Fathers of this period he also had some connection with the rapidly developing monastic life: his biography of Anthony made a deep impression in East and West and became the model for countless other biographies of monks.

Fifty years after Athanasius, CYRIL OF ALEXANDRIA (see **594**) took up arms almost as energetically against the doctrine of Nestorius. Of his numerous writings the dialogue *On the Unity of the Person of Christ* was already famous in ancient times. He also opposed the Emperor Julian's *Against the Galileans* in his *Against the books of the atheist Julian*.

While these two writers were completely taken up by the dogmatic struggle, DIDYMUS THE BLIND was carrying on the tradition of Origen in the school of Alexandria. Later, in 553, he also shared in the latter's condemnation, which explains why many of his books were lost or preserved under another name. Jerome who, like Rufinus, had been one of his pupils, translated his three books, *On the Holy Spirit*, into Latin.

Two poets follow the classical tradition. SYNESIUS OF CYRENE (370/5-413/4) a disciple of Hypatia, the famous woman philosopher, was appointed Bishop of Ptolemais for reasons which had but little to do with the faith, yet remained a Neoplatonic philosopher and, like Arnobius in the West, showed little understanding of the Christian religion. In his Platonic hymns he employs the Doric dialect according to the ancient tradition of the Greek chorus and on other occasions too follows classical models. In the same way NONNOS OF PANOPOLIS later follows the old Homeric tradition in his paraphrase of St John's Gospel. a poetising process which was, indeed, frequently applied in the West.

The Three Cappadocians, the brothers Basil (330-79) and Gregory of Nyssa († 394), and their friend Gregory of Nazianzus (329-90) occupy a prominent place in this period of full intellectual and theological expansion. All three come of a distinguished Christian and ascetic milieu and—a typical feature in this humanistically minded period—all received their education at the great schools of rhetoric, notably the university of Athens. This education left its mark upon their work. Their writings can be classed as pure 'literature', their aim being to achieve a polished style in the tradition of the late-classical schools of rhetoric. In addition to this they are strongly influenced by Neoplatonic philosophical thought. They create a baroque style in which the artifices of the later rhetoric are combined with the contemporary philosophical jargon which had introduced many of the old Mystery terms into a mystically-inclined philosophy. Theologically, they link up with the Alexandrian school and usually reflect clearly and succinctly the prevailing theological trends. Yet it would be inaccurate to consider them as typical of the Greek Christianity of the fourth century; they are merely an absorbing but by no means representative phenomenon.

BASIL (see **594**), his rhetorical studies completed, chose the ascetic coenobitic life, chiefly at the urging of his sister Macrina. He lived in Pontus, on the Iris, with a group of like-minded people. Together with Gregory of Nazianzus he compiled an anthology of the works of Origen (*Philocalia*), and his monastic rules also date from this period (see pages 171-72). Compelled by force of circumstance to return to active church life, he became Bishop of Caesarea in Cappadocia in 370 and, until his death, led the life of the pastor Bishop, anxious to preserve the purity of the doctrine and the unity of the Church. He has rightly been called the 'Roman among the Greeks' for he resembles in many ways the great Bishops of the West. His theological works owe much to Athanasius; in his *To the Young* he advocates the study of profane literature as a preparation for the study of the Holy Scriptures. His rhetorical training comes most to the fore in his homilies. His sermons on the *Six days of Creation* (*Hexaemeron*)—later pirated by Ambrose—are a rhetorical philosophical meditation upon the work of Creation.

GREGORY OF NYSSA, his younger brother, also started his career as a rhetorician. He too was ascetically inclined but, more or less under pressure from his brother, he became Bishop of Nyssa in 371. As Bishop and church politician he was a failure; he was more given to contemplation and strove to find a synthesis of faith and Neoplatonism. As a theologian he was more attracted to speculative theology, but none-the-less revised systematically the entire body of Church doctrine. In his *Great Catechetical Oration* he deals with the principal tenets of the

603. THE CLIVUS SCAURI on the Celio in Rome. Left, the 3rd century walls of the *titulus Bizantis* (house-church), now SS. Giovanni e Paolo. To the right was the house in which Gregory the Great was born.

604. THE THREE CHAPELS, entirely rebuilt in 1608, on the site of the Andreas monastery in the parental house of Gregory the Great; the middle one was perhaps the *oratorium*. From here Augustine left for Canterbury in 596.

Facing: monuments from Byzantine Rome.

605. WOMEN'S GALLERY in the memorial church of St Lawrence (579-90), rebuilt by Pelagius II and adorned with the apse mosaic which still exists today. Now S. Lorenzo fuori le mura.

606. S. MARIA ANTIQUA, founded by Greek monks in a pagan building on the Forum; 6th century.

607. S. AGNESE, founded by Honorius I (625-38,) above her tomb near the earlier church (see **135**). It too contains a women's gallery.

603

604

608/609

faith and in his *Life of Moses* attempts a mystical exegesis. Of his ascetic works the *On Virginity* had a wide influence. The rhetorical pathos of his moralising sermons is somewhat irritating.

The life of GREGORY OF NAZIANZUS (see **594**) is similarly devoted, after his training in the schools of rhetoric, to contemplation, pastoral care, and church polity; yet he too lacks Basil's sober practical sense. In Constantinople, where Theodosius had entrusted him with the care of those— few—who had remained true to the faith of Nicaea, he became the victim of intrigues and retired to lead an ascetic and literary life. Like Prudentius in the West he aspired to the creation of a many-sided Christian poetry. As an autobiographical document his *Autobiography* can be compared with the *Confessions* of Augustine, yet the spirit of this work, an anticipation of Abélard's *History of Disasters*, betrays an inspiration far different from that of Augustine's laudatory prayer of thanksgiving. As a theologian he follows the classical school: he gives a faithful picture of the purest philosophical thought of his time and milieu. Of his dogmatic sermons, the five *Theological Discourses* (27-31) delivered at Constantinople in 370 are deservedly famous.

Jerusalem. Syria produces a number of great writers who in thought and style are closer to the old tradition. CYRIL OF JERUSALEM († 386; see page 134) has left behind a number of catecheses which give us a picture of the liturgical life of the church of Jerusalem during the fourth century.

In contrast to the allegorical interpretations of the Scriptures furnished by the Alexandrians, the exegetes of the school of **Antioch** cling to the literal sense. THEODORE OF MOPSUESTIA († 428, a pupil of the pagan rhetorician Libanius) wrote a commentary on almost the entire Scripture. Considered orthodox during his lifetime, he was later (in 553) condemned as a Nestorian, apparently on the grounds of supposititious documents. Some of his writings, which for the greater part had been lost, have recently been rediscovered in a Syriac translation: his Christology appears to be orthodox.

Above and facing: monuments from Byzantine Rome.

608. APSE MOSAIC in S. Teodoro al Palatino, a small rotunda decorated by Theodore I (642-49). Son of the Bishop of Jerusalem, he heard in Rome the news that the Holy City had been taken by the Arabs.

609. AGNES between Pope Honorius (625-38), the founder of the church, and Pope Symmachus. Apse mosaic in S. Agnese (see **607**).

610. S. MARIA AD MARTYRES: the Pantheon, dedicated to all the martyrs (*Panmartyrion*) by Boniface IV (608-14). The first temple in Rome to be dedicated to the worship of Christ.

The glory of the school of Antioch is JOHN CHRYSOSTOM (354-407; see **594** and **596a**), considered to be the greatest of the Greek preachers. At first an ascetic, he entered the priesthood in Antioch and became Bishop of Constantinople in 398. His stern administration, his drastic action in combating abuses (and the Empress Eudoxia) led to his banishment. He is, above all, a pastor of souls and a preacher. His sermons, less exuberant in style than those of the Cappadocians, deal directly with the actual realities of life and are made arresting by a wealth of images. Following the Antioch tradition, he interprets the Scriptures according to the literal sense. His treatises *On the Priesthood* and *On Education* have continued to be read throughout the centuries. Of the two hundred and thirty-six letters written during his exile, the seventeen to Olympias constitute a remarkable document of humanistic spiritual guidance.

The fourth century is also the flowering time of the **Syrian** church. Its classical writer is EPHRAEM (*ca* 306-73), exegete, preacher, and poet. His writings, for the greater part in metrical form, have not yet been published in a critical edition and have received insufficient attention on the part of scholars. He exercised a great influence on Byzantine hymnology and in particular on the work of ROMANUS THE SINGER (6th century; see **249**), also a Syrian.

In the West, after 325, the Trinitarian struggle rages, especially in Gaul. Her HILARY OF POITIERS († 367) stirs up the clergy against the Arian-minded metropolitan Saturninus of Arles. Exiled to Asia by Constantius, he wrote his *On the Trinity* which made of him the 'Athanasius of the West'.

This flowering period is dominated by three figures: Ambrose, Jerome, and Augustine.

AMBROSE (born 339 at Trèves, † 397, see **600**), after a legal and rhetorical training, chose an official career, but when, as governor of Milan, he attempted to mediate in the struggle between Catholics and Arians, he was unexpectedly chosen Bishop by the people. As Bishop he remained a wise governor and a high-principled but clever politician. He dealt firmly with both the pagan reaction (Symmachus, in Rome) and with Justina the Empress-mother who was an Arian sympathiser. He maintained his spiritual authority even against Theodosius (see page 75). His training and wide reading made him an admired preacher who made a great impression upon the young Augustine. Most of his works indeed arose out of his sermons. As a theologian he showed no particular originality but knew infallibly how to choose from his sources (mostly Greek) those points which conformed with orthodox tradition and was at the same time capable of appealing to an audience of intellectuals influenced by Neoplatonism. In his exegesis he follows Origen; his *Hexaemeron* is based upon that of Basil, and in his *On the offices of the clergy*, a handbook for the clergy and church of Milan, he attempts to give a Christianised version of Cicero's *De officiis*. The *On the mysteries* and *On the Sacraments* (this too is now considered as authentic) give an idea of the instruction for the newly baptised (see pages 129 and 131). His most personal creation is the hymn intended to be sung in church, a poetic innovation in the West which was to dominate the religious poetry of the Middle Ages (for examples, see pages 72, 73, 148, 151).

The chief merits of JEROME (347-420) lie in the domain of Biblical textual criticism, exegesis, and ascetic spirituality. Born in Stridon, he studied in Rome and Antioch, where he learned Greek. He then proceeded to the desert of Chalcis (see Map 15a), learned Hebrew there, and became a pupil of Gregory of Nazianzus in Constantinople. Pope Damasus commissioned him to revise the Old Latin Bible translations, and this became his life work. Having encountered some opposition in Rome, he retired to the East with a few pious women whose spiritual director he was (see page 105). In Bethlehem he founded three convents and a monastery and concluded the critical revision (he used Origen's *Hexapla*) and translation (partly from the Hebrew) of the Holy Scriptures. With a sure feeling for style he eradicated from the old texts all that was no longer in accordance with contemporary linguistic usage and that he considered inaccurate, while preserving the hieratic style as far as possible. His commentaries are connected with his work as translator. His letters—some of them complete treatises—are important for their content but tasteless in style. He polemised against Origen and Pelagius.

AUGUSTINE (born at Thagaste 354; † 430 Hippo Regius) gives us, in his *Confessions*, in the form of a meditative prayer of thanksgiving, the story of his spiritual development up to his baptism by St Ambrose in Milan. After fully fifty years of controversy, the subjective and objective veracity of this account is now almost generally recognised. Augustine decided, after a searching inner struggle, to give up his position as teacher of rhetoric and to devote himself to the study of 'truth' while leading a life of continence. On his return to Africa this Christian-philosophical way of life was soon transformed into a wholly religious ideal. Having rather unexpectedly been ordained priest at Hippo Regius, he became Bishop of this city a short while afterwards, in 395. Although living with his clergy within a monastic community in this provincial town, he was none-the-less to dominate the ecclesiastical life of the period in word and writing for thirty-five years (see **597-9**). He is the great champion of orthodoxy in the West.

611

The whole of his life was devoted to combating heretics: Manichaeans, Arians, Donatists, Pelagians. His practice in polemics led him, however, to constructive theology: his *On the Trinity*, for example, was the final word in the controversy which raged about the Trinity. In his more than a thousand sermons he repeatedly provides a corrective to the all too intransigently formulated ideas so common in polemics, especially concerning the life of grace. His *City of God*, an audacious attempt at an apologetic theology of history, finds its pendant in the *Exposition of the Psalms*, which gives a purely Biblical interpretation of the drama of mankind. In *On Christian Doctrine* he deals with the relationship between profane and Christian culture. More than any other of the Western Fathers he was to determine the theological, cultural, and even political life of the centuries to come.

The Gallic writers of this period nearly all belong to monastic circles. SULPICIUS SEVERUS († 421) wrote a life of St Martin of Tours; JOHN CASSIAN (born 360) introduced Egyptian monasticism to Provence.

This period is brought to a worthy close by Pope Leo the Great (440-61) who not only defended Rome against Attila and Genseric but also fought for the true faith on many fronts. He is the first Pope after Damasus of whom we possess a personal literary work. In the beautiful Latin of his homilies, delivered on feast days, we seem to hear once again, in this time of inner decay and barbarian menace, the majestic voice of ancient Rome.

III. THE DECLINE

After 451 the time of greatness is past. In the East a certain self-confidence, feeling itself justified by the tradition of a great past, leads to a lack of creative activity; a desire is shown to render the ancient treasures accessible in Chain Commentaries and Anthologies. In the fifth century(?) the puzzling figure of PSEUDO-DIONYSIUS THE AREOPAGITE renews the attempt to achieve a synthesis of Christianity and Neoplatonism. The fifth and sixth centuries, however, see a late flowering in the exegesis of the school of rhetoric in Gaza. PROCOPIUS († *ca* 538) leaves, besides a series of Chain Commentaries, a collection of letters important for the history of culture. The seventh century produces one last great theologian, MAXIMUS CONFESSOR, who opposed Monophysitism and Monotheletism.

In the West, the spirit of St Augustine dominates the work of a host of epigones, and poetry flourishes again in a series of Bible paraphrases in which the classical poetic forms are used.

The entire culture appears to collapse in the West under the pressure of the barbarian invasions, yet in the regions which escape complete devastation, a humanistic spirit arises which looks back with a certain affectionate nostalgia upon former greatness while at the same time attempting to save what is still worth saving. Thus does BOETHIUS (480-514), at first right hand and then victim of Theodoric, seek his salvation in philosophy: *On the Consolation of Philosophy*. Theodoric's chancellor CASSIODORUS († 583) founds his humanistic monastery Vivarium (in Calabria; cf page 124 and **391**). Pope Gregory the Great draws attention in his *Dialogues*, written already in 'medieval' style, to the treasures of sanctity also to be found in the West, far from Egypt, and still later ISIDORE OF SEVILLE († 636) compiles his encyclopedic works.

And yet, when GREGORY OF TOURS (538-94) decided to write his *History of the Franks*, the first national, albeit moralising and legendary, history of a new, and for the Romans, barbarian people, it became clear that the time of the one, Imperial, Church, built up on the tradition of the classical οἰκουμενή—the 'inhabited world'—was gone for ever. But the foundations of a new unity have already been laid by BENEDICT OF NURSIA († 547, see **592**), of an élite that was to hand on the literary heritage of the first centuries, together with a superior spiritual tradition.

611. NESTORIAN STONE with inscription dating from the 7th century at Sianfu in China. This is the most eastward-lying monument of Early Christianity. Nestorianism—which after the 5th century had ceased to have any connection with the orthodoxy of the Eastern Roman Empire— spread from Persia into Turkestan and later into the north and northwest parts of China.

612-13. GOLDEN CHALICE with filigree, and paten inlaid with red glass; 6th century, found at Gourdon (Côte d'Or). *Paris, Cabinet des médailles.* The models and technique are still those of the late Roman craftsmanship, but the ornamentation, proportions, and execution are already typically Merovingian. The church in which these sacred vessels were used belonged to the young Burgundian kingdom. Even these small works of art which bring this book to a close are an unmistakable sign of the changing times: the golden age of the Early Christian Church has vanished for ever.

612

613

Epilogue

Early Christian culture is purely religious. It is a culture of exile, for the true believer 'has here no abiding dwelling place'. In so far as it none-the-less became a part of life during the last centuries of the Roman Empire it developed simply, almost imperceptibly, and by no means always as the result of compromise. For the new religion brought with it not only a new moral law and a revealed knowledge of the divine unknown to the Ancients. It brought also a world of ideas and images in which the premises of the Scriptures were blended, sometimes almost astonishingly, with those of the traditional Greek perception of reality. This is also true of the world of Christian art and literature.

What strikes us most here is the perfect harmony of word and image. Both arise from a trait peculiar to the Christians, that of viewing all reality in the light of the deep, profoundly Biblical sense of the figurative interrelation of all things: of Old and New Testament, of nature and divine intervention, of internal and external, of rite and reality. Hence it follows that even the simplest texts are profound, the images full of significance, the features of the portraits intense, their gaze meaningful. These people have a message to convey.

We find nothing of all this in the works of pagan contemporaries, who, from the time of the Antonines continue to live in the past and to reiterate ancient wisdom. Only the sarcophagi of the third century, a reflection of the Neoplatonic symbolisation of reality, have power to move us, and they form as it were a natural introduction to the Early Christian decorative motifs. The same is true in literature of a philosopher like Plotinus.

At the same time the Early Christian vision of reality strikes us, who come after and have inherited the medieval sensitiveness, as remarkably intellectualistic. This remains true even when it is shown to us in the poetic framework of an ever-present symbolism. Expressions of human emotion are lacking or are only esteemed for their moral worth. Indeed, the first note of lyricism in the history of Christianity is sounded by St Bernard and French Gothic art, and by the Franciscan movement in Italy.

The Christian church was the concern of all and the culture which it gradually shaped was one for the 'very many'. For, in contrast to the refined, purely literary culture of the Late Roman Empire, addressed solely to an élite, the world of faith was one in which all could feel at home. The very symbolism of the liturgy and the Biblical message, by its infinite richness of meaning ensured that there was something to appeal to all. The Scriptures were at the same time simple and profound, the Christian language popular and evocative. Christian art was plain and easy to understand but left endless scope to the imagination. It is not by chance that the great basilica, the outstanding achievement of the fourth century, is, both by its spacious interior and by its disposition, a house for multitudes and the first truly democratic piece of spatial architecture.

What has been the significance for future generations of these dramatic centuries, the third to the sixth?

For every Christian, Christian Antiquity is the *venerabilis antiquitas*, the venerable golden age when the water ran so clear close to the source even though the stream was not so broad as it was later to become. Among the Greek Christians the heritage of this time has been faithfully preserved up to the present day, albeit in a more hieratic form. The Slavonic peoples too, in matters of religion, are still guided by the teachings of the desert Fathers, the old tales of the martyrs, the hymns and liturgy of Antiquity; the rule of their faith is, after the Word of God, the authority of the eight oecumenical councils.

Western Christianity has a more turbulent spiritual history. Upon the period with which this book closes there followed a time of drastic impoverishment accompanied by a scant preservation of the very best. Boethius tried to save the philosophical, Cassiodorus the literary heritage of pagan Antiquity. Gregory the Great spoke with tenderness and pride of the majesty of the Roman past, for, he most probably thought, the days of the *imperium* would not return again. To the coming centuries *Roma mater*, *latinitas*, and *romanitas* remained words to conjure with, and classical Antiquity was endowed once and for all with that golden halo which, in our countries, it has never lost.

And yet this same Gregory the Great was one of those who resolutely set out to make the Church independent of the Empire as well as of the small barbarian kingdoms. He brought the faith, together with what culture it entailed, to the Arian Visigoths and to those Anglo-Saxons who, in the second generation, would already repay their talent with interest. St Benedict, that other Roman *paterfamilias*, created, unintentionally perhaps, that style of life in which, for a thousand years, the best sons of Roman and barbarian could meet together in the service of Christ.

And the Church, once almost identified with the doomed Empire, now stood alone and in these barren times scattered with lavish hand among the young nations, gifted, yet poor in culture, all the treasures of its vanished golden age. It gave them its language, mature and ready coined, the writings of its Fathers, the example of its confessors and martyrs, the service of God in spirit and truth of its majestic liturgy, and above all—notwithstanding much ancient wisdom, Roman statesmanship, Latin laws, Greek subtleties, Neoplatonic mysticism, and Egyptian asceticism—it gave them the most precious thing it had, its true *raison d'être*: the preaching of the word of God, the joyful message of the Kingdom and, in its never-ceasing sacramental signs, the Living Spirit of its Lord.

That light [Christ] is eternal life: and all that participate in that light, live; the night now fears the light, and, vanishing in fear, makes way for the light of the Lord.
All has now become light that does not wane, and the region of the sun's setting has become that of its rising. This is the meaning of the New Creation. For He who rides in his chariot high above all things, the 'Sun of righteousness', visits all mankind without distinction. In this he follows his Father who also 'causes the sun to rise' and the dew of truth to fall 'upon all mankind'.

CLEMENT OF ALEXANDRIA, *Protrepticus* II, 114: 2–3 (see **74**)

GEOGRAPHICAL INDEX

to the maps and plates

Former names: all in Latin spelling. This sometimes varies, especially in Africa (b instead of p; t instead of th). Words should be sought under both letters.

Modern names: given in brackets following ancient name. For eastern Arabian names the English form of transcription is used.

Location: this is indicated by reference to the division into provinces in force in the Roman Empire after A.D. 294 (see front endpaper; the provinces are found again on the main maps).

Dates: figures placed in brackets are the earliest known references in documents to the dioceses. Later dates are usually those of synods, earlier dates depend upon less precise evidence. (For the churches dating before A.D. 300 see the survey maps 1, 3/4, 5).

Abbreviations: the Roman numerals I-XIV accompanying names in Italy indicate the former *Regiones* of Augustus; beg. = beginning; dep. (with mod. French names) = department; cent. = century; Civ. = Civitas; dioc. = diocese; E = east; Gr. = Greek; i. = island; is. = islands; l. = lake; loc. = locality; m. doc. = documents relating to the martyrs; metrop. = metropolis; mon. = (monasterium) monastery; N = north; prov. = province; riv. = river; S = south; W = West. References to maps and plates are given at the end of each entry: map references in ordinary type, plate references in italic type.

Abarshar or **Nishapur**, in Chorassan, Persia; (409, 420): 36
Abasgi, people living south of the Caucasus (Abkhazia, USSR): 35, 36
Abbaitis, district in Lydia: 16a
Abbircella (Henchir en Naam, near Sidi Médiène), Abbirgermaniciana, in Proconsularis; (411): 3, 22
Abda or **Eboda**, in the Negeb, in Palaestina III; (325): 14, cf 15a and 17
Abd-el-Kadir, S Egypt: 17
Abdera, in Rhodope; (451): 19
Abdera (Adra), in Baetica; (589): 20, 25
Abeda, in Proconsularis; (411): 22
Abellinum, see AVELLINUM
Abila (Sukh Wadi Barada), in Abilene, prov. of Phoenice Libanensis; (445): 15a
Abila (Tell Abil), in Palaestina II in Peraea; city of the Decapolis; (518): 15a
Abithinae (Chaoud), in Proconsularis; (256): 22, 30, 33
Abiwerd, in Chorassan, Persia; (554): 35
Abkhazia, land of the Abasgi, Caucasus: 14
Aboba, near the old fortified town of Pliska, in Bulgaria: 14
Abrettene, district in Bithynia: 16a
Abrittus (Abtaat Kalesi), in Moesia II; (431): 14, 19
Abthungi (Henchir-Es-Souar?), in Proconsularis; (310): 22, 33
Abula (Avila), in Lusitania: 25, 40
Abunoteichus, see IONOPOLIS
Abu Simbel, in S Egypt: 17
Abusir, in Egypt: 14
Abydos, in Thebais II: 17
Abydus (near Çanak Kale), in Hellespontus; (451): 16a, 19
Abziri, in Proconsularis; (393): 22
Acalissus, in Lycia; (451): 14, 16a
Acampsis (Çoruh), riv. in Armenia: 16b
Acci (Guadix), in Carthaginiensis, Hispania; (302): 3, 20, 25, 40
Accon or **Ace** ('Akka), see PTOLEMAIS
Acelum (Asolo), X, in prov. of Venetia & Histria; (591, 598): 23
Achaia, prov. of dioc. of Macedonia: 2, 4, 19, 41b, 42b
Acheruntia (Acerenza) in Apulia, prov. of Apulia & Calabria; (499): 23
Achladeri, in Lesbos, Greece: 14
Achrida or **Lychnidus** (Ohrid, *Ital.* Ochrida), in Epirus Nova: 19
Achulla (Henchir Botria), in Byzacena; (484): 22
Achurean, riv. in Armenia: 16b
Acilicene, region on the Euphrates, Armenia: 16b
Acinipo (Ronda la Vieja), in Baetica; (302): 3, 25
Acmonia, in Phrygia Pacatiana; (before 300): 4, 16a
Acoris, mon. in Arcadia, Egypt: 17, 34
Acqui, see AQUAE STATIELLAE
Acre, in Palestine: 14
Acropolis (Agropoli), in Lucania, prov. of Lucania & Bruttii; (592): 23
Actipus, see ECDIPPA
Adada, in Pamphylia: 16a
Adam Klissi or **Tropaeum Traiani**, in the Dobrogea: 14
Adana (Adana), in Cilicia I; (325): 4, 14, 15a, 16a, 31
Ad Aquas Caesarianas or **Caesaris** (Youks), in Numidia; (256): 3, 22
Ad Aras (Tarmount), in Mauretania Sitifensis; (394): 20
Ad Badias (Badès), in S Numidia; (256): 12, 20, 22, 34
Addana, in Coelesyria: 14
Ad Dracones (Hammam Bou Hadjar), in Mauretania Caesariensis; (411): 20
Ad Ficum (El Ksar), in Mauretania Sitifensis; (411): 22

Adhorbaidjan (Azerbaijan), district between Mare Caspium and L. Matianus (the Caspian Sea and Lake Urmia); the great Atropatene; (beg. of the 5th cent.): 36
Adiabene, district between the Tigris and Lake Matianus; heart of ancient Assyria: 2, 36
Adiana, in Palaestina III: 17
Ad Lacum Regium (Henchir Taoukouch), in Numidia; (484): 22
Ad Maiores (Henchir Besseriani), in S Numidia; (411): 20, 22
Ad Medias (Taddert), in S Numidia: 22
Ad Olivam (Oundadja), in Mauretania Sitifensis; (411): 20
Ad Palman (Aouinet), in Byzacena: 22
Ad Perdices ('Ain Hamiett), in Mauretania Sitifensis; (411): 22
Adra or **Abdera** in Baetica, Hispania; (589): 40
Adraa (Der'a), in Arabia; (359): 15a, 32
Adramyttium (Edremit), in Asia; (431): 16a, 19
Adrassus (Balabolu?), in Lycaonia, loc. uncertain; (451): 14, 16a
Adrianopolis or **Hadrianopolis** (Edirne), metrop. of Haemimontus; (about 300): 4, 9, 19, 31
Ad Sinnada, in Mauretania Caesariensis; (484): 20
Ad Turres, in S Byzacena; (411): 22
Aduatica Tungrorum (Tongeren), in Germania II; (346, Servatius): 3, 25
Adulis (Zula), in Erythraea: 14, 17
Adurenses (Aire-sur-l'Adour), 40; see CIV. ATURENSIUM
Aeca or **Aecae** (Troia), in Apulia, prov. of Apulia & Calabria; (501, 502): 23
Aechinus or **Echinus** (Akhinos), in Thessalia; (431): 19
Aeclanum (Grotte, near Mirabella), in the land of the Hirpini, IV, prov. of Samnium; (408, 409, 418): 12, 14, 23, 30, 42b
Aegae or **Edessa** (Vódena), in Macedonia I: 19
Aegae, in Asia; (449): 16a
Aegeae or **Aegae** (Ayaş), in Cilicia II; (about 300): 15a, 16a, 31
Aegates (Egadi), is. near Sicily: 23
Aegiale, seat of bishop on Amorgus, prov. of Insulae: 19
Aegina (Aigina), i., in Achaia; 1, 4, 5, 19
Aeginium (Kalabaka), in Thessalia; (451): 19
Aegyptus (Egypt), imperial diocese I, Augustalis: 1, 2, 3, 4, 5, 6, 8, 9, 17, 32, 41b
— **Prima**, prov. of dioc. Augustalis: 17, 41b
— **Secunda**, prov. of dioc. Augustalis: 17, 41b
Aegysaus, in Scythia Minor: 14
Aelana or **Aila** ('Aqaba), in Palaestina III; (325): 17
Aelaniticus sinus (Gulf of 'Aqaba): 17
Aelia (Jerusalem), Hierosolyma (from A.D. 138), in Palaestina I; the first Christian community (from A.D. 30): 4, 5, 6, 7, 8, 9, 10, 11, 12, 15a, 17, 31, 32 (Egeria), 34, 35, 36, 39 (Byzantine city), 41b, 42b; *321-6*
Aeliae, in Byzacena; (411): 22
Aemilia, in Italia, part of *Regio* VIII; (before 294): 3
Aeminium (Coimbra), in Lusitania; (beg. of 5th cent.): 25
Aemonia, in Histria, prov. of Venetia & Histria: 23
Aenaria (Ischia), i. in mare Tyrrhenum: 23
Aenon prope Salim ('Aenon near Salim') in Palestine; cf. John 3: 23, and Egeria: 32
Aenus, in Rhodope; (343): 16a, 19
Aenus or **Phaeno** (Mesmiya, *Fr.* Mousmiyeh), prov. of Arabia (351): 15a, 17
Aequi, people from the neighbourhood of Lake Fucinus, prov. of Valeria: 23, 24
Aera or **Aere Bataneae**, also **Eres** (Es-Sanamen), in Arabia; (325, 451): 4, 15, 32

Aesinum or **Aesis** or **Esinum** (Iesi), in Umbria Transappenninica, prov. of Flaminia & Picenum, VI; (680): 23
Aethiopia (Abyssinia): 14, 17, 34
Aezani, in Phrygia Pacatiana; (325): 4, 16a
Africa, imperial diocese XI: 5, 6, 8, 9, 11, 34, 35, 41a
— **Proconsularis**, see PROCONSULARIS
Afrincatinum (Avranches), in Lugdunensis II; (6th cent.): 25, 40
Agarlabis, in Byzacena; (484): 22
Agatha or **Civitas Agathensis** (Agde), in Narbonensis I; (507): 26, 40
Agaunum (St-Maurice d'Agaune), in Alpes Poeninae & Graiae; in the region of the Civ. Vallensium; (mon. 515): 23, 25, 30, 40
Agbia ('Ain Hedja), in Proconsularis; (256): 3, 22
Agde, 26; see AGATHA
Agen, 13; see AGINNUM
Aggar (Sidi Amara), in Byzacena; (484): 22
Aggersel (Sidi Abd-er-Rahman El Garci), in Byzacena; (411): 22
Aghtznikh, prov. in Armenia: 16a
Aginnum (Agen), Civ. Aginnensium, in Aquitania II; (357): 10, 13, 25, 30, 42a
Agri Decumates, between the Danube and the Rhine: 3, 5
Agrigentum (Agrigento, formerly Girgenti), in Sicilia; (3rd cent., 578, 590): 3, 13, 20, 23, 25, 40, 42a
Aguada, in Lusitania: 40
Aguemoun ou Bekkar, in dep. of Oran: 13
Aguntum (Stribach, near Lienz, in Stiria), in Noricum Ripense; (6th cent.): 23, 25, 40
Ahnas, in Faiyum, Egypt: 14
Aiacium (Ajaccio), in Corsica; (591?, 609, 649): 23
Aigina, in the Bay of Salamis: 14
Aigosthina, Greece: 14
Aila or **Aelana** ('Aqaba or Eilat), in Palaestina III: 4, 17, 36
Aina, prov. near southern border of Arabia: 15a; see AENUS
Ainay, a suburb of Lyon: 13
'Ain Chorab, N Africa: 13
'Ain Fournou, = Furni?, N Africa; (256, 304): 13
'Ain Tamda, N Africa, = Tamada, Tamadi, Mauretania Caesariensis: 13
'Ain Tixter, N Africa: 13
'Ain Wif, (Thenadassa) in Tripolitana: 13
'Ain Zara, near Tripoli, in Tripolitana: 13
'Ain Zirara, in Numidia: 13; *356, 485*
'Ain Zoui, N Africa: 13
Aipolioi, in Cappadocia I: 16a
Aire-sur-l'Adour, in dep. of Landes, see CIV. ATURENSIUM
Aix-en-Provence, in dep. of Bouches-du-Rhône, see AQUAE SEXTIAE: *369* (baptistery)
Aksaray, Turkey; in Cappadocia: 14
Akthamar, on an i. in Lake Thospitis, Armenia; (monuments from 9th-10th cents.): 14, 16b
Alabanda, in Caria; (451): 16a, 19
Alaǧa Kalesi or **Yaila**, Turkey; in Lycia: 14
Alahan Monastir, see KOČA KALESI, in Isauria, in the Taurus: 14b
Ala Miliaria (Bénian), in Mauretania Caesariensis; (404): 13, 20
Alasehir, Turkey: 14; see PHILADELPHIA
Alba (Alba), in Carthaginiensis, Hispania: 20, 25
Alba (Aps, dep. of Ardèche), in Viennensis; (40); seat of bishop 5th cent. in Mélas, 517 in Vivarium (Viviers): 26
Alba Iulia (Apulum), in Dacia: 14b
Albania (Daghestan), in the Caucasus: 11, 14, 36

ARELATE — BARDA'AH

Arelate (Arles), in Viennensis; (256; cf Cyprian, *Letters* 68; 314): 3, 5, 7, 9, 11, 12, 25, 26, 30, 33, 34, 35, 39, 41a, 42a; for plates see Arles. Although under the jurisdiction of Vienna, the bishop in fact exercised metropolitan rights over a constantly changing region
Areopolis (Rabba), the ancient Rabbath-Moab, in Moabitis, in Arabia: 15a, 17
Arethusa (Er-Restan), in Syria II; (325): 15a, 16a, 31
Arezzo, 13; see Arretium
Argaeus Mons (Erciyas), near Caesarea, Cappadocia I: 16a
Argala, on Lesvos: 14
Argalaste, near Volos, in Greece: 14
Argalla, in Cappadocia I: 16a
Argamum, Dobrogea (Doloman): 14
Argentoratum or **Civitas Argentoretensium** (Strasbourg), in Germania I; (346, then 614): 25, 40
Argiza, in Hellespontus; (457): 16a, 19
Argus or **Argos** (Argos), in Achaia; (458): 14, 19
Arianzus, in Cappadocia III: 16a
Ariarathia, in Armenia II: 16a
Ariassus, in Pamphylia; (381): 16a
Arimathea (Rentis), in Palaestina I: 15a
Aricia (Ariccia), Latium Vetus, I, prov. of Campania: 24
Ariminum (Rimini), in Flaminia, VIII, prov. of Flaminia & Picenum; (313): 3, 9, 23, 25, 30, 33, 40
Arindela (Gharandel), in Palaestina III; (431): 15a, 17
Arisitum or **Vicus Arisitensis** (Ales; or: Hierle?), in Narbonensis I; (572): 26, 40
Arjona, in Baetica; (302): 3, 25
Arles, dep. of Bouches-du-Rhône: 13: *362-5, 366 (Aliscamps), 401, 423-4, 462, 464-5, 521, 551, 577 (sarcophagi)*; see Arelate
Arles-sur-Tech, in dep. of Pyr.-Or., in the Roussillon: 13
Armacha or **Armagh,** in Hibernia; (*ca* 445): 25, 40, 41a
Arma di Taggia, on the Riviera di Ponente: 13
Armenaz, in N Syria: 15b
Armenia or **Regnum Armeniae,** originally a vassal state of the Romans, later partly independent, partly under the Sassanian kings; 2, 4, 5, 7, 9, 11, 14 (inset), 34, 35, 36, 41b
— Prima, Rom. prov. in dioc. of Pontus; eastern boundaries variable; from the time of Justinian, Pontus Polemoniacus: 16a, 16b, 41b
— Secunda, Rom. prov. in dioc. of Pontus; also known as Melitene; from the time of Justinian, former Prima: 16a, 16b, 41b
— Tertia, from the time of Justinian, former Secunda
— Quarta, from the time of Justinian, east of the Euphrates: 16b
— Minor, prov. I and II, west of the Euphrates: 16b
— Alta, mountain country north of upper course of the Euphrates: 16b
Armorica (Brittany), inhabited by the Britones after A.D. 450: 11, cf. 40
Arna (Civitella d'Arna), in Umbria Cisappenninica, V, prov. of Tuscia & Umbria; (499): 23
Arnitha, in Rhodes: 14
Arnon (Wadi el-Mujib), tributary of the Jordan: 15a
Arpi (Arpe, near Foggia), in Apulia, II, prov. of Apulia & Calabria: 4, 23
Arpinum (Arpino), I, prov. of Campania: 23
Arras, see Civ. Atrebatum
Arretium, Aretium (Arezzo), in Tuscia Annonaria, VIII, prov. of Tuscia & Umbria; (3rd cent.?, 680): 3, 23, 25, 30, 33, 40
Arrubium (Măcin, in Dobrogea), in Scythia Minor: 19
Arsacal (Gole'a), in Numidia; (484): 22
Arsamea, in Commagene, prov. of Euphratensis: 16b
Arsamosata, in Sophene: 16b, 36
Arsanias (Murat), riv. in Armenia: 16b
Arsinnaria (Ras-el-abiad), in Mauretania Caesariensis;(484): 20
Arsharuni or **Theodosiopolis,** in Caranitis, Armenia: 16b
Arsinoe or **Cleopatris,** in Augustamnica I: 17
Arsinoe (Polis), on Cyprus; (451): 16a
Arsinoe or **Crocodilopolis** (near Medinet-el-Faiyum), in Arcadia: 4, 14, 17
Arsinoe or **Tauchira,** in Libya Superior, Cyrenaica: 21
Artashat, Artishat or **Artaxata** (near Kamarlu), former capital of Armenia, on the Araxes: 9, 14 (inset), 16b, 36
Artemisia, i. near Corsica: 23
Artynias (Lake Apolyont), l. in Hellespontus: 16a
Arvernum, Arverna or **Arvernis,** 30, 34, 35, 40, 42b; see Civ. Arvernorum
Arycanda, in Lycia; (311); site of famous anti-Christian inscription of A.D. 312: 4, 14, 16a
Arzanene (Gharzan), district north of the Tigris, Armenia: 16b, 36, 41b
Arzon, in Arzanene, Armenia; (224): 5, 16b, 36
Arzuges, people in S Numidia: 33
Ascalon or **Ashqelon** (near 'Askalan), in Palaestina I; (325): 4, 15a, 17, 31
Ascania (Lake of Iznik), l. in Bithynia: 16a
Asculum (Ascoli Piceno), in Picenum Surburbicarium, V; (451): 23, 41a
Ashtarak, in N Armenia: 14 (inset)
Ashtishat, Armenia: 7, 16b, 34, 36, 41b
Asia, imperial diocese IV: 4, 16a, 19, 41b
Asia, prov. of dioc. of Asia: 6, 16a, 19, 41b; before 294, prov.: 1, 2, 4
Asopus or **Asopophoebia,** in Achaia; (343): 19
Aspendus (Balkis), in Pamphylia; (325): 4, 14
Asphaltidis (The Dead Sea), l. in Palaestina: 15a
Aspona, in Galatia I; (451): 16a
Assava, in Mauretania Sitifensis; (411): 22
Assidonia, in Baetica: 40
Assisium, Asisium (Assisi), in Umbria Cisappenninica, V, Tuscia & Umbria; (649): 3, 23
Assuras (Zanfour), in Proconsularis; (*ca* 250; cf Cyprian, *Letters,* 65): 3, 22
Assus (Beramkoy), in Troas, prov. of Asia: 4, 14, 16a, 19
Asti, see Hasta
Astianene, district in Armenia: 16b
Astigi (Ecija), in Baetica; (302): 3, 20, 25, 30, 40; *372 (sarcophagus)*
Asturia, district in N Spain; (after 400): 40
Asturica (Astorga), until A.D. 453 metrop. of Gallaecia; (258): 3, 11, 25, 35, 40, 41a, 42a
Astypalaea (Astipalaia) i, prov. of Insulae; 14, 16a, 19
Aswan, in Egypt: 14; see Syene
Asyut, in Egypt: 14; see Lycopolis
Atarbechis, in Aegyptus I: 17
Atarneus, in Asia: 16a
Ategua, in Baetica; (302): 3, 25
Atella (S. Arpino near Aversa), I, in prov. of Campania; (465): 23, 30
Ateni, in Georgia: 14 (inset)
Aternus, riv. in Italy: 23
Athenae (Athens), in Achaia; (1st cent. (Paul); 325): 1, 4, 5, 6, 8, 9, 11, 14, 18, 19, 42b
Athenaeum, in Chersonesus Taurica: 16c
Athos Mons, in Macedonia I: 19, 34
Athribis, in Augustamnica II: 4, 17
At(h)ripe or **Monasterium Candidum** (Deir el-Ahmar), in Thebais I: 12, 14, 17, 42b
Atria (Adria), in Venetia, V, prov. of Venetia & Histria; (649): 23
Atrebates, see Civ. Atrebatum
Atripalda, 13; see Avellinum
Atrun (El), in Libya: 14
Attalea (near Akhisar) in Lydia; (343): 16a
Attalia (Antalya), in Pamphylia; (431): 1, 4, 5, 16a
Attanassus, in Phrygia Pacatiana; (451): 16a
Attuda, in Phrygia Pacatiana; (431): 16a
Auch, in dep. of Gers: 13; see Eliumberis
Aufidena (Alfidena), land of the Samniti, IV, prov. of Samnium, seat of bishop transferred to Trivento in 10th cent.; (494, 495): 23
Aufinum (Ofena), in the land of the Vestini, IV, prov. of Samnium; (475): 23
Augila, in Libya: 35
Augsburg, 13; see Augusta Vindelicorum
Augustae (at the mouth of the Ogust), in Dacia Ripensis; (431?): 19
Augustalis, dioc., Egypt & Libya: 17, 21; see Aegyptus
Augustamnica Prima, prov. of dioc. of Aegyptus: 17, 41b
— Secunda, prov. of dioc. of Aegyptus: 17, 41b
Augusta Praetoria (Aosta), in Alpes Poeninae et Graiae; (451, probably as early as 380): 23, 40
Augusta Rauracorum (Augst, near Basle) in Maxima Sequanorum; from the end of the 3rd cent.: Castrum Rauracorum or Rauracense (Kaiseraugst): 25
Augusta Suessionum (Soissons), in Belgica II; (*ca* 300?, 346): 3, 7, 25, 30, cf 40
Augusta Taurinorum or **Taurini** (Turin), in Alpes Cottiae? (under eccl. jurisdiction of Liguria); (probably *ca* 397, 408-423): 11, 12, 23, 26, 30, 42b
Augusta Treverorum or **Treveri** (Trèves, Trier), metrop. of Belgica I; (2nd cent; 314): 3, 5, 7, 9, 11, 12, 25, 30, 40, 41a, 42a; *155, 160, 162 (palace), 400 (sarcophagus)*
Augusta Vindelicorum (Augsburg), in Raetia II: 3, 25, 30, 40, 41a
Augustodunum or **Civitas Aeduorum** (Autun), in Lugdunensis I; (3rd cent.; 313, 314): 3, 6, 10, 25, 30, 40, 42a; 55 (*epitaph of Pectorius*)
Augustopolis, in Palaestina III; (431): 15a, 17
Auja el-Hafir, in the Negeb: 14
Aujila, 14; see Augila
Aulon Cilicius, strait between Cyprus and Isauria: 15a, 16a
Aulona (Vlonë, in Albania; *ital.,* Valona), in Epirus Nova; (458): 19
Auranitis (Jebel Druz and Hauran), region in Arabia: 15a
Aurariola, part of Visigothic Spain: 40
Aurelianum, -ani (Orléans), in Lugdunensis IV; (*ca* 340-50, 346): 25, 35, 40
Aurelianopolis, in Lydia; (325): 4, 16a, 19
Auria or **Aurensis** (Orense), in Gallaecia; (589): 25, 40
Aurocra, in Phrygia Salutaris; (451): 16a
Ausafa, see Auzafa
Ausona or **Vicus Ausona** (Vich, in Catalonia) in Tarraconensis: 25, 40
Ausugguru, in Numidia; (484): 22
Autenti, in Byzacena, loc. uncertain; (484): 1, 22
Autissiodurum (Auxerre), in Lugdunensis IV; (beginning of 4th cent.): 3, 25, 34, 40, 42a
Autrigonia, district in Cantabria; (6th cent.): 40
Autun, dep. of Saône-et-Loire: 13; *55*; see Augustodunum
Auxerre, in dep. of Yonne: 13; see Autissiodurum
Auximum (Osimo), in Picenum Suburbicarium; (599): 23
Auzafa, in Byzacena; (256): 3, 22
Auzia (Aumale), in Mauretania Sitifensis: 3, 20
Avan, in Armenia: 14 (inset)
Aveia (near Fossa), land of the Vestini, IV, prov. of Valeria; (465): 23
Avella or **Abella** (Avella), I, prov. of Campania: 23
Avellinum or **Abellinum** (Atripalda), I, prov. of Campania; (499, near Avellino): 23, 30
Avenio or **Civitas Avennicorum** (Avignon), in Viennensis; (439): 26
Aventicum (Avenches), in Maxima Sequanorum; (246); destroyed by the Alamanni; bishop's residence in Vindonissa (Windisch) after A.D. 550: 25, 35, 40, 42a
Avignon, in dep. of Vaucluse: 13, 26; see Avenio
Avila, see Abula
Avioccala (Sidi Amara), in Proconsularis: 22
Avranches, in dep. of Manche; see Afrincatinum
Axiopolis (Hinok, near Cernavoda), in Scythia Minor: 4, 14, 19, 31
Axumis (Aksum), in Ethiopia; (4th cent.): 17
Ayaş, (Aegaeae) in Turkey: 14
Ayaşin, in Turkey: 14
Azotus (Isdud), in Palaestina I; (325): 1, 4, 5, 15a, 17

B

Ba'albek, 14; see Heliopolis
Babamonitis, district in Paphlagonia: 16a
Bab el-Hawa, N Syria: 15b
Babisqa, N Syria: 15b
Babra, in Numidia; (484): 22
Babuda, in N Syria: 15b
Babutta, in N Syria: 15b
Babylon, south of the Euphrates: 7, 31, 36
Babylon (Cairo), in Augustamnica II; (449): 17, 34
Babylonia, district south of the Euphrates: 34
Bactria, region near the Oxus: 36
Badhisi, in Chorassan: (585): 36
Badimon, in Armenia II: 16a
Baecula (Baylen) in Baetica; (314): 3, 25
Baeterrae, see Biterrae
Baetica (Andalusia), prov. of dioc. XV, Hispania: 2, 3, 20, 25, 35, 40, 41a
Baetis (Guadalquivir), riv. in Baetica: 40
Bagai (Ksar Bagai), in Numidia (near the lakes): (256): 3, 9, 20, 22, 33
Bagaran, in N Armenia: 14 (inset)
Baghawat (El) (Hibe), in Thebais II: 14, 17: *345-7 (cupola frescoes in mausolea)*
Bagis, in Lydia; (325): 4, 16a
Bagnols, in dep. of Gard: 13
Bagrada(s) (Medjerda), riv. in Proconsularis: 22, 33
Bagrawand or **Bagravandene,** prov. in central Armenia: 16b
Bagtshisaray, in the Crimea: 14
Bahanna, in Byzacena; (411): 22
Bahnasa (El), Egypt: 14, 17
Bahrain, i. in the Persian Gulf: 36; see Tylus
Baiae, in Campania, I: 23
Baiana, in Numidia; (393): 22
Baiocae or **Civitas Baiocassium** (Bayeux), in Lugdunensis II; (6th cent.): 25, 40
Balabitene, in Armenia IV: 16b
Balabolu (Adrassus?), in Isauria: 14b
Balad, on the Tigris; (497): 36
Balaneae (Baniyas, on the coast), in Syria II; (325): 4, 15a, 16a
Balasfar, in Beit Madaye, east of the Tigris; (424): 36
Balbura, in Lycia; (381): 14, 16a
Balcić, south coast of Dobrogea: 14
Baleares (Balearics), is., prov. of dioc. of Hispania, from A.D. 369-86: 25, 41a
Balkh, in what was formerly Bactria: 36
Ballene Praesidium, in Mauretania Caesariensis; (484): 20
Balneum Regis (Bagnorea), in Tuscia Suburbicaria, VIII, prov. of Tuscia & Umbria; (600, 861): 23
Bambyce, see Hierapolis
Bamuqqa, in N Syria: 15b
Banbury, see Bannaventa
Bancorna, = Bangor Fawr: 25
Bangor (Bangor, Co. Down), mon. in Hibernia: 34, 40
Bangor Fawr (Bangor, Caernarvon), in Britannia: 25, 34, 40
Bangor Iscoed (in Flints., Wales), mon. in Britannia: 25, 34, 40
Baniyas, 14; see Paneas
Bannaventa (Banbury), in Britannia: 25
Baqirha, in N Syria: 15b
Baqusa, in N Syria: 15b
Bararus, in Byzacena; (484): 22
Barata (Binbirkalesi), in Lycaonia; (325): 4, 14, 16a
Barbalissus (Balis), in Euphratensis; (431): 15a
Barbe (Barbesula, near Torre de Guadiaro), in Baetica: 3, 25
Barce, in Libya Superior, Cyrenaica; (325): 4, 7, 14, 21
Barcelona, 13; see Barcino
Barcino (Barcelona), in Tarraconensis; (343): 3, 10, 11, 25, 30, 33, 35, 40, 42a
Barda'ah, on the Terteï, seat of the Albanian katholikos, 36

Bargylia, in Caria: 16a, 19
Barglyus Mons, in Syria II: 15a
Bari, 14; see BARIUM
Baria (Vera), in Carthaginiensis, Hispania; (302): 3, 20, 25
Baris (near Isparta), in Pisidia; (325): 16a
Baris, in Hellespontus; (451): 16a, 19
Barium (Bari), in Apulia, II, prov. of Apulia & Calabria; (465): 19, 23
Barqusa (Burpush, southwest of Damascus), in Phoenice Libanensis: 15a
Barletta, in Apulia: 14
Basel, Basle, see BASILEA
Basen, seat of bishop in Armenia: 16b
Basen or Phasiane, prov. in Armenia: 16b
Bashamra, in N Syria: 15b
Bashmishli, in N Syria: 15b
Basilica Therme or Aquae Saravenae, in Saravene, prov. of Cappadocia I; (451): 16a
Basilea (Basel, Basle), in Maxima Sequanorum; seat of bishop A.D. 346 in Castrum Rauracorum (Kaiseraugst), after A.D. 614 here: 25
Basilinopolis, in Bithynia: 16a
Baslania (Baza), in Baetica: 40, cf 25; see BASTI
Basra, 36; see PERAT
Bassiana (Ferryville), in Proconsularis; (349): 22
Bassianae (Dobrince), in Pannonia II: 19
Basti (Baza), in Carthaginiensis; (302): 3, 25; see BASLANIA
Batanae, in Euphratensis: 15a
Batanaea, district in Arabia: 15a
Batava, in Raetia II: 25
Bathnae, Bathanae or (Syr.) Sarug (Sürüç) in Osrhoëne; (381): 15a, 32, 34, 35, 36, 42b
Batuta, in N Syria: 15b
Ba'ude, in N Syria: 15b
Bav or Bau, see PBOV
Bawit, in Thebais I., mon. of Apollo: 14, 17, 34; 340
Bawiti (El), Egypt: 14; see OASIS MINOR
Bayeux, dep. of Calvados; see BAIOCAE
Bazas, dep. of Gironde; see VASATICA
Baziher, in N Syria: 15b
Bazufan, in N Syria: 15b
Beauvais, in dep. of Oise, see BELLOVACUM
Bechulla, in N Syria: 15b
Begerin, in Hibernia: 25, 40
Behyo, in N Syria: 15b
Beirut, see BERYTUS
Beja, see PAX IULIA
Beisan, isr. Beth Shean, in Palaestina II: 14; see SCYTHOPOLIS
Beit Armaiye, Pers. prov. in Mesopotamia (cap., Seleucia): 36
Beit Husaiye (Sahabad), Persian prov. east of the mouth of the Tigris; (224): 36
Beit Laphat or Gundishapur, city in Susiana; (224; 410 metrop. of Susiana): 36
Beit Madaye, Pers. prov. northeast of Ctesifon; (419): 36
Beit Maskene, Pers. prov. north of Seleucia; (224): 36
Beit Moksaye or Moxoene, Pers. prov. including Mokh; (409): 16b, 36
Beit Qatraiye, Pers. prov. S of Bahrain; (224): 36
Beit Selok or Karka de Beit Selok (Kirkuk), metrop. of Garamaea; E of the Tigris; already bishopric in A.D. 171; (224; 410 metrop.): 36
Beit Zabde, city in Zabdizene or Gerzira; already Christian ca A.D. 100: 1, 5, 36
Belali, in Proconsularis; (411): 22
Belbek, in the Crimea: 14
Belgica, prov.; divided in A.D. 294: 2, 3
— Prima, prov. of dioc. of Gallia: 25, 41a
— Secunda, prov. of dioc. of Gallia: 25, 41a
Belica (Belley), in Lugdunensis I; after A.D. 552 seat of bishop (transferred from Noviodunum): 26
Bellegarde, dep. of Gard, near Nîmes: 13
Belley, dep. of Ain: 26, see BELICA
Bellezma, dep. of Constantine, Algeria: 13
Bellovacum or Civitas Bellovacorum (Beauvais), in Belgica II; (6th cent.): 25, 40
Bellunum (Belluno), in Venetia, X, prov. of Venetia & Histria; (589, 591): 23
Belluza, in N Syria: 15b
Belovo, Bulgaria: 14
Benarno or Civitas Benarnensium (Lescar, in Béarn), in Novempopulana; (507): 25, 40
Bencenna, in Proconsularis; (411): 22
Beneventum (Benevento), land of the Hirpini, II, prov. of Samnium; (313): 3, 23, 40, 41b
Bénian, 13; see ALA MILIARIA
Benghazi, 14; see BERENICE
Bennafa (Oglet Khalifa), in Byzacena; (393): 22
Berenice (Benghazi), in Cyrenaica, prov. of Libya Superior; (325): 4, 7, 14, 21
Berenice Troglodytice, in Thebais II: 17
Bernicia, principality in Britannia: 40
Berga, in Macedonia I; (431): 19
Bergama, in Turkey: 14; see PERGAMUM
Bergomum (Bergamo), in Liguria, XI, prov. of Liguria & Aemilia; (before 397): 3, 23
Berja, in Andalusia: 13, 371 (sarcophagus)

Berish, in N Syria: 15b
Beriza, in Armenia I; (458): 16a
Beroe, in Scythia Minor: 19
Beroea (Veroia), in Macedonia I; (343): 1, 4, 5, 19
Beroea ad Belum (Aleppo, Haleb), in Syria I; (beg. 4th cent.): 4, 15a, 15b, 16a, 32, 34, 42b
Beroea or Irenopolis (Stara-Zagora, Bulgaria), in Thracia; (343): 19
Berre, dep. of Bouches-du-Rhône: 13
Bersabaea, Palaestina I: 15a
Bertrand-de-Comminges (St-), dep. of Hautes-Pyrénées: 13; see CIV. CONVENARUM
Berytus (Beirut), in Phoenice I; (324, 325): 4, 11, 15a, 42b
Besançon, dep. of Doubs, see VESONTIO
Besanduce (Khirbet der Sáad, near Beit Jibrin), mon. in Judaea, Palaestina II: 15a, 34
Bescera (Biskra), in S Numidia; (411): 20, 22
Bethammaris, in Euphratensis: 15a
Bethania (El-'Azariye), in Palaestina I; Lazarion, according to Egeria: 15a, 32
Bethel (Beitin), in Palaestina I: 15a
Bethlehem (Beit Lahm), in Palaestina I: 4, 9, 10, 12, 14, 15a, 17, 31, 32, 34, 42b; 129 (Church of the Nativity)
Bettir, in N Syria: 15b
Bewcastle, in Northumbria: 40
Béziers, dep. of Hérault: 26; see BITERRAE
Bida (Djemma Saharidj), in Mauretania Sitifensis; (484): 20
Biertan, in Rumenia: 14b
Bigastrium, in Baetica: 40
Bigorretana or Civitas Bigorritanorum (Bagnères-de-Bigorre), in what was formerly Novempopulana: 40
Bih-Shapur, city in Persia, m. doc.: 36
Bilbilis, in Tarraconensis (Cerro de Bambola, near Calatayud): 25, 42
Bilechas, tributary of the Euphrates, Osrhoëne: 15a
Billaeus (Filyos), riv. in Honorias: 16a
Bilta, in Proconsularis; (256): 3, 22
Bina or Vina, in Proconsularis; (393): 22
Binbirkalesi or Madenşehir, 'the 1001 churches', perhaps the ancient Barata in Lycaonia: 14
Binin, in N Syria: 15b
Birtha or Apamea (Birecik, on the Euphrates), in Euphratensis; (431): 15a, 36
Bisericuta, in Rumenia (Dinogetia): 14
Bist or Bust, in Sakastene, Persia; (544): 36
Bistue Nova, in Dalmatia; (530): 19, 23
Biterrae, Baeterrae or Civitas Beterriensum (Béziers), in Narbonensis I; (419): 9, 25, 26, 40
Bithynia, prov. before A.D. 294; after A.D. 294 prov. of the dioc. of Pontus: 1, 2, 4, 5, 6, 16a, 41b
Bithynium or Claudiopolis, in Honorias: 16a
Bitolj, see HERACLEA LYNCESTIS
Bituricae or Civitas Biturigum, later Bituriges (Bourges), metrop. of Aquitania I; (end of 3rd cent.): 3, 7, 25, 40, 41a
Bizica, (Henchir Bijga), in Proconsularis; (411): 22
Bizone, in Scythia Minor: 19
Bizya (Vize), in Europa; (343): 4, 16a, 19, 31
Bladia (Henchir Baldia), in Proconsularis; (411): 22
Blanda Iulia (Porta di Sapri?), in Lucania, III, prov. of Lucania & Bruttii; (592): 23
Blandus, in Armenia I: 16a
Blaundus, in Lydia: 16a
Blera (Bieda on the Via Clodia), in Tuscia Suburbicaria, VII, prov. of Tuscia & Umbria; (487): 23, 24, 30
Bobbio, mon. south of Pavia: 34, 40
Boeae, in southern part of Achaia: 4, 19
Bogaz Köy, in Galatia I: 16a
Boiodurum (Innstadt-Passau), in Noricum Ripense: 25
Bolan, pass in Afghanistan: 36
Bolnisi, in Georgia: 14 (inset)
Bologna, 13; see BONONIA
Bolsena, 13; see VOLSINII
Bolzano, formerly Bauzanum, or Pons Drusus: 13
Bône, dep. of Constantine, Algeria, near the ruins of Hippo Regius: 13
Bonna (Bonn), in Germania II: 13, 25, 30
Bononia (Bologna), in Aemilia, VIII, prov. of Liguria & Aemilia; (beg. of 4th cent; 381): 3, 23, 25, 30, 33, 40, 41a
Bononia (Vidin), in Dacia Ripensis: 4, 19, 31
Bonorvo, on Sardinia: 13
Borazi, in Yugoslavia: 14
Bordeaux, dep. of Gironde: 13; see BURDIGALA
Boreum (Gasr Bou Grada), in Cyrenaica, Libya Superior: 21
Borysthenes (Dnieper), riv. in Sarmatia: 36
Bosa, on Sardinia; seat of bishop?: 23
Boset, in Proconsularis; (411): 22, 33
Bosnia, in Yugoslavia: 14
Bosphorus or Panticapaeum (Kerch, Kersj), in Chersonesus Taurica; 4, 16c, 36
Bosphorus Cimmeruis (Strait of Kerch): 16c
— Thracius (Bosphorus), between Europa and Bithynia: 16a
Bostra (Busra, in the Hauran), metrop. of Arabia, with 17 suffragans; (324, 325): 4, 8, 10, 15a, 31, 36, 41b, 42b
Botrus (Batrun), in Phoenice I; (451): 15a
Bourges, dep. of Cher, see BITURICAE
Bovianum or Bovianum Undecimanorum (Boiano), land of the Samniti; (501, 503): 23

Boyole, N. of Pula, Istria: 13
Brać, 14; see BRATTIA
Bracara (Braga, Portugal), from A.D. 453 onwards the metrop of Gallaecia; (390): 11, 12, 25, 35, 40, 41a, 42a
Brad, in N Syria: 14, 15b
Braga, Portugal: 13; see BRACARA
Brattia (Brać), i. in Dalmatia: 19, 23
Bravron, in Attica, prov. of Achaia: 14
Bravonium, Bravinium or Brefi, in Wales, Britannia: 25, 35, 40
Bregenz, on the Bodensee; see BRIGANTIUM
Brescello, see BRIXELIUM
Brescia, 13; 157 (gold glass) 198, 520 (lipsanotheca); see BRIXL.
Breviglieri, in Tripolitana: 13
Briate (Brioude), in Aquitania I: 26; see also BRIVAS
Brieuc (St-), dep. of Côtes-du-Nord: 25; see BRIOCUM
Brigantium (Bregenz), in Raetia II: 25
Brigetio (Szöny, Hungary), in Pannonia I, necropolis: 19
Brignoles, in dep. of Var: 7, 13, 26; for plates see LA GAYOLLE
Brindisi, Apulia: 14; see BRUNDISIUM
Briocum (St-Brieuc), in Lugdunensis III: 25, 34, 40
Brioni, i. on the coast of Dalmatia: 13; mon. before 847?
Brioude, in dep. of Haute-Loire: 26; see BRIATE
Britannia, prov. before A.D. 294: 2, 3, 9, 11; after A.D. 294 imperial diocese XII divided into 5 provinces: 25, 34, 41a
— Prima, prov. of dioc. of Britannia: 25, 41a
— Secunda, prov. of dioc. of Britannia: 25, 41a
Britonia, in Gallaecia; (572): 25, 40
Briula, in Asia; (431): 16a, 19
Brivas, Vicus Brivatensis or Briate (Brioude): 34
Briviesca, N Spain: 13
Brixellum (Brescello), in Aemilia, VIII, prov. of Liguria & Aemilia; (451): 23
Brixia (Brescia), in Venetia, X, prov. of Liguria & Aemilia (543), 5 bishops: 3, 7, 10, 23, 25, 30, 42a; for plates see BRESCIA
Brixworth, England: 13 (7th cent. church), 40
Brundisium (Brindisi), in Calabria, II, prov. of Apulia & Calabria; (492, 496): 4, 19, 23, 30
Bruttii (Lucania &), see LUCANIA & BRUTTII
Bruzus, in Phrygia Salutaria: 16a
Btirsa, in N Syria: 15b
Bubastis (Zagazig), in Augustamnica II: 17
Bubon, in Lycia; (381): 16a
Bucolia (Abukir), in Aegyptus I: 17
Budrum Kalesi, 14; see CASTABALA
Buhen, in S Egypt: 17
Bukhara, in Sogdiane: 36
Bulbitinum (Ostium), one of the 7 mouths of the Nile: 17
Bulla, in Proconsularis; (484): 22
Bulla Regia (Hammam Darradji), in Proconsularis; (256): 3, 20, 22, 23
Burdakli, in N Syria: 15b
Burdigala (Bordeaux), metrop. of Aquitania II; (314): 3, 7, 9, 10, 12, 25, 40, 41a, 42a
Burdj el-Derum, N Syria: 15b
Burdj Haida, in N Syria: 15b
Burguillos, in Estremadura, Spain: 13
Burgundarholm (Bornholm): 11
Bursa, Arabia: 14; see BOSTRA
Bursa, Turkey: 140 see PRUSA
Busentum, small riv. in Bruttii: 11
Busiris, in Aegyptus II: 4, 17
Bust, see BIST
Buthrotum (Vutrinos), in Epirus Vetus; (458): 19
Buto, in Aegyptus II; (431): 17
Buto, l. in the Nile Delta: 17
Buxentum (Capo della Foresta, near Policastro), in Lucania, III, prov. of Lucania & Bruttii; (501, 502): 23
Byblus (Jbail), in Phoenice I; (381): 4, 15a
Byllis (Balish, in Albania), in Epirus Nova; (458): 19
Byzacena, prov. of dioc. of Africa: 20, 22, 33, 41a
Byzantium (Istanbul), in Europa, refounded after A.D. 320 as Constantinople; 2nd cent.: 4, 5
Bznunikh, bishopric in Armenia: 16b

C

Cabalia, district in Lycia: 16a
Cabarsussi, in Africa; loc. uncertain: 9
Cabasa, metrop. of Aegyptus II; (431): 17, 41b
Cabeza del Griego, central Spain near Saelices, prov. Cuenca, 13; see ARCAVICA
Cabillonum or Castra Cabillonum (Chalon-sur-Saône), (346), ca A.D. 470 seat of a bishop: 40
Cabira, ancient name for Neocaesarea in Pontus: 16a
Cabra, in Baetica; (302): 25
Cabrera, near Barcelona: 13
Cades Barnea, in Palaestina III: 17
Cadi, near ruins of Aezani, Phrygia Pacatiana: 6, 14
Cádiz, see GADES
Cadmus Mons, in Phrygia Pacatiana: 16a
Cadurci or Civitas Cadurcorum (Cahors), Aquitania I; (6th cent.): 25
Caeliana, in Numidia, loc. uncertain; (484): 22
Caenopolis, in Thebais II: 17

CAERE — CHELLES

Caere (Cerveteri), in Tuscia Suburbicaria, VII, prov. of Tuscia & Umbria; (499): 24
Caerleon, see ISCA
Caerwent, in Britannia: 13, 25
Caesaraugusta (Zaragoza), in Tarraconensis, Hispania, gradually became the metrop. in place of Tarraco; (before 300): 3, 12, 25, 30, 34, 35, 40, 41a, 42a
Caesarea, in Bithynia; (325): 4, 16a
Caesarea or **Mazaca** (Kayseri), metrop. of Cappadocia I; (325): 4, 5, 7, 8, 9, 10, 14, 31, 32, 34, 35, 36, 41b, 42b
Caesarea Mauretaniae (Cherchel, dep. of Oran), in Mauretania Caesariensis (314): 3, 13, 20, 30, 33, 40, 41a; *354 (mensa)*
Caesarea Palaestinae or **Turris Stratonis** (Kaisariye), in Palaestina I; 1st cent.; (325): 1, 4, 5, 8, 9, 10, 14, 15a, 31, 32, 41b, 42b
Caesarea Philippi or **Paneas** (Baniyas), in Phoenice I; (325): 15a
Caesaria, in Numidia; (484): 22
Caesariani (Kessaria), in Numidia; (303): 22
Caesena (Cesena), in Flaminia, VIII, prov. of Flaminia and Picenum; (603): 3, 23
Cagliari, 13; see CARALES
Cahors, dep. of Lot: 13; see CADURCI
Caicus (Bakyr), riv. in Asia and Lydia: 16a
Cairo, in Egypt: 14
Cala (Chelles), mon. north of Paris: 34
Calabria (Apulia &), see APULIA & CALABRIA
Calafora (Calahorra), 40; see CALAGURRIS NASSICA
Calagurris Fibularia (Loarre), in Tarraconensis; (302): 3, 7, 25
Calagurris Nassica (Calahorra), in Tarraconensis; (before 310): 3, 12, 25, 30, 42a
Calama (Guelma, dep. of Constantine), in Numidia: 3, 10, 12, 20, 22, 30, 33, 40
Calamona, in Phoenice Libanensis: 15a
Caldey, i. off the coast of Wales, with mon.: 34
Cales (Calvi), I, in prov. of Campania; (499): 23
Callatis (Mangalia), in Scythia Minor: 14, 19
Calleva Atrebatum (Silchester), in Britannia: 25, cf 13
Calliana, i. off the coast of India: 36
Callinicum Nicephorium (Ragga), in Euphratensis, frontier post; (388): 15a, 36
Callipolis (Gelibolu, Gallipoli), in Europa, on the Hellespont; (536): 16a, 19
Callipolis or **Anxa** (Gallipoli), in Calabria, II, prov. of Apulia & Calabria; (551, 593): 23
Callirrhoe or **Edessa,** in Osrhoëne: 15a
Calycadnus (Göksu), riv. in Isauria; 16a
Calydon, in Achaia, Greece: 14
Calymna (Kalimnos), i., in prov. of Insulae: 19
Calynda, in Lycia; (458): 16a
Camaracum or **Civitas Camaracensium** (Cambrai), in Belgica II; (346, then 6th cent.): 25, 40
Camelodunum (Colchester), in Britannia: 25
Camerina, in Sicily: 23
Camerinum (Camerino), in Umbria Transappenninica, V, prov. of Tuscia & Umbria; (465, 496, 550, 560): 23
Caminus, i. in prov. of Insulae: 16a
Camirus, in Rhodes, prov. of Insulae: 19
Campania, in prov. of Italia Suburbicaria; the former *Regio* I, i.e. Latium Vetus, Latium Adiectum, and Campania itself: 23, 41a
Camulianae or **Iustiniopolis,** in Cappadocia I; (553): 16a
Canatha (Kanawat), city of the Decapolis, in prov. of Arabia: 14, 15a
Candida Casa or **Witherna** (Withern, Strathclyde), in Caledonia: 9, 25, 34
Candra, in Bithynia: 16a
Canopicum (Ostium), one of the 7 mouths of the Nile: 17
Canopus or **Menuthis,** in Aegyptus I; (404): 17, 31; *316*
Canosa, see CANUSIUM: 23
Canoscia, south of Arezzo: 13
Canterbury, 13; see CANTUARIA
Cantuaria (Canterbury, Kent), in Britannia: 13, 25, 35, 40
Canusium (Canosa), in Apulia, II, prov. of Apulia & Calabria; (343): 23
Cap Bon, Chr. ruins northwest of Carthage, at Kélibia, in Tunis: 13
Capena, in Tuscia, near Rome, prov. of Tuscia & Umbria: 24
Capharnaum (Tell Hum), in Palaestina II: 1, 7, 15a, 31; *35 (synagogue)*
Caphergamala (Kfar Gamba, at Beit Jamal, S of Hartuv), in Palaestina I: 15a, 31
Capidava, in Scythia Minor: 19
Capitolias (Beth Ras), in Palaestina II; (325): 4, 15a
Cappadocia, Rom. prov. before A.D. 294; after A.D. 294 reduced to central region; prov. of dioc. of Pontus; in A.D. 371 divided by Valens into Prima and Secunda; in A.D. 536 into Prima, Secunda, and Tertia (although Nyssa remained within the ecclesiastical province of Caesarea): 1, 2, 4, 5, 7, 16a, 32, 34, 36, 41b
— Prima, prov. of dioc. of Pontus: 16a, 41b
— Secunda, prov. of dioc. of Pontus: 16a, 41b
— Tertia, prov. of dioc. of Pontus: 16a, 41b
Cappadox (Delice), tributary of the Halys, in Cappadocia: 16a
Capraria (Capraja), i. near Corsica: 23, 33, 34
Capreae (Capri), i., near Misenum, in prov. of Campania: 23
Capsa (Gafsa), in S Byzacena; (256): 3, 20, 22, 33, 34
Capsus, in Numidia; (411): 22
Capua (Santa Maria di Capua Vetere), in prov. of Campania, I; (313, 314): 3, 23, 30, 40, 41a, 42a
Caput Ciliani (Gouéa), in Mauretania Caesariensis; (484): 20
Caput Saltus Horreorum ('Ain Zada), in Mauretania Sitifensis; (484): 22
Caput Vada (R. Kaboudia), promontory in Byzacena: 22
Caraiatha, in Arabia: 15a
Carales or **Caralis Locus** (Cagliari), in Sardinia; in a certain sense the metrop. of the island; (314): 3, 10, 23, 25, 30, 33, 34, 40, 41a, 42a
Caralis (Beysehir), l. in Pisidia and Lycaonia: 16a
Carana or **Theodosiopolis** or **Arsharuni,** in Caranitis, Armenia: 16b
Caranitis, district in Armenia: 16b
Carcabia, in Tripolitana; (393): 21, 22
Carcaso or **Ecclesia Carcassonensis** (Carcassonne), in Narbonensis I; (after A.D. 550; 589): 25, 40
Carcassonne, in dep. of Aude; see CARCASO
Carcesa, in Baetica: 25; see CARTEIA, CARTERA
Carcinites sinus, north of the Chersonesus Taurica: 16c
Cardagköy, in Turkey: 14
Caria, prov. of dioc. of Asia: 16a, 19, 41b
Cariathaim, in Arabia: 17
Caričin Grad, Serbia, see LUSTINIANA PRIMA: 14, 19
Carinae or **Hiccara,** (near Palermo in Sicily; mod. Carini lies more to the east): 23
Carith (Krit), brook in Palaestina II: 32
Carmalas (Samanli), tributary of the Sarus, in Cilicia and Cappadocia: 16a
Carmania (Kermen), prov. in Persia: 36
Carmeia or **Carmeianum** (near Monte Gargano), in Apulia, prov. of Apulia & Calabria; (501, 502): 23
Carmelus (Mons), in Phoenice I: 34
Carnavonia (Caernarvon), in Britannia; (465): 11, 25
Carneas (Khirbet en-Nile), according to Egeria, Dennaba, in the land of Job: 15a, 32; see NEAPOLIS in Arabia
Carnuntum (Altenburg), in Pannonia I: 19
Carnutum, see CIVITAS CARNOTENSIUM
Carpasia (Rizokarpasa), in Cyprus; (400): 15a, 16a
Carpathus (Karpathos), i. in prov. of Crete; (343, 536): 16a, 19, 35, 42b
Carpentoracte (Carpentras), in Viennensis; (439): 13, 26, 40
Carpentras, 13, 26; see CARPENTORACTE
Carpi (Henchir Mraissa), in Proconsularis: 22
Carrhae or **Charan** (Haran), in Osrhoëne; Charra, according to Egeria: 4, 15a, 31, 32, 34, 35, 36
Carrobia (S.), in Majorca: 13
Carsioli, in the land of the Aequi: 24
Carsium, in Scythia Minor: 19
Cartagena, 25; see CARTHAGO NOVA
Carteia, in Baetica: 40; see CARSESA, CARTERA
Cartennae (Ténès), in Mauretania Caesariensis; m. doc.; (before 310): 3, 20, 40
Cartera, in Baetica: 20; see CARCESA, CARTEIA
Carthaginiensis, prov. of dioc. of Hispania: 20, 25, 41a
Carthago, in Proconsularis; not according to eccl. law but in actual fact metrop. of Roman Africa from the 4th cent. onwards; (2nd cent.): 3, 5, 6, 7, 8, 9, 10, 11, 12, 13, 20, 22, 30, 33, 34, 35, 40, 41a, 42a; *353 (mensa Cypriani)*
Carthago Nova or **Carthago Spartaria,** in Carthaginiensis, Hispania; metrop. until A.D. 531; (302): 3, 20, 25, 40
Cartili (Bordj-Uled-Damus or Duplein), in Mauretania Caesariensis; (484): 20
Carula, in Baetica: 25
Caryanda, in Caria: 19
Caryanda, in Lycia: 14
Carystus (Palaiokhori near Káristos), in Euboea, prov. of Achaia; (458): 19
Casae Medianae (El Madher), in Numidia; (411): 22
Casae Nigrae (Negrine), in Numidia; (305): 22
Casanarello, in Apulia, near Lecce: 14; *469 (mosaic)*
Cashel, in Ireland: 25, 40
Casinum (S Germano), in Latium Adiectum, I, prov. of Campania; (465): 23
Casiotis, district in Syria I: 15a
Casium, in Augustamnica I, near the sea; (431): 17
Cassandrea or **Potidaea,** in Macedonia I: 19
Castabala or **Hieropolis** (Budrum Kalesi), in Cilicia II; (324, 325): 4, 14, 15a, 16a
Castellane or **Civitas Salinensium** or **Salinae** (Castellane), in Narbonensis II; (439–42, afterwards disappeared) 26
Castellamare di Stabia, in Gulf of Naples; see STABIAE
Castellum Novas (on an ieland, near Caorle), near Iulia Concordia, in Venetia, X, prov. of Venetia & Histria; (599): 23
Castellum, in Numidia (484): 22
Castellum Ripae or **Castrum Ripae,** in Mauretania Sitifensis; (484): 22
Castel Sant' Elia, near Nepi, in S Etruria: *438 (ambo)*
Castiglione, in dep. of Alger: 13
Castiliscar, north of Zaragoza: 13
Castra Martis, in Dacia Ripensis; (343): 19
Castra Nova (Perrégaux), in Mauretania Caesariensis; (484): 20
Castra Puerorum (Les Andalouses), in Mauretania Caesariensis; (inscription, A.D. 353): 20
Castrum Cabillonum (Chalon-sur-Saône), in Lugdunensis I: 30
Castrum Divionum (Dijon), in Lugdunensis I: 30
Castrum Tingitii (Orléansville, dep. of Alger), in Mauretania Caesariensis; basilica, inscr.; (324): 3, 20
Castrum Tituli, in Numidia; (484): 22
Castrum Trinorciense (Tournus), in Lugdunensis I: 30
Castulo (Cazlona, ruins), in Carthaginiensis, Hispania; (302): 3, 25
Catalaunum or **Durocatalaunum** (Châlons-sur-Marne): 40
Catana or **Catina** (Catania), in Sicily; (before 305; 515, 558): 4, 17, 23, 30
Catania, 14; see CATANA
Cataonia, district in Cappadocia, prov. of Armenia II: 16a
Cataracts of the Nile, 1st cataract in Thebais IIa, 2nd outside the Empire: 17, 34
Cattaro or **Kotor,** see RISINIUM
Cauca (Coca, in Castile), in Hispania: 9
Caucoliberi (loc. uncertain, north of Gerona), in Tarraconensis; (516): 25
Caudium (near Montesarchio), in land of the Hirpini, II, prov. of Samnium; (499): 23
Caunus, in Caria; (359): 16a
Caurium, in Lusitania: 40
Cavaillon, in dep. of Vaucluse: 26; see CAVELLIO
Cavellio or **Civitas Cabellionum** (Cavaillon), in Viennensis; (396): 26
Cayster (Kösuk), riv., prov. of Asia: 16a
Caxa, mon. in Sicily: 23, 34
Caziona, in Baetica: 40
Cebar, in Byzacena: 22
Cedamussa, in Mauretania Sitifensis; (484): 22
Cediae or **Cedias** (Henchir Ounkif), in Numidia; (256): 3, 22, 30, 34
Cedoniae (Sibiu, Romania), in Dacia, which was conquered by Trajan, north of the Danube: 19
Cedri Libani, in Phoenice I; 14
Cefalo, on Kos, Gr. Archipelago: 14
Cefalù, on Sicily: *593 (mosaics of the Fathers)*
Celaenae, opposite Apamea Cibotus, Pisidia: 16a
Celeia (Celje), in Noricum Mediterraneum: 23, 25
Celeiu (Sucidava), in Rumenia: 14
Celenderis (Gilindire), in Isauria; (381): 15a, 16a
Celerinae (Guebeur Bou Aioun), in Numidia; (411): 22
Celje, in Yugoslavia: 14; see CELEIA
Cellae (Kherbet Zerga), in Mauretania Sitifensis: (484): 20, 22
Cellae (Henchir 'Ain Zouarine), in Proconsularis; (411): 22
Cellae Picentinae (Kolib el Kolin), in Byzacena: (641): 22
Çeltikçi, in Phrygia: 14
Cemenelum or **Civitas Cemenelensium** (Cimiez, near Nice), in Alpes Maritimae; (439): 26
Cenannus or **Cenondae** or **Kells,** mon. in Ireland: 25, 40; cf 34
Cenas (Îles Kenaïs), i. and mon. in Byzacena; (411): 22, 34
Cenondae, see CENANNUS
Cenchreae, near Corinth, in Achaia: 1
Cenomannica or **Cenomannum** (Le Mans), in Lugdunensis III; (5th cent.; 453): 25, 40
Centula (St-Riquier, dep. of Somme), mon. in Gallia: 13, 34
Centumcellae (Civitavecchia), in Tuscia Suburbicaria, VII, prov. of Tuscia & Umbria; (314): 3, 23
Centuriones (El Kentour), in Numidia; (305): 3, 22
Cepha or **Hesna de Kepe** (Hasankeyf), on the Tigris, in Mesopotamia; seat of a bishop under Amida; (451): 16
Cephallenia (Kefalinnia), i., in Epirus Vetus: 4, 5, 19
Cephro, in Aegyptus I: 4, 17
Ceramus, in Caria; (431): 16a, 19
Ceramussa, in Numidia; (411): 22
Cerasus later **Pharnacia** (Girasun), in Pontus Polemoniacus; (431): 16
Cercina (Kerkenna), i. and town near Byzacena; (484): 20, 22, 33, 34, 40
Cerillae (Cirella, ruined, near Laos), in Bruttii, III, prov. of Lucania & Bruttii; (649): 23
Cervia, see FICUCLAE
Cerynia (Kerenia), in Cyprus: 16a
Cestria, in Isauria; (451): 16a
Cestrus (Ak), riv. in Pamphylia: 16a
Ceus, i., in prov. of Insulae: 19
Ceuta, see SEPTA
Ceyreste, see CITHARISTA: 26
Chafagi Aamer, in the Jebel Nefuça, Tripolitana: 13
Chagny, in dep. of Saône-et-Loire: 13
Chalce (Khalkia), i., in prov. of Insulae: 16a, 19
Chalcedon (Kadi-Köy), in Bithynia; (325): 4, 5, 9, 11, 12, 16a, 19, 31, 34
Chalcis, in Thessalia; (343): 19
Chalcis, in Phoenice I: 15a
Chalcis (Khalkis), on Euboea, prov. of Achaia: 4, 19
Chalcis ad Belum (Kennesrin), in Syria I; (381): 15a, 16a, 34, 42b
Chalon-sur-Saône, in dep. of Saône-et-Loire, see CABILLONUM
Châlons-sur-Marne, in dep. of Marne; see DUROCATALAUNUM
Chamanene, district in Cappadocia III: 16a
Chaqqa or **Shaqqa,** 14; see MAXIMIANOPOLIS
Characmoba (prob. Kerak), in Arabia: 15a, 17; *see 324 (on map of Madaba)*
Charadrus (Haladran), in Isauria; (451): 16a
Chartres, in dep. of Eure-et-Loire; see CIV. CARNOTENSIUM
Chelles, in dep. of Seine-et-Oise: 34; see CALA

CHEMMIS — CTESIPHON

Chemmis, 17; see PANOPOLIS
Chenoboscium, mon. in Thebais II: 17, 34
Cherchel, 13; see CAESAREA MAURETANIAE
Cheretapa, in Pamphylia: 16a
Cherronesus, see APAMEA CHERRONESUS
Chersonesus or **Sebastopolis** (Sebastopol, in the Crimea), in the Chersonesus Taurica: 4, 7, 11, 16c, 36
Chersonesus, in Crete; (458): 19
Chersonesus Taurica (Crimea), outside the Empire: 2, 4, 16c, 36, 41b
Chester, see DEVA
Chino, in Aegyptus I; (325): 17
Chinon, in dep. of Indre-et-Loire: 34; see MONASTERIUM CAIONENSE
Chius (Khios), i. and town in prov. of Insulae; (448): 4, 14, 19, 31
Chiusi, 13; see CLUSIUM
Choba (Ziama), in Mauretania Sitifensis; (484): 20, 22
Choba, in Syria I: 4
Choma, in Lycia; (381): 16a
Chonacara or **Chonachora** or **Comocharra** (Oara, on the road to Homs? or: S of Damascus?), in Phoenice Libanensis; (458): 15a
Choulans, suburb of Lyon: 13
Chora, in Samos: 14
Chorassa(n), (Khurasān) formerly in Persia; (409): 36
Chorzianene or **Chorzene** (district of Gurzan), in Armenia IV: 16b
Chrysopolis (Uskudar), on the Bosphorus, in Bithynia; (4th cent.): 4, 16a, 19
Chullu (Collo), in Numidia; (411): 20, 22
Chur, in Switzerland; see CURIA
Chusira (La Kessera), in Byzacena; (484): 22
Chytri (near Kythrea), in Cyprus; (451): 15a, 16a
Cibalianae, in Byzacena; (256): 3, 22
Cibalae or **Cibalis** (Vinkovci), in Pannonia II: 4, 19, 30
Cibyra, in Caria; (325): 4, 16a
Cierus later **Prusias,** in Honorias: 16a
Cilibia, (Henchir Kelbia), in Proconsularis; (411): 22
Cilicia, district around Caesarea Cappadocia: 16a
Cilicia, prov. (divided after 294): 1, 2, 4, 15a, 16a
— Prima, prov. of dioc. of Oriens: 15a, 16a, 41b
— Secunda, prov. of dioc. of Oriens: 15a, 16a, 41b
Cilli, 13; see CELJE
Cillium or **Cilium** (Kasserine), in Byzacena; (256?): 22, 33, 34
Cimiez, near Nice, dep. of Alpes-Maritimes: 26; see CEMENELUM
Ciminas Mons, mountain on the boundary of Hellespontus and Asia: 16a
Ciminius (Lago di Bracciano), l. in Tuscia: 24
Cincar (Henchir Tengar), in Proconsularis; (411): 22
Cingulum (Cingoli), in Picenum Suburbicarium, V; (555, 560): 23
Cinna, in Galatia I; (4th cent.): 4, 16a
Circei, on the Mons Circeus, Campania: 23
Circesium, frontier fortress at the meeting of the Chaboras and the Euphrates, in Euphratensis (near Bassira, at the mouth of the Khabur); (431): 9, 36
Çirga, in Isauria, finds now at Adana Museum: 14
Cirta (Constantine, Algeria), in Numidia; (256): 3, 5, 7, 9, 20, 22, 33, 34, 40, 41a, 42a
Cisamus, on Crete; (343): 19
Ciscisus, *Gr.* **Kuskusos,** in Cappadocia I: 16a
Cissa (i. near the coast of Rignano) in Histria, X, prov. of Venetia & Histria; (seat of bishop A.D. 571-7, 586-7, 589, 680; since the 8th cent.): 23
Cissi (Cap Djinet), in Mauretania Sitifensis; (411): 20
Citharista (La Ceyreste, formerly an island, now 6 km. NNE. of La Ciotat), on the coast of Viennensis: 26
Citharizon, in Armenia IV: 16b
Citium (Kition-Larnaca), in Cyprus; (381): 15a, 16a
Cius, in Scythia Minor: 19
Cius (Gemlik, *Gr.* Gio), in Bithynia; (4th cent.): 4, 16a
Cività Castellana, north of Rome: 13
Civitas Agathensis, see AGATHA
Civitas Albigensium (Albi), Aquitania I; (5th cent.): 25, 30, 40
Civitas Arvernorum (Clermont-Ferrand), in Aquitania I, later Arvernum, Arverni, Arvernis, Arverna, still later Claromontanum; (*ca* 300): 3, 7, 13, 25, 26, 30, 40
Civitas Articlavorum later **Virodunum** (Verdun), in Belgica I; 4th cent.; (346): 25, 40
Civitas Atrebatum later **Atrebates** (Atrecht, Arras), in Belgica II; (7th cent.): 25, 40
Civitas Aturensium or **Adurense**s (Aire-sur-l'Adour), Novempopulana; (507): 25, 40
Civitas Ausciorum (Auch), (5th cent.): 25, 40; see ELIUMBERIS
Civitas Bigorritanae or **Turba ubi ostra Bigorra** (Tarbes), Novempopulana; (507): 25
Civitas Boiatium (prob. Buch, near Arcachon), seat of bishop disappeared 5th cent., not on Map 25
Civitas Cadurcorum, see CADURCI
Civitas Carnotensium (Chartres), later Carnutum, in Lugdunensis IV; (beg. of 4th cent.): 3, 25
Civitas Ceutronum later **Tarantasia** (Tarantaise), in Viennensis; (450): 26
Civitas Consoronnorum (-annorum) later **Consoronni** (Couserans & bishopric of St-Lizier), in Novempopulana; (*ca* 500, 507): 25, 40
Civitas Convenarum (St-Bertrand-de-Comminges), in Novempopulana; (4th cent.; 507): 10, 25, 42a
Civitas Coriosopitum later **Coriospitum** (Quimper, dep. of Finistère), in Lugdunensis III, in Armorica; Breton bishopric end 5th cent.: 25, 40
Civitas Elloronensium (Oloron), in Novempopulana; (507): 25
Civitas Encolismorum or **Civitas Encolismensium** (Angoulême); in Aquitania II, later Encolisma; (beg. of 5th cent.); see ENCOLISMA
Civitas Equestrium, see NOVIODUNUM (Nyon); 552; afterwards Belica; later bishopric at Saint-Claude)
Civitas Lexovionum, later **Lexovium** (Lisieux), in Lugdunensis II; (538): 25, 40
Civitas Mediomatricum later **Mettis** (Metz), in Belgica I; formerly Divodurum Mediomatricorum (end of 3rd cent., 346): 25, 40
Civitas Meldensium (Meaux), in Lugdunensis IV; later called Civ. Melduorum, or Meldae; (6th cent., 549): 25, 34, 40
Civitas Mimatensium or **Civitas Gabalum** or **Gabalis,** (Mende, in the Gevaudan), originally Vicus Mimatensis; (314): 25, 26, 40
Civitas Namnetum or **Portus Namnetum,** later Namnetum, Namnetes (Nantes); (374): 25, 40
Civitas Nemetum (Speyer), in Germania I, originally Civ. Noviomagus; (346, then 614): 25, 40
Civitas Ossismorum later **Ossismi** (originally Carhaix, then St-Pol-de-Léon), in Armorica, prov. of Lugdunensis II; end of 5th cent. seat of a bishop; (453): 25, 40
Civitas Rutenorum, see SEGODUNUM
Civitas Santonum later **Santones** (Saintes), in Aquitania II; (511): 25, 30
Civitas Segesteriorum or **Segestero** (Sisteron), later Sistaricum, in Narbonensis II; (516): 26
Civitas Senonum later **Senones** (Sens, dep. of Yonne), the old Agedincum; metrop. of Lugdunensis IV; (end of 3rd cent.): 3, 7, 25, 30, 40
Civitas Tricassium later **Tricasses** or **Tricenses** (Troyes, dep. of Aube), in Lugdunensis IV; (4th cent.): 25, 30, 40
Civitas Vangionum later **Vangiones** (Worms), formerly Civ. Borbetomagus, in Germania I; (346, then 614): 25, 40
Civitas Vellavorum or **Vellavi** or **Anicium** (Le Puy-en-Velay, dep. of Haute-Loire), in Aquitania I; (4th or 5th cent.): 25, 26, 40
Civitas Veromanduorum, (St-Quentin), in Belgica II; (511; seat of bishop of this *civitas* in 4th cent.; later Noviodunum (Noyon): 25, 30
Civitavecchia, see CENTUMCELLAE
Città di Castello, see TIFERNUM TIBERINUM
Claromontanum, see CIV. ARVERNORUM
Classis or **Portus Ravennae** (Classe, south of Ravenna), in Flaminia, VIII, prov. of Flaminia & Picenum: 13, 23, 40; *265 266, 268, 269, 270, 449, 457-60, 470, 540 (Sant' Apollinare in Classe) and 269, 270 (sarcophagi)*
Claternae (Quaderna), VIII, in prov. of Flaminia & Picenum; (378-9): 23
Claude (St-), in dep. of Jura; see CONDATISCO
Claudiopolis (Mut), in Isauria; (325): 16a
Claudiopolis or **Bithynium** (Bolu), metrop. of Honorias; (beg. of 4th cent.): 4, 16a, 41b
Clazomenae, in prov. of Asia; (431): 16a, 19
Cleopatris or **Arsinoe,** in Augustamnica I: 4, 17
Clermont-Ferrand, 13; see CIV. ARVERNORUM
Cliternia, in land of the Sabini, prov. of Samnium: 24
Clogher, in Hibernia: 25, 40
Clonard, mon. in Hibernia: 25, 34, 40
Clonfert, mon. in Hibernia: 25, 40
Clonmacnoise, in Hibernia: 25, 40
Cloyne, in Hibernia: 25, 40
Cluentum (Civitanova), in Picenum Suburbicarum, V; (494, 495, 496): 23
Cluj or **Klausenburg,** in Romania: 14; see NAPOCA
Clupea (Kélibia), in Proconsularis, northeast of Carthago; (411): 20, 22
Clusium (Chiusi), in Tuscia Suburbicaria, VII, prov. of Tuscia & Umbria; (322; inscription of *ca* 290 (Mustiola)): 3, 13, 23, 30, 33, 40; *191 (cathedral)*
Clysma (Suez), in Arcadia; (347): 17, 31, 32, 34
Cnidus (near Cape Krio), in Caria; (451): 16a, 19
Cnossus, in Crete; (2nd cent.): 4, 5, 6, 19, 42b
Čoban-Dere, in Bulgaria: 14
Cochaba, in Phoenice Libanensis: 15a
Coelesyria (*Gk.* Suria Koiles), Syria I and II combined: 15a, 32, 41b
Collegno, in Piedmont: 13
Collo, in dep. of Constantine, Algeria: 13
Colluthion, near Alexandria, in Aegyptus I: 4, 17, 34
Coloe, in prov. of Asia: 16a, 19
Coloe, in Lydia; (431): 16a
Colonia or **Archelais** or **Garsaura** (Ak-Saray), in Cappadocia III; (325): 16a
Colonia Agrippina, or **Civitas Agrippinensium,** metrop. of Germania II; (2nd cent.; 314): 3, 5, 7, 9, 11, 12, 13, 25, 30, 40, 42a
Colonia Equestris, see NOVIODUNUM (Maxima Sequanorum)
Colonia Germe, in Galatia II; (553): 16a
Colonia Traiana (Xanten), in Germania II: 25, 30, 40
Colopene, district in Armenia I: 16a
Colophon, in prov. of Asia; (431): 14, 16a, 19
Colossae, in Phrygia Pacatiana; (1st cent.; Paul), 1, 4, 5, 16a
Columnata (Waldeck-Rousseau), in Mauretania Caesariensis (484): 20
Colzim, Mons, see MONS S. ANTONII
Comana Chruse or **Hierapolis,** in Armenia II; (325): 4, 16
Comana Pontica (Gumenek), in Helenopontus; (325): 4, 7, 12 16a, 31, 42b
Comba, in Lycia: 16a
Comba da Bande (S.), in Portugal: 13
Commagene, district west of the Euphrates; upper course belongs to prov. of Euphratensis: 15a, 16b, 36
Como, 13; see COMUM
Comoara or **Comocharra** or **Chonacarra,** in Phoenice Libanensis: 15a
Complutum (Alcalá de Henares), in Carthaginiensis, Hispania (before 310): 3, 25, 30, 40
Compsa (Conza), in land of the Hirpini, II, prov. of Samnium (743): 23
Compulteria or **Cubulteria** (near Treglia), I, in prov. of Campania; (6th cent.): 23
Comum (Como), in Liguria, XI, prov. of Liguria & Aemilia (374-97, first bishop): 3, 13, 23, 30
Conana, in Pisidia: 4, 16a
Concordia, see IULIA CONCORDIA SAGITTARIA
Condatisco (St-Claude, in dep. of Jura), mon. in Maxima Sequanorum, later Cundat and Monasterium Sancti Claudii (6th cent.): 25, 34, 40
Condeixa a Velha, in Portugal: 13; see CONIMBRIGA
Confluentes (Koblenz), in Germania I: 13, 25
Conimbriga (Condeixa a Velha), in Lusitania: 13, 25, 40
Consentia (Cosenza), in Bruttii, III, prov. of Lucania & Bruttii (597, 599, 603): 23
Consilinum (Sala Consilina in the Val di Tamagro?), in Lucania, III, prov. of Lucania & Bruttii: 23
Consoronni, 40; see CIV. CONSORONNORUM
Constanta, in Romania: 14; see TOMI
Constantia (Coutances), in Lugdunensis I; (6th cent. 511): 25, 40
Constantia (Konstanz), in Raetia I: 25, 40
Constantia, in Mesopotamia, east of Edessa; (381): 15a
Constantia or **Salamis,** in Cyprus: 15a, 16a
Constantia, see GAZA
Constantina (Buracq, west of Ledja), in Arabia; (381): 15a
Constantina, see TELA
Constantine, in dep. of the same name: 13; see CIRTA
Constantinopolis, formerly **Byzantium,** in Europa; (2nd cent.): 9, 10, 11, 12, 16a, 19, 31, 34, 35, 36, 37 (containing all the monuments), 41b, 42b; *for plates see* ISTANBUL
Convenarum, see CIV. CONVENARUM
Copia, 23; see THURII
Copti (Egypt): 35
Coptus (Ooft), in Thebais II: 17
Cora (Cori), in Latium Adiectum, I, prov. of Campania: 24
Coracesium (Alanya), in Pamphylia; (381): 16a
Corada, 15a; see GERODA
Corbridge, see CORSTOPITUM
Corcyra (Kerkira, *Ital.* Corfu), i. and town off Epirus Vetus; (beg. of 4th cent.): 4, 19
Corduba (Córdoba), in Baetica; (302, 325): 9, 10, 13, 20, 25, 30, 40, 42a; *375 (Visigothic altar)*
Corduca or **Gorduca** or **Gordyene** (Botan, in Kurdistan), *Pers.* Beit-Kardu, *Arm.* Kordukh, in Corduene, Armenia, 16b
Corfinium or **Valva** (Pentima, near Corfinio; now the site of the Basilica Valvensis, or San Pelino, not far from Raiano), in land of the Paeligni, IV, prov. of Samnium; (404, 405): 23
Corinthus (Korinthos), metrop. of Achaia; (1st cent., Paul): 1, 4, 5, 6, 10, 19, 31, 41b, 42b
Coriospitum, 40; see CIV. CORIOSOPITUM
Corippia, 16c; see ANAPA
Coronaea, in Achaia; (343): 19
Coropissus (Dağ Pasari), in Isauria; (325): 1, 4, 14, 16a
Corsica, i. and prov.: 3, 23, 30, 33, 41a
Corstopitum (Corbridge), in Britannia: 25
Corycus (Meriamlik), in Cilicia I; (381): 14, 15a, 16a, 31, 32
Corydallus, in Lycia; (375): 16a
Cos (Kos), i. and town in prov. of Insulae; (325): 4, 16a, 19
Cossura, i., off Proconsularis: 20
Cotyaeum (Kutahya), in Phrygia Salutaris; (before 300): 16a, 31
Cotyora, in Pontus Polemoniacus: 16b
Coutances, see CONSTANTIA
Cratea or **Flaviopolis** (Gerede), in Honorias; (431): 16a
Crediton, in Wessex: 40
Cremna, in Pisidia: 16a
Cremona (Cremona), in Liguria, XI, prov. of Liguria & Aemilia; (451): 23, 40
Creta (Kriti, *Eng.* Crete), i. and prov.: 1, 2, 4, 5, 16a, 19, 31, 35, 41b, 42b
Crocodilopolis, see ARSINOE
Cromna, in Paphlagonia: 16a
Croton (Crotone), in Bruttii, III, prov. of Lucania & Bruttii; (551, 592): 19, 23
Ctesiphon, on the left bank of the Tigris, opposite Seleucia (a little farther to the north); capital of the Sassanian kings; (the Persian *katholikos,* on the other hand, resided in Seleucia, which had begun to flourish again discreetly after the destructions of A.D. 116 and 163): 36; see SELEUCIA

Cucusus (Göksun), in Armenia II: 16a, 31
Cugat de Vallès (S.), in Catalonia: 13
Cuicul (Djemila, in dep. of Constantine), in Numidia; (256): 3, 13, 20, 22, 33; *350-1, 407, 420 (baptistery)*
Cululi, in Byzacena; (256): 22
Cuma, see Cumae
Cumae (Cuma), in I, prov. of Campania; (465): 3, 23, 30
Cures or Cures Sabinorum (Monteleone, near Correse), later S. Anthimi; in land of the Sabini, IV, prov. of Valeria; the former municipium Trebula Mutuesca (465, 487, 499, 501): 23, 24
Curia (Chur), in Raetia I: 25, 30, 40
Curium (Episkopi), in Cyprus; (431): 16a
Curubis (Korba), in Proconsularis; (258): 3, 22
Cusae, in Thebais I: 4, 17
Cybistra, in Cappadocia II: 4, 16a
Cydonia (Khania), in Crete: 19
Cymae or Cyme, on the coast of prov. of Asia; (431): 16a, 19
Cynegia Chora, desert west of Chalcis ad Belum, in Syria I, rich in monastic foundations: 15a, 15b, 16a, 34
Cynopolis Inferior, in Aegyptus II: 17
Cynopolis Superior, in Arcadia: 4, 17, 31
Cyparissiae (Kiparissia), in Achaia; (343): 19
Cyprus, i. and prov. of the dioc. of Oriens; after A.D. 450 ecclesiastically autonomous: 1, 2, 4, 5, 9, 12, 15a, 16a, 31, 32, 35, 41b, 42b
Cypsela (Ipsala), in Rhodope; (553): 19
Cyrenaica, region of the Pentapolis; also in a wider sense, a prov. of Libya Superior: 21
Cyrene (Gureina), in Cyrenaica: 1, 4, 5, 7, 10, 14, 21, 42b
Cyrrhestica, region around Cyrrhus, in Euphratensis: 15a, 16a
Cyrrhus, in Euphratensis; (325): 4, 12, 15a, 16a, 31, 42b
Cyrus (Kura), riv. south of the Caucasus: 36
Cysis, in Thebais II: 17
Cythera (Kithira), i. and town in prov. of Achaia: 14, 19
Cytorus, in Paphlagonia: 4, 16a
Cyzicus (south of Erdek), in Hellespontus; (325): 4, 9, 12, 14, 16a, 19, 31, 41b, 42b

D

Dabravina, in Yugoslavia: 14
Dacia Citerior (Romania), north of the Danube, from A.D. 107-275 Roman: 2, 4, 5
Dacia, dioc. VIII: 41b
Dacia, prov. of the dioc. of Dacia, divided into:
— Mediterranea: 19, 41b
— Ripensis: 19, 41b
Dadybra (Iskilip or Çerkes?), in Paphlagonia; (451): 16a
Daghestan, 14 (inset), 36; see Albania
Dağ Pasari (Coropissus?) in Isauria: 14
Dailam, region south of the Caspian Sea; (224): 36
Dakuk, in Garamea, near Beit Selok: 36
Dalisandus, in Isauria, loc. uncertain; (381): 16a
Dalloza, in N Syria: 15b
Dalmatia, before A.D. 294, a province: 2, 4; after A.D. 395 prov. of dioc. of Illyricum: 11, 19, 23, 25, 30, 41b
Damascus (Dimisho, or Es-Sham), metrop. of Phoenice Libanensis, with 13 suffragans; (1st cent.): 1, 4, 5, 14, 15a, 16a, 31, 32, 36, 41b
Dana, in N Syria: 15b; see Addana
Danaba (Mehin), in Phoenice Libanensis, near Evaria; (541): 15a
Danubius, see Ister
Daphnae, in Augustamnica; (432): 17
Daphne, near Antioch, Syria I: 4, 14, 15a, 16a; *288 (laurel wood), 161, 290 (mosaics)*
Daphnousia, in Greece: 14
Dara, Mesopotamia, seat of bishop founded A.D. 507 under Amida; later titulary metrop.: 31, 36
Darabgerd, in Persia; (424): 36
Dardania, prov. of dioc. of Illyricum: 19, 41b
Dardanus, in Hellespontus; (451): 16a, 19
Darin, near Bahrain; (409, 430): 36
Dariro, mon. near Tralles, prov. of Asia: 34
Darnis (Derna) metrop. of Libya Inferior, Marmarica; (431): 14, 21, 41b
Dar Qita, in N Syria: 15b
Dascylium (Daskili), in Bithynia; (680): 16a, 19
Daskarta, near Arbela, east of the Tigris; (419): 36
Dax, see Aquae Tarbellicae
Dazibyza, in Bithynia: 16a
Dazimon, mon. in Helenopontus: 16a
Dea (Die), in Viennensis; (4th cent., 325?): 3, 13, 26, 40
De Baricis, in Mauretania Sitifensis: 22
Debeltum, in Haemimontus; (2nd cent.): 4, 5, 19
Dehes, in N Syria: 15b
Deir Abu Fana, in Egypt, west of the Nile, mon.: 14
Deir Abu Hennis, near Antinoe, east of the Nile, mon.: 14
Deir Abu Magar, in the Wadi Natrun, mon.: 17
Deir Amba Pshoi, in the Wadi Natrun, mon.: 17
Deir Baramus, in the Wadi Natrun, mon.: 17
Deir Dosy or Mon. S. Theodosii, near Jerusalem: 14
Deir el-Abiad or Mon. Rubrum, near Sohag, Egypt: 14
Deir el-Ahmar or Mon. Candidum, near Sohag, Egypt: 14, see Athripe
Deir el-Magma, in Thebais II, mon.: 17

Deir el-Medinah, in central Egypt, *581-2 (monastery in the temple)*
Deir es-Suriani, in the Wadi Natrun, mon.: 17
Deir es-Salib, in Thebais II, mon.: 17
Deir es-Shuhada, in Thebais II, mon.: 17
Deir Manin or Turmanin, in N Syria, ruined mon.: 15b
Deir Sambil, in N Syria, ruined mon.: 15b
Deir Sem'an or Telanissus, in the Jebel Sem'an, mon.: 15b
Deir Seta, in Syria: 15b; *304 (baptistery)*
Deir Solaib, in Syria II, west of the Orontes, mon.: 15a
Deir Tell'Ade or Teleda, south of the Oenoparas, mon.: 15a, 15b
Dellys, 13; see Rusuccurru
Delminium (Zupanjac, in Duvno Polje), in Dalmatia: 19, 23
Delphi (Delphoi), in prov. of Achaia: 14, 19
Delus or Delos (Dhilos), in prov. of Insulae (451): 14, 19
Demetrias, in Thessaly; (431): 14
Demre, in Lycia: 14; see Myra
Dendera, see Tentyra
Dennaba, in Arabia (according to Egeria): 32; see Neapolis
Der'a, in Arabia: 32; see Adraa
Der'aman, in N Syria: 15b
Der Balyzeh, in Egypt: 8
Derbe, in Lycaonia 14 m. NE of Laranda, = 25 km. NE; the site was identified in 1957); (381): 1, 4, 5, 14, 16a
Dercos, in Europa, NW of Istanbul, on the Terkos Gölü: 16a, 19
Dere Ağçi, in Turkey: 14
Derna, in Libya Superior: 14; see Darnis
Dertona, in Alpes Cottiae, under ecclesiastical jurisdiction of Liguria; (381): 23
Dertosa (Tortosa), in Tarraconensis, Hispania; (516): 25, 40
Derxene, on the Euphrates, district in Armenia: 16b
Desertum Indicum, west of the Indus: 36
— Iudae, in Palaestina III: 15a
— Libycum, in Libya Inferior: 21, 35
— Persicum, in central Persia: 36
— Pharan (according to Egeria): 32
Deva (Chester), in Britannia: 25
Dhilos, 14; see Delus
Dia, in Honorias (Akçakosa): 16a
Dia, i., north of Crete: 19
Diana (Zana), in Numidia; (411): 22
Dianium, i., in Tyrrhene Sea: 23
Dianium, in Carthaginiensis, Hispania: 25, 40
Dibus, see Diu
Dices (Henchir Sidi Salah Or Sadik), in Byzacena; (411): 22
Didyma, in Caria, south of Miletus: 16a, 19
Die, 13, 26; see Dea
Digne, 26; see Dinia
Dijon, in dep. of Côte d'Or: 30; see Castrum Divionum
Dindymus Mons, in Phrygia Pacatiana: 16a
Diner, 14; see Apamea Cibotus
Dinia or Civitas Diniensium (Digne), in Alpes Maritimae; (ca 360-70): 26
Dinogetia, (Bisericuţa) in Scythia Minor: 19
Diocaesarea (Uzuncaburç) in Isauria; (4th cent.): 4, 15a, 16a
Diocaesarea or Nazianzus, in Cappadocia III: 16a
Diocaesarea or Sepphoris (Sefuriye), in Galilaea, in Palaestina II; (536): 7, 15a
Dioclea, in Phrygia Salutaris; (451): 16a
Diocletianopolis, in Thessalia; (343): 19
Diolcus, mon. in Aegyptus II in the Nile Delta: 17, 34
Diomedeae, is., north of Mons Garganus: 23
Dion, in Greece: 14
Dionysiana, in Byzacena; (256): 3, 22
Dionysias (Suweida), in Arabia; (325): 4, 15a
Dionysiopolis, Phrygia Pacatiana; (451): 16a
Dionysiopolis (Gruni), in Scythia Minor: 19
Dioscoridis (Socotra), i. in Indian Ocean: 7
Dioscurias (Sukhumi), in Georgia, USSR), on the Pontus Euxinus (6th cent.): 35, 36
Dioshieron, in prov. of Asia; (451): 16a
Diospolis or Lydda, in Palaestina I: 1, 4, 5, 11, 15a, 17, 31
Diospolis (Akçakosa), in Honorias: 16a
Diospolis magna or Thebae (Medinet-Habu), in Thebais II: 17
Diospolis parva or (Copt.) Hou (Hau), in Thebais II: 17
Diu or Dibus (Port. Diu), off the west coast of India: 7, 36
Dium, in Palaestina II: 15a
Dium, in Macedonia I; (343): 19
Divodurum Mediomatricorum, 3; see Civ. Mediomatricum
Diyarbakir, see Amiba, on the Tigris: 14 and 14a
Djebar, in dep. of Oran: 13
Djémila, 13; see Cuicul
Djerba, 13; see Girba
Djivari, in Georgia: 14 (inset)
Doara or Odogra, in Cappadocia III: 16a
Doberus, in Macedonia Salutaris; (343): 19
Docimeum, in Phrygia Salutaris; (343): 16a
Doclea, in Praevalitana; (451): 19
DodecascIoenus, south of the Imperial frontier, outside Thebais II: 17
Dodona, in Epirus Vetus; (431): 5, 14, 19
Dol, in dep. of Île-et-Vilaine: see Dolus
Doliche (Tell Duluk), in Euphratensis; (324, 325): 4, 15a, 16a
Doliche, in Epirus Vetus: 19
Dolichiste (Kekova), i. off the coast of Lycia: 16a

Doloman, Dubrogea: 14
Dolus (Dol), mon. in Lugdunensis III; seat of bishop in 5th cent.?: 25, 34, 40
Domanitis, region in Paphlagonia: 16a
Domitiopolis (Dindebol?), in Isauria; (451): 16a
Doornik, 13; see Tornacum
Dor, 14; see Dora
Dora (Dor), in Palaestina I; (518): 15a
Dorylaenum (Dor), in Phrygia Salutaris; (325): 4, 16a
Dougga, in Tunisia: 13; see Thucca
Dovin or Dwin or Dvin, on the Araxes in Armenia: 14 (inset), 16b
Down or Downpatrick, in Ireland: 11, 25, 40
Drepanum promontorium, in Thebais I: 17
Druas (Henchir Bou Dries), in Byzacena; (411): 22
Drusilana (Khanget El Kedian), in Proconsularis; (411): 22
Druz (Jebel), see Jebel Druz
Druzipara or Drusipara (Karistiran), in Europa; (beg. of 4th cent.): 4, 16a, 19, 31
Dubrovnik, in Dalmatia: 14; see Epidaurus
Ducatus Beneventanus, Friuli, Spoleti, Romanus, in the 6th cent.: 40
Duel, in Austria: 13
Dulichium, in Thessalia; (5th cent.): 19
Dumium, (Dume) in Gallaecia; (561): 25, 35, 40, 42a
Dunapentele (formerly Intercisa), in Hungary: 14
Dunaszekesö, in Hungary: 14
Dunwich, in East Anglia: 13, 25
Durazzo, in Albania: see Dyrrhachium
Dura-Europos (Es-Salihiye), on the Euphrates, frontier fortress: 5, 7, 14; *37-9, 68 (synagogue), 51, 52, 62, 71, 403 (house church)*
Durius (Douro), riv. in Hispania: 40
Durocatalaunum or Civitas Catalaunorum later Catalaunum (Châlons-sur-Marne), in Belgica II; (ca 300?, 346): 25
Durostorum (near Silistra, Bulgaria), in Moesia II; (300): 4, 10, 19, 31, 42b
Durovernum, 25; see Cantuaria
Durrow, mon. in Ireland: 13, 25, 40
Dusa, in Byzacena: 22
Düverlü-Airai, west coast of Turkey: 14
Duvillaun, island before the west coast of Ireland: 25, 40
Dwin or Dovin, 9, 14, 16b; see Dovin
Dyarbakir, on the Tigris: 14; see Amida
Dyrrhachium or Epidamnus (Durrës, in Albania), metrop. of Epirus Nova: 19, 41b

E

East Anglia, in Britannia: 40
Eauze, see Elusa
Eblin, in N Syria: 15b
Eboda (Abda), in Palaestina III: 4, 15a, 17, 34
Ebora (Evora), in Lusitania: 25, 40
Eboriacum (Faremoutiers, near Meaux), mon. south of Meldae: 34
Ebredunum or Civitas Ebrodunensium (Embrun), metrop. of Alpes Maritimae; (350-60): 25, 26, 33, 40, 41a
Ebroicum (Evreux), in Lugdunensis II; (6th cent., 511): 25, 40
Eburacum or Eboracum (York), in Britannia, prov. of Valentina; (314): 3, 9, 25, 34, 40, 41a
Ebusus (Ibiza), on one of the Pityusae Is., prov. of Baleares: 25
Ecdaumava or Gadamava, in Galatia I: 16a
Ecdippa or Actipus, in Phoenice I: 15a
Echinus or Aechinus, in Thessalia; (431): 19
Echmiadzin or Etchmiadzin, in Armenia, near Valarshapat: 14 (inset), 16b, 36
Ecija, in Baetica: 13; *51, 372 (sarcophagus)*; see Astigi
Edessa or Callirrhoe (Urfa, in Iraq), metrop. of Osrhoëne with 11 suffragans; (mid. 2nd cent. Chr.; ca 200 letter of K. Abgar IX to Christ; first Bishop Palut, ca 200): 1, 5, 6, 7, 8, 9, 10, 11, 12, 15a, 31, 32, 34, 35, 36, 41a, 42b
Edessa or Aegae (Edhessa), in Macedonia I: 4, 5, 19
Egara or Tarrasa (Tarrasa), in Tarraconensis; (516): 25
Egitania, in Lusitania; (411?, 589): 25, 40
Egivard, in Armenia: 14 (inset)
Egypt, 13; *327-47, 510, 556*; see Aegyptus
Eisenstadt, in Austria: 14
El 'Adra, in Thebais II, mon.: 17
Elaea, see Elea
Elam or Persis or Persiana (Fars), prov. in Persia: 36
El Asabaa, in the Jebel Nefuça, Tripolitana: 13
El Asmunein, in Egypt: 14
Elataea, in prov. of Achaia; (343): 19
Elberris, 40; see Illiberris
Elea, or Elaea, in prov. of Asia; (451): 16a, 19
Elche, 13; see Ilici
Elena, or Elna or Ecclesia Elnensis (Elne, dep. of Pyr.-Or.), in Narbonensis I; (after 550; 571, 589): 13, 25, 40
El Entaiye, in Transjordan: 14
Elephantaria (Mouzaiville), in Mauretania Caesariensis; (484): 20
Elephantaria (Sidi Said), in Proconsularis; (393): 22
Elephantine (near Aswan), i. in Nile, in Thebais II: 17
Eleusa or Sebaste (Ajas), in Isauria; (434): 14, 15a, 16a
Eleutherna (Elevtherna), in Crete; (451): 19

KHIRBET HASS — MACEDONIA

Khirbet Hass, N Syria: 15b
— Qumran, on NW bank of the Dead Sea, where the famous scrolls were found; Essene community: 1, 5, 6
Khyber Pass, in the Hindu Kush: 36
Kildare, in Ireland: 25, 40
Killabuonia, in Hibernia; 25, 40
Kilmalkedar, W Ireland: 13, 40
Kirkuk, 36; see Beit Selok
Kithira, 14; see Cythera
Kizil-Oren, in Pisidia: 14
Klosterneuburg, near Vienna: 14
Koblenz, 13; see Confluentes
Koča Kalesi or **Alahan Monastir,** cupola church in Isauria: 14; *314 (cupola church)*
Kokanaya, N Syria: 15b
Koljane, in Yugoslavia: 14
Köln, 13; see Colonia Agrippina
Koma, in Arcadia, Aegyptus: 4, 17
Konya, 14; see Iconium
Konstanz, see Constantia, in Raetia
Kordukh, town and seat of Bishop in Armenia; formerly Corduca in Corduene: 16b; see Corduca
Korinthos, in Greece: 14
Korkaya, in N Syria: 15b
Kos, 14; see Cos
Kriti, Crete, 14; see Creta
Ksar Bagai, in dep. of Constantine; formerly Bagai, in Numidia: 13
Ksar el-Kelb, in dep. of Constantine: 13; see Vegesela
Kseybe, in N Syria: 15b
Kutaisi, in Georgia (USSR): 14 (inset)
Kynae (Qani), near Seleucia-Ctesiphon; (424): 36
Kyzillik, in Pamphylia: 14

L

Labicum (near Monte Compatri), in Latium Vetus, prov. of Campania; (313–649): 24
Lacedaemon (Sparti), in prov. of Achaia: 4, 5, 19
Lacene, in Byzacena: 22
Lachmidae (Kingdom of the), southwest of the Euphrates; (from 4th cent. onwards; 6th cent. Chr., from 633 under Islam): 35, 36 (shows Hira, the capital)
Lacobriga (Lagos), on S coast of Lusitania: 40
Lactora or **Civitas Lactoratium** (Lectoure), in Novempopulana; (507): 25, 40
Ladenburg, see Lopodunum
Lagania or **Anastasiopolis** (Beypazari), in Galatia I; (451): 16a
La Gayolle, see Gayolle (La)
Lagbe, in Pamphylia: 16a
Lagos, see Lacobriga
Laibach or **Ljubljana,** see Emona
Lamasba (Henchir Merouana), in Numidia; (256): 3, 22
Lambaesis (Lambèse), in Numidia; (246): 3, 5, 7, 20, 22, 30, 33
Lambiridi (Kheret-Ouled Arif), in Numidia; (411): 22
Lamdia (Medea), in Mauretania Caesariensis; (411): 20
Lamecum or **Lameca** (Lamego, in Portugal), in Lusitania; (beg. of 5th cent.; 589): 13, 25, 40
Lamia (Lamia), in Thessalia; (431): 19
Lamiggiga (Pasteur), in Numidia; (411): 22
Lamos or **Lamus,** in Isauria; (458): 16a
Lampsacus (Lapseki), in Hellespontus: 4, 9, 14, 16a, 19, 31
Lampsili, in Numidia; (411): 22
Lamsorta (Henchir Mafouna), in Numidia; (411): 22
Lamus, riv. in W Cilicia; (438): 15a, 16a
Lancarna, mon. in Britannia: 34
Lancarvan, in Britannia: 35, 40, 42a
Landava (Llandaff, in Wales), in Britannia; (512): 25, 40
Langres, see Lingones
Lanuvium, in Latium Vetus, southeast of Rome: 24
Laodicea ad Lycum (Eskihisar, near Denizli), metrop. of Phrygia Pacatiana (1st cent.; cf Rev. 1:12 and 3:14–22); (325): 1, 4, 5, 9, 16a, 41b
Laodicea (El Ladhiqiya), in Syria I; (2nd cent.; 251, 325): 4, 5, 10, 15a, 16a, 31, 42b
Laodicea Catacecaumene or **Combusta** ('the burnt') (Yorgan Ladik, in Turkey), in Pisidia; (332): 14, 16a
Laodicea Libani (Tell-Nebi-Mend, south of lake of Homs), in Phoenice Libanensis; (431): 15a
Laon, see Laudunum
Lapethus, in Cyprus; (451): 16a
Lappa, in Crete; (451): 19
Laranda (Karaman), in Lycaonia; (325): 4, 5, 14, 16a
Lar Castellum, in Mauretania Caesariensis; (411): 20
Lares (Henchir Lorbeus), in Procunsularis; (256): 3, 22
Larinum (Larino Vecchio), in IV, prov. of Samnium; before 294 belonging to Apulia; (*ca* 493): 23
Larissa (Larisa), metrop. of Thessalia; (4th cent.): 5, 19
Larissa (Shelzar), in Syria II; (325, 414): 4, 15a
Laryma, in Caria: 16a
Lasaea, in Crete: 19
Latini, tribe in Latium: 24
Latium, divided into Latium Vetus and Latium Adiectum, together with Campania formed *Regio* I, and after 294 became prov. of Campania: 23
Latmos Mons, mountain range in Caria, northeast of Miletus; many monasteries: 14, 16a, 19, 34
Latopolis, in Thebais II: 17, 34
Laudunum (Laon), in Belgica II; (6th cent., 549): 25, 40
Lauriacum (near Lorch at confluence of the Enns and Danube, in Austria), in Noricum Ripense: 3, 11, 25, 30, 34, 40
Lauro, in Carthaginiensis, Hispania; (302): 3, 25
Lausanna or **Losonna** (Lausanne), in Maxima Sequanorum; (at the end of the 6th cent. the Bishop, of Civ. Helvetiorum had his seat here instead of as previously at Vindonissa (Windisch)); 25, 40
Laus Pompeia (Lodi), in Liguria, XI, prov. of Liguria & Aemilia; (381): 23, 33
Lauzandus, in Isauria: 16a
La Valetta, in Malta: 13
Lavantthal, in Austria: 13
Laviansene, district in Cappadocia, prov. of Armenia I: 16a
Lavinium, south of Rome, in Latium Vetus: 24
Lazica, region on the Phasis, south of the Caucasus: 35, 36
Lazon, in Garamaea, Persia: 36
Lebda, 13; see Leptis Magna
Lebedus, in Asia; (449): 16a, 19
Lebinthus, i., in prov. of Insulae: 16a, 19
Lebrija, in Andalusia, south of Seville: 13
Lecce, see Lippia
Leda, in Kriti (Crete): 14
Ledja or **Trachonitis,** in prov. of Arabia: 14, 15a
Ledrae, in Cyprus: 4, 16a
Legio (León), in Gallaecia; (258): 3, 25, 40
Legionum Urbs or **Isca** (Caerleon), in Britannia: 3, 25, 30
Le Mans, see Cenomannica
Le Mas d'Aire, near Aire-sur-l'Adour (formerly Civ. Aurensium), dep. of Landes: 13; *367 (sarcophagus)*
Lemellef (Bordj Rhedir), in Mauretania Sitifensis; (362): 20, 22, 30
Lemeneia (Bardsey), i., off Britannia: 25, 40
Lemnus (Lemnos), i., near prov. of Achaia: 14, 19
Lemovices or **Civitas Lemovicum** (Limoges), in Aquitania I; (*ca* 250: the local martyr Martialis; 6th cent.): 3, 12, 25, 40, 42b
Lemta, 13; see Leptis Minor
Lentia, in Noricum Ripense: 25
Lentini, in Sicily: 14
León, 13; see Legio
Leontium (Leontini), in Sicily; (602): 23
Leontopolis, metrop. of Augustamnica II; (by 300): 4, 17, 41b
Leontopolis, also in Augustamnica II but more to the south: 17
Leptis Magna or **Neapolis** (Lebda), in Tripolitana; (*ca* 200): 3, 5, 13, 21; *437 (ambo)*
Leptis Minor (Lemta), in Byzacena; (256): 3, 20, 22
Le Puy-en-Velay, 26; see Civ. Vellavorum
Lérida, 13; see Ilerda
Lérins (Ile de) or **Saint-Honorat,** 13, 26; see Lerinum
Lerinum (Ile de Lérins, Ile St-Honorat), i., in Narbonensis II; mon.: 12, 13, 25, 26, 33, 34, 40, 42a
Lerus (Leros), i., in prov. of Insulae: 16a, 19
Lesbus (Lesvos), i., near prov. of Asia; (4th cent.): 14, 16a, 19
Lescar, see Benarno
Lesui, in Mauretania Sitifensis; (411): 20
Lesvos, 14; see Lesbus
Lete, in Macedonia I; (451): 19
Letopolis, in Aegyptus I: 4, 17
Lexovium or **Civitas Lexovionum** (Lisieux, in Normandy), in Lugdunensis II; (6th cent.; 538): 25, 40
Liberalia (Liqua), in S Numidia; (411): 20, 22
Libanus Mons (Libanon), in Phoenice Libanensis: 15a, 32
Libya or **Cyrenaica and Marmarica,** province formerly combined with Crete: after 294 divided into:
— Inferior or **Marmarica,** prov. of dioc. Augustalis: 21, 41b
— Superior or **Cyrenaica** (with the Pentapolis), prov. of dioc. Augustalis: 21, 41b
Libyca Palus, south of Numidia: 20, 22, 33
Licata, in Sicily: 13
Liger (Loire), riv. in Gallia Lugdunensis and Aquitania: 40
Ligugé, 13; see Monasterium Locogiagense
Liguria, before 294 prov. equivalent to the former Transpadana: 3
Liguria & Aemilia, after 294 prov. of Italia Annonaria (made up of the sections Liguria from *Regio* XI and Aemilia from *Regio* VIII): 23, 25, 41a
Lilybaeum or **Lilibaeum** (Marsala), in Sicily; (417, 418): 20, 23
Limnai, in Cappadocia II: 16a
Limoges, see Lemovices
Limyra, in Lycia; (375): 16a
Lincoln, see Lindum
Lindisfarne or **Holy Island,** off the coast of Northumbria: 34, 40
Lindum (Lincoln), in Britannia: 3, 9, 25, 40
Lindus (Lindos), in Rhodes, in prov. of Insulae: 19
Lingoles (Langres), in Lugdunensis I; formerly Civ. Lingonum, later also Lingonica; (after 300, 346): 25, 30, 40
Lipara (Lipari, on the main island of the Isole Eolie, near Sicily); (501, 526 mon., 806 Gr. mon.): 23
Liparaeae (Isole Eolie), is., near Sicily: 23
Lippiae or **Lipia** or **Lupiae** (Lecce), in Calabria, II, prov. of Apulia & Calabria; (553, 595): 23
Lisboa, Lisbon, 13; see Ulisipo
Lisieux, see Lexovium
Lismore, in Hibernia: 25, 40
Lissus (Lesh, *Ital.* Alessio), in Praevalitana; (592): 19
Lita (Litani), riv. in Phoenice I: 15a
Liternum (Torre di Patria), in Campania, I: 23
Livias, in Peraea, in Palaestina I; (431): 15a, 32
Lizier (St-), in dep. of Ariège; seat of Bishop after Couserans: 25, 40; see Civ. Consoronnorum
Llancarvan, 25; see Lancarvan
Llandaff, see Landava
Llantwit, mon, in Britannia: 13, 25, 34, 40
Lobbes, mon. in Henegouwen, Belgium: 34
Locri (Torre di Gerace?), in Bruttii, III, prov. of Lucania & Bruttii; formerly Locri Epizephyrii; (391, 598): 23
Lodève, 26; see Luteva
Lodi, see Laus Pompeia
Loja, in Andalusia: 13
Lomello, in Lombardia: 13
Londinium (London), in Britannia; (314): 3, 9, 25, 40
London, see Londinium
Lopadion, in Hellespontus: 16a
Lopodunum (Ladenburg), in Germania I: 25
Lorch, 13; see Lauriacum
Lorica or **Eliocroca** (Lorca), in Carthaginiensis: 40
Lorium (Buccea, between La Bottaccia and Castel di Guido, west of Rome), in S Tuscia Suburbicaria, prov. of Tuscia & Umbria; later Sylva Candida or Santa Rufina; (3rd cent.): 24
Losonna, see Lausanna
Louth, in Ireland: 25
Luca (Lucca), in Tuscia Annonaria, VII, prov. of Tuscia & Umbria; (343, 344): 3, 13, 23, 33
Lucania & Bruttii (modern Basilicata and Calabria), originally *Regio* III, prov. after 294: 23
Lucania, N part of *Regio* III, as above: 30
Lucca, 13; see Luca
Luceria (Lucera), in Apulia, II, prov. of Apulia & Calabria; (*ca* 493–4): 23
Lucq-de-Béarn, in dep. of Basses-Pyrénées, north of Oloron: 13
Lucus Augusti (Lugo), in Gallaecia; (5th cent., 589): 25, 40
Ludro, in Dalmatia; (530): 19
Lugdunensis, before 294 prov. of Gallia: 3; in 294 divided into two, and in 386 into four: 25, 41a
— Prima (Lyonnais and Burgundy, as far as Langres): 25, 26, 41a
— Secunda (Normandy), up to 386 forming part of III: 25, 41a
— Tertia (Brittany, Maine, Anjou), from 386 onwards: 25, 41a
— Quarta or **Senonia** (Ile-de-France and surrounding district, as far as Nivernais), from 386 onwards, until then part of I: 25, 41a
Lugdunum or **Civitas Lugdunensium** (Lyon), metrop. of Lugdunensis I; (*ca* 150, first Bishop Pothinus, died 177): 3, 5, 6, 7, 12, 25, 26, 30, 33, 35, 40, 41a, 42a
Lugo, see Lucus Augusti
Lugura, in Numidia; (484): 22
Lullingstone Park, near Eynsford, Kent: 4th century frescoed house-chapel: 13
Luna or **Lunae** (Luni), in N Tuscia Annonaria, VII, prov. of Tuscia & Umbria; (465): 23
Lunda, in Phrygia Pacatiana: 16a
Luperciana, in Byzacena; (256): 22
Lusitania (Portugal), prov. of dioc. of Hispania: 3, 25, 40, 41a
Lutetia Parisiorum, later **Parisii** (Paris), in Senonia, i.e. Lugdunensis IV; (*ca* 300): 3, 7, 9, 25, 40
Luteva or **Civitas Lutevensium** (Lodève), in Narbonensis I; (422): 26, 40
Luxor, on the Nile, in Thebais II: 17
Luxovium (Luxeuil, in dep. of Haute-Saône), mon. in Gallia: 34, 40
Lycaonia, prov. of dioc. of Asia, from 371: 1, 16a, 32, 41b
Lychnidus or **Achrida** (Ohrid), in Epirus Nova; (343): 19
Lycia, prov. of dioc. of Asia: 16a, 31, 41b
Lycia & Pamphylia, prov. before 294: 4
Lycopolis (Asyut), in Thebais I; (325): 14, 17, 34
Lycus (Kelkit), riv. in Pontus: 16a, 16b
Lydda or **Diospolis** (Ludd), in Palaestina I; (324, 325): 15a, 31; see Diospolis
Lydia, prov. of dioc. of Asia: 16a, 19, 41b
Lyon, 26; see Lugdunum
Lysa, in Palaestina III: 17
Lysimachia, in Europa; (451): 16a, 19
Lysinia, in NW Pamphylia; loc. uncertain: 16a
Lystra (near Katyn-Saray), in Lycaonia; (1st cent.): 1, 4, 5, 14, 16a

M

Ma'annata, in N Syria: 15b
Ma'aret en-Numan, in N Syria: 15b
Ma'aret-Mesrin, in N Syria: 15b
Maastricht, see Traiectum ad Mosam
Mabbug, 35; see Hierapolis in Euphratensis
Macaria(e), in Dalmatia; (530): 19, 23
Macedonia, before 294 Rom. prov.: 1, 2, 4; after 294 Imperial dioc. VI, the central part of Macedonia, divided into:

Q

R

W

X

Y

Z

INDEX OF PERSONS AND THINGS

in the maps, plates, and text

Information mentioned on the maps is not repeated in this index. See also the back endpaper for information about authors.

Abbreviations: a. = author; B. = bishop; C. = confessor (persecuted but not martyred); catac. = catacomb; Chr. = Christian; Emp. = Emperor; Gr. = Greek; K. = king; Lat. = Latin; m(m). = martyr(s), (followed by place of martyrdom or cult, or sites of memorial churches, often places of pilgrimage; see survey Maps 28, 30, 31); mon. = monastery; mos. = mosaic; p. = poet, poetess; rhetor. = rhetorician; S. = Sanctus, Sancta, San; St = Saint; Ste = Sainte; sarc. = sarcophagus; Syr. = Syrian. References to maps and plates are given at the end of each entry; map references in ordinary type, plate references in italic type.

INDEX OF AUTHORS AND INSCRIPTIONS

The numbers refer to the pages of this volume

NOTES TO THE MAPS

Endpaper I. Map 41 a, b. *Division of the Roman Empire into Prefectures, Dioceses, and Provinces.* This Map shows the division of the Empire into 120 provinces, 15 dioceses, and 4 prefectures, which resulted from the administrative reform of the Emperor Diocletian (284-305) Subsequent modifications were slight: between 294 and 400 certain provinces were divided up (the date of division can be found in the region concerned; see for example Cappadocia I, II, III), and in consequence their number was increased from Diocletian's 114 to 120. A new diocese was also created during the fourth century: Western Illyricum (modern Austria, Hungary, Yugoslavia west of the Danube).

The provinces ceased to correspond with the earlier ones, which were either senatorial or imperial, and fewer in number, and these few were considerably larger. This former division can be seen on Map 3/4 which covers the period from A.D. 100 to 300. In the East the new division survived until the middle of the Byzantine period and, in the West, until the collapse of the Empire following the barbarian invasions.

The provinces were grouped into dioceses (Gr. διοίκησις, an administrative district), and these in their turn, after Constantine, into four great imperial divisions called prefectures. These last coincide more or less with the four-fold form of imperial government introduced by Diocletian (the 'tetrarchy': two Augusti and two Caesars). The prefects were at the head of the closely-knit all-powerful bureaucracy characteristic of this period. Also characteristic of the state of the Empire is the fact that the official residence of each of these prefects lay close to the imperial frontier.

Of the four prefectures, the first was made up of what was then called 'the East' (Oriens), that is, Thrace (Bulgaria), 'Asia', and Pontus (Asia Minor, now Turkey), Syria, Palestine, Egypt, and Libya. From 334 onwards the capital was Constantinople; before this Diocletian usually resided in Nicomedia. The dioceses are shaded in shades of red and purple. The second prefecture was composed of the central section of the Balkan peninsula, Greece, Crete, and a few other islands (see Map 19); the capital was Sirmium (Srem or Mitrovica on the Danube). The dioceses are shown in blue-green. Both these parts of the Empire spoke Greek; the language of the two remaining sections was, on the contrary, Latin: see the linguistic frontier on the Map. The third prefecture embraced the central district between the Danube and the Sahara, i.e. Italy and Africa; Mediolanum (Milan) was the capital. The dioceses are shown in light-brown. The fourth included the countries of the West from almost the boundary of modern Scotland to the northern part of Morocco, i.e. Britain, Gaul, the Seven Provinces, and Spain; the capital was Augusta Treverorum (Trier/Trèves). The four dioceses are shaded in blue-green.

This division, introduced just before the Church of the martyrs obtained official status and gradually became a typically Imperial Church, is of the utmost importance, since, in the East especially, it laid the foundation of the later ecclesiastical administration. For in the East, at this period the centre of Christendom, the ecclesiastical division coincided almost exactly with the civil framework. The civil metropolises (capitals of provinces, all indicated upon the Map) became the sees of the ecclesiastical metropolitans or archbishops (literally 'bishops of the mother cities'). They are indicated upon the Map by a double-barred cross. This, however, does not hold good for the West. In Africa one cannot speak of metropolitans: the bishops of the provincial capitals (Carthage, Cirta, Caesarea) had no hierarchical precedence. In Spain and southern Gaul several sees within the one province enjoyed special privileges (see Map 25). Italy itself enjoyed a special position. In the diocese of Italia Annonaria (roughly north of the line Elba-Ancona, including much of the region beyond the Alps) Milan and Ravenna, both of which had, for a time, been the official residence of the Western Roman Emperors, became ecclesiastical metropolises, to be followed later, in some sense, by Aquileia (see Maps 11 and 12). Italia Suburbicaria ('under the Urbs', suburban), the whole of Italy south of the Apennines, including the islands, came completely under the jurisdiction of the 'papa' or Pope of 'the City' (Rome).

The imperial division given here can be found on the detailed Maps 15, 16, 17, 19, 20-2, 23, and 25, and on the Maps 13/14 and 42a, b. This endpaper can thus be said to provide the key to the whole series. The coloured boundary crossing the sea indicates the frontier between the Western and Eastern part of the Empire, from ca 395 onwards.

Map 1. *The Earliest Churches.* The churches we know to have been founded in the first century, including those founded by Peter and Paul and those mentioned in Rev. 1-2. Districts where Christianity is known to have spread rapidly (e.g. Bithynia, as appears from Pliny's letter) are shown in light red. The earliest documents are those of the New Testament and the Letter of Clement.

Map 2. *The distribution of Christianity by A.D. 300.* The focal points lie in the East, in Asia and Phrygia especially; more than two hundred churches also already existed east of the Euphrates. In the West the region of Proconsularis (west of Carthage) occupies the first place. This Map must be viewed in connection with Map 3/4.

Map 3/4. *Churches Founded before the Persecution by Diocletian (304).* Here the churches, in so far as they are shown, are shown separately (compare with the rough estimates on Map 2). They are known principally from the lists of members of certain famous synods, held shortly after 304—those Elvira (Granada), Arelate (Arles) and Rome—and from the first Oecumenical Council of Nicaea (325). For this last the principal authority is the critical list established by Ernst Honigmann (*Byzantion*, 14, 1939, 17-76). The provincial boundaries, in red, are those of the pre-Diocletian period. See above.

Map. 5. *The Church in the Second Century.* The principal personages and events are localised, as far as possible, in red.

Map 6. *Christian Writers of the Second Century.* Alexandria and Rome are important centres; in Palestine the apocryphal literature is also indicated. For further information concerning this and other Maps dealing with authors, see pages 173-4, on 'Christian literature and the Fathers of the Church'.

Map 7. *The Church in the Third Century.* The individual churches are not indicated here but are given, all together, on Map 3/4. What is included here serves merely to illustrate church history, with events and persons indicated in red. At the same time the earliest Christian monuments are given (within thin black rules). These are preserved at Brignoles in Provence and Trèves (sarcophagi), in Rome (remains of house-churches, the earliest catacombs, and the oldest sarcophagi), in Naples (catacombs), and at Dura-Europos on the Euphrates (house-church) (see Plates 40-108: where all the principal monuments dating from the third century are shown). For the house-churches in Rome see Map 29.

Map 8. *Christian Writers of the Third Century.* See text, pages 174-7.

Map 9. *The Church in the Fourth Century.* Only the main themes of church history (and a few political data, as background) are summarised here. For the individual churches one should consult the detailed Maps 15-25 and the Index, where the name of each bishopric is accompanied by the date of the earliest known mention.

Map 10. *Christian Writers of the Fourth Century.* See text, pages 177-81.

Map 11. *The Church in the Fifth Century.* The main themes of ecclesiastical history are shown against the background of the political changes resulting from the collapse of the Empire in the West and the emergence of the barbarian kingdoms inside Roman territory.

Map 12. *Christian Writers of the Fifth Century.* See text, pages 179-81. In the East the great ecclesiastical circumscriptions (patriarchates) are given in full colour; for the regions where the Nestorians and Monophysites gradually came to dominate the majority of the churches, see Map 36.

Map 13/14. *Early Christian Monuments, 300-600.* This Map surveys what has been preserved of the flowering of Early Christian art in the fourth, fifth, and sixth centuries—as well as of the so-called Early Byzantine art which flourished in the sixth century in the Empire of Justinian. In Syria, between Antakya and Aleppo, a great many monuments are found close together (inside the rectangle indicated by a thin dotted line); these can be found separately on Map 15b. The monuments of the great centres are also given on separate Maps: those of Rome on Map 27:9, those of Ravenna on Map 38, those of Jerusalem on Map 39, and those of Constantinople on Map 37.

Few monuments have been preserved intact: most of these have been illustrated in this Atlas (Plates 126-609); they form four-fifths of the illustrations. For the hundreds of localities which are indicated as possessing one or more basilicas, one should only imagine a ground-plan which can be reconstructed from the foundations, with perhaps fragments of a mosaic floor and remains of walls and columns or pillars.

Only the most important monuments are indicated. In the regions of dense Christian population (Asia Minor, Africa) the number of monuments shown is obviously determined by the space available; in the outer provinces also smaller monuments are given. The most important centres are distinguished by red dots. As far as the inscriptions are concerned, only in Spain are the places of origin more or less indicated in full; lack of space makes this impossible elsewhere. Famous ivories, precious metal work, textiles, and manuscripts are localised, but not museum collections as such. Capital **S** indicates an important sarcophagus, small **s** a less important one.

Inset map. The earliest churches of Armenia and Georgia can be dated only approximately.

Map 15a. *Coelesyria, Phoenice, Palaestina, Arabia.* Upon this and all other detailed Maps of the Empire (Maps 16, 17, 19, 20, 21, 22, 23, 25) all known bishoprics are indicated with their original names in the Latin spelling. The modern names, further particulars, and references to the Plates, can be found in the Index. The principal monastic foundations and other celebrated localities are also given. Matters referring to church history, however, are to be found in the 'historical' Maps (1-12 and 35-6). The green areas are regions especially rich in Early Christian ruins.

Map 15b. *Early Christian Monuments between Antioch and Beroea.* The sites are indicated by their modern names; the ancient names, when known, are also given in red. The symbols are the same as those used in the general monument map (13/14), on which this region is also outlined. See Plates 288-300.

Map 16a. *Asia and Pontus, with Part of the Diocese of Oriens.* Bishoprics and ecclesiastical divisions. For the patriarchates see Map 12. The imperial boundary with the Parthian kingdom (on Map 16b) changes continually according to the fortunes of war (see Map 36). That given here is thus to a certain extent arbitrary. Armenia belongs alternately to each power and sometimes to neither. For the bishoprics east of the Euphrates see Map 36.

Map 17. *The Diocese of Egypt (or diocesis Augustalis).* This Map shows also the neighbouring Palaestina Tertia, a province forming part of the Diocese of Oriens. Nearly all the bishoprics lie in the Nile valley (shaded in green). Egypt is the cradle of monastic life; the earliest monasteries and some later ones are indicated by red dots. They lie usually in or upon the fringe of the desert. For the western part of this diocese, Libya, see Map 21. At the margins of the Map can be found particulars of the outer regions of Early Christendom; at the foot, of Aethiopia and Nubia, at the right margin, of southern Arabia (Yemen), both far beyond the Empire.

Map 18. *Alexandria.* The pagan monuments are shown in black; some of them have been transformed into churches (see caption). Nothing in this city (from the 2nd cent. onwards the centre of Greek-speaking Christianity) has been preserved to remind us of its Christian past, apart from a small catacomb and a few ivories, textiles, manuscripts, and icons attributed to Alexandrian workshops (Plates 329-38 and 552-6). Nothing is known of the sites of the churches and *martyria* mentioned in the texts. Even this plan of Alexandria is largely conjectural.

Map 19. *The Dioceses of Illyricum, Dacia, Macedonia and Thracia, with Part of the Diocese of Asia.* Only the eastern part of Illyricum is shown; the western half can be found on Map 23. The province of Insulae (the Greek Archipelago with Rhodes) was under the jurisdiction of the Procunsul of Asia and he himself depended immediately upon the Emperor. The Map shows the bishoprics and the ecclesiastical circumscriptions, which coincided with the civil.

Map 20. *The Diocese of Africa.* Only in Mauretania are the bishoprics shown in full. Those of the four eastern provinces are given on Maps 21 and 22.

Map 21. *Tripolitana and Libya.* The latter province forms part of the diocese of Egypt and the prefecture of the East. Towns were only to be found in the coastal region: in the interior there existed nothing but small frontier forts (see Map 13, remains).

Map 22. *Numidia, Proconsularis, and Byzacena.* These three provinces formed one of the most densely populated regions of the Empire; they also furnished Rome with corn (*annona*). Here, too, lay one of the main centres of Latin Christianity; about A.D. 400 there existed roughly about 500 bishoprics, Catholic and Donatist. The names are known principally from the lists of Bishops who attended the Synod of Hippo in 393 and the debate in 411 at Carthage about the stamping out of the Donatist schism. Names are also found in the 'Notitia provinciarum et civitatum Africae' a document dating from the time of the Vandal persecution, in which 448 Catholic Bishops are named. Not all the names are localised, nor is it always certain in which cities and villages a Catholic Bishop or a Donatist or even a Bishop of both churches resided. In the Index the names are followed by the dates of the documents in which they are mentioned. The earliest, mentioned in the Synod of 256, are distinguished by red dots; they can also be found on Map 3.

Map 23. *The Diocese of Italia Suburbicaria and the Chief Part of Italia Annonaria.* The northern part of Italia Annonaria (Raetia and Noricum) is not visible here (it can be found on Map 25); on the right is the western part of Illyricum (the remainder is shown on Map 19). The provinces indicated here do not coincide with the old 'Regiones' of the time of Augustus. In the Index, however, each bishopric is followed by the 'Regio' in which it is situated.

The boundary between the two Italian dioceses crosses the provinces of Tuscia and Umbria, so that one speaks of Tuscia Annonaria and Tuscia Suburbicaria; in Umbria the boundary is formed by the Apennines, so that here one speaks of Umbria Cisappenninica and Transappenninica,; the Index shows in which half each bishopric lies. Tuscia is also known as Etruria.

Map 24. *The Environs of Rome.* The Map shows the bishoprics lying close to the city which later, in the Middle Ages, were called 'Suburbicarian'. It also shows the roads leading to the city (the old *viae consulares*), upon which lie the cemeteries and catacombs (see Map 28).

Map 25. *The Dioceses of Britannia, Gallia, the Seven Provinces, Hispania, Italia Annonaria, with the western part of Illyricum.* All the bishoprics known to have existed before 600 are mentioned; those founded in the 6th cent. are underlined in red; the earliest, dating from before 300, are found on Maps 3 and 5. The bishoprics in Gaul correspond with the *civitates* of the 'Notitia Galliarum'. In the south and centre of the country they all survived the incursions of the barbarians from 410 onwards, and in the north the greater part remain.

In contrast to the Eastern Empire, the ecclesiastical divisions correspond only rarely with the civil. This sometimes leads to several ecclesiastical spheres of influence in one province: e.g. that of Toletum (Toledo) and Carthage (Cartagena) in Carthaginiensis; of Caesaraugusta (Zaragoza) and Tarraco (Tarragona) in Tarraconensis; of Arelate (Arles), Vienna (Vienne), and Massilia (Marseille) in Narbonensis. The imperial capital and seat of the whole western *praefectura Galliarum*, Augusta Treverorum (Trèves), had no especial ecclesiastical precedence, except perhaps as the see of the metropolitan of Belgica Prima.

In Britannia there are no fixed provincial boundaries. The Romans withdrew from the country shortly after 400. Hibernia (Ireland), shaded in red, was never part of the Roman Empire. A few of the many monastery-bishoprics of the Celtic church which flourished there from the 4th cent. onwards are shown. Compare, too, Maps 34 and 40.

Mauretania Tingitana (at the tip of Morocco) is reckoned with Spain in civil matters and with Africa for ecclesiastical.

Map 26. *The Rhône Provinces.* In consequence of the peculiar position of the bishop of Arelate (Arles; see Map 9) the ecclesiastical and civil districts diverged considerably. Only the civil, which in the 5th cent. fell under barbarian occupation, are given here; the modern name of every bishopric is given in red. Nearly all these old bishoprics survived until 1791 and many exist even today.

Map 27. *Early Christian Rome, 300-800.* All the Christian architectural monuments are given here: those from 300 to 500 in solid black, from 500 to 700 in red with black, from 700 to 800 in red. In order to complete the picture, those dating from between 800 and 1000 are added, although they fall outside the compass of this Atlas; they are, however, inseparably connected with the earlier monuments. It has not been thought necessary to indicate whether they still exist, have been much restored, or have disappeared altogether (like the old basilica of St Peter in the Vatican); this is sufficiently clear from the text accompanying the many Plates which are listed in the Index under 'Rome'. *Diaconiae* are social relief institutions, attached to a church and run by monks. These institutions were introduced into Rome by monks from Greece in the 8th cent. For the *tituli* see Map 29. The street plan of *ca* 600 is naturally for the greater part conjectural.

Map 28. *The Roman Cemeteries and Memoriae, 100-520.* All lie outside the walls of Aurelian. Of the 38 *memoriae* which once existed, eleven remain either as churches or as ruins. There are in addition five underground sanctuaries (*cryptae*), each linked with the corridors of a catacomb. One memorial church, that of Sts John and Paul, lies within the city walls (*Regio* II). In addition to the cemeteries (mostly underground, i.e. catacombs) and cemetery basilicas (*basilicae coemeteriales*), the names of the principal martyrs are also given, in red, near the cemetery in which they are buried (for further information see Map 30/31).

Map 29. *The Roman Tituli, 200-600.* Tituli are the parish churches of early Christian Rome. Twenty-one already existed as clandestine churches (*domus ecclesiae* = house-church) during the persecutions, before 313 (in black); five were founded later (red, outlined in black). Remains of the earlier churches still exist here and there (indicated by . ˙ .). They mostly bore the name of the person by whom they were founded (*titulus* = name-board); later, when the relics of the martyrs were transferred from the catacombs to within the city churches, the old name usually made way for that of the holy martyr (for example, *titulus Aemilianae*, the *titulus* of Aemiliana, becomes *basilica Quattuor Coronatorum*, i.e. Church of the Four Crowned Martyrs from Pannonia).

Map 30/31. *Memoria and Martyriae of the Martyrs and the Holy Places.* The early Christians made pilgrimages to the 'Holy Places' (the lands of the Bible - Palestine, and Gessen, Sinai, and the place of the Crossing of the Red Sea) and to the sanctuaries built upon the graves of the martyrs. The first are shaded in green (see Plates 319-26 and, in the text, pages 105-6); the most frequented *martyria* and *memoriae* (of the martyrs) are shown by red dots; the localisation is according to H. Delehaye, *Les origines du culte des martyrs* (Bruxelles, 1933); for Rome see Map 28. For the monuments in honour of the martyrs see Plates 479-513.

Map 32. *Egeria's Pilgrimage to the Holy Places.* See text pages 106-7. The red line indicates the route followed; the interrupted section is hypothetical.

All the place-names mentioned by Egeria are included, in her own spelling, beside the classical names, and also the monuments and sites to which she refers. The journey took place in 414-6 (formerly the date was thought to have been 395-6).

Map 33. *The Life of Augustine.* The principal events and persons who played a rôle in his life, localised as far as possible, are shown in red, notably in Thagaste, Carthago, Hippo, Madaurus, Rome, and Milan, with appropriate dates. Apart from his youthful voyage to and from Italy, Augustine never again travelled by ship; he travelled overland, even to Caesarea Mauretaniae, 300 miles from Hippo, when he was 62. See text, page 176 and Plates 597-9. See also Maps 10 and 12.

Map 34. *Monastic Life, 300-700.* Origin and spread are indicated by lines and arrows which, starting from Egypt, the home of monasticism (see Map 17), point to the zones where lie the most numerous and the earliest centres; these are shaded in light brown. The Irish-Celtic area, completely dominated by the monastic ideal, is shaded in red; the red dots elsewhere are communities founded by Irish-Celtic monks. Of the numerous communities in Italy of the sixth and later centuries only those are shown which are linked with the person of St Benedict and with that of Pope Gregory; from the parent monastery of the latter, Roman monasticism spread to Britannia (black dotted line, from Rome to Canterbury and Wearmouth-Jarrow). The Italian and Romano-British monasteries are indicated by green dots. *Regula mixta* (in the key) means a Rule of life devised out of many existing Rules; it is, for example, not certain where and by whom the Rule of St Benedict was followed before the sixth and seventh centuries.

A few of the seventh-century foundations between the Rhine and Loire are also indicated with open dots, but in no particularly coloured background since it is difficult to determine whether these belonged to any definite type.

Map 35. *The Age of Justinian, especially in the East* (the West is dealt with in Map 40). This Map contains data concerning the church history of the 6th cent. Right, near the edge, the areas where the Bishops and faithful were not in accordance with the decisions of the Councils of Ephesus (431) and Chalcedon (451), respectively the Nestorians and Monophysites, who gradually departed from the orthodox Church of the Empire, thus bringing about the inner dissociation of the hinterlands (Syria, Mesopotamia, Armenia, and Egypt) from the Roman Empire. The Nestorians, banned from the Empire, found a precarious refuge in the Sassanian kingdom (Persia); the Monophysites are found especially in Syria, Armenia, and Egypt (where they are known as Copts). For Persia see Map 36.

Map 36. *The Churches of Persia and Neighbouring Countries.* Of the Persian churches the metropolitan sees are indicated in red, (including some of the later ones, from after 700 until *ca* 1000). The ordinary churches are indicated by black dots. The most important Monophysite bishoprics, both within and without the Persian kingdom, are indicated by blue dots.

The Nestorian *katholikos* (patriarch) resided at Ctesiphon, the Armenian (Monophysitic) at Valarshapat, later Etchmiadzin.

Map 37. *Constantinople, 200-600.* Those monuments dating between 300 and 600 of which remains have been preserved are shown in black; these are walls, churches, cisterns (water reservoirs), triumphal columns, and the ruins of palaces. For convenience later monuments are indicated in red. The ground area of the Great Palace (with the Great Church and the hippodrome) is shaded in light red (see Plates 245-54).

Map 38. *Early Christian Ravenna.* Only those monuments which came into existence between 300 and 600 and are still extant are shown (in black). Modern names are given in red; churches with mosaics are underlined. The town walls are late medieval. Upper left: political data for the period 402-751; below: prominent bishops; lower right: data concerning Classis, with S. Apollinaris, which lies to the south.

Map 39. *Jerusalem, 500-700.* Situation before the destruction by the Persians in 614; the monuments of the Arabian conquerors, after 638, are also given in darker green (El 'Aqsa mosque, and the 'Dome of the Rock' or Qubbet es-Saqra). One fact which immediately strikes the eye is the displacement of the city; the ancient Jewish town is within the red fortification; the new, Aelia, is walled around in black. The wall of Empress Eudocia (5th cent.) indicated the expansion to the south, by which the Christian city, a town of churches and monasteries, exceeded the former city area by a third. The complex of the Holy Sepulchre lies to the left of the *cardo maximus* (main colonnaded street) outside the walls of the Jewish city (see Plates 320-36, Map of Madaba).

Map 40. *The Church in the West in the Sixth Century.* See Map 35, which gives both East and West. On Map 40 are found: (1) data concerning church history; (2) the writers and poets (see Map 35 and, especially, Map 42a); (3) all bishoprics, with the names common in the 6th cent. which often differ in spelling from the earlier, on Map 25 (in Spain the name has sometimes been changed entirely); (4) newly-founded bishoprics, underlined in red; (5) the principal centres and persons of the Celtic monastic church (the Scoti).

Endpaper 2. Map 42a, b. *The Early Christian Writers, 100-700.* All the authors successively named upon literature Maps (Maps 1, 6, 8, 10, 12, 35, and 40) are collected here; and, naturally, those dealt with on pages 173-83 in the chapter on 'The Apostolic Fathers and Early Christian literature'. The underlining indicates in which language their works were written, Greek, Latin, or Syriac.

Those authors whose residence and place of origin or work are not definitely known are placed wherever scholars are accustomed to localise them (the treatise *Ad Diognetum*, for example, 2nd cent. in Asia; Commodianus, of whom nothing further is known, somewhere in Provence), with a question mark.

ACKNOWLEDGEMENTS

Alinari, Fratelli, Florence 18, 29, 31, 36, 42, 58, 60, 61, 65, 69, 76, 77, 88, 90, 105 113, 157, 167, 177, 187, 191, 196, 199, 200, 213, 239, 256, 272, 402, 438, 451ab, 454-6, 468, 472, 477, 479, 480, 514, 520, 522, 529, 532, 533, 603 – Anderson, Rome 2-8, 15-17, 19-23, 25-7, 33, 34, 44-7, 59, 67, 85, 94, 111, 114, 117, 121, 122, 128, 130, 131, 133, 137, 168-70, 175-6, 184, 198, 206-8, 210, 212, 219, 221-3, 225, 232, 234-6, 238, 249, 257-8, 260-4, 267, 270, 327-8, 331-4, 467, 470, 473-4, 476, 478, 487, 490-5, 501-8, 516, 519, 523, 525, 530-1, 541, 543, 562, 566-7, 572, 593, 595, 596ab, 609-11 – Archives Photographiques, Paris 147, 220, 242, 306 – Bayerisches Nationalmuseum, Munich 197 – Bodleian Library, Oxford 592a – British Museum, London 378, 475 – Bromostampa, Milan 188 – Bromostampa, Turin 143 - Buzi, F., Milan 195 - Cadel, Trieste 415 - Caisse des Monuments Historiques, Paris 369 – Carlsberg Glyptotek, Copenhagen 14, 28, 337 – Combier, L., Mâcon 352-3 – Corpus Christi College, Cambridge 392 – Crystal, London 129 – Dept. of Antiquities, Jerusalem 584 – Deutsches Archäologisches Inst., Rome, 41, 534-5, 547, 550, 614 – Dumbarton Oaks 444 – Ediz. E.S., Ravenna 432 – Eichacker, Algiers 407 – Elsevier Uitg. Mij., Amsterdam, 254 – Felicetti, Rome 552, 554 – Fotocelere, Turin 233 – Fotocielo, Rome 127, 224, 226-7, 259, 265 – Gabinetto Nazionale Fotografico, Rome 139-40, 144, 193, 211, 217, 383, 386-8, 397, 421, 426, 428-9, 515, 549, 579, 608 – Gallerie Vaticane e. Ist. d. Arch. Cr., Rome 48-50, 53, 57, 78-84, 86-7, 89, 91-3, 101, 158-9, 165, 321, 356, 396, 399, 481-2, 485-6, 488-9ab, 536, 548, 557-8, 561, 564, 568-71, 573, 580, 594 – Grigolon, Grado, Italy 273-5 – Grollenberg, L.H., o.p., Nijmegen 35, 288-9, 297-9, 319, 581-2, 585-90 – Heyden, A.A.M. van der, Bussum 40, 98, 100, 106, 108, 116, 125, 174, 194, 278, 280, 284-5, 362, 366, 405, 413, 462, 464-5, 517-8, 538, 591 – Inst. Français d'archéologie, Beirut 71, 294 – Inst. di Studi, Liguri 419 – Kestner Museum, Hanover 338 – Koninklijke Bibliotheek, The Hague 183, 186 – Kunsthistorisch Instituut, Nijmegen 10, 110, 112, 118-9, 138, 151-6, 160-2, 179, 182, 189-90, 192, 202-5, 287, 290-2, 307-10, 335-6, 344, 376, 385, 393, 418, 604 – Lévy & Neurdein, Paris 357 – Mar, Nice 370 – Monte Cassino 592b – Moscioni, Rome 66 – Musée du Bardo, Tunis 453 – Museo delle Terme, Rome 398 – Museo Lateranense, Rome 95, 97 – Muzio, Milan 602 – National Museum of Antiquities, Edinburgh, page 118 (inset) – Nuellens, Aix-la-Chapelle 1 – Ofalac, Algiers 348-51, 404, 420, 583 – Omniafoto, Turin 228-31 – Patuelli, R., Ravenna 537 – Piccardo, Albenga 416 – Richter, E., Rome 605 – Rylands Library, Manchester 379 – Sender, Istanbul 245 – Service d'antiquités, Algiers 354-5 – Sibbelee, H., Amsterdam 32, 107, 109, 120, 123-4, 132, 136, 171-3, 185, 209, 214, 400, 448, 466, 498, 606-7 – Soprintendenza, Trieste 141-2, 271, 276-7, 411 – Stampa Angeli, Terni 266 – Tarantola, Ravenna 268-9, 540 – Velzen, Th. van, Breda 43, 64, 103, 163, 363-5, 368, 401, 417, 422-3, 424ab, 434, 521, 526, 528, 544, 551, 577 – Victoria and Albert Museum, London 342 – Ward Perkins and Goodchild, Archaeologia 95 (1953) 358-61 – Worcester Art Museum, Mass. 293 – Yale University, Gallery of Fine Arts, New Haven, Conn. 51-2, 62, 72, 403.

ILLUSTRATIONS FROM BOOKS

Ars Hispaniae II 371-5 – Deichmann, *Frühchristliche Kirchen Roms* 126, 135 – Du Mesnil du Buisson, *Les Peintres de la synagogue de Doura-Europes* 37-9, 68 – Felicetti-Liebenfels, *Ikonenmalerei* 553, 555-6 – Gischia-Mazenod, *Les Arts primitifs français* 612 – Malraux, *Bas-reliefs, Sc. Mondiale, Monde chrétien* 12, 13, 24, 30, 243, – Skira, *Peinture byzantine* 248, 286, 384; *Peinture romaine* 9, 11, – Schneider, *Hagia Sophia* 250-3 – Wilpert, *Katakombenmalereien* 560 – Wilpert, *Sarcofagi* 102, 104, 164, 166, 367, 527.

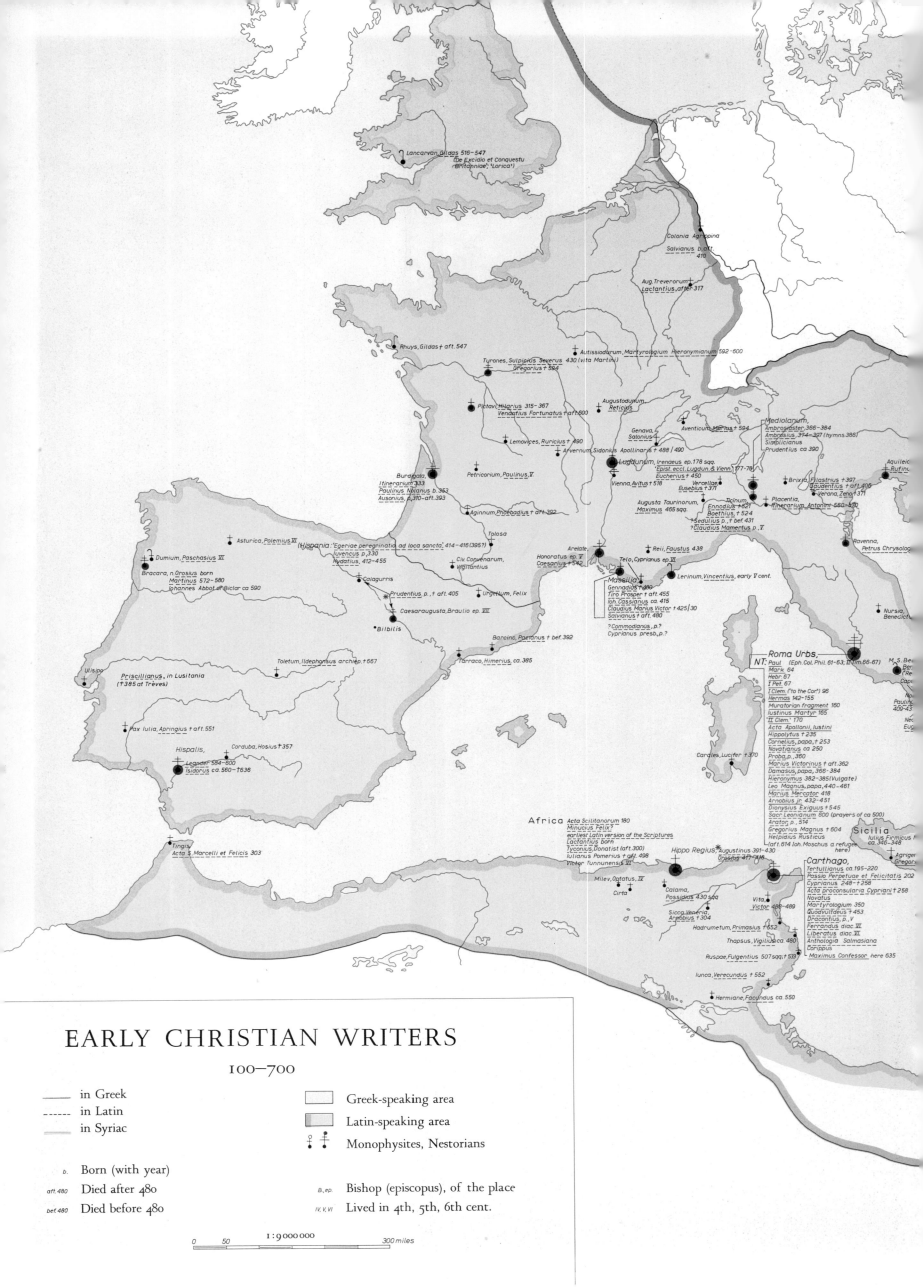

EARLY CHRISTIAN WRITERS

100–700

——— in Greek	▨ Greek-speaking area
------ in Latin	▨ Latin-speaking area
═══ in Syriac	⚲ ☩ Monophysites, Nestorians

b. Born (with year)

aft.480 Died after 480

bet.480 Died before 480

B.,ep. Bishop (episcopus), of the place

IV, V, VI Lived in 4th, 5th, 6th cent.

0   50   300 miles

1:9 000 000